PUBLIC FINANCE IN A CHANGING WORLD

Also by Peter Birch Sørensen

TAX POLICY IN THE NORDIC COUNTRIES (*editor*)

Public Finance in a Changing World

Edited by

Peter Birch Sørensen
Professor of Economics
University of Copenhagen
Denmark

First published 1998 by
MACMILLAN PRESS LTD
Houndmills, Basingstoke, Hampshire RG21 6XS
and London
Companies and representatives
throughout the world

ISBN 0–333–68221–1

A catalogue record for this book is available
from the British Library.

This book is printed on paper suitable for recycling and
made from fully managed and sustained forest sources.

10   9   8   7   6   5   4   3   2   1
07 06 05 04 03 02 01 00 99 98

Printed and bound in Great Britain by
Antony Rowe Ltd, Chippenham, Wiltshire

Contents

List of Tables   vii

List of Figures   viii

Preface   ix

Acknowledgements   x

Notes on the Contributors   xi

Public Finance in a Changing World: Introduction and Summary
Peter Birch Sørensen   1

Part I   Alternative Perceptions of Government

1   The Role of the State in Fiscal Theory
    Richard A. Musgrave   35

2   Government Role and the Efficiency of Policy Instruments
    Vito Tanzi   51

Part II   The Welfare State, Entrepreneurship and Employment

3   Social Insurance, Incentives and Risk-Taking
    Hans-Werner Sinn   73

4   Unemployment in the United States: The Problem and a
    Proposal
    Robert Haveman   101

5   Unemployment and Public Finance in Europe
    Frederick van der Ploeg   126

Contents

Part III   Public Finance with Many Jurisdictions

6   Factor Mobility and Redistributive Policy
    David E. Wildasin   151

7   Theory and Practice of Confederate Finances   193
    Dubravko Mihaljek

8   Reform and Coordination of Company Taxes in the European
    Union
    Sijbren Cnossen   221

**Part IV   Economies in Transition: Raising Revenue and
            Allocating Property Rights**

9   Tax Reform in Transition Economies: Experiences from the
    Croatian Tax Reform Process of the 1990s
    Manfred Rose and Rolf Wiswesser   257

10 The Sales Policy of the *Treuhandanstalt* as a Privatization
    Strategy
    Gerlinde Sinn   279

Index   297

List of Tables

2.1   The growth of general government expenditure, 1870–1994   54
2.2   The size of revenue from financial repression   61
2.3   Seigniorage revenue in 26 developing countries, 1984   62
2.4   Tax revenue from implicit financial taxation in selected
      countries, 1971–86 averages   63
4.1   Net new jobs created in ten countries, 1979–93   102
4.2   Unemployment rates in the United States, by age and race   104
4.3   Percentage allocation of males aged 18–64 across
      work-pattern categories, 1973–92   104
4.4   Variance of logarithm (VLN) of earnings, 1973–91, male
      workers aged 18–64   107
4.5   Expenditures by government on education, training and
      employment, and social services/other, United States,
      1970–92   112
5.1   OECD unemployment rates, 1993   129
5.2   OECD sectoral trends in employment growth, 1979–90   130
5.3   Unemployment benefit replacement rates by duration, 1991   139
5.4   Number of unemployed per staff member in employment
      offices and related services, 1992   141
8.1   European Union taxes on company earnings in 1996   224
8.2   Tax rates on labour and capital income in the Nordic countries 241

List of Figures

3.1 Private insurance versus social insurance 77
3.2 Risk productivity, ideal insurance and redistributive taxation 84
3.3 Moral hazard 89
3.4 The excessive welfare state 90
3.5 The redistributive paradox 92
3.6 The optimal tax problem 95
3.7 Optimal taxation and the redistributive paradox 96
4.1 Changes in earnings across the earnings distribution, year-round, full-time male workers aged 25–64, 1973–93 106
4.2 Changes in earnings across the earnings distribution, year-round, full-time female workers aged 25–64, 1973–93 107
4.3 Real hourly wages for men, by level of education, 1973 and 1993 108
4.4 Earnings of cohorts of men aged 25–34, by education, 1975–90 109
4.5 Poverty in the United States, 1959–94 111
4.6 Public expenditures on labour market programmes, as a percentage of GDP 114
6.1 Attainable distribution of income with migration 159
6.2 Fiscal transfers and migration with and without mobility costs 173
9.1 Determination of the personal allowance in the Croatian income tax system 273

Preface

This volume brings together a selection of papers which were originally presented at the 51st Congress of the International Institute of Public Finance on 'The Changing Role of the Public Sector: Transitions in the 1990s', held at Universidade Nova in Lisbon in August 1995.

All papers were subsequently refereed and edited for publication. As editor, I am grateful to the many anonymous referees who helped seeing the papers through to the final stage.

Copenhagen

PETER BIRCH SØRENSEN

Acknowledgements

The editor and publishers are indebted to Kluwer Academic Publishers for permission to reprint, in Chapter 1, the article by Richard A. Musgrave, 'The Role of the State in Fiscal Theory', *International Tax and Public Finance*, July 1996, vol. 3, no. 3, pp. 247–58, and, in Chapter 3, the article by Hans-Werner Sinn, 'Social Insurance, Incentives and Risk Taking', *International Tax and Public Finance*, July 1996, vol. 3, no. 3, pp. 259–80; and The Institute for Fiscal Studies for permission to reprint, in Chapter 8, the article by Sijbren Cnossen, 'Company Taxes in the European Union: Criteria and Options for Reform', *Fiscal Studies*, November 1996, vol. 17, no. 4, pp. 67–97.

Notes on the Contributors

Sijbren Cnossen is Professor of Economics, Erasmus University, The Netherlands.

Robert Haveman is Professor of Economics, University of Wisconsin, United States.

Dubravko Mihaljek is Economist, International Monetary Fund.

Richard A. Musgrave is Adjunct Professor of Economics, University of California at Santa Cruz, United States.

Frederick van der Ploeg, MP, The Hague, is Professor of Economics, University of Amsterdam, The Netherlands.

Manfred Rose is Professor of Economics, University of Heidelberg, Germany.

Gerlinde Sinn is Economist, University of Munich, Germany.

Hans-Werner Sinn is Professor of Economics and Director of Centre for Economic Studies, University of Munich, Germany.

Peter Birch Sørensen is Professor of Economics, University of Copenhagen.

Vito Tanzi is Director of the Fiscal Affairs Department, International Monetary Fund.

David E. Wildasin is Professor of Economics, Vanderbilt University, United States.

Rolf Wiswesser is Economist, University of Heidelberg, Germany.

Public Finance in a Changing World: Introduction and Summary

Peter Birch Sørensen[*]

In recent years many governments throughout the world have struggled to adapt their fiscal systems to rapidly changing circumstances. This process is perhaps most obvious in the former socialist countries of Eastern Europe. Under the previous socialist regimes governments derived a large part of their revenues from the profits of state-owned enterprises, and many important public services were provided by the enterprises directly to their employees rather than being delivered via the public budget. With the transition to a market-oriented economic system based primarily on private enterprise, Eastern European governments have had to design new systems of taxation and social security almost from scratch, often in a very difficult and unstable environment. The changing political landscape in Eastern Europe has also led to the emergence of new nations and jurisdictions, thereby raising new challenges of intergovernmental fiscal coordination.

While the trend in Eastern Europe has been towards the creation of new independent jurisdictions, governments in Western Europe have renounced on national autonomy in some areas of public policy, most notably trade policy, in an effort to integrate their economies. This development has raised the issue of how national fiscal systems can be designed and coordinated so as to avoid tax-induced distortions of the flows of trade and production factors. In other parts of the world, including North America and Asia, governments have likewise taken steps to break down regional trade barriers to pave the way for increased mobility of goods, services, and factors of production.

In addition, the general market-driven tendency towards increased international economic integration forces many governments to adapt their

* I wish to thank Robert Haveman and Andreas Haufler for helpful comments on an earlier draft of this chapter.

1

systems of public finance to an environment in which economic activities are becoming increasingly mobile and hence increasingly difficult to tax, and where public services and transfer payments may to a growing extent come to be enjoyed by immigrants and not just by the native population.

Developments in labour markets also contribute to the changing environment for public finance. In many countries, especially in Europe, high and rising rates of structural unemployment impose a growing burden on public budgets. According to many observers, the economic disincentives implied by the tax-transfer systems of advanced welfare states are partly responsible for the high rates of equilibrium unemployment in Western Europe. Under this view reforms of the systems of taxation and social insurance are needed to bring down unemployment. In North America unemployment is lower, but wage inequalities are growing, and unemployment is becoming highly concentrated on low-skilled workers and on members of racial minorities. To counter these disturbing trends, some observers have called for changes in the tax-transfer system which will lower the tax burden on low-paid workers and improve their incentives to seek work.

As a result of all of these developments, recent years have witnessed an intensified debate among economists and policy-makers on the changing role of the state and the need for reforms of the systems of public finance. Without pretending to offer a comprehensive treatment of all of the complex issues alluded to above, the present volume brings together a number of contributions dealing with the role of the government and its budget in a changing world. The first part of the book discusses alternative perceptions of government and the way we measure its activities. The second part focuses on the modern welfare state and its impact on entrepreneurship and employment, while the third part shifts attention to some important problems of public finance in a multijurisdiction setting. The fourth and final part concentrates on the problems of raising government revenue and of allocating property rights in economies in transition.

In the sections below I shall try to summarize the main messages of the ten chapters of the book and to show how they are linked.

I ALTERNATIVE PERCEPTIONS OF GOVERNMENT

The first two chapters, by Richard Musgrave and Vito Tanzi, deal with alternative perceptions of the state and its activities. While Richard Musgrave describes alternative normative views of the role of government as they have evolved over the centuries, Vito Tanzi is mainly concerned with the problem of how the impact of government on the economy can and should be measured.

The Role of the State in Historical Perspective

At a time when the role of government is being reconsidered and in some cases fundamentally changed, it is useful to step back and consider how scholars have changed their perceptions of the proper fiscal role of the state over the centuries.

This is the task which Richard Musgrave sets for himself in Chapter 1. Going back to the origins of modern economic theory in the eighteenth century, he starts by describing the classical view of the 'service state', as expounded by Adam Smith and his followers. As is well-known, the classical view of government developed as a reaction against the previous interventionist practices of mercantilism. Convinced that a *laissez-faire* economy based on the 'system of natural liberty' would offer the best institutional framework for the accumulation of the wealth of nations, Adam Smith argued that the role of the state should be limited to corrections for obvious market failures and to the provision of basic public goods, including law and order, national defence and basic physical infrastructure. Alluding to the ensuing positive externalities, Smith also called for the state to provide basic education for the poor. It would thus be unwarranted to see Smith as an advocate only of a minimal nightwatchman state.

Professor Musgrave finds a clear continuity of thought in the development of the theory of public goods from David Hume and Adam Smith to Knut Wicksell and Paul Samuelson. Non-rivalry in or non-excludability from the consumption of certain goods causes market failure. This must be overcome by the service state and its political process which serves to reveal the citizens' preferences for public goods. The state thereby assists the invisible hand to approximate what the market would have done.

While early classical writers saw no role for the state in adjusting the distribution of income determined by the market, public finance scholars inspired by utilitarian ideas gradually came to accept the idea that income redistribution is a legitimate function of government. John Stuart Mill was an important transition figure in this context by insisting that the tax system could be used to ensure a fair distribution of income without compromising the superior role of the market as the main mechanism guiding the allocation of resources. Following developments in welfare economics, Anglo-Saxon writers unfolded a vision of what Richard Musgrave terms the 'welfare state' whose functions extend beyond the provision of public services to correction of the distribution of income. The modern theory of optimal taxation – which studies how redistributive taxes can be designed so as to minimize the ensuing loss of economic efficiency – may be viewed as a culmination of this theoretical tradition.

From Adam Smith to the present day, Anglo-Saxon public finance theorists have tended to define social welfare as a function solely of the private welfare of the individuals who make up society, and they have seen the role of the state as that of helping to ensure the best possible satisfaction of individual needs, somehow weighted through the political process. By contrast, nineteenth-century scholars such as Albert Schäffle, Lorenz von Stein and Adolph Wagner, writing in the German tradition of *Finanzwissenschaft*, developed an alternative vision of the 'communal state' which had needs and functions beyond those derived directly from individual preferences. In this organic or 'holistic' view of the state, society is seen as more than just the sum of its individual parts. On the one hand, citizens have private needs which may be satisfied in the marketplace, but as members of a community they also have communal needs, the satisfaction of which requires action by the state, potentially in a wide range of areas of social life. The perceived character of communal needs varied significantly from one writer to another. Some saw the state as an organic entity separate from individual citizens, with its own distinct needs and functions, having a moral character superior to the profit-seeking activities of individuals acting in the market-place. Others saw the state as the coordinating agent whose actions manifested the communal desires of the collective of citizens united by a common set of social values. As Musgrave describes, the idea of the communal state gradually lost its appeal during the twentieth century, in part because writers in the *Finanzwissenschaft* tradition failed to provide a clear definition of the crucial concept of 'communal needs' which might serve as an operational guideline for delineating the boundaries of state action. However, although not mentioned by Musgrave, the influence of the *Finanzwissenschaft* tradition in continental Europe may help to explain why modern European welfare states have expanded their activities beyond those that seem warranted by the need to correct for market failures and for inequities in income distribution.

An alternative explanation for the growth of government may be that various pressure groups, including politicians and civil servants, have the power to secure expansion of government activity in areas serving their special interests. This observation brings us to the fourth vision of the state mentioned by Musgrave: a perspective which does not seek primarily to offer normative criteria for the fiscal actions of government, but rather to explain why governments often fail to act in the 'efficient' or 'optimal' manner prescribed by welfare economics. This perspective, characterized by Musgrave as the model of the 'flawed state', shifts the focus from market failure to government failure. Although rooted in the writings of Italian scholars in the late nineteenth and early twentieth century, this view of the state is most clearly represented by the public choice school led by James Buchanan. Writers in this tradition often analyse the implications for government behaviour of the existence of rent-seeking interest groups, including self-interested governmental agents. One typical prediction is that the government sector will tend to overexpand as a result of these forces. Public choice theorists have therefore studied the possibility of containing government growth through constitutional constraints which limit the scope for rent-seeking behaviour.

The evaluation of alternative institutional frameworks for government requires some normative criteria against which government performance can be judged. Thus, whether one adopts the approach of the public choice school or the more traditional approach of welfare economics, the study of public finance ultimately presupposes some sense of what the good society can and should be like. As noted by Musgrave, this is what gives the field of public finance its special appeal.

Defining and Measuring the Impact of Government

In Musgrave's definition, the discipline of public finance studies the fiscal tools of the state and how they can best be used to meet the goals of public policy. Usually these fiscal tools have been thought of as taxes, transfers and government purchases of goods and services, all of which are recorded in the public budget. However, in Chapter 2 Vito Tanzi argues that the narrow focus on these conventional fiscal policy tools often causes economists and policy-makers to overlook the many subtle ways in which government impacts on the economy. For political or administrative reasons, governments are often unable to pursue their goals by introducing explicit taxes and public expenditures. Rather than adjusting their ambitions in the light of the available fiscal policy tools, policy-makers frequently react to these constraints by resorting to more indirect policy instruments such as various types of regulations which enable them to pursue their objectives in a less controversial or in an administratively simpler manner. According to Tanzi, this causes a kind of 'institutional failure' much akin to the government failures highlighted by the public choice school: compared to ordinary taxes and transfers, the indirect policy tools adopted are less effective in influencing the policy targets or imply larger unintended side effects. For these reasons they typically lead to greater distortions of the economy or to large gaps between intended and actual changes in target variables. In addition, because policy intervention through regulations does not give rise to explicit taxes and public expenditures, an outside observer focusing on the size of the public budget will tend to underestimate the impact of government on resource allocation and income distribution.

To give an example: a government wishing to subsidize the housing costs of poor families could do so most naturally via direct tax-financed subsidies targeted at low-income families. Yet governments often resort to the non-fiscal instrument of rent controls which do not cause an expansion of the public budget but nevertheless work very much like a tax on the landlord combined with a subsidy to the renter. However, in the long run rent controls may lead to a serious shortage of housing supply, and the benefits of low rents may not always accrue to the most needy families. Tanzi mentions several other examples of such 'quasi-fiscal' regulations which are essentially substitutes for taxing and spending actions of the government, and he reports estimates of the quantitative importance of two common quasi-fiscal activities. One of these is 'financial repression', defined as controls on financial intermediaries coupled with controls on international capital flows. Another is the seigniorage which the government obtains from its monopoly power over money creation. The estimated implicit government revenue from these sources often amounts to several percentage points of GDP, and according to Tanzi they are only the tip of the iceberg of quasi-fiscal activities.

Thus, Tanzi's contribution strongly suggests that public finance economists must study a wider range of policy instruments if they wish to understand the impact of government on the economy. Quasi-fiscal activities seem particularly common in developing countries where the availability of conventional tax and spending instruments is often limited. Indeed, part of the recorded historical growth of government in the developed industrialized countries may simply reflect the fact that quasi-fiscal controls have been replaced by ordinary fiscal tools, in which case the growth record seems less dramatic.

II THE WELFARE STATE, ENTREPRENEURSHIP AND EMPLOYMENT

The chapters by Musgrave and Tanzi contribute to our understanding of the background for the emergence of the so-called welfare state. The three subsequent chapters, by Hans-Werner Sinn, Robert Haveman and Frederick van der Ploeg, take a closer look at the tax-transfer systems of modern welfare states and their impact on risk-taking activities and labour market activity.

As already hinted at by Musgrave and Tanzi, public and political opinion on the proper role of government tends to move in long cycles. Reflecting the dismal performance of the capitalist economies during the interwar years and the ensuing social problems, the first decades following the Second World War saw widespread public support for a more active role for government in important areas such as health, education and social insurance. However, in recent decades the advanced welfare states in the OECD area have faced growing scepticism. This is hardly surprising, for even if part of the recorded growth of government may be due to a switch from quasi-fiscal regulations to more conventional fiscal instruments, the government sector has indeed expanded greatly since the early postwar years. Moreover, the unintended negative side effects of various welfare state policies have become more obvious as tax and transfer rates have increased and as larger sections of the population have come to rely on government for income support. As a result, a growing number of critics have announced their desire to 'roll back' the welfare state, and many OECD governments have cut back substantially on a number of welfare programmes.

The contributions to Part II may be seen as a warning that, in this process of trimming the welfare state, policy-makers should be careful not to throw away the baby with the bathwater. While fully recognizing the need to design welfare state policies with a careful view to their impact on economic incentives, the authors point out that redistributive policies do not always lead to an inferior allocation of resources.

Social Insurance and Risk-Taking

The redistributive tax policies of the welfare state are often blamed for discouraging risky economic activities, thereby hampering the entrepreneurship which is a vital source of prosperity and growth. In Chapter 3, Hans-Werner Sinn takes issue with this view. Sinn argues that, when seen in a proper long-term and intergenerational perspective, the so-called redistributive welfare state policies may be Pareto-improving social insurance policies which tend to stimulate risk-taking. If families are risk-averse and cannot predict the future careers of their children, it seems likely that they benefit *ex ante* from welfare state policies which redistribute resources from the lucky rich to the unlucky poor, even if those families whose children end up in the high-income groups of society may lose from such policies *ex post*. *Ex-ante*, the expected variance of children's outcomes is lower with the welfare state in existence than it would be without the welfare state. Since voluntary private insurance contracts must be based on actuarial principles, they cannot offer the same type and amount of income insurance as the social safety net of the welfare state. Sinn supports this claim by presenting empirical evidence which suggests that welfare state activities crowd out private insurance activity only to a very limited extent, thus indicating the imperfect substitutability of the two forms of insurance. He goes on to argue that, because the provision of public services and public income transfers represent income insurance in an *ex ante* expected utility sense, the welfare state may actually encourage risky economic activities with high expected returns, thereby raising national income and welfare relative to the benchmark case of *laissez-faire*. At the same time, recognizing the well-known moral hazard problems, Hans-Werner Sinn acknowledges that very high tax-transfer rates may generate welfare losses by stimulating excessive risk-taking and discouraging private efforts at loss prevention.

To illustrate these ideas, Sinn sets up a very simple general equilibrium model which describes how private risk-taking behaviour and welfare is affected by private market insurance and by redistributive taxation. In particular, the model highlights how the distribution of pre-tax incomes changes as a result of the changes in risk-taking activity induced by redistributive taxation. As a benchmark, Sinn uses the model to identify the constrained Pareto-optimal resource allocation which could be implemented via so-called 'ideal market insurance' under conditions of perfect monitoring where insurance companies can tailor insurance premiums precisely to the actions of each individual agent. In practice this Pareto optimum cannot be attained either through the market or through government intervention, because imperfect and asymmetric information generates problems of moral hazard. In an intergenerational perspective, the government has the advantage that it can use redistributive taxation to insure against risks that cannot be insured in the private market. On the other hand, redistributive tax-transfer policies generate moral hazard because it is administratively impossible to grant full tax deductibility of all relevant private opportunity costs of loss prevention, interpreted in a broad sense to include all private efforts at avoiding income shortfalls. Sinn shows that, with no deductibility of the private costs of loss prevention, redistributive taxation will generate *too much* risk-taking relative to the hypothetical optimum with ideal market insurance. The reason is that redistributive taxation lowers the variance of expected private returns to risky activities while at the same time discouraging efforts at loss prevention. With high rates of taxation it is even possible that the redistributive activities of government will generate a lower level of welfare for the representative agent than a situation with no government intervention at all. As noted by Sinn, this seems to be the situation which the critics of the welfare state have in mind.

However, the main result of Sinn's analysis is that, even if problems of moral hazard are unavoidable, a welfare state applying a proper dose of redistributive taxation can achieve a higher level of consumer welfare than a *laissez-faire* economy. Furthermore, at the second-best optimal level of redistributive taxation Sinn shows that one of two paradoxical situations must prevail: in the first possible case the amount of risk-taking and the ensuing income losses are so high that a reduction of risk-taking would not only generate a more equal distribution of pre-tax incomes but would also raise national income per capita. In other words, less pre-tax inequality would be associated with a higher rather than a lower mean income. In the other possible case the second-best redistributive tax policy will lead to a situation where a small increase in the tax rate would stimulate risk-taking to such an extent that both pre-tax *and* post-tax incomes would become more unequally distributed (in absolute terms), that is, attempts at further redistribution would only generate further inequality!

In an uncertain economic environment where agents trade off higher expected returns against higher risks, the standard view that higher redistributive taxes will always reduce inequality, but invariably at the expense of lower mean incomes, may thus be much too simplified. Hans-Werner Sinn's contribution serves to remind us that we may not yet fully understand the potentially beneficial efficiency effects of redistributive welfare state policies.

Unemployment and Public Finance in the United States

Just as the welfare state is often blamed for discouraging entrepreneurship, its tax policies and income support programmes are also frequently accused of eroding work incentives and keeping low-income families caught in an 'unemployment trap' or a 'poverty trap' by making it difficult for them to improve their earnings by seeking work. In Chapter 4 Robert Haveman discusses how the tax-transfer system could be reformed to alleviate the problems of unemployment and poverty in the United States. In so doing, he puts the recent reform of US welfare programmes into critical perspective.

As a background to his reform proposals, Robert Haveman starts out by documenting the trends in employment, earnings and poverty in the USA since the 1970s. Compared to Western Europe, where employment has generally been stagnating and unemployment has risen dramatically, the US labour market has been an impressive job generator and has displayed no trend rise in unemployment. However, the median real hourly wage in the USA has fallen by 6 per cent from 1973 to 1993, and unemployment has become much more concentrated on the young, on members of ethnic minorities, and on individuals with little or no education. Moreover, earnings inequalities have increased greatly: male workers at the lowest tenth percentile of the earnings ladder took a 23 per cent cut in their real earnings between 1973 and 1993, whereas male workers at the highest tenth percentile experienced a real earnings increase of more than 7 per cent over the same period. The earnings premium obtained by college graduates relative to workers with a high school degree or less also increased from about 30 per cent in 1979 to over 70 per cent by the early 1990s. At the same time the proportion of the US population falling below the official poverty line rose from 11.1 per cent in the early 1970s to 14.5 per cent in 1994.

As Haveman observes, one might have expected US policy-makers to have responded to these developments by taking steps to improve the labour market opportunities for low-paid workers and minority groups and to counter the tendency towards sharply increasing income differentials. In fact the opposite seems to have happened. During the period when the bottom of the US labour market virtually collapsed, the US federal government significantly reduced the share of federal expenditure allocated to employment and training programmes for low-skilled workers. In addition, the recent reform of the US welfare system involving cuts in the eligibility for various safety net programmes is expected to drive 200 000 to 300 000 low-skilled benefit recipients into the labour market where they will be earning the minimum wage which in real terms has already fallen to about 75 per cent of its level in 1981.

According to Haveman, this labour market strategy fails to consider the serious problem of declining earnings for low-skilled workers which has come to characterize the US labour market. While recognizing the desirability of encouraging low-income earners to seek work rather than collect benefits, Haveman proposes measures to strengthen the demand side as well as the supply side of the market for low-skilled labour.

On the demand side, he suggests the introduction of an employer-based marginal employment subsidy. Under such a scheme an employer would receive a subsidy or tax credit amounting to (say) 50 per cent of the first (say) 10 000 dollars of wages paid to (say) the first 50 workers hired above (say) 102 per cent of the firm's previous year's employment. By limiting the marginal subsidy to a maximum base level of individual annual earnings, such a programme would increase the relative demand for low-paid workers. Furthermore, by granting the subsidy only to increases in employment above some base amount, the taxpayer cost of the programme would be limited. Inevitably, there would be some windfall to employers who would have expanded their employment in any case, but this would not eliminate the tendency for the subsidy to twist relative demand in favour of low-paid workers.

On the supply side, Robert Haveman suggests the introduction of a wage rate subsidy to workers earning a wage rate below some target level. The hourly subsidy would amount to some percentage of the difference between the target and the actual hourly wage. According to Haveman, such a policy would have three unambiguous merits: first, it would increase the net income from work relative to income from welfare and unemployment benefits, thereby tending to 'make work pay'. Second, even though increased labour supply would result in some fall in pre-subsidy wage rates, the subsidy would tend to raise net earnings at the bottom end of the pay scale, thus alleviating the poverty problem. Third, by increasing labour supply, the subsidy would offset the adverse employment effect of the existing minimum wage policy. On the debit side, Haveman notes that the fall in the subsidy generated by an increase in the market wage rate would increase the effective marginal tax rate on wage rate increases for low-paid workers, thereby reducing their incentive to move up the earnings ladder via education, training and job search. He also recognizes the administrative problem that employers would have to keep records of hourly wage rates, and that the authorities would have to undertake some auditing to ensure that employers and employees do not collude by reporting a lower than actual wage rate in order to split the benefit from the resulting subsidy payment.

Yet Haveman argues that the potential administrative problems can be overcome and that the taxpayer cost of a targeted marginal employment subsidy scheme combined with a targeted wage rate subsidy will be much lower than the cost of obtaining a similar increase in low-skilled employment via the implementation of public service employment programmes.

The Welfare State and Unemployment in Europe

In Chapter 5 Frederick van der Ploeg discusses the unemployment problem and possible public finance remedies from a European perspective. As a starting point he surveys the anatomy of unemployment in Western Europe. Similar to the US situation, unemployment in Europe tends to be concentrated among the young and the low-skilled members of the labour force. However, labour turnover is generally much lower in European countries than in the USA. Once unemployed, the average European worker therefore has a smaller chance of quickly finding a new job. This may be one reason why long-term unemployment makes up a much larger proportion of total unemployment in Europe. European employment growth has been slow in recent decades, and van der Ploeg points out that most of the new jobs have been opened in the public sector. Since the 1970s unemployment in Europe has become higher and much more persistent than in the United States. On the other hand, earnings differentials in Europe have generally been fairly stable, in contrast to the sharp increase in wage dispersion of the USA, and real wage growth has been higher on the European side of the Atlantic.

As already noted by Robert Haveman in the preceding chapter, this experience suggests that policy-makers may face an unpleasant trade-off between an American-style package of rapid employment growth, high and rising wage inequality, and slow wage growth versus a European-style package of slow employment growth, low and steady wage inequality, higher wage growth and high unemployment. Apparently the extensive European social safety net combined with minimum wages and union practices have prevented downward wage adjustment and widening wage differentials between skilled and unskilled workers, but at the cost of growing unemployment, especially among the low-skilled.

Frederick van der Ploeg notes that most European systems of unemployment compensation are indeed fairly generous and may be responsible for high reservation wages at the bottom end of the pay scale. However, convinced that the bulk of unemployment in Europe is involuntary, he points out that substantial cuts in unemployment benefits would have undesirable implications for income distribution. As an alternative, he advocates tighter administrative controls of unemployment benefit schemes to ensure that benefits go only to those who are actively seeking work, combined with a number of fiscal reform measures designed to promote employment.

To provide some analytical background to his reform proposals, van der Ploeg briefly reviews the effects of taxation in the conventional neoclassical model of a competitive labour market. In this standard framework a fall in the average tax rate on labour income (keeping the marginal tax rate constant) will have a negative effect on employment by generating a negative income effect on labour supply. On the other hand, for a given average tax rate, a fall in the marginal labour income tax rate (that is, a less redistributive tax system) will raise aggregate employment by eliciting a positive substitution effect on labour supply.

By contrast, in imperfect labour markets those effects of taxation are completely reversed. Van der Ploeg illustrates this by sketching a search model where imperfect information forces workers and firms to engage in costly search activity before vacancies can be matched with unemployed job seekers. A job match involves a rent which is the sum of expected search costs for the firm and the worker, including forgone wages and profits. This rent is split between the worker and the firm in a bilateral wage-bargaining process. Because employed workers capture part of the rent, their utility is strictly higher than that of the unemployed job seekers. In this sense the search frictions generated by imperfect information cause involuntary unemployment, even in the absence of monopolistic union practices. The share of the rent which will be captured by the worker will depend on his 'threat point' or 'outside option', that is, his alternative income in case bargaining breaks down and the firm and the worker split up. This alternative income consists of after-tax unemployment benefits plus whatever income the worker might be able to earn in the informal economy, that is, in the underground economy and in household production activities.

In this setting with search frictions a fall in the average tax rate on labour income (keeping the marginal tax rate constant) will induce wage moderation and thereby stimulate employment, because it raises the net income from work relative to the net income obtainable from the worker's outside option. The moderating effect on wage rates will be particularly strong if the fall in the tax burden applies only to labour income but not to benefit income, or if a large part of the worker's alternative income derives from the informal economy. On the other hand, for a given average tax rate a fall in the marginal tax on labour income will generate higher wage rates and lower employment. With a lower marginal tax rate it becomes less costly for the employer to offer the employee some given increase in the after-tax wage by raising the pre-tax wage rate, and hence it becomes advantageous for workers and firms to shift part of the rent from job matches towards workers through higher wages. In addition, the higher marginal tax rate will tend to raise the number of persons employed, because it provides an incentive to bargain for a reduction in work hours. Van der Ploeg goes on to point out that these effects of average and marginal tax rates in imperfect labour markets are very robust, since they also materialize in union models and efficiency wage models of wage formation and employment.

Against this analytical background, Frederick van der Ploeg proceeds to argue for the introduction of an Earned Income Tax Credit (EITC) in Europe, that is, a credit against the tax on labour income which is gradually phased out as the worker's income from labour increases. According to van der Ploeg, such an EITC would stimulate employment in two ways. For one thing, by reducing the average tax rate on low-income earners and raising their net income gain from employment relative to unemployment and activity in the informal economy, it would induce more active search activity and moderate wage pressures at the lower end of the pay scale where unemployment is higher. Second, because the gradual phasing out of the tax credit would increase effective marginal tax rates on labour income over a long interval, this increase in tax progressivity would imply a further incentive for wage moderation, in line with the above theoretical analysis. The reader will note that the proposed EITC would work much like Robert Haveman's proposal for a wage rate subsidy to low-income earners, although the EITC is not as directly targeted at individuals with low earnings capacities. The novelty of van der Ploeg's analysis is that there might be an additional argument for this kind of policy in an imperfect labour market where higher tax progressivity tends to moderate wage claims. Like Haveman, van der Ploeg recognizes that increased tax progressivity may have some detrimental side effects, including reduced incentives for skill upgrading in the income interval where the EITC is phased out. Clearly, such negative side effects must be accounted for when policy-makers attempt to identify the 'optimal' level of EITC.

As a possible means of financing tax cuts for low-income wage-earners, van der Ploeg calls for a rise in environmental taxes on polluting activities, such as higher taxes on energy use, although he is careful to point out the conditions which must prevail if such a 'green' tax reform is to yield a 'double dividend' in the form of higher employment as well as an improved environment. His analysis suggests that a double dividend will occur only if pre-existing energy taxes are moderate and if there is a sizeable informal economy generating substantial untaxed incomes for the unemployed. The point is that while people working in the informal economy escape labour income taxes, they cannot escape the consumer price effects of higher indirect taxes on energy. A shift from labour income taxes to energy taxes will therefore moderate wage claims to the extent that wage rates in the official labour market are influenced by the real net income obtainable by workers in the informal economy.

Frederick van der Ploeg suggests two further fiscal weapons against the European unemployment problem. First, to counter the tendency for the long-term unemployed to become alienated from the labour market, he argues for temporary wage subsidies for this category. According to his proposal, the subsidy should be larger if the worker has been longer unemployed and engages in training. By making the individual subsidy temporary, it should be possible to avoid serious crowding-out effects on workers who are already employed. Second, pointing to the importance of new firms for long-term job growth and to capital market imperfections hampering the start-up of new businesses, he suggests a number of fiscal incentives for the start-up of new firms, arguing that such incentives for entrepreneurship will often be more beneficial than the creation of additional public sector jobs for the unemployed.

Finally, van der Ploeg warns that the ongoing process of fiscal consolidation in many European countries has tended to involve cuts in productive public spending on education, training and infrastructure which may harm employment and growth in the long run. In their efforts to make room for employment-promoting cuts in taxes on labour income, he believes that European governments should rather cut into income transfers to well-to-do families and try to make public service production cheaper by making it more efficient.

III PUBLIC FINANCE WITH MANY JURISDICTIONS

The contributions to Part II pointed to a number of reasons why redistributive fiscal policy may be justified not only by appeal to concepts of fairness and equity, but also because a properly designed redistributive policy may improve the functioning of the economy by stimulating employment and risk-taking. Against this background it is obviously important to study how the redistributive policies of an individual jurisdiction are affected and constrained by the policies of other jurisdictions in the contemporary world where new policy-making jurisdictions and political entities are entering the world economic scene, and where goods, services and in particular factors of production are becoming increasingly mobile across jurisdictional boundaries.

The interjurisdictional fiscal interdependencies also raise the question of how the governments in a region might best design a constitutional framework which can promote mutually advantageous fiscal coordination while respecting the desire of individual jurisdictions to maintain a high degree of autonomy. Because capital is a particularly mobile factor of production, it is of special interest to investigate whether and how the system of capital income taxation can be designed so as to accommodate desires for national autonomy in tax policy without seriously distorting international capital flows.

The chapters in Part III, by David Wildasin, Dubravko Mihaljek and Sijbren Cnossen, address all of these issues.

Factor Mobility and Redistributive Policy

In Chapter 6 David Wildasin discusses the scope for and the effects of redistributive fiscal policy in a multijurisdiction world with factor mobility, offering an interpretation and synthesis of a number of important contributions to the literature on this topic. Since most writers on the economic implications of factor mobility have concentrated on the effects of capital mobility, David Wildasin deliberately chooses to focus most of his attention on the consequences of labour mobility which have been much less researched. One of his messages is that many issues of international public finance are becoming increasingly akin to those arising in the context of local public finance so that it seems natural to search for general principles of 'open economy public economics' which can be applied in a variety of different policy contexts with factor mobility.

To understand how fiscal policy works in a setting with factor mobility, it is necessary to grasp the general economic implications of factor mobility in the absence of government intervention. Wildasin therefore starts out by reviewing the effects of factor mobility on resource allocation and income distribution without specific reference to government policies. At first, he notes that factor market integration can improve the efficiency of factor allocations. To the extent that factor returns reflect marginal productivities, the movement of labour and capital from areas with low returns to areas with high returns will tend to raise aggregate incomes.

In principle, this raises the possibility that all citizens of the integrating regions may gain from integration. However, as Wildasin points out, factor mobility will most likely affect the distribution of income. In the country of origin, the emigration of a mobile factor will tend to raise the return to that factor while reducing the return to complementary immobile factors. By contrast, in the country of destination the immigration of the mobile factor will depress that factor's return while raising the return to the local immobile factors. Even if world income per capita goes up as a result of the efficiency gain from migration, it is therefore quite possible that some factor owners will lose not only in relative but also in absolute terms.

The third point raised by Wildasin has been less widely recognized: in a world where idiosyncratic economic shocks are not evenly distributed

across space, factor mobility enables individuals to escape the consequences of adverse location-specific shocks by moving to another location. Factor mobility may thus help to insure against income risk, and from
an *ex ante* perspective this may be seen as a welfare improvement for all
owners of mobile factors in an expected utility sense.

Having reviewed the most basic effects of factor mobility, David
Wildasin turns to some of its fiscal dimensions. His first observation is
that factor mobility may raise the efficiency cost of income redistribution
and limit the effectiveness of redistributive policies. Within a given jurisdiction it will be very difficult to impose net fiscal burdens on the owners
of highly mobile factors, since the burden may be escaped through emigration. Similarly, attempts by a single jurisdiction to redistribute income
towards a highly mobile factor may cause such an inflow of the factor that
the local fisc cannot sustain the pressure and is forced to give up its policy.
More generally, since mobility causes an increase in the supply elasticities
of mobile factors, it tends to raise the deadweight losses associated with
redistributive policies affecting these factors.

The political system is likely to respond to the higher cost of redistribution attributable to increasing mobility by pursuing less ambitious redistributive policies. According to Wildasin, whether this is to be welcomed
or not depends on one's view of government. If government is seen as a
benevolent maximizer of social welfare, trading off efficiency losses
against equity gains, increased mobility will worsen the terms of this
trade-off so that social welfare may fall, even if mobility tends to raise
average income. On the other hand, those who emphasize 'government
failure' in the sense explained by Richard Musgrave in Chapter 1 have
often argued that many redistributive policies result from the political
pressures of special interest groups exploiting the fiscal tools of the state
for their private rent-seeking purposes. In this view actual redistribution
may well go from the poor to the rich, rather than in the opposite direction,
and increased factor mobility may then improve equity as well as
efficiency by reducing the scope for redistribution. Given the different
political systems and institutions across the world, it is conceivable that
increased mobility may lead to social welfare gains in some countries
while generating losses in other countries.

Wildasin also observes that while mobility may limit the effectiveness
of redistributive policy, it may also reduce the benefits from such policy
(assuming that the benefits are indeed positive). If mobility helps to insure
against income risk, as mentioned earlier, increases in mobility would
seem to reduce the need for redistributive social insurance policies. More
precisely, factor mobility tends to shift the incidence of income risks away

from mobile towards immobile factors of production. If the income risks associated with immobile factors such as land can be diversified through financial markets whereas the income risk associated with labour cannot, it seems likely that increased labour mobility has the potential to reduce overall income risks, thus reducing the need for publicly provided social insurance. However, as Wildasin points out, it is also possible that higher mobility leads to an increase in certain uninsurable income risks so that the benefits from redistributive policy will not necessarily fall.

Because the factor flows induced by the fiscal policies of one jurisdiction may generate positive or negative spillovers on other jurisdictions, they provide a rationale for intergovernmental grants to internalize these externalities. For instance, Wildasin notes that transfers from a rich to a poor jurisdiction may reduce the incentives for inefficient migration of labour in response to fiscal differentials, thereby benefiting both jurisdictions. The potential benefits from fiscal coordination may also provide a motive for a group of neighbouring jurisdictions to form a federation with a common central government which may implement interjurisdictional transfers and assume responsibility for some redistributive policies which cannot be carried out effectively at lower levels of government. This observation takes David Wildasin into a rich discussion of the determinants and consequences of changes in jurisdictional structure.

In the final part of his chapter Wildasin discusses how important the fiscal impacts of labour mobility are likely to be in practice. It is often argued that labour mobility is not a serious constraint on national fiscal policy because labour seems to be rather immobile across countries in most parts of the world. As Wildasin's analysis makes clear, this argument is too imprecise and superficial. First of all, the absence of significant recorded cross-border flows of labour during a given time period is no proof that labour is immobile. An alternative explanation could be that the economic incentives to migrate have already been eliminated through migration in some earlier time period, or that these incentives have been neutralized because government policies have already responded to the threat of migration. Second, even if the major part of the labour force is more or less immobile, fiscal policy may still be significantly constrained if there is a marginal group of individuals who are relatively mobile. With high mobility at the margin, many fiscal measures will have the same effects as if all workers were mobile. Similarly, though there may be high fixed (pecuniary and psychological) costs of moving from one country to another, a change in fiscal policy may still induce substantial migration flows by raising the net gain from migration above the fixed cost of moving for a large number of individuals.

Furthermore, the time horizon adopted for the purposes of analysis is very important, since labour tends to be much more mobile in the very long run than in the short run. For this reason, and because the assimilation of immigrants in a country is a time-consuming process during which the economic characteristics of the immigrant and his descendants are likely to change substantially, Wildasin argues that the implications of labour mobility ought to be studied in a long-term dynamic perspective. In such a perspective the empirical assessment of the economic and fiscal effects of migration becomes rather complicated, but also quite an intellectual challenge.

Confederacy as a Fiscal Constitution

David Wildasin noted how perceived economic gains as well as fiscal externalities arising from integration may induce a group of independent jurisdictions to enter into some form of political union to promote integration and to internalize the spillovers. He also briefly described how perceived adverse changes in the interjurisdictional distribution of the benefits from cooperation may induce an individual jurisdiction to secede from such a union.

In Chapter 7 Dubravko Mihaljek suggests that the institutional framework offered by confederacy may be a particularly appealing form of cooperation to many of the new jurisdictions which have recently emerged on the world scene or which may emerge in the future. In a *confederation* the central government derives its authority from individual member states which voluntarily decide to delegate decision-making powers to the confederation in certain limited and well-defined policy areas. Moreover, the member states of a confederation retain the right to secede in accordance with procedures laid down in the confederate constitution. By contrast, in a *federation* the lower-level governments derive their authority from the central government which decides to decentralize policy-making in certain areas while retaining supremacy in all other policy areas not explicitly left to member states. Furthermore, in a federation secession from the union is generally considered unconstitutional.

Because of its stronger constitutional position, the central government of a federation tends to be better equipped to ensure fiscal coordination between member states. From the narrow perspective of economic efficiency, the federal form of organization may therefore be preferable to the looser confederate form. However, as emphasized by Mihaljek, the jurisdictions contemplating the formation of a political union will often have a strong political preference for retaining as much autonomy as possible, including autonomy in most fiscal affairs. In such a situation a confederation may be the preferred alternative to the perceived straitjacket of a federation and may still offer important political and economic benefits from cooperation.

Historically most confederations have either dissolved into fully independent nations of evolved into federations. Some observers have therefore claimed that confederations are inherently unstable. Against this background Mihaljek carefully reexamines the fiscal history of five confederations: the Confederate States of America (1777–89), Switzerland (1815–48), Germany (1871–1919), the former Yugoslavia (1972–90), and China (1988–93). He concludes that the economic and fiscal problems in all of these confederations were due to specific historical circumstances and exogenous events such as war (the Confederate States of America), foreign military pressure combined with a weak administrative capacity to collect taxes (Switzerland), excessive expenditures on armaments (Germany), violent nationalist forces rooted in history and released by the erosion of communist party power (Yugoslavia), and an irrational division of tax bases between the central and the regional governments (China).

Absent such unique factors and exogenous disturbances, Mihaljek sees no reason why the confederate form of organization should not be economically viable. He points out two economic motives for a country to enter a confederation. First, from an *ex ante* perspective the confederation may provide some insurance against *ex post* bad economic outcomes to the extent that it involves fiscal transfer mechanisms favouring member states which experience a fall in their relative income position. Second, because a confederate constitution typically guarantees internal free trade and sometimes also free factor mobility and a monetary union, it offers the benefits of economic integration without requiring member states to give up independence in key areas of sovereignty.

Mihaljek proceeds to discuss issues in the design of confederate finances on the premise that members of confederations would maintain a high degree of political and constitutional sovereignty. Given the importance usually attached to policies involving interpersonal income redistribution and social security, he argues that the member states of a confederation would not want to delegate such policies to the confederate authority. Moreover, since preferences for core public services may vary considerably across member states, Mihaljek sees no basis for introducing elaborate horizontal fiscal equalization schemes and vertical matching grants with the purpose of ensuring roughly similar levels of taxation and public service provision throughout the confederation. However, he does see an important role for interregional transfers to compensate for wide economic disparities, arguing like David Wildasin that such transfers from rich to poor regions can be efficiency-enhancing, for instance by preventing socially disruptive migration flows and by helping to keep backward regions open to free trade.

As far as stabilization policy is concerned, Mihaljek points out that the central government budget of a confederation will typically be so small that stabilization cannot be carried out effectively at the confederate level. This policy branch will thus have to be left to member states, but some coordination is necessary to avoid negative spillovers. Mihaljek argues that the most effective framework for fiscal policy coordination is one that develops agreements about broad and reasonably flexible fiscal rules and establishes mechanisms for regular discussion and coordination of budgetary strategies. He points to successful German and Belgian experiences with this type of policy coordination between central and state governments.

Turning to expenditure assignment, expenditure on defence and on regulation activity serving to implement free trade may be natural candidates for confederate functions, but again, the bulk of expenditure would be assigned to member states. In areas where public goods and services are regional in character, Mihaljek argues that horizontal regional cooperation agreements may be more efficient than intervention involving the confederate authority. Given that confederate expenditures are likely to be limited, Mihaljek believes they could be easily financed through sources such as joint external tariff revenues and lump-sum contributions from member states. In this way member states would not have to give up or share any of their major tax bases, in line with the assumed desire for national autonomy in taxation. However, with tax policy left entirely at the discretion of member states, the issues of tax competition and tax coordination arise. According to Mihaljek, tax competition is likely to bring about a gradual convergence of tax levels so that there would be no need for confederations to insist on tax harmonization. He does not discuss whether convergence is likely to take place around the 'proper' level of taxation and spending. However, as several previous chapters of the book have suggested, the answer to this question is likely to depend on the view of government one adopts, that is, whether government is seen as a 'Leviathan' tending to overexpand in the absence of constraining forces such as fiscal competition, or whether the political process is believed to secure a level and composition of public spending roughly in line with voter preferences.

In summary, Dubravko Mihaljek argues that, in a world where nations value their sovereignty, confederations have the advantage that they enable member states to reap most of the benefits of economic integration while still allowing them to exercise independent powers in key areas of policy-making.

Capital Income Taxation with Multiple Jurisdictions

In Chapter 8 the need to respect national preferences for a high degree of autonomy in tax policy is also an important premise for Sijbren Cnossen. Cnossen discusses how capital income taxes and in particular company taxes in the European Union can be reformed and coordinated. This has been a recurrent theme of theme of the European tax policy debate and an issue of growing importance as the increasing mobility of capital has exposed the weaknesses of the existing systems of capital income taxation ever more clearly.

Under the current corporate tax systems the tax burden on investment varies greatly depending on the legal form in which investment takes place (that is, company form or non-company form), the choice of financing of investment (debt versus equity), the dividend policy of the company (that is, whether profits are retained or distributed), the tax status of the recipient of the return (whether the recipient is a private investor, a corporate investor or a tax-exempt institution), and the place of residence of the investor (domestic versus foreign residence). In general, the tax system tends to favour debt finance over equity finance and retention over distribution of profit, even though all EU countries except The Netherlands have taken steps to mitigate the double taxation of dividends. Cnossen argues that the deductibility of interest from the corporate tax base combined with the growing importance of foreign and tax-exempt institutional investors causes excessive reliance on debt finance and a serious erosion of the capital income tax base. He therefore calls for a fundamental reform of the European systems of capital income taxation. As guidelines for reform, he appeals to the principles of neutrality and subsidiarity embedded in the treaties of Rome and Maastricht. Neutrality implies that competition should be the mechanism for allocating economic resources in the EU and that European firms should be able to compete on equal terms. In the field of capital income taxation, this means that tax systems should be designed so as to minimize the distorting impact on investment decisions, inducing firms to react to market signals rather than to tax incentives. The still evolving concept of subsidiarity implies a presumption in favour of decentralization. As far as possible, policy functions should be exercised by member states, although each member is obliged to consider the effects of its actions on other member states.

Inevitably, there is some tension between the two principles. While tax neutrality tends to require a substantial degree of international tax harmonization, subsidiary requires that each member state be granted as much tax autonomy as is consistent with the goals of free trade and free competition. According to Cnossen, subsidiarity implies that tax policy must be based on a clear set of common rules for the division of tax bases among member states but that these rules must enable each member state to operate its own tax system without the need for day-to-day cooperation with other member states in the form of information exchange, cross-border audits and so on.

Neutrality in taxation requires that all forms of capital income be taxed uniformly and just once – neither more nor less. In the domestic sphere this means that the differential tax treatment of different kinds of return and different types of investors must be brought to an end. In the international sphere, neutrality means that cross-border investment should be neither overtaxed nor undertaxed relative to domestic investment and, preferably, that the international allocation of investment should not be influenced by tax factors.

The latter observation takes Sijbren Cnossen into a discussion of the source principle versus the residence principle of capital income taxation. Under the source principle income is taxed in the country where it is earned. Under the residence principle income is taxed in the country where the investor resides. Under current European tax systems, corporate source equity income tends to be taxed in accordance with the source principle whereas the residence principle applies to the taxation of returns to debt-financed investment. In theory, a consistent application of the residence principle to all forms of capital income would ensure that the international allocation of investment would be unaffected by tax considerations because an investor would face the same effective tax rate no matter where he decided to invest. However, effective implementation of the residence principle would require extensive cooperation among national tax administrations, thereby violating Cnossen's principle of 'operational independence' of tax systems. In particular, Cnossen does not believe in the possibility of effective residence-based taxation of the return to debt-financed investment, due to the difficulties of monitoring foreign source interest income. If interest is to be taxed at all in a world of growing capital mobility, the tax will have to be levied at source. To Cnossen, source-based taxation is thus the only viable solution to the problem of the eroding capital income tax base. Unfortunately the source principle may distort the cross-country allocation of capital, because investors will face different tax rates in different locations. The source principle thus invites

tax competition, giving each country an incentive to attract foreign investment or taxable 'paper profits' (reallocated through the transfer-pricing of
multinationals) by offering a lower tax rate than other countries. To
prevent such beggar-thy-neighbour policies, Cnossen argues for an EU
agreement on a minimum corporate tax rate below which no member state
can go.

From this point of departure, Cnossen proceeds to discuss a number of
options for a European company tax which have been debated in recent
years. The first option is a system of so-called full integration in which all
company earnings, whether retained or distributed, are allocated to shareholders and taxed in their hands. Under such a system, the corporate tax
would serve only as a withholding tax to be credited against the shareholder's final tax liability. For a number of reasons, Cnossen does not
believe full integration to be a viable system. First, it is administratively
difficult to impute retained profits to individual shareholders. Second,
because of the high marginal personal income tax rates in most EU countries, full integration would imply a substantial increase in the tax burden
on investment financed by retentions, thereby discouraging investment.
Third, the taxation of all corporate source income at progressive personal
tax rates makes sense only under a residence-based system of worldwide
income taxation, but the residence principle is difficult to put into practice,
as mentioned above.

As an alternative to full integration, some writers have proposed a so-
called dual imputation system which aims at effective, one-level taxation
of interest and dividend income. Under this system, interest would no
longer be deductible from the corporate tax base, but the recipients of
interest as well as dividends from corporate sources would receive a credit
for the underlying corporate tax against their final tax liability. According
to Cnossen the main problem with this system is that it would greatly
increase the effective tax rate on corporate source interest income, thereby
raising the cost of corporate capital to a level which might have detrimental effects on investment in the EU.

Instead of eliminating the tax bias against equity finance by raising the
effective tax on interest, one could reduce the tax burden on equity by
allowing companies to deduct a normal rate of return on their equity base
from their taxable income. Combined with interest deductibility, this
would turn the corporation tax into a neutral tax on pure profits. Yet
Cnossen argues against this solution because it would erode the corporate
tax base even further and violate the established right of source countries
to tax all returns on (equity-financed) investment generated within their
jurisdiction.

A cash-flow tax which allows immediate expensing of all investment while disallowing interest deductibility would be an alternative method of levying tax only on rents, because such a system can be shown to leave the normal return to investment free of tax. However, transition to a cash-flow tax would be a radical departure from current practice and would not ensure overall neutrality of capital income taxation unless the return to all forms of saving were exempted from personal income tax.

These criticisms leave Sijbren Cnossen with only two remaining options for capital income tax reform. One is the comprehensive business income tax (CBIT) which taxes all corporate earnings at source at the corporate level. Thus, under the CBIT interest payments are no longer deductible from the corporate tax base, but on the other hand dividends and interest are no longer taxed at the level of the recipients, be they individuals or companies.

The other remaining option – and the one preferred by Cnossen – is a version of the so-called dual income tax, recently introduced in the Nordic countries. Under this system all forms of capital income (including corporate income) are taxed at a low flat uniform rate while labour income continues to be taxed at higher progressive rates. In Cnossen's version, dividends are tax-exempt at the shareholder level, having already borne capital income tax at the corporate level. Interest continues to be deductible from the corporate tax base, but a withholding tax constituting the final tax liability is levied when interest is paid out to all domestic or foreign debtholders, be they individuals, companies or institutional investors. Thus, neither interest nor dividends are subject to personal tax, and capital gains on shares are taxed only in so far as they exceed the accumulated amount of after-tax profits retained in the corporation. When dividends are paid out of income exempt from corporate tax, a compensatory tax is levied at the corporate level to ensure that such income does not escape tax altogether. Designed in this way, the dual income tax is effectively equivalent to the comprehensive business income tax, but the continuation of interest deductibility in the calculation of taxable corporate profits implies that the dual income tax will seem closer to current tax practice.

The advantage of the dual income tax is that it would enable EU member states to separate the taxation of capital income from the taxation of labour income and to set the capital income tax rate at a fairly low level so as to prevent serious problems of capital flight out of Europe. Even so, Cnossen believes that it would require a coordinated move by the EU, the USA and Japan towards withholding taxes on interest income to prevent tax-induced capital outflows from Europe. For this reason, and because a consistent dual income tax of the type proposed by Sijbren Cnossen would eliminate a large number of current tax privileges, his proposal may still be too ambitious to be implemented at the present stage of European integration. Still, Cnossen's thorough discussion should certainly provide ample food for thought for all economists and policy-makers interested in European tax problems.

IV ECONOMIES IN TRANSITION: RAISING REVENUE AND ALLOCATING PROPERTY RIGHTS

As we have just seen, some of the most urgent problems of tax policy in Western Europe arise from tension between national desires to pursue independent fiscal policies on the one hand, and, on the other hand, the pressure for tax coordination and tax harmonization stemming from the process of economic integration. In the emerging market economies in Eastern Europe, governments face the even more basic problem of designing new tax systems which may compensate for the loss of previous revenue sources such as profits from state-owned enterprises and generate additional funds for the many pressing needs of the public sector, including the need to finance new social insurance systems to cope with the risks faced by citizens in a market economy. Another immense challenge for governments in transition economies is that of finding an appropriate procedure for moving from public to private ownership of the means of production: a unique task for which there is no precedent.

In the final part of this volume, Manfred Rose, Rolf Wiswesser and Gerlinde Sinn discuss these issues.

Designing a Tax System for an Economy in Transition

Like Sijbren Cnossen, Manfred Rose and Rolf Wiswesser analyse the complex problems of capital income taxation (Chapter 9). However, because Rose and Wiswesser are concerned with the design of a tax system which accounts for the special circumstances and needs of a transition economy, their policy recommendations are somewhat different from those of Sijbren Cnossen.

In the former socialist economies of Eastern Europe investment was not guided by the relative price signals derived from the open world market. With the transition to a market economy open to foreign trade with the Western world, the price structure in most of these economies has changed significantly, making much of the previously accumulated capital stock unprofitable and hence economically obsolete. Similarly, the transition to a market economy has reduced the relative demand for many of the skills accumulated under the socialist regime and has generated excess demand for several other skills. Hence, transition economies often suffer from a severe relative shortage of (marketable) physical and human capital, and according to Rose and Wiswesser the tax system must allow for this problem. The makers of tax policy must also account for the lack of administrative experience with complex income tax systems of the type operated in the West. The need for administratively simple solutions to the many problems of income taxation is thus particularly strong in a transition economy. On the other hand, while the factors mentioned above impose special constraints on tax policy, the governments of the former socialist economies also face the unique opportunity of being able to redesign the tax system almost from scratch. This should provide more room for manoeuvre in constructing a simple and consistent tax system, whereas tax reformers in the West are often constrained by the fact that taxpayers have adapted their circumstances to existing tax rules over a long period.

Manfred Rose and Rolf Wiswesser were members of a group of German tax experts who were asked to advise the newly independent government of Croatia on the design of a new system of income taxation. In Chapter 9 Rose and Wiswesser describe the new Croatian tax system, implemented on 1 January 1994 and designed much in line with the recommendations of the authors. The Croatian tax reform is unique and likely to attract interest from a wide international audience, since it appears to represent the first attempt in the world to implement a fully consistent consumption-based system of personal income taxation.

Rose and Wiswesser start by describing the criteria which guided the Croatian tax reform. Among those criteria were a number of time-honoured taxation principles such as tax neutrality and horizontal and vertical taxpayer equity. In addition, Croatian tax reformers paid special attention to the need for administrative simplicity, the need to strengthen Croatian public finances, and, first and foremost, the need to stimulate capital formation by avoiding tax distortions to savings and investment decisions. In line with the advocates of consumption-based taxation, Rose and Wiswesser argue that, by taxing the normal return to saving, the conventional income tax violates horizontal equity and discourages capital formation, because it imposes higher capitalized lifetime tax burdens on individuals with relatively high savings during the early stages of life, and because it reduces the private net return to saving below the social (pre-tax) return to investment. Agreeing with this view, Croatian tax reformers decided to opt for a tax system which would exempt the normal return to saving from tax.

In principle this goal can be achieved through a cash-flow consumption tax which Rose and Wiswesser choose to denote the 'savings-adjusted income tax' (SAIT). Under an SAIT, tax is levied on the taxpayer's cash receipts from all sources minus his cash outlays on the acquisition of all forms of assets. Savings are thus deductible from the tax base so that tax is levied only on consumption. At the business level, the cash-flow tax would take the form of a tax on the net distributions from corporations to shareholders. Hence, under cash-flow taxation taxpayers can accumulate the return to their savings without having to pay tax. However, in the Croatian context a cash-flow tax was considered too difficult to administer, because it would require tax collectors to record all the cash-flow transactions of taxpayers. It was also considered a disadvantage of the cash-flow tax that the full deductibility of all outlays on savings and investment would erode government revenues in the critical transition phase where levels of capital formation are expected to be high and rising.

As an alternative to the cash-flow tax Croatian tax reformers therefore chose to define the tax base on the basis of more conventional income accounting principles, but to allow a deduction for the normal return to saving. Such an 'interest-adjusted income tax' (IAIT) is easier to administer, and it will be principle imply the same present value of lifetime tax as the cash-flow tax.

For the self-employed the IAIT is implemented by allowing a deduction of an imputed normal return to depreciable assets. Provided the imputed rate of return corresponds to the taxpayer's discount rate, such a system will guarantee a zero rate of tax on the return to the marginal investment while ensuring that tax is collected on pure profits from intramarginal investments. If depreciation for tax purposes happens to exceed true economic depreciation, the taxpayer's asset base is written down correspondingly. This implies a fall in deductible 'normal' returns which exactly offsets the benefit from accelerated depreciation so that no investment distortion arises. The neutrality of the IAIT is also preserved under conditions of inflation, because the tax system provides for full nominal interest deduction for equity-financed as well as debt-financed investment.

Business firms which are statutorily obliged to keep commercial financial accounts are taxed according to similar principles, being allowed to deduct an imputed return on their net equity from the base of the business profit tax (the reader will note that this corresponds to the allowance for corporate equity discussed by Sijbren Cnossen in the previous chapter). For individual taxpayers the normal return to financial savings is exempt from tax partly by excluding interest from the tax base, and partly by granting a deduction for contributions to pension funds, allowing the funds to accumulate interest earnings free of tax, and subjecting pensions to tax, in line with cash-flow tax principles.

Despite a considerable lowering of marginal tax rates compared to the previous primitive system of schedular income taxation, the 1994 Croatian tax reform led to a marked increase in income tax revenue due to the abolition of a huge number of tax preferences. The reform thus helped to secure the short-term stabilization of the Croatian economy, but, as Rose and Wiswesser note, only time will tell whether the reform will also be sufficiently effective in stimulating capital formation and economic development.

Even so, the Croatian tax reform is highly noteworthy because it indicates that it is possible to construct a consistent consumption-based tax system which can also be administered. Moreover, the different approaches to capital income taxation recommended in Chapters 8 and 9 also serve as reminders that different economic and institutional contexts often call for different policy solutions to similar problems.

Selling Off the Family Silver

The transition from a planned economy based on state ownership of productive assets to a market economy based on private property is a gigantic social experiment. Arguably, the most fundamental aspect of this transition process is the privatization of the previously public-owned assets.

In Chapter 10 Gerlinde Sinn undertakes a critical analysis of the privatization process in East Germany following the German reunification in 1990. Like Manfred Rose and Rolf Wiswesser, Gerlinde Sinn stresses the fact that capital is scarce in a transition economy. When markets are liberated and factor prices are brought in line with relative scarcities, high returns on capital should then be expected, and successful privatization should lead to an investment boom which would gradually bring real wages and living standards in the East up to Western standards.

At the end of 1994 the *Treuhandanstalt* – the government institution responsible for privatization of the formerly state-owned East German assets – closed its doors, having completed its privatization programme in less than four years. Measured by the speed of privatization, the performance of the *Treuhand* was thus an indisputable success. However, Gerlinde Sinn argues that this 'success' was bought at a very high cost – indeed at an unnecessarily high cost – to the citizens of East and West Germany. Since several Eastern European countries have not yet completed the process of privatization, Gerlinde Sinn's discussion is not only of

historical interest, but may also carry important lessons for future privatization policy in other countries.

Ultimately, the criterion for successful economic transformation must
be that it leads to the maximum possible rise in welfare in a present-value
sense. In principle, it is still too early to rule out the possibility that this
criterion will ultimately be met in the German case. However, as Gerlinde
Sinn points out, the short-term costs of economic transition in East
Germany have been enormous. Total East German employment has
dropped dramatically. Prior to unification, the East German state of
Saxony had the highest industrial employment in all of Europe, whereas
post-unification East Germany has become a deindustrialized region.
Stimulated by high investment subsidies, new capital formation in East
Germany has been quite strong recently, but during the early 1990s non-
subsidized investment in West Germany was even stronger. Finally, while
the sale of public assets via the *Treuhand* was expected to bring in considerable revenue to the German government, the actual realized sales proceeds were only one-tenth of the original revenue estimate.

To many observers, this performance has been very disappointing, considering that the starting position of the *Treuhand* seemed very favourable
compared to the situation prevailing in other transition economies. Thus,
since East Germany essentially took over the well-established legal and
political institutions which had generated a high degree of economic and
political stability in West Germany, East Germany appeared to offer a
much safer investment climate than any other Eastern European country.
The bulk of direct investment by Western investors in Eastern Europe has
indeed been channelled to East Germany, but, as already mentioned,
investment activity has nevertheless been insufficient to prevent a catastrophic rise in unemployment.

Undoubtedly, one highly important reason for this development was the
wage policy pursued in Germany. When the German monetary union was
established, the currency conversion of the East German mark caused a
fourfold increase in wages in the East German export sector which was
previously responsible for 40 per cent of East German GDP. Following
this, the process of unionization in East Germany led to a further wage
explosion so that in the end East German wages rose to more than ten
times their original level within four years. As noted by Gerlinde Sinn,
this wage policy was strongly influenced by an unholy alliance of West
German unions and employers' associations. Western unions wanted to
avoid the immigration of an East German industrial reserve army, and
Western employers wanted to hinder low price competition from their own
back yard. Obviously, there was no way in which East German productiv-

ity growth could keep pace with the sky-rocketing wage rates, and millions of East German wage-earners therefore inevitably ended up being priced out of the labour market.

Nevertheless, Gerlinde Sinn argues that the specific privatization strategy pursued by the *Treuhandanstalt* also hampered successful privatization and transformation. First, and most importantly, the *Treuhand* made the mistake of trying to sell off all of East Germany's capital stock at once. Such a policy gives rise to a serious stock-flow problem, since the value of the existing capital stock is many times larger than the current flow of national savings in any developed economy. To pave the way for an absorption of the previously public-owned East German assets into private portfolios, the German government would have had to repay some of its debt by using the proceeds from the asset sales to retire government bonds from the market. In fact, however, quite the opposite thing happened: the German government budget deficit rose dramatically, because of increased expenditure on transfers to the East to alleviate the consequences of mass unemployment. Alternatively, the sale of *Treuhand* assets could have been financed by a massive inflow of capital from abroad. In the early 1990s German net capital imports did in fact increase, but far less than was needed to absorb all of the East German assets, and only at the cost of a sharp increase in interest rates and a concomitant appreciation of the D-mark which contributed significantly to the breakdown of the fixed exchange rate arrangement within the European Union.

Another difficulty stemmed from the policy of reprivatization, that is, the policy of returning to the (heirs of the) original owners the real assets which had been expropriated when the communist German Democratic Republic had been formed. Because the property rights to these assets turned out to be rather hard to identify, many potential new investors were deterred from investing in East German assets because of fears that they would subsequently be faced with a legal claim by (descendants of) the original owners.

A third difficulty was caused by the fact that the *Treuhand* tried to sell the firms it controlled as single units. Since many of these units were very large, there were few potential investors who were able to mobilize the financial resources needed to buy these firms. In many cases this policy ruled out the possibility for small investors to enter the market, and combined with the attempt to sell off all East German assets at once, it seriously depressed the sales prices obtained by the *Treuhand*.

The sale of East German firms as single units also implied that many sales took the form of mergers with capital-rich West German companies. Gerlinde Sinn therefore argues that the sales policy of the *Treuhand* failed to promote one of the important goals of privatization, that is, that of fostering economic efficiency by creating more competition. Instead, the *Treuhand* privatization method led to an increased concentration of German industry.

Essentially, then, the East German capital stock was taken over by West German and foreign investors at rock-bottom prices, amounting to a near give-away. The East German population, formally the original owners of the assets, ended up owning less than 10 per cent of the privatized assets. Apart from the policy of selling East German firms as single units, there were two more reasons for the low East German participation in the privatization process. First, East Germans owned few financial assets which they could sell off to finance the purchase of shares in East German firms. Second, East German financial assets were converted into D-marks at an exchange rate much less favourable than the one applied in the conversion of wage rates.

Were there other and better ways in which the privatization of the East German economy could have been implemented? Gerlinde Sinn argues that there were indeed: given that the sale of East German assets brought in so little government revenue anyway, the assets could have been distributed free of charge to the East German population in the form of shares in firms or shares in holding companies and funds controlling the firms. This would have given East Germans a source of non-labour income which could have paved the way for a more moderate wage policy and a higher rate of employment. Moreover, the necessary import of know-how and management skills from the West could have taken the form of joint ventures with Western firms, with East Germans supplying minority shares equal to the value of the old capital stock, and Western firms supplying majority shares in the form of new capital necessary for the restructuring of East German firms.

Some German economists, including Gerlinde Sinn, did in fact propose such a privatization strategy right after German unification, but they were overruled. However, policy-makers in other transition countries still struggling with the problems of privatization may draw many useful lessons from her analysis.

This completes my attempt to summarize and synthesize the contributions to this volume. Needless to say, my summary has had to be rather selective, and in some cases my interpretation of the authors undoubtedly has a personal and subjective bent. I now invite the readers to study the chapters in this book for themselves to benefit from their richness.

Part I
Alternative Perceptions of Government

1 The Role of the State in the Fiscal Theory

Richard A. Musgrave

Public finance explores the fiscal tools of the state and how they can best be used to meet the goals of public policy. It is not surprising therefore to find different theories of state to be associated with different approaches to public finance. How fiscal instruments function is a matter of economics, but the purposes to which they are put depend on the image of a 'good society' and the state's role therein. Fiscal theory, therefore, is not a matter of economics only; and that, I will add, is its particular appeal.

That link is here sketched in a historical perspective, from its eighteenth-century beginnings up to the modern period. Four pairings of state and fiscal theory are distinguished. The first, which I call the service state, performs a quite limited though essential role. It is to repair certain leaks in the efficient functioning of the market as a provider of goods and to do so in a way which stimulates what would have been a market solution. The second, which I refer to as the welfare state, admits distributional concerns. The state now seeks to correct the market-determined distribution of income and wealth, moving it towards what society views as efficient or fair. In both these models the state implements the choice of individuals and their preferences. A third model, let me call it the communal state, differs. Policy goals are now set by the state's own needs or, put more moderately, by the public (as distinct from private) needs of its members. This leaves a fourth perspective, of what I will call the flawed state. Fiscal theory here no longer focuses on a normative solution, as did the first three, but on the state's failure to obtain it, be it for technical reasons or, worse, the pursuit of self-interest by its controlling agents. Focus switches from market failure to state failure.

These four patterns, to be sure, are pure or ideal types only. Any one state at a given time offers a mixed picture. Aspects of the service and welfare functions typically coexist, and even quite individualistic societies serve some communal interests. Nor will the best-run state be free of flaws and abuses. The four models nevertheless reflect distinct visions and have shaped public finance traditions in various countries. Thus English,

American and Scandinavian thought has moved in the service and welfare frames, the German tradition has been rooted in the communal setting, while Italian authors early on took aim at the state as a flawed institution.

I   CORRECTING MARKET FAILURE: THE SERVICE STATE

Public finance, in the English tradition, grew from the same soil as did classical economics and developed as an integral part thereof. Its roots may be found in Adam Smith and his *Wealth of Nations*. The mercantilist model with its policy of intervention and enrichment of the state was rejected. Focus shifted to the individual as the driving force in society and to the promotion of individual welfare. Government was discharged of the responsibility of 'superintending the industry of private people' (to quote Adam Smith), and reliance placed on the 'obvious and simple system of natural liberty that will establish itself of its own accord' (Smith, 1776, p. 180). Guided by the discipline of a competitive market, the invisible hand secures an efficient outcome, thereby reconciling self-interest with the common good.

The state is no longer at the centre, but still has an important role to play. The state, 'according to the system of natural liberty', has three duties to perform, 'duties of great importance indeed, but plain and intelligible to common understandings' (Smith, 1776, p. 180). They include the protection of society against foreign invasion and of each member against injustice from others. In addition, they call for

> erecting and maintaining those public institutions and those public works which, tho they may be in the highest degree advantageous to a great society are, however, of such a nature that the profits could never repay the expense to any individual or small number of individuals, and which it therefore cannot be expected that any individual or small number of individuals should erect. (Smith, 1776, p. 211)

Basic education of the poor is needed as well since 'the state derives no inconsiderable advantage from their instruction' (Smith, 1776, p. 269).

Externalities as a source of market failure were recognized and dealt with. Nor was Smith the first to see the problem. Half a century earlier, David Hume had observed how two neighbours can agree to drain a meadow but a thousand persons cannot, since each will try to lay the whole burden on others. To quote, 'thus bridges are built, by the care of government which 'tho composed of men subject to all human infirmities, becomes by one of the finest and most subtle of human inventions possible a composition which is, in some measure, exempted from all these infirmities' (Hume, 1739, p. 539). Government is needed, put in modern terms, to overcome the free-rider problem in the presence of public goods.

The same theme was resumed by John Stuart Mill. 'While *laissez-faire* should be the general practice' (Mill, 1848, p. 314), 'there is a multitude of cases in which governments, with general approbation, assume powers and execute functions ... which conduce to general convenience' (p. 150). The legal system protection and education are again noted and, following Smith, intervention is extended to a

> variety of cases in which important public services are to be performed, while yet there is no individual especially interested in performing them, nor would any adequate remuneration naturally or spontaneously attend their performance ... No one would build lighthouses from motives of personal interest as there is no mode of intercepting the benefit on its way to those who profit by it, unless rewarded out of a compulsory levy by the state. (Mill, 1848, p. 342)

From Hume to Smith to Mill, the core problem of public finance or, as now called, of 'public economics', was thus recognized early on; but a precise formulation only emerged in the 1880s and 1890s. Austrian authors including Sax and Wieser joined with a group of Italians – Panteleoni, Mazzola, Einaudi, De Viti de Marco among them (see Buchanan, 1960) – to integrate the meadow and lighthouse problems into the newly emerging marginal utility theory of value. Market failure in the provision of public goods was now traced to their non-rival and/or non-excludable nature. Nevertheless, the efficient provision of public as that of private goods was to be subject to the same rule, that is, the equating of price payable by consumers with their marginal utility derived. But implementation of the rule differs. Consumers of private goods are charged the same unit price and may choose different amounts. Consumers of public goods are provided with the same amount but are charged different prices in line with their marginal evaluations. Benefit taxation thus offers an efficient solution.

Wicksell readily accepted this principle as a 'law of fiscal economy' but questioned it as a 'prescription for fiscal action' (Wicksell, 1896, p. 81). For benefit charges to be assessed, preferences have to be known and the problem of preference revelation had to be confronted. Unlike the market for private goods where consumers must reveal their preferences by bidding, consumers of the jointly available and non-rival public goods may act as free-riders. Linked tax-expenditure voting is needed to overcome the problem. Voting their preferences, individuals will generate a level of public services and tax prices in line with benefit taxation. Conducted ideally under a unanimity rule, this would come about as a voluntary process. In practice a qualified majority has to do, so as to limit transaction costs and to avoid obstruction by a minority. An element of coercion enters as compliance with the voting outcome must be required. Extended later by Lindahl's market analogy (Lindahl, 1919), an equilibrium is reached at the intersection of the supply schedule with an aggregated demand schedule, arrived at by vertical addition of individual demand curves. Thus the basis had been laid for a public choice approach to budget determination.

This development should have been hailed by English authors since it offered a solution analogous to a market outcome. But written in Italian and German, the new school remained undiscovered. Even though Pigou's *Economic of Welfare* (1920) dealt with externalities, concern was with public bads, not goods. His fiscal treatise, *A Study in Public Finance* (1928), addressed taxation as a problem of welfare economics, with minimal attention to the expenditure side of the budget. There is no reference to the Wicksell–Lindahl model. The spirit of the 1880s and 1890s entered English language discussion only a decade later. A paper based on my doctoral dissertation examined the contribution of Wicksell and Lindahl (Musgrave, 1939), a contribution by Bowen followed (1943) and a lively discussion of social goods appeared in the 1950s and 1960s.

Two lines of development emerged. One line, led by Samuelson, set aside Wicksell's concern with the revelation problem by postulating an omniscient referee to whom preferences are known. Based on that premise, the efficient solution would require the marginal rate of substitution of public for private goods in production to equal that in consumption (Samuelson, 1954). This more general solution bypassed the issue of tax pricing, although Wicksell's and Lindahl's earlier benefit tax formulation still qualified as a special case. Along a second line, various types of goods were examined and the problem of preference revelation was explored (Musgrave, 1959; Head, 1962; Buchanan, 1968). Public choice as a new field developed and became a natural extension of public finance (Buchanan and Tullock, 1962).

As one follows the theory of public goods and its development, there is a clear continuity of thought from Hume and Smith to Wicksell and Samuelson. Non-rival consumption and/or non-excludability causes market failure. That failure is to be overcome by the service state and its political process needed to secure preference revelation. The state thereby joins with the invisible hand to approximate what the market does for the case of private goods. As Smith put it, this is a duty 'of great importance indeed', reaching well beyond the function of a minimal or 'nightwatchman' state. This completes my review of the service state and its primary task of securing a Pareto-optimal provision of public goods. I now turn to the welfare state and its concern with distribution.

II ADJUSTING DISTRIBUTION: THE WELFARE STATE

Adam Smith, as we have seen, thought the provision of public services of great importance, but he did not call upon the state to redistribute income. He largely accepted Locke's dictum that entitlement to earnings is given by natural law. 'Wherever there is great property there is great inequality', and civil government must protect 'that valuable property, which is acquired by the labour of many years' (Smith, 1776, p. 199). Accumulation is needed for commerce to flourish and must be undertaken by the rich. They can consume only so much and gain little from 'the baubles and trinkets which are employed in the economy of greatness' (Smith, 1759, p. 304). A limited support of the poor was called for, but beyond this is the distribution of income was to be left to the market to determine.

Nevertheless, considerations of fairness in the distribution of the tax burden inevitably arise and have to be considered. 'The subjects of every state', as Smith claimed in his first maxim of taxation, 'ought to contribute towards the support of the government, as nearly as possible, in proportion to their respective abilities; that is in proportion to the revenue which they respectively enjoy under the protection of the state ... In the observation or neglect of this maxim consists what is called the equality or inequality of taxation' (Smith, 1776, p. 306). The principle is not easily interpreted, since it appears to combine two distinct rules, that of ability to pay with that of benefit taxation. Smith may have viewed both the benefit derived and the recipient's ability to pay for it as measured by the revenue obtained under the state's protection, so that the two indices coincide. Perhaps so, but thereafter the ability-to-pay principle was applied to the distribution of the tax burden only, quite independent of benefits received. Fiscal analysis came to be divided into two distinct parts, with problems of taxation on one side of the ledger and problems of expenditures on the other.

From Mill on, ability-to-pay taxation was viewed in terms of sacrifice incurred. Various versions of equal sacrifice – equal absolute, equal proportional and equal marginal sacrifice – were developed. With Edgeworth

(1897) and later on Pigou (1928), equal marginal sacrifice was crowned the 'correct' version. Reading 'equal marginal' as 'least total' sacrifice, the paradigm shifted from fairness to welfare maximization. Given (1) a fixed amount of income available for distribution as well as (2) a uniformly applicable and declining marginal utility of income function, Bentham's utilitarian case for income equalization and progressive taxation, advanced almost a century earlier (Bentham, 1789, p. 3; 1802, p. 305), was restated. The quest for a 'fair' distribution of the tax burden had become an efficiency-based rule of welfare economics. Lockean entitlement had been discarded and the welfare state (as I use the term here) emerged.

The development of taxation theory thereafter paralleled that of welfare economics. The challenge of good taxation was how to collect the needed revenue at the least cost to society. The framework had been set but two problems soon arose. First, the earlier premise of known, comparable and cardinal utility functions was questioned and replaced with the construct of a social welfare function. Based on the subjective view of individual members of society an attempt was made to derive a social welfare function from conditions under which a rearrangement would yield mutual gains (Bergson, 1938). Though appealing in some contexts, the formulation hardly resolves the choice between alternative tax burden distributions along the optimality frontier, where some stand to lose while others gain. Nor will allowance for A's satisfaction derived from redistribution to B give the answer, as the initial state of distribution remains to be decided. More recently, attempts have been made to rationalize the derivation of a social welfare function, based on the ethical premise of distributive choice from behind a veil of ignorance. Using an assumption of extreme risk aversion a maxi-min solution is derived (Rawls, 1972); or, formulated in utilitarian terms, the solution is shown to depend on the prevailing patterns of risk aversion (Harsanyi, 1955). The question remains, however, how that function comes to be revealed. The Wicksellian voting process provides an answer. Alternatively, policy outcomes may be ranked on the basis of assumed shapes of the social welfare function (Atkinson, 1983, p. 310), based on the author's own preference meant to reflect the community's like or dislike of inequality.

A second development, from Dupuit (1844) through Marshall (1890) to Pigou (1928) was to refine the measure of tax burden. Concern with burdens extending beyond the amount collected, to be sure, was not new. Bentham and Edgeworth argued for equalizing taxation on the assumption of a fixed income base, but then qualified that conclusion by allowing for detrimental taxation effects on the available base. With Pigou's announcement effects of taxation, that general concern was measured more rigorously in terms of the excess burden or deadweight loss, which results as economic choice is interfered with. Blossoming out later into optimal taxation (Diamond and Mirrlees, 1971), 'good taxation' was no longer only a matter of distributing the burden correctly but also (and as some would have it, primarily) one of raising funds so as to minimize the total burden. With deadweight loss tending to rise at the square of the marginal rate of tax (Harberger, 1974), the utilitarian case for progression was weakened.

As in the context of the service state, the close link of fiscal theory to general economics, now as welfare economics, is again evident. Given two goals, policy coordination is now needed. As the goals of the service and welfare state are combined, the tax system is confronted with two seemingly incompatible tasks. On the one hand, in order to secure preference revelation, the tax and public service budget should be voted upon jointly, with taxation on a marginal net benefit basis. On the other, in order to maximize welfare and secure an optimal distribution, a tax-transfer system based on a social welfare function is needed. Wicksell, aware of this problem, noted that for benefit taxation to be equitable as well as efficient, the underlying distribution of income from which benefit taxes are drawn must also be just (Wicksell, 1896, p. 143). In this spirit, two fiscal branches are required, including one to provide and finance public services in line with the benefit rule, and another to adjust the state of pretax distribution (Musgrave, 1959).

The linkage of fiscal analysis to economic theory, as found in the theory of public goods and distribution, was to micro-theory. A further linkage to macro-theory emerged with Keynesian economics in the 1930s. Compensatory finance was added as a new function of the service state, needed to overcome market failure now in maintaining full employment (Hansen, 1941; Lerner, 1944). Coordinating stabilization with the government's more traditional service and distribution functions again called for a multiple branch approach (Musgrave, 1959). Public finance, *qua* functional finance (Lerner, 1994), became the heart of macroeconomics, but that role ebbed and focus returned to the more traditional functions of the public sector. Most recently there has been added a new vision offered by the increasingly international setting of fiscal affairs, integrating fiscal issues even more closely with other phases of economic life.

III   THE COMMUNAL STATE

I now turn to a third model. Here the state is no longer a mere handmaiden to overcome externalities or to add distributional adjustments, made in line with the private preference of its members. Where before the perspective was essentially individualistic, the state or community, as distinct from its private member individuals, now has its own role to play. Individuals and community interact in the broader frame of society and its changing forms. This is the communal setting of *Finanzwissenschaft* in the nineteenth-century German tradition. Unnecessary to add, fiscal analysis in modern Germany has joined the standard pattern and no longer suffers (or benefits) from that tradition.

Finanzwissenschaft in that setting did not develop as an integral part of *Volkswirtschaft* or general economics. Its status as a distinct science is reflected in a long sequence of specialized treatises, in contrast to the British tradition where fiscal issues were dealt with in the context of general studies. Where the history of German *Finanzwissenschaft* counts a dozen or two major volumes, the British contains a handful only. This is not to say that *Finanzwissenschaft* disregarded the insights of *Volkswirtschaft* in the conduct of fiscal affairs. They were allowed for, but in the context of goals peculiar to the interests of the state. This view traces back to mercantilism and its political economy, the kameralist's teachings of the seventeenth and especially the eighteenth century. Designed to conduct the economic affairs of the prince, detailed systems of fiscal administration were developed, and taxation became a major concern as proceeds from public land and regalia became insufficient. Beyond maintaining the court, the state was to coordinate the various branches of the economy, providing linkages through the provision of road systems and other public works. Dealt with as a guide to practical application rather than formal theory, a tradition was laid for attention to administrative detail and to changing public institutions.

Concern with the interest of the state also derived from the philosophical setting in which *Finanzwissenschaft* developed. English authors, as noted before, proceeded from the models of Locke and Hume, a society organized to protect and meet private interests, leaving the state with a service function only. That vision also appeared in the German scene as Kant's view of the individual's place in the state differed little from that in the English model. However it did not prevail. With the rise of romanticism from Fichte, List and Schelling to Hegel, with its rejection of eighteenth-century rationalism, an alternative perspective took over. Focused on the whole rather than its parts, the interest of the state became a primary concern. Added thereto was the balkanized setting of German jurisdictions and the search for a unifying state. The emergence of *Finanzwissenschaft* has thus been described as 'an original national product, a characteristic expression of the German spirit' (Meisel, 1926, p. 246).

An early and extreme version of the romantic view, as advanced by Adam Müller perceived the state as 'the totality of human affairs' (Müller, 1809, vol. 1, p. 48). Competition and exchange are rejected in favour of reciprocity and value creation. Focus is on the communal linkage of individuals within the state. Taxes are viewed as 'holy contributions' (vol. 1, p. 56) paid in return for the invisible spiritual capital which the state renders, and by which economic effort is made effective for the benefit of the whole (vol. 2, p. 445). 'The value of a thing is its significance for the state and its continuing renewal' (Spann, 19, p. 101).

Not all German authors argued in this statist frame. Among the earlier contributors, Jakob (1821) in particular built on Adam Smith, as did Hermann (1832) and, by way of transition, Rau (1837). Thereafter the communal theme prevailed, if in more moderate form. While the image of a personified state as subject of its own needs faded out, individuals remained to be seen in two distinct roles, as private persons with private needs and as members of the community with communal needs. Attention to communal needs prevailed, if in varying forms, in the writings of von Stein, Schäffle and Wagner, the 'triad' of authors – *das Dreigestirn der Finanzwissenschaft* (Beckerath, 1952, p. 416) – who, in the closing decades of the nineteenth century gave *Finanzwissenschaft* its characteristic form.

Stein, the most subtle of the three, viewed the state as including individuals in two forms, (1) as equals in the human community, and (2) as unequals in society (von Stein, 1885, part 1, p. 5). Seen in Hegelian fashion as a struggle between the two roles, there eventually emerges a civic society, a '*staatsbürgerliche Gesellschaft*', where the two are reconciled. The state's fiscal function is to serve community life in all its forms. Taxes must be raised to render services, but the capital of the private sector must be protected so as to recreate the state's base. There is no uniquely correct tax system. As society evolves, so do the forms in which revenue is obtained. Levies are needed at all stages, but the idea of taxation as the contribution of free and equal individuals emerges only with the citizen state (part 2, p. 439). Transformation of economy and state interact and Schumpeter's concept of the *Steuerstaat* (1918) was anticipated. Stein's sweeping design is impressive, but the concept of communal needs, though essential to his construct, remains unclear. Instead, his argument shifts to the spirit of the service function when holding that outlays are to be made 'where the service cannot be obtained by the single individual through private purchase' (1885, part 2, p. 97).

Schäffle, moving from a philosophical to a biological perspective, viewed society as a set of interacting organisms. Each has its function but prevails only as a part of the whole. Coordination among the parts is

required and 'the purpose of the state is the realization of communal interests through the exercise of a uniform will' (1896, vol. 2, p. 433). The
highest principle of *Finanzwissenschaft* is the proportional coverage of
state and private needs (1873, vol. 2, p. 110), an early view of Pigou's
later principle of equating public and private net benefits at the margin.
While the benefits of the state must exceed its costs, the state may secure
benefits where private undertakings would be unprofitable. It must provide
where the services cannot be contributed 'bit by bit' through the individual
members of the community (p. 113), but again without explanation why
this should occur.

Schäffle's organic view of society and the individual's place therein
also shaped the approach to taxation. Critical of the 'objective' view of the
tax base as a set of factor shares as developed by British authors from
Smith on, Schäffle sought to develop a more subjective approach (1861).
With focus on the individual's place in society, the definition of the tax
base is related to the individual's personal position and sources of taxable
capacity. From this the concept of income as accretion was to emerge.
Foreshadowed already by Hermann (1832) and culminating in the contribution of Schanz (1896), that concept later became Germany's most
important contribution to the international body of fiscal literature, especially as it developed in the United States following the Second World
War (Haig, 1921; Simons, 1950). I regret to add that its principled
approach to tax base design may be lost in the current climate of tax
reform.

Wagner, the most influential of the three, rejected the 'purely individualistic' theory of state underlying the economics of Adam Smith, as well
as the socialist model which disregards individual motivation and endan-
gers liberty. A compromise between the two views is needed (Wagner,
1892, p. 23). The institutions of property and competition have to be
adapted where needed to serve the public good. The narrow and rationalis-
tic view of the state is replaced by a historical and organic perspective,
leaving the state not as a necessary evil but as a positive force and (not
unlike Hume's previously noted formulation!) 'the highest form of communal economy' (Wagner, 1883, p. 7).

The issue of motivation is raised and three forms are distinguished –
individualistic, communal and charitable. The first is served by the market,
self-interest and exchange. The last involves voluntary action only. The
communal principle falls in between. It calls for a variety of services, in
particular 'where needs, though experienced by the individual, can be met
only in common and in the common interest'. Humans being as they are,
the communal principle does not prevail and compulsion is required.

Though needs are experienced by the individual, burden allocation in line with benefits received (as had been held by Sax) is rejected. Holding that benefit shares cannot be assigned in the case of truly communal wants, Wagner required taxation in line with ability to pay (Wagner, 1880, p. 17; 1890, part 2, p. 223).

Two further aspects of his contribution should be noted. First, there is his well-known law of expanding government activity. The needed scope of public services, as was also argued by Adam Smith, must be seen in an historical context. They are subject to change and the need will rise with income and technical progress (Wagner, 1883, vol. 1, p. 76). Next, there is his principle of social policy, '*sozialpolitisches Prinzip*', calling for social programmes and taxation to moderate inequalities in the market-determined distribution of income. Unlike its derivation from utilitarian principles of welfare maximization in the English tradition, such moderation is seen as needed as a matter of social justice. Adequate levels of existence and a broad participation in cultural values are to be provided for by the modern state (Wagner, 1890, p. 207). With Wagner, a leading figure of the 'pulpit socialists' (*Kathedersozialisten*) of Bismarck's time, taxation thus assumed the double function of financing public services and of distributional adjustment.

After the high period of the triad, *Finanzwissenschaft* lost steam. When a renewed period of lively discussion emerged during the 1920s, the earlier tradition was resumed. Unwillingness to build on the economic nature of public goods still prevailed. Ritschl offered resumption of an extreme version of the romantic strand (Ritschl, 1931), while Colm built on Wagner's model. Policy choices are to be made by whoever runs the state, and the economist's prime task is limited to planning and executing their implementation (Colm, 1927). The discussion also was enriched by offerings in fiscal sociology, but outcomes fell short of the high expectations which Schumpeter earlier held for that approach.

As we compare the service, welfare and communal models, the first most readily fits the frame of economic analysis. The distinction between public and private goods, as non-rival and rival, is straightforward and may be drawn in the economist's conventional terms. The state of distribution and effective preferences based thereon are taken as given. Benefit taxation in principle offers an optimal solution. Only the revelation problem and how to resolve it remains puzzling. Moving to the welfare model, the state of distribution is no longer given. Distribution and with it the distribution of the tax burden itself becomes a concern of policy. The safe heaven of Pareto optimality is lost and policy shifts into the more precarious, though not less important, world of welfare economics.

But economics, or what economists call economics, it still is. The communal model is more troublesome. Where the distinction between private and public goods is straightforward, that between communal and private wants is complex, a concept involving psychological and philosophical dimensions. The more sensible contributors to the communal model, to be sure, dropped the hard-line view of the state as itself the subject of wants, but a distinction between the individual's concern as a private person and as a member of the community remained. This has been both a minus and a plus for *Finanzwissenschaft.*

On the minus side, concern with the distinction between private and communal wants tended to crowd out that between private and public goods. As a result, the development of public goods theory, a natural part of the service model, was largely overlooked. Yet there was no need for this, since the two problems differ and do not overlap. Private wants may be met by public goods just as public wants may call for satisfaction by private goods. By failing to distinguish the two issues and linking public goods to communal and private goods to private wants, *Finanzwissenschaft* was kept from addressing the lighthouse problem on its own terms, thereby losing linkage with standard economics.

On the plus side *Finanzwissenschaft* should not be faulted for introducing communal concerns. Such concerns, to be sure, are not the kind of thing economists like to deal with, but that need not render them foolish. The idea of the state 'as such' having its own needs can be readily rejected; but the distinction between the role of individuals as private persons and as members of their community deserves serious consideration. As we know only too well, the community concept carried to romantic extremes has its risks, threats which are avoided within the safe haven of self-interest. Yet, to view the world as based on private and self-interest-oriented concerns only leaves out a significant part of the social setting in which individuals function, viewed in either a normative or a positive perspective. The challenge for public finance is not to disregard that issue, but to address it in a fruitful way. My concept of 'merit goods' was meant as a nudge in that direction (Musgrave, 1959, 1987).

IV POLICY FAILURE: THE FLAWED STATE

It remains to note a fourth model, a perspective which does not view the state and its fiscal instruments in normative terms, but as flawed institutions. Focus shifts from market failure to public sector failure.

The Italian literature of the 1880s and 1890s again enters. It not only made pioneering contributions to the marginalist school but also to its opposite view. In its extreme form, Pareto denied the applicability of economic analysis and logical choice to the public sector (Pareto, 1916). Individuals as acting agents are replaced by a rule of rotating elites and their pursuit of minority interests. Fiscal affairs are seen as class struggle, but unlike Marx, the concept of elites and classes is seen more broadly and not in economic terms only. Also critical but in a more moderate vein, Puviani (1897) pointed to inefficiencies in fiscal choice which arise as government seeks to create fiscal illusions, designed to hide the burden of taxation and to exaggerate the benefits of outlays. Absent a unanimity rule, Barone stressed the coercive nature of the fiscal process (Buchanan, 1960).

The shift from a normative to a positive and critical view of fiscal operations has received massive support in recent decades. One line has addressed the technical issues inherent in arriving at a satisfactory voting outcome. Following Wicksell's early concern with voting as a means of preference revelation, public choice has explored the role of coalitions, strategy, and the political process in which voting choices are made. The feasibility of an efficient outcome was questioned by Arrow's impossibility theorem and simple formulations such as the median voter model have been rejected. A second line has addressed the role of governmental agents, politicians and bureaucrats. Constructive leadership is set aside, with emphasis placed on self-serving behaviour. Abuse of deficit finance is seen to generate inefficient and excessive budgets, calling for new policy instruments and constitutional restraints on governmental action (Brennan and Buchanan, 1977). Attention also shifted from the functioning of the fiscal system in a closed setting to its operation in an open economy with intergovermental competition and decentralization seen as a remedial factor.

I will not undertake here to assess the validity of these concerns and their proposed remedies. Voting imperfections, as I see them, may induce deficient as well as excessive budgets; and governmental agents, including politicians (or statesmen?) and bureaucrats (or civil servants?) may lead as well as mislead (Musgrave, 1981). Much depends on the time and place under consideration. Moreover, attention needs to be paid to the formation of social forces, interest groups and classes, not only to the strategic behaviour of individual agents. The concept of government failure, by its own logic, also implies an image of how to do it right. Doing it right, as we all agree, calls for efficient implementation of set goals. But it also calls for choosing the goal, a sense of what the good society should and can be like, and of the state's role therein. Thereby fiscal theory, in its various traditions, reaches beyond Pareto optimally and connects with an underlying theory of state. This, to be sure, is troublesome since it places public finance at the boundary where efficiency and value considerations are difficult to keep apart. But, as I noted at the outset, this also is what gives our field its particular appeal.

References

Atkinson, A.B. (1983) *Social Justice and Public Policy* (Brighton: Wheatsheaf).

Beckerath, Edwin von (1952) 'Die Neuere Geschichte der Deutschen Finanzwissenschaft', in W. Gerloff and Neumark, F. (eds), *Handbuch der Finanzwissenschaft*, 2nd. ed. Vol. 1 (Tübingen: Mohr).

Bentham, Jeremy (1789) *The Principles of Morals and Legislation* (New York: Haffner, 1948).

_____ (1802) 'Principles of the Civil Code', in J. Bowring (ed.), *The Works of Jeremy Bentham*, Vol. 1 (New York: Russell and Russell, 1962).

Bergson, Abraham (1938) 'A Reformulation of Certain Aspects of Welfare Economics', *Quarterly Journal of Economics*, Vol. 52, pp. 310–34.

Bowen, Howard (1948) *Toward Social Economy* (New York: Rinehart).

Brennan, Geoffrey and James M. Buchanan (1977) 'Towards a Tax Constitution for Leviathan', *Journal of Public Economics*, Vol. 8, pp. 255–74.

Buchanan, James M. (1960) 'La Scienza delle Finanze: The Italian Tradition in Fiscal Theory', in James M. Buchanan, *Fiscal Theory and Political Economy* (Chapel Hill: University of North Carolina Press).

Buchanan, James M. and Gordon Tullock (1962) *The Calculus of Consent* (Ann Arbor: University of Michigan Press).

Buchanan, James M. (1968) *The Demand and Supply of Public Goods* (Chicago: Ranol Mcnally).

Colm, Gerhard (1927) *Volkswirtschaftliche Theorie der Staatsausgaben* (Tübingen: Mohr).

Diamond, Peter and James A. Mirrlees (1971) 'Optimal Taxation and Public Production I: Production Efficiency and II Tax Rules', *American Economic Review*, Vol. 61, pp. 8–27; 261–72.

Dupuit, J. (1844) 'On the Measurement of the Utility of Public Works', reprinted in *International Economic Papers*, Vol. 2 (1952).

Edgeworth, F.Y. (1897) 'The Pure Theory of Taxation', *Economic Journal*, Vol. VII, pp. 46–70, 226–38, 550–71.

Haig, A. (1921) *The Federal Income Tax* (New York: Columbia University Press).

Hansen, Alvin (1941) *Fiscal Policy and Business Cycles* (New York: Norton).

Harberger, Arnold (1974) *Taxation and Welfare* (Boston, Mass.: Little, Brown) p. 35.

Harsanyi, John (1955) 'Cardinal Welfare, Individualistic Ethics and Interpersonal Comparisons of Utility', *Journal of Political Economy*, Vol. 73, pp. 309–21.

Head, John (1965) 'The Welfare Foundations of Public Finance Theory', reprinted in Head (1974) *Public Goods and Public Welfare* (Durham, Dahe University Press).

Hermann, F. (1832) *Staatswirtschaftliche Untersuchungen* (new edn, Munich: Ackermann, 1874).

Hume, David (1739) *A Treatise of Human Nature*, Selby-Biggs (ed.) (1888) (London: Oxford University Press).

Jakob, L.H. von (1821) *Die Staatsfinanzwissenschaft* (Halle: Hemmerde & Schwetschke).

Lerner, Abba (1944) *The Economics of Control* (New York: Macmillan).

Lindahl, Erik (1919) *Die Gerechtigkeit der Besteuerung* (Lund: Gleeerupska).

Locke, John (1689) *Two Treatises of Government*, P. Laslett (ed.) (1960) (London: Mentor).

Marshall, Alfred (1890) *Principles of Economics* (London: Macmillan).

Meisel, Franz (1926) 'Geschichte der Deutschen Finanzwissenschaft im 19. Jahrhundert bis zur Gegenwart', in W. Gerloff and F. Meisel (eds), *Handbuch der Finanzwissenschaft I*, 1st. ed. (Tübingen: Mohr).

Mill, John Stuart (1848) *Principles of Political Economy* (London: Penguin Classics, 1985).

Müller, Adam (1809) *Die Elemente der Staatskunst* (Berlin: Öffentliche Vorlesungen), Jacob Butterfield (ed.) (Vienna: Wiener Literarische Anstalt).

Musgrave, Richard A. (1939) 'The Voluntary Exchange Theory of the Public Economy', *Quarterly Journal of Economics*, Vol. 53, pp. 213–37.

____ (1959) *The Theory of Public Finance* (New York: McGraw-Hill).

____ (1981) 'Leviathan Cometh, or Does He?', in Helen E. Ladd and Nicholas Tideman (eds), *Tax and Expenditure Limitations* (Washington, DC: Urban Institute Press); also in Richard A. Musgrave (1986) *Public Finance in a Democratic Society*, Vol. II (New York: New York University Press).

____ (1992) 'Social Contract, Taxation and the Standing of Deadweight Loss', *Journal of Public Economics*, Vol. 49, pp. 369–81.

Musgrave, Richard A. and Alan Peacock (eds) (1958) *Classics in the Theory of Public Finance* (London: Macmillan).

____ (1987) 'Merit Goods', in J. Eatwell (ed.), *The New Palgrave*, Vol. 3, pp. 452–3 (New York: Macmillan).

Pareto, Alfredo (1916) *The Mind and Society* (New York: Harcourt Brace).

Pigou, A.C. (1920) *The Economics of Welfare*, 4th edn (London: Macmillan).

____ (1928) *A Study in Public Finance* (London: Macmillan).

Puviani, Amilcare (1897) *Teoria della Illusione nelle Entrate Publiche* (Perugia). See also James M. Buchanan (1960).

Rau, Karl-Heinrich (1837) *Grundsätze der Volkswirtschaftslehre* (Leipzig: Winter).

Rawls, John (1972) *A Theory of Justice* (Cambridge, Mass.: Harvard University Press).

Ritschl, Hans (1931) *Gemeinwirtschaft und Kapitalistische Marktwirtschaft* (Tübingen: Mohr).

Samuelson, Paul A. (1954) 'The Pure Theory of Public Expenditures', *Review of Economics and Statistics* (November) pp. 387–9.

Sax, Emil (1887) *Grundlegung der Theoretischen Staatswirtschaft* (Wien). Also in Richard A. Musgrave and Alan Peacock (1958).

Schäffle, Albert (1861) 'Mensch und Gut in der Volkswirtschaft', *Deutsche Vierteljahrsschrift*, pp. 232–307.

____ (1873) *Das Gesellschaftliche System der Menschlichen Wirtschaft*, 3rd edn, Vol. 2 (Tübingen: Laupp).

_____ (1896) *Bau und Leben des Sozialen Körpers*, 2nd edn, Vol. 2 (Tübingen: Laupp).

_____ (1880) *Die Grundsätze der Steuerpolitik* (Tübingen: Laupp).

Schanz, Georg (1896) 'Der Einkommensbegriff und die Einkommenssteuergesetze', *Finanzarchiv*, Vol. 13, pp. 1–87.

Schumpeter, Joseph A. (1918) 'Die Krise des Steuerstaates', reprinted in Joseph A. Schumpeter (1956) *Aufsätze zur Soziologie* (Tübingen: Mohr).

Simons, Henry C. (1950) *Federal Tax Reform* (Chicago, Ill.: University of Chicago Press).

Smith, Adam (1759) *The Theory of Moral Sentiments*, edited by E. West (1959) (New Rochelle: Arlington House).

_____ (1776) *The Wealth of Nations*, Vol. 2 (London: Everyman's Library, Dent & Sons, 1910).

Spann, Othmar (1929) *Die Haupttheorien der Volkswirtschaftslehre* (Leipzig: Quelle).

von Stein, Lorenz (1885) *Lehrbuch der Finanzwissenschaft*, Parts 1 and 2, 5th edn (Leipzig: Brockhaus).

Wagner, Adolph (1883) *Finanzwissenschaft*, Erster Theil, 3rd edn (Leipzig: Winter).

_____ (1890) *Finanzwissenschaft*, Zweiter Theil, 2nd edn (Leipzig: Winter).

_____ (1892) *Grundlegung der Politischen Oekonomie*, Erster Theil, Erster Halbband, 3rd edn (Leipzig: Winter).

Wicksell, Knut (1896) *Finanztheoretische Untersuchungen nebst Darstellung und Kritik des Steuerwesens Schwedens* (Jena: Fischer). Also in Richard A. Musgrave and Alan Peacock (1948) *Classics in the Theory of Public Finance* (London: MacMillan).

2 Government Role and the Efficiency of Policy Instruments*

Vito Tanzi

I CURRENT DEBATE ON THE ROLE OF GOVERNMENT

For the past decade, a raging debate has been going on about the role that the public sector should play in the contemporary world. The collapse of the centrally planned economies and the real, or alleged, failures of the welfare state in mixed economies have brought about an in-depth reevaluation of that role in an environment that is much more pro-market than was the case in recent decades. As this and other recent economic conferences confirm, perhaps, at no other time has so much attention been paid, by economists, political scientists and policy-makers, to what the government should do.

In this largely normative debate, some economists argue in favour of a minimalist state, in which the government should have very limited functions essentially justified by the narrow application of economic arguments related to market failure such as the existence of externalities, public goods, monopolies and informational deficiencies. These economists reveal much faith in the market and little faith in the actions of the government. Others argue that the retreat of the state from many activities, and a more timid role for it, would lead to many problems such as the growing incidence of crime (and especially of organized crime), the growth of poverty, a progressively less even income distribution, and so forth. They justify a larger government role by recourse to the Musgravian functions, such as allocation of resources, when the market fails to do so optimally; the redistribution of income, when the market generates a distribution that is not considered fair by society; and the stabilization of economic activities, when the automatic working of the market leads to

* Paper presented at the 51st Congress of the International Institute of Public Finance, Universidade Nova, Lisbon, Portugal, 21 August 1995. The views expressed are strictly personal. Comments received on an earlier draft from Roberta Gatti, Agnar Sandmo and Ludger Schuknecht were much appreciated.

economic instability accompanied by unemployment, inflation and balance of payments disequilibrium.

In modern and complex societies the objectives pursued by the government have become broader and more difficult to define. For example, it is now better recognized that the private sector may fail to allocate resources optimally not just at a moment in time, but intertemporally, thus justifying public sector intervention *vis-à-vis* many new areas that involve different periods such as the environment, research and pensions. The distribution of income has also acquired more facets as governmental intervention has been justified not just by the uneven size distribution of income but, with increasing frequency, by income differences which may arise because of gender, age, and ethnic, regional and physical characteristics of individuals. Even the stabilization function has become more multidimensional and now it may relate to output, employment, price level, balance of payment, public debt, level of public spending and level of taxation.

A quantitative impression of what a minimalist state might imply in terms of the level of public spending is provided by the historical statistics, for the 1870–1913 period, shown in Table 2.1. It will be seen that government expenditure, as a share of GDP, was much lower a century ago than in later years. These low shares of public spending were not exhibited by primitive societies but by societies that were quite advanced and sophisticated. However, in that period the state did not engage in activities such as higher education, provision of health services, social security and public welfare on a mass scale, unemployment compensation, and many others that are now common.

An impression of the level of expenditure needed by an extended role of the public sector is provided by statistics for recent years, especially for the so-called welfare states among the industrial countries. Table 2.1 provides these statistics. It will be seen that, for some countries, total public spending has exceeded 50 per cent of GDP and has even approached or exceeded 60 per cent of GDP. For the group of countries reported in Table 2.1, public spending, as a share of GDP, grew from an average of around 10 per cent at the beginning of the twentieth century to 45 per cent in recent years.[1] These data refer to market-oriented industrial countries. In the centrally planned economies that characterized Eastern Europe, the role of the state was even more extended.

II   THE 'EFFICIENCY' OF POLICY INSTRUMENTS

The economic discussion on the role of the state has been conducted in terms of market failure, emphasized by those who wished to justify a larger role, or in terms of government failure, emphasized by those who wished to limit that role (see Stiglitz, 1995). Among the latter, a particularly influential group has been that associated with the public choice school. The components of this group have shown how rent-seeking by special interests and other bureaucratic behaviour lead to the growth of government expenditure and to the failure of public policy in achieving its stated objectives (see Mueller, 1989).[2] In the public sector, principal–agent problems are common and the difficulty of writing precise but not excessively constraining contracts or instructions for the behaviour of agents acting on behalf of the public sector leads to results that are often at odds with the objectives of the policy-makers. In many countries, corruption on the part of some public officials adds to the problem (see Tanzi, 1995).

In this chapter, I wish to focus on a different aspect of the role of government, an aspect that is related neither to traditional market failure nor to government failure in the public choice sense. Broadly, it can be defined as institutional failure. This aspect has been largely ignored in the literature and especially in the public finance literature. It relates to the gap that often exists between government goals and the availability of fiscal instruments necessary to pursue those goals and how governments react to that gap. Because the policy instruments are the vehicles that must implement, or are supposed to implement, the intentions of the policy-makers, when these instruments are not available or are not efficient, difficulties may arise.[3] When this gap exists, there are two possibilities: either the policy-makers give up pursuing some of their objectives or, at least, they modify their objectives to make them consistent with the available instruments; or they continue to pursue the same objectives but they do so through reliance on less efficient instruments.

Unfortunately, the second possibility seems to be more common, thus resulting in poor economic policy and in a more confused role of the state. The final results from governmental action are, thus, often different from the intended results. In this context, the 'efficiency' of a policy instrument is defined *à la* Tinbergen: an instrument is efficient when a modest change in it brings about a significant change in the policy objective pursued through the use of that instrument (see Johansen, 1965, pp. 12–14). It is thus not the usual allocative definition of efficiency.

Economists and political scientists generally associate the scope and the importance of the public sector (or, putting it differently, the role of the government) with the share of public spending or tax revenue in national income. Public finance courses deal with taxing and spending and ignore monetary or foreign trade policy because the latter is not supposed to deal with *fiscal* objectives. Also, these courses generally do not discuss regulations.[4] The implicit assumption is that those objectives can only be

Table 2.1   The growth of general government expenditure, 1870–1994 (in per cent of GDP)*

	Later nineteenth century About 1870[1]	Pre-First World War 1913	Post-First World War 1920	Pre-Second World War 1937	Post-Second World War 1960	1980	1990	1994
General government for all years								
Australia	18.3	16.5	19.3	14.8	21.2	31.6	34.7	37.5
Austria	–	–	14.7[2]	20.6	35.7	48.1	48.6	51.5
Canada	–	–	16.7	25.0	28.6	38.8	46.0	47.4
France	12.6	17.0	27.6	29.0	34.6	46.1	49.8	54.9
Germany	10.0	14.8	25.0	34.1	32.4	47.9	45.1	49.0
Ireland	–	–	18.8	25.5	28.0	48.9	41.2	43.8
Japan	8.8	8.3	14.8	25.4	17.5	32.0	31.7	35.8
New Zealand	–	–	24.6	25.3	26.9[2]	38.1	41.3	35.7
Norway	5.9	9.3	16.0	11.8	29.9	37.5	53.8	55.6
Sweden	5.7[2]	10.4	10.9	16.5	31.0	60.1	59.1	68.8
Switzerland	16.5	14.0	17.0	24.1	17.2	32.8	33.5	37.6[3]
United Kingdom	9.4	12.7	26.2	30.0	32.2	43.0	39.9	42.9
United States	7.3	7.5	12.1	19.7	27.0	31.8	33.3	33.5
Average	10.5	12.3	18.7	23.2	27.9	41.3	42.9	45.7

Table 2.1   (Continued)

	Later nineteenth century About 1870[1]	Pre-First World War 1913	Post-First World War 1920	Pre-Second World War 1937	Post-Second World War 1960	1980	1990	1994
Central government for 1870–1937, general government thereafter								
Belgium	–	13.8	22.1	21.8	30.3	58.6	54.8	54.8
Italy	11.9	11.1	22.5	24.5	30.1	41.9	53.2	53.9
Netherlands	9.1	9.0	13.5	19.0	33.7	55.2	54.0	54.4
Spain	–	11.0	8.3	13.2	18.8	32.2	42.0	45.6
Average	10.5	11.2	16.6	19.6	28.2	47.0	51.0	52.2
Total average	10.5	11.9	18.2	22.4	27.9	42.6	44.8	47.2

* Table assembled by Vito Tanzi and Ludger Jchuknecht.
[1] Or closest year available for all columns.
[2] Central government data for this year, New Zealand: 1960–1970.
[3] 1992 instead of 1994.

Sources: European Commission (1995) *Tables on General Government Data*; OECD (1994, 1995) *Economic Outlook*; B. Mitchell, 'International Historical Statistics', various issues; Acha Hernandez (1976) 'Datos Basicos para la Historia Financiera de España'; Bureau of Census (1975) 'Historical Statistics of the U.S.A.'; N.G. Butlin (1984) *Select Comparative Economic Statistics, 1900–1940*, Source Paper No. 4, The Australian National University, Canberra; P. Flora *et al.* (1983) *State Economy and Society in Western Europe*, Vol. I, St James Press, Chicago; R. Delorme and C. Andre (1983) *L'Etat et L'Economie.*

pursued through tax and public expenditure instruments. The higher the level of taxation or of public spending, the greater the role of the government in the economy is assumed to be. On this assumption, the government plays a much larger role in Sweden than in Japan and in industrial countries than in developing countries. Those who wish to impose constitutional limits on the level of taxation ought to be pleased with its level in developing countries.

Developing countries are generally characterized by: (a) an income distribution that is less even than in industrial countries;[5] (b) less stable macroeconomic developments, as measured by fluctuations in output, prices, or balance of payments outcomes; and (c) more pervasive market failure due to lack of information, prevalence of monopoly or monopolistic practices, and externalities of various kinds.[6]

While the evidence available points to a greater *need* for governmental action in developing countries as compared with industrial countries, it is the latter that exhibit a much larger role for the government when that role is measured by levels of taxation and public spending. On average, the level of taxation and public spending, measured as a share of GDP, is at least twice as large in industrial countries as in developing countries. As pointed out above, this difference cannot be explained by a lower need for public sector intervention in developing countries. It is, rather, explained by these countries' difficulties in raising tax revenue. For a variety of reasons, which cannot be discussed here, the developing countries are far less successful at collecting taxes than the industrial countries. Does this mean that the policy-makers of the developing countries scale down their policy objectives to reflect this reality? An argument will be made in the next section that, often, governments that cannot raise a desired level of tax revenue do not scale down their role in the economy but, rather, they attempt to pursue that role through non-fiscal instruments. Thus, the role of the government is not reduced, but the way in which that role is pursued is changed. These other instruments are largely, but not exclusively, *quasi-fiscal activities and quasi-fiscal regulations*. These are activities not connected with the budget but which can have effects broadly similar to those of fiscal actions.

Quasi-fiscal activities and regulations have also been important in industrial countries when the desire to maintain a larger role for the government has collided with the reality of inadequate tax revenue. In some cases, as for example in Italy for much of the 1970s and part of the 1980s, this led to the creation of quasi-fiscal activities within the financial system which allowed the government to finance its public debt more cheaply (see Bruni, Penati and Porta, 1989). In other cases, such as the United States in the 1980s, this led to the use of quasi-fiscal regulations often referred to as unfunded mandates to local governments and to private enterprises.

III THE IMPORTANCE OF QUASI-FISCAL ACTIVITIES AND REGULATIONS

If a government wanted to encourage an economic activity, it would normally be best if it did it through a subsidy to that activity given through the budget. If a government wanted to discourage an economic activity, it would be best if it did it through a tax. This is the standard Pigouvian way of dealing with both positive and negative externalities. In reality, however, and especially in developing countries, the economic encouragement or discouragement of certain activities is often not done through the budget but through other means, mainly quasi-fiscal activities or quasi-fiscal regulations.[7] These are *fiscal* actions carried through *non-fiscal* instruments. They are, thus, *outside* the budget, replacing the spending–taxing function of the budget.

In a well-working market economy, regulations should be limited to helping define the rules of the game and to protecting the citizens against particular risks. Thus, the government could regulate the merger of firms, to maintain competition; it could require child vaccination, to ensure health; it could regulate the sale of pharmaceutical products for the same reason; it could determine traffic rules and require drivers' licences to ensure traffic safety; it could regulate banks and insurance companies to protect their customers against unwarranted behaviour by those who run those institutions, and so on. Within limits, these are considered legitimate regulatory activities on the part of the public sector. They would not be considered quasi-fiscal regulations. The function of a driver's licence or of traffic regulations cannot be replaced by a tax and a subsidy.

Quasi-Fiscal Regulations

However, assume that the government wants to help poor families by subsidizing the rental cost of their lodgings.[8] It could do it with an explicit subsidy to the relevant families given through the budget and financed through taxation. Without discussing the merit of this policy, this would be a normal use of the taxing–spending instruments of governments. Assume, however, that the tax or other ordinary resources of the government are limited, but that the government still wants to pursue its objective of subsidizing the rental expenditures of poor families. A quasi-fiscal regulation that will broadly promote this objective is rent controls. Rent controls are equivalent to a policy that subsidizes the rentees and taxes the rentors.[9] In other words, rent controls replace the function of the budget and thus reduce the level of taxation and the level of spending while still broadly pursuing the government objectives. The fact that the end result of this governmental action is likely to be less efficient in terms of the objective sought than if it were done through the budget is part of our story, but it does not change the reality that rent controls are substitutes for actions that could be taken through the budget. There are many other examples of quasi-fiscal regulations from zoning laws to uncompensated and obligatory military service.

Quasi-Fiscal Activities Through the Foreign Exchange System

Assume that a country exports coffee and imports medicines and that the government wants to subsidize the use of medicines by taxing the coffee producers. A conventional though not economically efficient,[10] governmental policy would be to tax the exporters of coffee, thus raising the level of taxation, and to subsidize the importers of medicines, thus raising the level of public spending. However, the government may have difficulties (administratively or politically) in pursuing this course of action. An administratively or politically easier alternative is to use the exchange rate mechanism to promote the same social objective by using appreciated exchange rates for the import of medicinals and for the export of coffee.[11] The government compels the coffee exporters to sell to the central bank their foreign exchange earnings for which they receive a smaller amount (in domestic currency) than they would have received if they had been free to sell their foreign exchange in the market. The government then sells this foreign exchange (also at an appreciated rate) to the importers of medicines, who buy their medicines more cheaply (in domestic currency). Once again, taxing (the coffee producers) and subsidizing (the users of medicines) has taken place without an apparent effect on the level of taxation and on the level of public spending. The unwary observer, who used the conventional data on taxing and spending, would conclude that the role of the government in that country is more limited than it actually is.

The above example can be extended to the export of other agricultural products and, especially, to the export of mineral products. In each case, the exporters are forced to yield to the government, at an overvalued exchange rate, the foreign exchange that they earn.[12] Thus, *de facto*, these exporters are being taxed sometimes at very high rates. When the foreign exchange is provided to the importers of particular products, also at an overvalued exchange rate, the net result is similar to that of a budgetary subsidy to the goods that use this exchange rate for imports. Multiple exchange rate regimes are very common (see IMF, 1994). Depending on the coverage of the special rates, the quasi-fiscal taxes and subsidies they entail can be substantial.

Quantitative import restrictions are also often used by many countries. These also provide implicit subsidies to some groups and implicit taxes to others. However, it is often difficult to quantify these effects.

Quasi-Fiscal Activities Through the Financial System

Quasi-Fiscal activities are often carried out *through the financial system* and can take many forms. But they all result in the implicit taxation of some groups (depositors, holders of cash) and in the implicit subsidy of other groups (borrowers, banks with problem loans, government). In all cases, they do not result in explicit tax revenue or public spending. They thus lead to lowering of the ratios of taxes or public spending in GDP. A comprehensive analysis of this aspect is not possible here.[13] We limit ourselves to a few examples.

In some cases, the financial institutions are required to lend to enterprises or to the government at below market interest rates.[14] Or, some financial institutions can benefit from preferential rediscounting practices with the central bank and can thus pass on an implicit subsidy to those who borrow from them. Or, highly risky borrowers can get the loans at an interest rate that does not reflect the risk. Or, some borrowers can borrow at a risk-free rate because the government (or some part of it such as the central bank) guarantees the loans. In still other cases, the government gets subsidized credit by forcing banks to hold uncompensated or undercompensated high reserve requirements at the central bank. In most cases, 'control on international capital flows [are] coupled with controls on domestic financial intermediaries' (Giovannini and De Melo, 1993, p. 953). These controls result in 'financial repression' which is a form of implicit taxation.

We have provided examples of governmental activities that are common especially among developing countries and economies in transition and that result in implicit taxation. This taxation is at times accompanied by implicit subsidies to particular groups while in other cases it is for the benefit of the government that can thus pursue some of its objectives without raising explicit taxes. Inflationary finance, that is, the direct lending by the central bank to the government, is an example of a quasi-fiscal operation that is mainly an implicit tax (on holders of cash) collected by the government. Up to a certain point, this tax increases with the level of inflation.

In the next section, we provide available quantitative estimates of *some* of these activities. These are by no means all the channels through which what are essentially fiscal objectives of the government are pursued through the use of non-fiscal instruments. In some way, what we have shown is just the tip of the iceberg.

IV   SOME QUANTIFICATION

In the previous section, we have provided examples of quasi-fiscal activities and quasi-fiscal regulations that can proxy for the spending and taxing actions of the government. We have argued that these activities and regulations allow the government to play a larger role without having to raise taxes or spend more. We have no way of quantifying all of these quasi-fiscal activities and even less the quasi-fiscal regulations. If we could, we would attempt to answer the question: by how much would the tax level and the spending level have to rise to replace the implicit taxes and subsidies with conventional or explicit taxes and government spending? Yet some idea of the dimensions involved can be obtained from the analysis of a few specific quasi-fiscal activities. Here we report some available estimates.

Giovannini and De Melo (1993) have estimated the implicit taxes that the governments of various countries obtain from 'controls on international capital flows coupled with controls on domestic financial intermediaries' (p. 953). These controls allow governments to finance themselves at artificially low interest rates. The authors emphasize that their estimates are minimum estimates because they limit their calculations to the interest that the government saves on servicing its debt. They are thus likely to substantially underestimate the true scope of quasi-fiscal 'revenue' from the financial sector.

Table 2.2 reports these estimates for 24 countries. The table shows that revenue from financial repression can be very high both as shares of GDP and as shares of (conventionally measured) tax revenue. For the years reported, these implicit taxes raised more than 5 per cent of GDP in Mexico and in Zimbabwe and smaller but still large amounts in several other countries. Greece, Portugal, and Turkey are the only European countries in the table, each raising a little over 2 per cent of GDP from this source. The unweighted average for the whole group is 2 per cent of GDP and 9 per cent of government revenue.[15]

Table 2.2   The size of revenue from financial repression

Country	Sample	Revenue from financial repression	
		Percentage of GDP	*Percentage of tax revenue*
Algeria	1971–1987	4.30	11.42
Brazil	1983–1987	0.48	1.57
Colombia	1980–1984	0.24	2.11
Costa Rica	1972–1984	2.33	12.76
Greece	1974–1985	2.53	7.76
India	1980–1985	2.86	22.38
Indonesia	1976–1986	0.00	0.00
Jamaica	1980, 1982	1.38	4.74
Jordan	1978–1987	0.60	2.40
Korea	1975–1987	0.25	1.36
Malaysia	1974–1981	0.12	0.31
Mexico	1984–1987	5.77	39.65
Morocco	1977–1985	2.31	8.89
Pakistan	1982–1983	3.23	20.50
Panama	1977–1987	0.69	2.49
Papua New Guinea	1981–1987	0.40	1.90
Philippines	1975–1986	0.45	3.88
Portugal	1978–1986	2.22	6.93
Sri Lanka	1981–1983	3.40	19.24
Thailand	1976–1986	0.38	2.57
Tunisia	1978–1987	1.49	4.79
Turkey	1980–1987	2.20	10.89
Zaire	1974–1986[1]	0.46	2.48
Zimbabwe	1981–1986	5.50	19.13

[1]   The sample for Zaire does not include the years 1981, 1982, and 1983.
Source: Giovannini and De Melo, 1993, p. 959.

Maxwell Fry (1993) has estimated, for 26 countries, the seigniorage that the government received from its monopoly over money creation in 1984.[16] This is revenue *additional* to that from financial repression. When this seigniorage leads to inflation, it is a kind of excise tax whose revenue is obtained by multiplying the tax rate (that is, the current inflation rate) by the tax base which is the 'geometric average of beginning-of-year and end-of-year values of currency in circulation plus bank reserves'

Table 2.3   Seigniorage Revenue in 26 developing countries, 1984

	Seigniorage tax revenue	
Country	*Percentage of GNP*	*Percentage of government current revenue*
Algeria	1.6	n.a.
Argentina	7.4	46.5
Brazil[1]	2.5	9.1
Chile	0.9	2.7
Cote d'Ivoire	0.4	1.5
Egypt	7.5	16.7
Ghana[1]	0.7	6.2
Greece	3.1	8.7
India	1.0	7.6
Indonesia	0.7	6.2
Korea[3]	0.1	1.4
Malaysia[3]	0.1	0.5
Mexico	7.2	41.9
Morocco	1.7	6.8
Nigeria[3]	0.9	5.1
Pakistan[2]	0.5	2.6
Peru[1]	8.7	58.0
Philippines	2.4	22.1
Portugal	5.3	14.6
Sri Lanka[2]	0.8	3.4
Tanzania[4]	3.1	18.6
Thailand[3]	0.2	1.3
Turkey[3]	2.6	13.9
Venezuela	1.5	5.7
Yugoslavia	9.8	132.8
Zaire[2]	3.0	16.1

[1] 1985.
[2] 1986.
[3] 1987.
[4] Seigniorage, 1985.
Source: International Financial Statistics and World Bank, World Tables
1989–90: Socio-economic Time-series Access and Retrieval System,
Version 1.0 (Washington, DC: World Bank, March 1990). Taken from
Fry, 1993, p. 11.

Table 2.4   Tax revenue from implicit financial taxation in selected countries, 1971–86 averages (percentages of GDP)

Country	Rate of return method	Cash-flow method
Ghana	6.8	4.8
Somalia	4.9	4.3
Zaire	7.8	7.2
Zambia	4.3	4.0

Source: Arranged from Table 2 in Chamley, 1991, pp. 524–5.

(Fry, 1993, p. 10). Fry's estimates are shown in Table 2.3. Once again, the revenue importance of these implicit taxes is striking. In five countries (Argentina, Egypt, Mexico, Peru and Yugoslavia) this unorthodox revenue source generated more than 7 per cent of GDP and large proportions of tax revenue. Once again, these estimates pertain to 1984. Major changes have taken place since then in some of these countries.

Christopher Chamley (1991) has also attempted to estimate the tax revenue from implicit financial taxation in four African countries – Ghana, Somalia, Zaire and Zambia – for the 1971–86 period. He has used two alternative methods for this calculation.[17] The *average* revenues for the whole period, shown as percentages of GDP, are given in Table 2.4.

Once again, the importance of this implicit source of revenue is obvious. The yearly estimations, shown in Chamley's article, indicate a great variability of this source. In particular years, it provided much higher values than those shown in Table 2.4. Revenues from financial repression are also estimated in some of the chapters dealing with specific developing countries in Easterly, Rodriguez and Schmidt-Hebbel (1994).

Unfortunately, there are no good estimates of the implicit taxes and subsidies associated with multiple exchange rate systems, domestic price controls, or quantitative restrictions on trade. The bits of evidence indicate that these taxes or subsidies may be very high. For example, Brian Pinto (1989, p. 329) has estimated that the implicit marginal tax rate on exports by Ghana was 91 per cent. This implicit tax was a consequence of the overvaluation of the exchange rate.

V CONCLUDING REMARKS

This chapter has addressed some issues related to the positive role of the government. It has highlighted the fact that governments can pursue their roles in various ways and through various instruments. These instruments extend well beyond the range of taxes and public spending which are the ones that attract most attention especially from public finance economists. The use of quasi-fiscal activities and quasi-fiscal regulations is common among countries. These are non-fiscal instruments used to achieve or to influence the same objectives as those pursued through taxes and government spending.

While all countries use, to some extent, these other instruments, much greater prevalence of their use is found in developing countries and, to a lesser extent, in poorer industrial countries. Economies in transition also make much use of them. The information available suggests that quantitatively – in terms of the percentage of GDP that would be needed to replace them with explicit taxes and public spending – these other instruments, in developing countries, may be as important as the traditional tax and spending instruments.[18] Because the developing countries have levels of taxation which, as percentages of GDP, are only about half as large as those of the industrial countries, it can be concluded that through the use of these quasi-fiscal instruments, the governments of developing countries attempt to play roles which may not be too different from those of the governments of industrial countries. They just do it with different tools. Thus, those who favour a minimalist role for the state should not get excited when the tax level of a country is low until they assure themselves that traditional tax sources have not been replaced by less traditional, or hidden, implicit taxes.

We could formulate a general hypothesis, which, admittedly, has not been fully proven in this chapter. With inevitable variance around the mean – due in part to the random presence of more or less conservative governments at given times and in given countries – most governments would like to play broadly similar roles. When the taxes they can raise are not sufficient to finance the desired expenditures, they tend to rely on less orthodox, non-tax instruments. Perhaps a corollary of this general hypothesis is that *governmental goals change more over time than across space*.[19] Demonstration effects might explain the tendency for the governments of various countries (adjusting again for the political colouring of the party in power) to try to promote similar goals and to play similar roles. When these roles change over time, they tend to change for all countries.

Public finance specialists and, perhaps, most other economists believe that *fiscal* instruments are more efficient than *quasi-fiscal* instruments in pursuing the role of the state. Economists normally prefer taxes over regulations, and direct budgetary subsidies over subsidies given through quotas, subsidized credit and so on. In this context, the term 'efficiency' has two distinct meanings: as defined by Tinbergen, and as generally used by economists (that is, having to do with a Pareto optimum and the allocation of resources). On both grounds, economists as a group tend to prefer fiscal to other instruments. However, in particular cases – such as for inflationary finance – some major economists, such as Phelps (1973) and Dixit (1991), have argued that the economic efficiency of particular instruments can only be judged in the context of a general equilibrium approach. Thus, a *priori* one cannot be sure that taxation is always preferable to inflationary finance. Furthermore, the alternative of raising more tax revenue may not be available and the marginal benefit of public spending may be very high. This latter point was made for multiple exchange rates by E.M. Bernstein as far back as 1950 when he wrote:

> The case of multiple [exchange] rates as a tax service ... does not rest on its economic merit. It rests rather on the fact that it is easy to impose ... [and] that it is easy to enforce ... These are not good reasons for preferring one type of taxation to another. They may, however, have the merit, in countries with budgetary difficulties, of being better than no additional taxes. (pp. 236–7).

Still, most economists now believe that these alternative revenue sources are very inefficient. Furthermore, the particular case for inflationary finance (the case discussed by Phelps and Dixit) is considerably weakened when one takes into account the loss in tax revenue that often accompanies high inflation in the presence of significant collection lags (see on this Tanzi, 1978).

The above discussion leads to some rather uncomfortable conclusions. Current attitudes and thinking show a strong preference for (a) purely fiscal over quasi-fiscal tools for promoting the government's goals; (b) economically efficient over distortionary taxes; (c) the complete separation of fiscal from monetary policy and the elimination of monetary repression – the preference for this separation is evident from the many papers now available arguing for the complete independence of central banks which would eliminate the quasi-fiscal role played by these institutions;[20] and (d) the removal of all impediments to trade and especially those associated with multiple exchange rates and quantitative restrictions.[21]

These preferences will, in time, significantly reduce the instruments and the controls available to governments to pursue their goals. This is clearly desirable and consistent with a greater dependence on the market. If governments can scale down their goals to make them consistent with their reduced ability to control and with the greater role given to the market, the reduction in the use of quasi-fiscal instruments and in the total resources that the governments have controlled through explicit and implicit taxes will lead to a healthier economy. However, if governments cannot moderate their objectives, and/or do not find market-friendly ways of promoting them,[22] then fiscal deficits might become more common than they have been because governments may not reduce, or may even increase, spending in the face of reduced resources. This problem will be of particular relevance to developing countries and to economies in transition:[23] first, because these countries are the ones that have relied the most on quasi-fiscal instruments; and second, because these countries will have greater difficulties in raising needed revenue from efficient tax sources. In these countries, the need to moderate the ambitions of governments and to build strong revenue sources from efficient tax systems will be particularly great. Major reforms in taxes and in public spending will be an essential feature of future developments.[24]

The discussion in the chapter may have also relevance for institutions such as the European Union which has been given important responsibilities but limited taxing and spending powers. On the basis of the discussion in this chapter one would forecast that the EU would have a particular tendency in relying on regulations for achieving its objectives.

Notes

1. This increase was due mainly to governmental policies rather than to technical factors, often summarized under the term of 'Wagner's Law'.
2. The contribution of the 'New Italian School' through the work of Alberto Alesina, Guido Tabellini and others is also relevant in this context.
3. Of course, the availability of policy instruments depends on the availability of good institutions. Here we focus on the instruments rather than the institutions.
4. Johansen (1965, pp. 22–5) lists the main instruments at the government's disposal, including monetary policy, prohibitions, and the government's own business activity but then limits the fiscal policy instruments to payments to the government (taxes) and payments from the government.
5. Gini coefficients are generally much higher in developing countries than in developed countries.
6. In its *World Development Report 1983*, the World Bank attempted to construct 'indices of price distortions' for many developing countries. It is not

clear how accurate is the picture provided by this heroic attempt. See p. 60 of that report.

7. In the environmental area, regulations have often been used in industrial countries. These often have a quasi-fiscal effect. Of course, tax incentives and tax expenditures are also used to achieve this objective.

8. This could be considered the subsidization of a merit good.

9. Please note that the burden of the tax is not on the general taxpayers but on those who own the houses that are rented.

10. Please note that in this sentence, efficiency refers to the allocative concept rather than to the concept as defined earlier.

11. The fiscal or revenue effect of multiple exchange rates has been recognized for a long time. See Bernstein (1950) and Sherwood (1956).

12. Alternatively, they may be forced to sell their products domestically at prices which are well below the world price for that product. This is frequently the case with petroleum, which, in oil-producing countries such as Nigeria, Iran, Venezuela, Russia and other countries, is sold at low prices. In this case, the implicit taxation of the oil sector and the implicit subsidies to oil consumers do not appear in the budget. In these countries, the implicit taxes on the producers and the implicit subsidies to the producer may be very large.

13. See, for it, G.A. Mackenzie (1994); Mackenzie and Stella (forthcoming); Maxwell Fry (1993); and Christopher Chamley (1991).

14. In particular circumstances, especially when the inflation rate is high and the interest rates are low, the implicit subsidies to those who borrow can be huge. As these subsidies are not shown in the budget, a country can have high inflation even when the formal budget appears to be in balance. This was the case in Brazil in years past.

15. Please note that the table refers to years in the 1970s or the first half of the 1980s. In some of the countries covered the situation in the 1990s may be very different.

16. Earlier estimations are available in Fischer (1982).

17. The reader is sent to the original article for details.

18. This is also especially true in economies in transition.

19. This may explain, for example, why there is much less variation in taxing and spending for industrial countries at a point in time than there is over time. Please refer again to Table 2.1.

20. A progressively larger number of countries have been introducing legislation that makes the central bank an independent agency.

21. The tendency is also to remove impediments to capital movements.

22. The Chilean-initiated experiment of privatizing the pension system is an example of a market-friendly way to promote a governmental objective.

23. In Russia, for example, the central bank had, until recently, directly financed at highly negative interest rates the activities of state enterprises. To some extent, the financing compensated the enterprises for the social expenditures they were carrying (see Tanzi, 1993). If the enterprises no longer finance these social expenditures, the budget may have to take over some of them.

24. For a discussion of related issues see Tanzi and Schuknecht (forthcoming).

References

Bernstein, E.M. (1950) 'Some Economic Aspects of Multiple Exchange Rates', *IMF Staff Papers*, vol. 2, pp. 224–37.

Bruni, Franco, Alessandro Penati and Angelo Porta (1989) 'Financial Regulation, Implicit Taxes, and Fiscal Adjustment in Italy', in Mario Monti (ed.), *Fiscal Policy, Economic Adjustment and Financial Markets* (Washington: IMF pp. 197–230.

Chamley, Christopher (1991) 'Taxation of Financial Assets in Developing Countries', *The World Bank Economic Review*, vol. 5, no. 3, pp. 513–33.

Dixit, Avinash (1991) 'The Optimal Mix of Inflationary and Commodity Taxation with Collection Lags', *IMF Staff Papers*, vol. 38, pp. 643–54.

Easterly, William, Carlos Alfredo Rodríguez and Klaus Schmidt-Hebbel (eds) (1994) *Public Sector Deficits and Macroeconomic Performance* (Oxford: Oxford University Press).

Fischer, Stanley (1982) 'Seigniorage and the Case for a National Money', *Journal of Political Economy*, vol. 90, pp. 295–313.

Fry, Maxwell J. (1993) 'The Fiscal Abuse of Central Banks', IMF Working Paper 93/58.

Giovannini, Alberto and Martha De Melo (1993) 'Government Revenue from Financial Repression', *American Economic Review*, vol. 83, no. 4, pp. 953–63.

International Monetary Fund (1994) *Exchange Arrangements and Exchange Restrictions: Annual Report*.

Johansen, Leif (1965) *Public Economics* (Amsterdam): North-Holland).

Mackenzie, George A. (1994) 'Hidden Government Deficit', in *Finance & Development*, vol. 31, no. 4, pp. 32–5.

Mackenzie, George A. and Peter Stella *Quasi Fiscal Operations of Public Financial Institutions* (Washington, DC: IMF), October Occasional Paper 142.

Mueller, Dennic C. (1989) *Public Choice II* (Cambridge: Cambridge University Press).

Musgrave, Richard (1959) *The Theory of Public Finance* (New York: McGraw-Hill).

Phelps, Edmund S. (1973) 'Inflation in the Theory of Public Finance', *Swedish Journal of Economics*, vol. 75, pp. 67–82.

Pinto, Brian (1989) 'Black Market Premia, Exchange Rate Unification, and Inflation in Sub-Saharan Africa', *The World Bank Economic Review*, vol. 3, no. 3, pp. 321–38.

Sherwood, Joyce (1956) 'Revenue Features of Multiple Exchange Rate Systems: Some Case Studies', *IMF Staff Papers*, vol. 5, pp. 74–107.

Stiglitz, Joseph (1995) 'Role of Government in the Contemporary World', paper presented at the IMF Conference on Growth and Income Distribution, Washington, 1–2 June.

Tanzi, Vito (1978) 'Inflation, Real Tax Revenue, and the Case for Inflationary Finance: Theory With an Application to Argentina', *IMF Staff Papers*, vol. 25, no. 3, pp. 417–51.

—— (1993) 'The Budget Deficit in Transition: A Cautionary Note', *IMF Staff Papers*, vol. 40, no. 3, pp. 697–707.

—— (1995) 'Corruption, Arm's Length, and Markets', in G. Fiorentini and S. Peltzman (eds) *The Economics of Organized Crime* (Cambridge: Cambridge University Press).

Tanzi, Vis and Ludger Schuknecht 'The Growth of Government and the Reform of the State', in a book to be edited by Andres Solimano (University of Michigan Press) (forthcoming).

Tinbergen, Jan (1952) *On the Theory of Economic Policy* (Amsterdam: North-Holland).

Part II

The Welfare State, Entrepreneurship and Employment

3 Social Insurance, Incentives and Risk-Taking

Hans-Werner Sinn
*

I INTRODUCTION

The welfare state has come under heavy attack in recent years. It has been blamed for reducing international competitiveness, for lowering work incentives and for reducing the economy's growth rate. In short, the welfare state is seen as an institution that makes the distribution of the slices more equal, but incurs a large cost in terms of reducing the size of the cake.

Economists have not always held such a negative view. In the 1950s, most economists saw the welfare state as a useful and necessary historical development. Atkinson (1991, 1995) is right when he argues that it is time to reconsider the basic functions of the welfare state and warns on the economic consequences of 'rolling back' this state. Apart from the benefit of stabilizing the political system and avoiding social unrest, the welfare state's main achievement is the social insurance it provides in an uncertain world. Social insurance (as defined in this chapter) cannot be equated with, or limited to, the activities which legally are subsumed under this term. Instead, it includes all redistributive budget flows that reduce the variance in people's real living standards. The risk of not having a successful career is substantial for young, and even more so for unborn, children. Knowing these risks, parents may well opt for a programme of income redistribution to insure their children against bad luck in terms of missed opportunities, illness, injuries and an unfavourable endowment of innate abilities. The whole system of redistributive taxation involves social insurance, as does the provision of public goods. Every road and every school building can be seen as part of social insurance if it is financed with taxes that deviate from the benefit taxation criterion by making the rich net contributors and the poor net receivers of economic resources.[1] In modern societies, the

* The author gratefully acknowledges research assistance by Claudio Thum and useful comments by two anonymous referees.

government budget is by far the largest risk-absorption device available, generating a protection similar to, but larger than, the protection offered by private insurance companies (see Section II).

Ironically, in some countries, the largest part of what is phrased 'social insurance' does not, in fact, contain many insurance elements. In Germany, for example, the pay-as-you-go public pension system is based on a strict equivalence principle implying that a person's pension is proportional to his previous contributions to the system. The pension system is primarily an intergenerational transfer device; its insurance aspects are of secondary importance.

It is often argued that the welfare state has to trade off equity against efficiency goals, that inefficiency is the cost of charity. This view is not compatible with the social insurance interpretation since redistribution is itself an efficiency-enhancing activity. The redistribution of market incomes through the government budget can be justified and explained on the basis of individual ethics without resort to utilitarian assumptions.

While the insurance against various kinds of risks is the main allocative function of the welfare state, it would be too narrow to see this function in the context of given risks only. Typically, insurance stimulates risk-taking and induces various kinds of moral hazard effects. Social insurance can hardly be an exception.

Up to a certain extent, risk-taking is the beneficial part of the behaviour changes brought about by redistributive taxation. It has many dimensions. The most important one is probably a person's educational or occupational choice. A young person faces a large variety of options differing with regard to the expected lifetime income and the riskiness of this income. In many countries, one end of the spectrum is defined by tenured employment in the government sector with low pay, few opportunities for advancement, and nearly perfect security. The other end of the spectrum consists of entrepreneurial activities that involve both a large risk of failure and the chance of winning a fortune. Between these extremes there is a multitude of other options densely covering the whole range.

Social insurance, like private insurance, makes people more daring since the government takes an equal share in the gains and losses resulting from their economic decisions. It makes people jump the dangerous chasms which otherwise would have put a halt to their economic endeavours.

It may, in fact, make them too eager to jump. The safety net provided by social insurance may actually imply that people do not try hard enough to succeed, become careless, and take too dangerous short-cuts in the mountainous life paths. This is the moral hazard problem that limits the usefulness of any insurance contract.

Surprisingly, there is not much literature on the welfare economics of risk-taking and redistributive taxation. It is true that there are many contributions on taxation and risk-taking including Ahsan (1974, 1976), Allingham (1972), Atkinson and Stiglitz (1980, ch. 4), Bamberg and Richter (1984), Buchholz (1987), Kanbur (1979) and Sandmo (1977). The literature dates back to Domar and Musgrave's (1944) paper and extends it in various directions. However, it concentrates on fiscal rather than redistributive taxation and is, with few exceptions, not concerned with welfare judgements.

There is also a more recent strand of literature including contributions by Diamond, Helms and Mirrlees (1980), Eaton and Rosen (1980), Varian (1980), Rochet (1991) and Mirrlees (1995) which studies the problem of optimal redistributive taxation in the context of various types of income and health risks. This literature is explicitly concerned with welfare judgements, but it is silent about the issue of risk-taking. In Varian's important paper, for example, there is an exogenous additive income risk whose size cannot be manipulated by individual action.

This chapter tries to reconcile the two apparently unrelated strands of literature by studying the allocative implications of redistributive taxation in the context of risk-taking and moral hazard effects. Among other things it will analyse a problem of optimal taxation with endogenous risk-taking.[2]

The lack of interest in the welfare state's influence on risk-taking may result from an ambiguity in the effect of fiscal taxation on risk-taking once found by Feldstein (1969) and Stiglitz (1969) as well as from the more technical aspect that two-parametric characterizations of probability distributions and preference functions are perceived as inferior to direct expected utility maximization. The chapter offers a solution to both problems. The ambiguity will be shown to disappear under redistributive taxation, and the use of the linear distribution class methodology of Meyer (1987) and Sinn (1983, 1990) will make it possible to use a $\mu - \sigma$ approach with only a little loss in generality.

II SOCIAL INSURANCE; MARKET INSURANCE AND REDISTRIBUTION: SOME FUNDAMENTAL ISSUES

Social insurance systems in the narrower sense of the word are often criticized on the grounds that they involve redistributive elements. Redistribution and insurance, it is maintained, are two completely distinct activities that should not be confused, since inequality is not the same as risk.

This view sharply contradicts the insurance interpretation of the welfare state, and it is misleading for at least two reasons. First, risk-taking has implications for the realized degree of inequality in the economy, because the more people dare the larger will be the income gap between those who succeed and those who fail. If the redistribution of incomes stimulates risk-taking it will therefore also bring about a more unequal pre-tax distribution of incomes. The chapter will study some of the relevant problems involved.

Second, an unequal society involves a substantial risk for a young entrant who does not know which position he will take over. Admittedly, even such a person's prospects may be partly determined through his inherited endowment. But the younger the person, the larger will be the uncertainty and the greater the need for insurance.

Life is a random walk whose path can only partly be manipulated by men's decisions. By the very nature of this random walk, a person's income is more predictable in the short run than in the long run. Seen from today, next year's income is not very risky and so it may appear difficult to interpret income redistribution as insurance. But the income 40 years from now is much less predictable, and many people would agree that a redistribution of that income would be insurance.

Insurance and redistribution are two sides of the same coin. Every insurance contract involves a redistribution from the lucky to the unlucky, and most redistributive measures can be interpreted as insurance when the time-span between assessing and taking these measures is sufficiently long. Understanding redistribution as insurance is simply a matter of making the judgement before the veil of ignorance has been lifted.

Writers like Friedman (1953), Harsanyi (1953, 1955), Rawls (1971) and Buchanan and Tullock (1962) have earlier clarified this issue in somewhat different contexts, and, in a sense, the principle of judging behind the veil of ignorance can even be attributed to Kant's (1785) *categorical imperative*. The crucial point to note here is that it is necessary to make the judgement not only *behind* a fictitious veil of ignorance, but *before* the veil is actually lifted. For everyone in society, there was a time where the veil still hid his destiny.

The issue is less philosophical than it seems because it has very practical implications for the relationship between private and social insurance. A number of authors including Bulow and Summers (1984), Gordon (1985), Kaplow (1991, 1992) and Konrad (1991) have demonstrated that, under certain conditions, social insurance cannot improve the allocation of risks beyond what the markets can do. With perfect risk markets, the government cannot improve the allocation of resources, and even with imper-

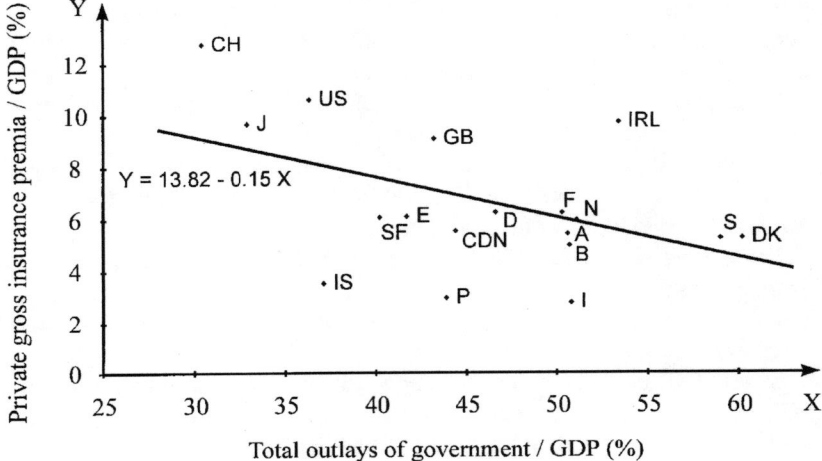

Figure 3.1   Private insurance versus social insurance

Source: OECD (1990) *Historical Statistics 1960–1988*, table 6.5, p. 68 (Paris);
OECD (1994) *Insurance Statistics Yearbook 1985–1992*, table 1.1, p. 18
(Paris); OECD (1994) *National Accounts: Main Aggregates 1960–1992*,
vol. 1, table 13, pp. 124–5 (Paris).
Note: The data include all countries for which OECD statistics are available. All
data refer to the year 1988.

fect markets it may not do better if the reasons for the imperfection, typically problems of asymmetric information, apply to the government as
well as private insurers. If the government decides nevertheless to introduce additional insurance it will simply crowd out private insurance one
by one.

There is some empirical evidence for a crowding-out effect. While there
is no significant cross-country correlation between the size of social security transfers and the revenue of the private insurance business, there is a
significant negative relationship between total government outlays and
private insurance revenue.[3] An increase in the government share in GDP
by one percentage point reduces the share of private insurance premia in
GDP by 0.15 percentage points. Figure 3.1 illustrates the findings.

The empirical findings reemphasize the point made in the introduction
that social insurance in the narrower sense of the word often does not
include much insurance and that all government outlays, even public
expenditure for goods and services, should be considered as part of social
insurance. They also show, however, that the crowding-out effect is far
from perfect. It is true that some government insurance competes with

private insurance, but the crowding-out effect is 15 per cent rather than 100 per cent as predicted. Obviously, by far the largest part of social insurance covers risks for which otherwise no private insurance would be available.

Private insurance covers specific contingencies. Typically there is a very narrowly defined set of circumstances under which a private insurance company pays indemnification. Social insurance, by way of contrast, is an all-inclusive insurance that protects against the risks of lifetime careers. The two kinds of insurance are not easily comparable.

The timing problem could be the reason why private insurance is not available for the kinds of risks covered by redistributive taxation. The issue can best be understood from the perspective of parents with young children or even parents-to-be because for them the veil of ignorance has not yet been lifted. These parents do not know which innate abilities their children have been endowed with, they fear that their children may suffer from illnesses and injuries, they are afraid of bad teachers and friends, they are concerned about missing job opportunities and bad choices, they are afraid that their children may become unemployed, and they hope, but cannot be sure, that a successful marriage will be possible. The welfare state cannot eliminate these risks, but, by offering a redistribution contract between successful and unlucky children, it can help mitigate the consequences.

Under the present liberal constitutions prevailing in Western countries, similar private redistribution contracts are inconceivable. They would not be allowed since they would come close to bondage, a system long overcome in these countries by the course of history. It would have to be acceptable for parents to allocate substantial fractions of their children's incomes to private institutions without their offspring having the chance to modify, or even nullify, the decision when they become adults.

Private redistribution contracts have to 'wait' until a person has reached the legal state of adulthood, but by then most of the veil of ignorance will have been lifted. When both the insurer and the insuree have the same knowledge about the inequalities then existing they will not be able to find a mutually agreeable redistribution contract. And when the insuree has superior knowledge, there will be the typical adverse selection problem, analysed so frequently in the insurance literature. Full coverage pooling equilibria are not feasible since the good risks will not participate, and, at best, there can be a separating equilibrium where only bad risks find enough coverage. All too often, insurance for the good risks will not be available at all.[4]

Barr (1992) has recently argued that the non-existence of risk markets due to adverse selection is the major explanation and justification for social insurance. Unlike private companies, he maintains, the government can force individuals to participate and thus avoid adverse selection. This argument is correct, but incomplete, since it neglects the timing problem.

Judged at the time when private contracts can be settled (that is, after adulthood has been reached), the imposition of force by the government is not a Pareto improvement since it makes the good risks worse off. At best, the government intervention can be defended with the Kaldor criterion, that the good risks lose less than the bad risks gain from enforcing a pooling equilibrium so that compensation would be theoretically feasible. Judged at a time early enough before adulthood, when the veil of ignorance has not yet been lifted, the same kind of force may be a Pareto improvement, because all parents welcome the insurance which the enforced redistribution implies. Adverse selection becomes a convincing allocative argument for government intervention if social insurance can cover a longer time-span than private insurance so that part of the inequality hampering the latter can be insured as risk by the former.

The reason societies have excluded bondage contracts and rely so much on an individual's voluntary decision at the time of adulthood is a deep sociological and legal question. But it is a matter of fact that this exclusion has made it necessary to develop career insurance through the welfare state rather than through the private insurance market.

Apart from the legal difficulties of having private 'career insurance' contracts, a crucial aspect contributing to the historical development of the welfare state can probably be seen in the growing importance of the provision of public goods motivated by other reasons. As was described so vividly by Wagner (1876) and Timm (1961), industrialization, urbanization and the general development of the exchange economy required a more than proportional increase in public expenditure for infrastructure, justice and education. Given that this expenditure was necessary it was plausible to finance it with redistributive rather than poll or benefit taxes. Introducing redistributive elements into the tax system had the advantage of providing social insurance without involving additional transactions or administrative costs. The marginal administrative cost of making an existing tax system redistributive may have been negligible or even negative. Setting up a private insurance solution from nothing would certainly have been the more expensive solution.[5]

III   RISK TAKING, INSURANCE AND REDISTRIBUTIVE TAXATION

Social insurance through redistributive taxation cannot be well understood if it is seen as the insurance of given risks. The behavioural changes induced by social insurance must also be taken into account. It is frequently argued that these behaviour changes are a sign of moral hazard which, as such, reduces the benefit from insurance. However, this view does not harmonize well with the beneficial effects that the Domar–Musgrave literature attributes to risk-taking. Indeed it is one of the great advantages of insurance that it makes risks bearable that otherwise would have prohibited economic activities. Henry Ford once said that New York would not have been built without the help of the insurance system, and it seems appropriate to add that the rise of Venice to the position of the world's richest city in the fourteenth and fifteenth centuries is inconceivable without the invention of a modern insurance system. Under the protection of the *foenus nauticum* and the various derivatives invented at the time, the Venetian merchant fleet risked making journeys to the most remote corners of the Mediterranean (later even to the Atlantic), collecting astronomical gains from trade.[6]

The beneficial effects of insurance are not limited to cases of active entrepreneurship. Even a reduction in loss prevention brought about by insurance can, in principle, be seen as a beneficial effect. When insurance under equivalence rating is cheaper than prevention there is no reason to denounce a substitution of these two activities a moral hazard. Cruciger (1921, p. 6n.) reports an interesting example from Hamburg's merchant fleet. For a long time, the fleet used to be accompanied by convoy ships whose task was to protect it against piracy. The maintenance of the convoy ships was expensive, though, and so there is small wonder that the introduction of an efficient insurance system in the eighteenth century rendered the convoy ships superfluous. Substituting insurance for convoys increased the profitability of Hamburg's merchant fleet and contributed to its success as continental Europe's most important harbour.

Equally spectacular examples do not seem to be available for social insurance, since social insurance helps with many different and diffuse risks rather than with well-specified and particular economic risks. Still, there is every reason to suspect that, in principle, beneficial risk-taking effects of a similar kind can be expected from social insurance, too. Under the protection of the welfare state people can avoid costly private protection measures like precautionary saving, job diversification, ultra-tenured employment contracts, offspring maximization or health fetishes. And they can dare to change jobs, to move to another house, to seek employment in risky industries, to open their own business, or to engage in a risky but profitable investment in human capital. The persistent structural change associated with industrial development would certainly face more resistance than it does if the welfare state did not spread its safety net to protect the large numbers of losers typically brought about by such a change. Interestingly enough, even the Venetian merchant fleet was not protected only by the newly created private insurance business, it received substantial public protection, too. While private insurance covered the loss of cargo, the galleys were owned by the state, which completely absorbed their risk of loss and destruction.

The risk-taking effects of market and social insurance are similar but not identical. To analyse the differences formally, let us assume a conventional formulation of a decision problem under uncertainty well-known in the insurance literature,[7] but represent the choice problem in $\mu - \sigma$ space in order to be able to speak meaningfully about 'risk-taking'. The $\mu - \sigma$ formulation can be used without any loss of generality, if it is assumed that all distributions belong to the same linear distribution class. Any von Neumann–Morgenstern utility function can be exactly represented by indifference curves in $\mu - \sigma$ space that are well-behaved and have properties that relate in an obvious way to the properties of the respective von Neumann–Morgenstern function.[8] Neither quadratic utility nor normality in the distributions has to be assumed.

Let m be a family's income in the case of good luck, e its effort in the sense of loss prevention expenses, and L the random loss. 'Prevention expenses' should, in the present context, be best thought of as a family's educational effort before the adulthood of its offspring. For the time being effort is assumed to be a loss of (taxable) market income. Section IV analyses the case where effort is a loss of (non-taxable) non-market income. Without insurance, income is

$$Y = m - e - L \qquad\qquad \text{(no insurance) (3.1)}$$

It is assumed that

$$L = \lambda\,(e)\,\theta \qquad\qquad\qquad\qquad (3.2)$$

where λ ($\lambda' > 0$, $\lambda'' \varnothing 0$, $\lambda' \rightarrow -\infty$ as $e \rightarrow 0$) is a function reflecting diminishing marginal returns to effort and θ ($\theta \varnothing 0$) is the random state of nature.

Now suppose there is an ideal *market insurance* covering the fraction τ of the losses and costing a premium p. An ideal market insurance is defined such that the premium is 'fair' in the sense of covering the individual's expected loss, not only in a symmetrical market equilibrium, but also when the individual decides to deviate from this equilibrium. With ideal insurance, income becomes

$$Y = m - e - L(1 - \tau) - p \qquad\qquad \text{(market insurance) (3.3)}$$

where[9]

$$p = \tau \cdot EL \qquad \text{(market insurance) (3.4)}$$

Abstract from the fact that, for the reasons explained, market insurance is not available for the kinds of risk considered.

Suppose alternatively that there is *social insurance* through redistributive taxation where τ is now the tax rate. Post-tax income is

$$Y = (m - e - L)(1 - \tau) + t \qquad \text{(redistributive taxation) (3.5)}$$

The variable t is a non-stochastic transfer (monetary and public goods) from the state, which has to satisfy a balanced budget requirement. In the case of a symmetrical equilibrium with identical individuals this requirement becomes

$$t = \tau(m - e - EL) \qquad \text{(redistributive taxation) (3.6)}$$

Equation (3.6) ensures that each individual receives a fair transfer in the sense that its expected net contribution of resources to the state is zero. This resembles the fair insurance condition (3.4). A crucial difference, however, is that, unlike the insurance premium p, the transfer t cannot be tailored to the individual's behaviour. If one individual deviates from the other individuals' prevention behaviour, it will have to reckon with a violation of equation (3.6) in the sense that its expected net contribution of resources to the state deviates from zero.

It is assumed that the individual risks are stochastically independent so that the law of large numbers ensures that any residual risk remaining with the insurance companies or the government is negligible in a large economy. With positively correlated risks there is no, or only little, scope for insurance, and with negatively correlated risks consolidation is particularly easy. The assumption of stochastic independence is a special, but not an implausible, assumption, lying in the middle of the spectrum of possibilities.

Equations (3.1)–(3.6) imply different choice sets in $\mu - \sigma$ space whose shapes depend on the way effort affects the loss distribution and the way losses are insured.

Consider first the problem of how the individual's probability distribution of income gross of insurance is affected. The pre-insurance mean and standard deviation are given by

$$\mu = m - e - \lambda(e)E\theta \qquad \text{(no insurance) (3.7)}$$

and

$$\sigma = \lambda(e)R\theta \qquad \qquad \text{(no insurance) (3.8)}$$

where R is the standard deviation operator. Denote the opportunity set described by (3.7) and (3.8) the 'self-insurance line'. The self-insurance line is represented in Figure 3.2. Its slope is

$$\frac{d\mu}{d\sigma} = \frac{\partial\mu/\partial e}{\partial\sigma/\partial e} = \frac{-\dfrac{1}{\lambda'(e)} - E\theta}{R\theta} \qquad \qquad \text{(no insurance) (3.9)}$$

Obviously, the self-insurance line is concave and has a maximum where λ' $(e)E\theta = -1$. This is the point where the cost of a marginal unit of effort equals the expected loss reduction it brings about. Increasing effort means moving from right to left along the self-insurance line. There is always a reduction in risk and in the expected loss with such a move, but the reduction in the expected loss will only be able to overcompensate the cost of effort in some initial range.

In the absence of insurance the individual will pick a point like T where an indifference curve is tangent to the self-insurance line. The point is to the left of the maximum, indicating that the individual chooses more effort than necessary to maximize income. Obviously, risk aversion – the positive slope of the indifference curve – implies that some expected income is sacrificed in order to lower the risk. To turn it the other way round, the individual operates at a point of his efficiency frontier where a little more risk tolerance would generate a little more expected income.

There are two interesting aspects of this simple result. The first aspect is that risk-taking is productive. The reason for the productivity of risk-taking is the same as the reason why, in general, the marginal productivity of factors of production is positive. Because the use of a factor is an *unwanted* activity, a firm operates at a point of its opportunity set where it compromises between the goal of minimizing this activity and maximizing another activity which is wanted. Increasing the unwanted activity a little makes it possible to increase the wanted one too: the unwanted activity is productive. Think of the old debate between von Böhm-Bawerk (1888, pp. 328–62) and Fisher (1907, pp. 64n.) about the productivity of 'waiting' (which we today call capital). Fisher showed nicely that it is only the preference for not waiting which explains why waiting is productive. Seen this way, Pigou (1932, pp. 771–81) was right when he called risk a 'factor of production' with the same status as the better-known factors like capital and labour.[10]

The second interesting aspect of the result is that market insurance and redistributive taxation may be able to bring risk productivity into operation. If risk aversion is the reason for a positive marginal productivity of risk, then an effective reduction of this aversion through insurance will increase the expected income.

Consider the *ideal market insurance* first. From (3.2), (3.3) and (3.4) it follows that expected income and its standard deviation are given by

$$\mu = m - e - \lambda(e)E\theta \qquad \text{(ideal market insurance) (3.10)}$$

and

$$\sigma = (1 - \tau)\lambda(e)R\theta \qquad \text{(ideal market insurance) (3.11)}$$

The equations indicate that ideal market insurance does not change the mean, but reduces the standard deviation of income. For reasons that will become clear in a moment denote the opportunity set resulting from (3.10) and (3.11) the 'redistribution line'. With ideal market insurance, the redistribution line is the individual opportunity locus of decision alternatives as perceived by the insuree. The redistribution line is represented in

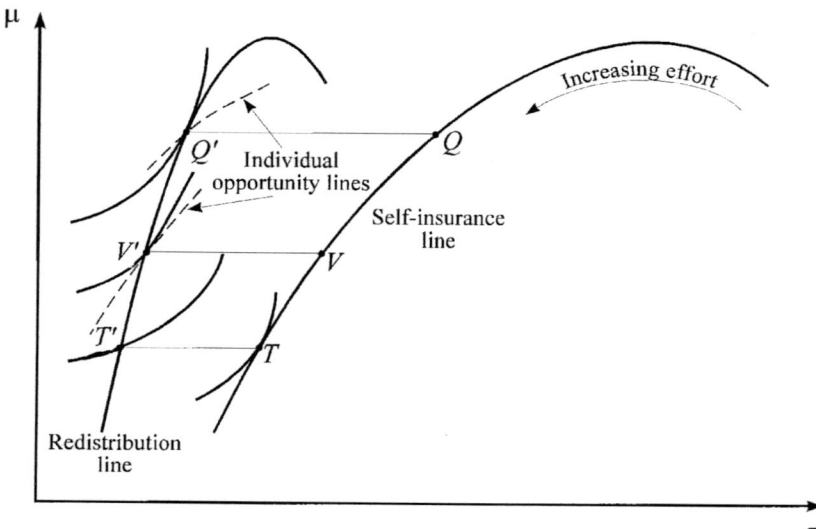

Figure 3.2   Risk productivity, ideal insurance and redistributive taxation

Figure 3.2. It can be constructed from the self-insurance line by shifting each point horizontally towards the abscissa where the percentage move equals the degree of coverage. The slope of the redistribution line equals

$$\frac{d\mu}{d\sigma} = \frac{1}{1-\tau} \cdot \frac{-\dfrac{1}{\lambda'(e)} - E\theta}{R\theta} \qquad \text{(ideal market insurance) (3.12)}$$

A comparison with (3.9) shows that, with any given effort level, the slope is $1/(1 - \tau)$ times the slope of the self-insurance line. The individual's optimum on this line is a point like Q' which is the analogue of point Q on the self-insurance line. If the individual did not change his behaviour, insurance would result in point T'. Q' is above T', since at point T' the indifference curve is flatter and the redistribution line is steeper than at T, indicating that the point of tangency is above T'.

Before this result is interpreted, consider the case of *redistributive taxation* next. If (3.6) is inserted into (3.5) the individual's choice problem obviously becomes isomorphic with the choice problem under ideal insurance, as represented by (3.3) and (3.4). However, as noted already, such a procedure would not make sense since it is the characteristic of redistributive taxation that the individual cannot affect the amount of transfers or public goods received through a manipulation of the taxes he pays. Thus the 'individual opportunity line' in the case of redistributive taxation is only given by (3.5) where (3.6) is just an equilibrium condition which has to hold but which the individual cannot incorporate into his own decision problem other than by taking the right amount of t as given. The mean and standard deviation of (3.5) are given by

$$\mu = [m - e - \lambda(e)E\theta](1 - \tau) + t \qquad \text{(ideal redistribution) (3.13)}$$

and

$$\sigma = (1 - \tau)\lambda(e)R\theta \qquad \text{(ideal redistribution) (3.14)}$$

Depending on the level of t, these equations imply alternative individual opportunity lines as illustrated in Figure 3.2. The slope of these lines is again given by

$$\frac{d\mu}{d\sigma} = \frac{-\dfrac{1}{\lambda'(e)} - E\theta}{R\theta} \qquad \text{(ideal redistribution) (3.15)}$$

as in the absence of taxation (see equation 3.9). Thus the slope at any given point of the individual opportunity line is equal to the slope at the corresponding point of the self-insurance line. This is illustrated in Figure 3.2 for two alternative positions of the individual opportunity line. The individual opportunity line can be seen as resulting from a parallel leftward shift of the self-insurance line.

A redistributive equilibrium is a situation where the individual has made his optimal choice and the government has chosen its transfer so as to balance its budget. In the figure this is a situation where an individual opportunity line is tangent to an indifference curve and where, at the same time, this point of tangency is located on the redistribution line. It must be on the redistribution line since (3.5) and (3.6) imply that only on this line is the government budget balanced, given the tax rate. The redistributive equilibrium is in a point like V'. V' is above T' since at T' the indifference curve is flatter than at T while the individual opportunity line has the same slope as at T. V' is below Q', since at Q' the redistribution line has the same slope as the indifference curve, but the individual opportunity line has always a lower slope than the redistribution line.

The interpretation of this result is straightforward if one decomposes the move from T to V' into a move from T to T' and from T' to V'. The two components indicate a double benefit from redistributive taxation. The first is the insurance effect. People's expected utility increases, since part of their uncertainty is removed. The second is the risk-taking effect. People prefer to translate part of the gain in safety into a higher expected income by taking more risks. This in itself increases expected utility a second time. Although in the case considered the increase in risk-taking comes about through a reduction in the self-insurance effort, the effect cannot be considered as a moral hazard effect. A moral hazard effect would reduce everyone's expected utility in a symmetrical equilibrium. The risk-taking effect makes everyone better off. Both the insurance effect and the risk-taking effect are strict Pareto improvements.

While the risk-taking effect is welfare-increasing it is not large enough. This becomes clear if the allocation is compared with a Pareto-optimal allocation. Given the rate of coinsurance τ, the constrained Pareto optimum is at Q', the point reached with ideal insurance. Ideal insurance is one where the insurer tailors the premium precisely to the action the individual chooses. This implies that insurance creates a double incentive for risk-taking: the required marginal compensation for risk-taking (the indifference curve slope) declines with a reduction in risk and the marginal return to risk-taking (the right-hand side of 3.12) increases. The individual perceives the redistribution line as his feasible opportunity set.

In contrast, redistribution only creates the first type of incentive, the decline in the required marginal return to risk-taking. In order for redistributive measures to create the second type as well it would be necessary to tailor the public transfer *t* to the individual action, which is an unrealistic requirement.

While risk-taking is too small under redistributive taxation, the effect as such is unambiguous. This is in striking contrast to the verdict by Feldstein (1969) and Stiglitz (1969) that once ended the discussion about the Domar–Musgrave effect. Both authors found the risk-taking effect to be ambigous under a general class of von Neumann–Morgenstern utility functions, but it is important to realize that they considered fiscal rather than redistributive taxation; that is, a taxation where the taxpayer does not in any sense enjoy the benefits from the public expenses which he finances. Under fiscal taxation the expected income declines which, in itself, increases the required marginal compensation to risk-taking when the utility function exhibits decreasing absolute risk aversion. Under redistributive taxation this effect is absent since the expected income is not changed. A formal proof that the required marginal compensation to risk-taking will indeed fall when σ decreases while μ is constant is given in Sinn (1990).[11]

IV MORAL HAZARD

The previous section analysed risk-taking under idealized conditions. The ideal insurance was one with equivalence rating where the premium was tailored to the individual decision, and the ideal redistribution was such that the tax base was identical with the argument of the individual's utility function. The tax that comes closest to the one analysed is a cash-flow tax for business investment where, however, all variables would have to be interpreted in present-value terms.

In many respects, reality is remote from the ideal situation analysed. Community rating is typical for many market insurance situations, because the insurer has inferior knowledge of the individual's actions, and imperfect deductibility of effort is a typical problem for tax systems.

Effort can have many more dimensions than are captured by equation (3.2). Equation (3.2) depicts the role of effort *ex ante*, before the dice of destiny are cast. Equally important is effort *ex post*, when the uncertainty has been resolved. Actually, most of the conventional theory of tax distortions concentrates on this type, and to analyse it here would mean taking coals to Newcastle. In principle, *ex post* moral hazard (or tax distortions under certainty) would have to be represented by downward shifts of the self-insurance and redistribution lines.

For the purposes of this exposition, it may instead be useful to concentrate on the problems resulting from distorting *ex ante* effort as analysed in different contexts by Ehrlich and Becker (1972), Shavell (1979) and Sinn (1978). Assume that effort is no longer a loss of market income but leisure or non-market income given up for the purpose of controlling risk. Let n be the total amount of leisure or non-market income available. Abstract from the multidimensionality of the problem by assuming that income, effort, leisure or non-market income, losses and public transfers can all be expressed in terms of the same good. Admittedly this is a courageous assumption for a tax theorist, but it is one that helps concentrate on the distortion in risk-taking. The tax is now an idealized version of a labour income tax with a labour–leisure distortion. Instead of (3.5) and (3.6) one gets

$$Y = (m - L)(1 - \tau) + n - e + t \qquad (3.16)$$

and

$$t = \tau\,(m - \mathrm{E}L) \qquad (3.17)$$

Using (3.2), the mean and the standard deviation become

$$\mu = [m - \lambda(e)\mathrm{E}\theta](1 - \tau) + n - e + t \qquad (3.18)$$

and

$$\sigma = (1 - \tau)\lambda(e)\mathrm{R}\theta \qquad (3.19)$$

The corresponding slope of the individual opportunity line is

$$\frac{d\mu}{d\sigma} = \frac{1}{1 - \tau}\cdot\frac{-\dfrac{1}{\lambda'(e)} - (1 - \tau)\mathrm{E}\theta}{\mathrm{R}\theta} \qquad (3.20)$$

Note that t has to be taken as given in the derivation of the individual opportunity line. A redistributive equilibrium, however, must satisfy (3.17) and so the solution where an indifference curve is tangent to the individual opportunity line must again be on the redistribution line. (Equations 3.16 and 3.17 yield the same opportunity set in $\mu - \sigma$ space as 3.3 and 3.4 or 3.5 and 3.6). Figure 3.3 illustrates the solution.

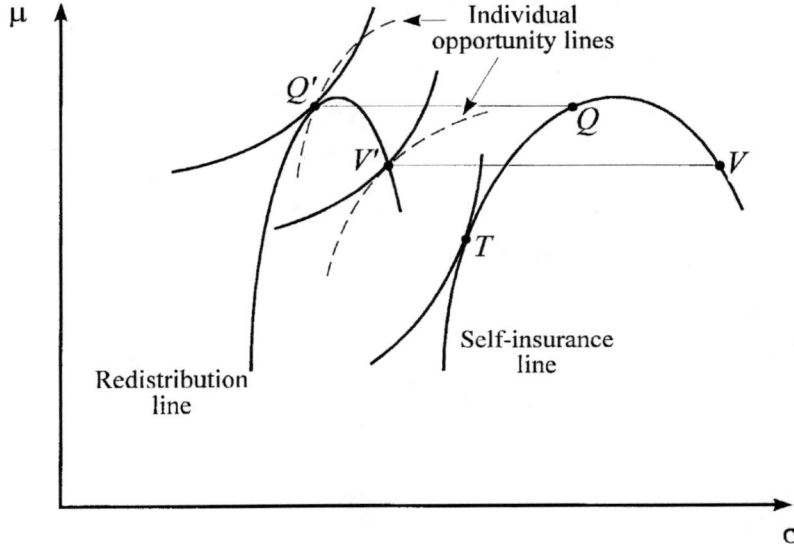

Figure 3.3   Moral hazard

A comparison between (3.20) and (3.12) shows that with $\tau > 0$, the slope of the individual opportunity line with moral hazard will always be larger than that of the redistribution line which, as was shown earlier, itself exceeds that of the individual opportunity line without moral hazard. This implies that effort is too small relative to a constrained Pareto optimum given the tax rate, and there is too much risk-taking. The solution may even be to the right of the maximum of the redistribution line (and of the self-insurance line) as illustrated in the figure.

It is now no longer clear that risk-taking is beneficial, and it is even possible that there is a net loss of utility from the imposition of the welfare state. Figure 3.4 illustrates this. In the limit as $\tau \to 1$, the redistribution line converges to a straight line on the ordinate such as $B'V'$ where the indifference curve slope is zero.[12] Clearly, setting (3.20) equal to zero and letting τ approach unity implies that $\lambda' \to -\infty$ and $e = 0$. The individual makes no effort, the pre-tax distribution is represented by V, and the post-tax distribution is represented by V'. V' is on a lower indifference curve than the *laissez-faire* optimum T. The overdrawn welfare state creates net welfare losses which is what the critics of the welfare state seem to have in mind.

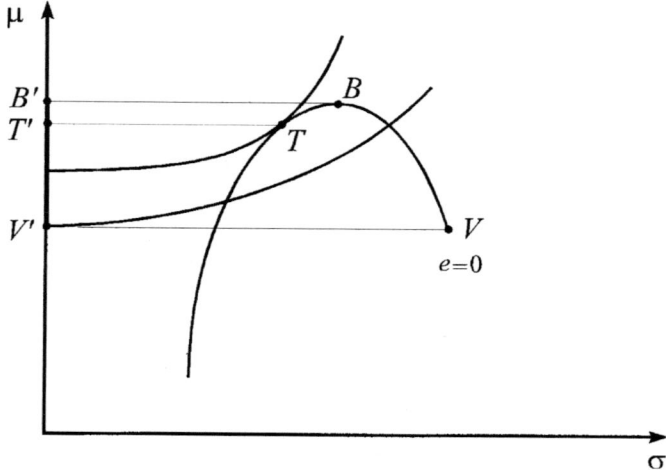

Figure 3.4   The excessive welfare state

To conclude the discussion of moral hazard note that in this case, and only in this case, the tax problem becomes isomorphic with the insurance problem. Moral hazard in the insurance problem results from community rating which implies that the premium is not tailored to the individual action while the insurance company's budget constraint, equation (3.4), still has to hold in an insurance equilibrium. If the companies cannot observe the individual actions, they can still use experience rating to make sure that (3.4) is satisfied and their expected indemnification costs are covered. Calculating μ and σ for (3.3) with given p gives the same expression for the slope of the individual insurance line under market insurance as (3.20) and therefore the same type of excessive risk-taking solution as under redistributive taxation without deductibility of effort.

Taken together, the results of this and the previous section suggest that there is a chance to design a tax system where, despite imperfect deductibility of effort, the optimal amount of risk-taking may be generated. With a full deductibility, there is too little risk-taking. With no deductibility, there is too much risk-taking. There should be an intermediate solution where redistributive taxation is able to generate the optimal amount of risk-taking that could be expected from ideal insurance with equivalence rating.

V REDISTRIBUTION AND INEQUALITY

There is an extensive literature on the effect of taxation on inequality, but nearly all contributions assume a fixed pre-tax distribution and disregard possible repercussions from redistributive taxation to the pre-tax distribution of incomes.

There are a number of possibilities for such repercussions, all having in common that pre-tax incomes become more unequal when the government tries to equalize post-tax incomes. One possibility is simply that the supply of the taxed factors of production is elastic so that the tax burden can be fully shifted to the inelastic factors and the net-of-tax rewards of the taxed factors stay constant. A small open economy is a particularly good example for this case. Another possibility is that efficiency wages require a given net-of-tax distribution of incomes so as not to violate the non-shirking constraints. A third possibility is that tax-induced risk-taking makes the pre-tax distribution more unequal. Kanbur (1979) has considered this case in a model with risky occupational choices and intersectoral migration, and there is also a discussion of related phenomena in Boadway and Wildasin (1990). The first to have used this argument seems to have been Friedman (1953).

The easiest possibility for modelling the problem is to assume that there is an economy with *ex ante* identical individuals who have the same preferences and who are endowed with the same set of probability distributions from which they can make their choices. If it is assumed that the probability distributions are stochastically independent across the individuals, in a large economy it will turn out that the realized income distribution is identical with each person's chosen probability distribution. If, say, the chosen probability distribution indicates that the probability of having an income of between $100 000 and $101 000 is 3 per cent, then the percentage of people whose income turns out to be in this range is just this 3 per cent. The law of large numbers converts a probability *ex ante* into a relative frequency *ex post*.

If we apply this idea to the choice problems analysed in the two previous sections it turns out that μ and σ are not only the mean and standard deviations of the probability distributions faced *ex ante*, but also the average per capita income and its standard deviation as realized *ex post*. The trade-off between expected income and risk turns out to be a trade-off between average income and equality, and the indifference curves become social indifference curves representing unambiguously the society's evaluations of income distributions. The point where an indifference curve enters the ordinate indicates Atkinson's (1970) 'equally distributed equivalent income' for all income distributions located on this indifference curve.

Ideal redistribution as analysed in Section III makes the pie bigger and its pre-tax distribution more unequal. Moral hazard as analysed in section IV may or may not bring about further increases in the size of the pie, but it will definitely make pre-tax inequality even greater.

However, how post-tax inequality will be affected is not clear because the insurance and risk-taking effects counteract one another.

If the self-insurance line is strongly curved in the relevant range there is little scope for changes in pre-tax risk, and the insurance effect will dominate. In the extreme case one may think of a kink in the self-insurance line which implies that the individual does not react to an increase in redistributive taxation, and only the insurance effect prevails. If, on the other hand, the self-insurance line is sufficiently straight, that is if there are approximately constant returns to risk-taking, the opposite may be true. Figure 3.5 illustrates this case.

Abstract for a moment from moral hazard and consider the case of ideal redistribution. The redistribution line is now linear, too, and it has a slope

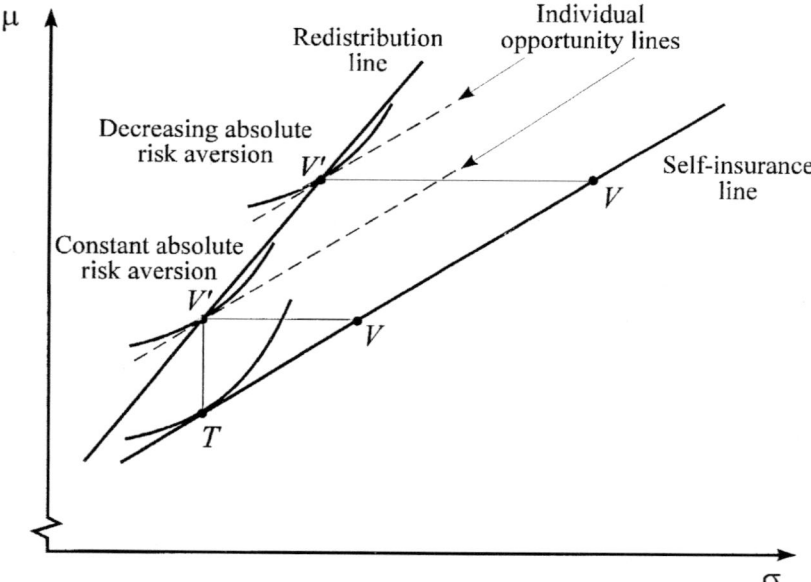

Figure 3.5   The redistribution paradox

$1/(1 - \tau)$ times that of the self-insurance line (see 3.12 and 3.15) While the *laissez-faire* solution is T on the self-insurance line, the redistributive equilibrium is characterized by a point on the redistribution line where an indifference curve is tangent to one of the dashed individual opportunity lines. The individual opportunity line has the same slope as the self-insurance line (see 3.9 and 3.15) but, depending on the level of public transfers, it can have different positions.

The interesting question is whether the solution point is to the right or to the left of the *laissez-faire* point T, that is, whether redistributive taxation increases or decreases post-tax inequality. The answer depends on whether absolute risk aversion is an increasing or a decreasing function of expected income, because the direction in which absolute risk aversion changes with an increase in μ is the same as the direction in which the indifference curve slope changes when μ increases, given σ.[13] In the borderline case where absolute risk aversion is constant, the point of tangency, V' in the figure, happens to be vertically above the *laissez-faire* point T, which indicates that redistributive taxation will not affect the post-tax inequality of incomes.

In the realistic case of decreasing absolute risk aversion, the indifference curve slope declines if μ increases with given σ, and so the point of tangency with an individual opportunity line must be to the right of the *laissez-faire* point T. There is a 'redistribution paradox'. Redistributive taxation makes the post-tax income distribution more unequal because people prefer to translate more than 100 per cent of the increase in safety and equality into risk-taking in order to be able to enjoy a larger size of the pie.[14]

While this paradoxical result has been derived under the assumption of ideal redistributive taxation, it is immediately obvious from the discussion of the previous section that it will hold *a fortiori* if there is a moral hazard effect in terms of excessive reduction in prevention effort and, correspondingly, excessive risk-taking and inequality. Thus it seems that, under the conditions analysed in this chapter, the only crucial assumption necessary for the taxation paradox to hold is constant returns to risk-taking. Future research will have to clarify to what extent this particular feature can be expected in real choice problems under uncertainty.

Regardless of how post-tax inequality changes, it will always be true in the present model that pre-tax inequality rises when there is more redistributive taxation. This aspect sheds new light on the positive correlation between income inequality and redistributive taxation that has found so much attention recently in papers by Alesina and Rodrik (1994), Perotti (1992), and Persson and Tabellini (1994). These authors argue that a high level of pre-tax inequality implies a political equilibrium with high redistributive taxes which, since taxes on capital income are included, tends to reduce the growth rate of the economy. The present analysis is not a contradiction to this view since an optimally designed welfare state may indeed react to an exogenous increase in the riskiness of the individual's pre-tax opportunity set (a rightward shift of the self-insurance line) with a tax increase. However the present analysis makes it clear that the causality could also be the reverse of how the authors interpret their empirical findings. More inequality in pre-tax incomes may well be the result rather than the cause of more redistributive taxation.

VI   THE OPTIMAL TAX PROBLEM

What do we learn from the foregoing analysis for the design of an optimal redistributive tax system?

An important but not very surprising lesson is that the tax base should coincide as closely as possible with the argument of people's utility function. This means, in particular, that effort should be deductible. It is true that risk-taking would be too small under such conditions, but the policy would definitely avoid the severe allocation problems that otherwise will have to be expected. It would err on the right side, since risk-taking would always be welfare-increasing relative to the situation where taxpayers do not change their behaviour. Cash-flow taxes, and all taxes that allow for an immediate deduction of investment expenses and other outlays, would be optimal, but the income tax in its usual form would be less desirable. On the one hand, depreciation *pro rata temporis* means that, in present value terms, there is imperfect deductibility of 'effort' in terms of investment outlays. On the other hand, labour income taxation fails to make allowance for the leisure given up, perhaps the most important 'effort' involved.

As little can be done about the distortions in the labour–leisure choice and a number of other distortions, there is a problem of optimal redistributive taxation balancing the advantages and disadvantages at the margin.

Suppose the moral hazard model of Section IV applies and the government wants to choose a tax rate so as to maximize the representative agent's expected utility, knowing what this agent's reactions are. Clearly it will be true, as is well-known from similar problems in the insurance literature,[15] that the optimal coinsurance rate is between zero and one. In the present context, the first bit of redistributive taxation has a positive first-order effect on utility via the insurance effect but, since risk-taking is optimal when there is no taxation, only a second-order effect via the resulting change in risk-taking. And the last bit of redistributive taxation, when τ has approached unity, will reduce utility via a reduction in expected income but will not be able to change utility due to a change in post-tax risk, because there is no risk aversion 'in the small' (the indifference curves enter the ordinate perpendicularly).

A more interesting question is what the optimality condition says. In principle, there are two possibilities for an optimal redistributive tax system. They are illustrated in Figures 3.6 and 3.7. For any given tax rate τ there is a well-specified redistribution line as illustrated in Figures 3.2 and 3.3 with a unique redistributive equilibrium. Plotting the alternative equilibria resulting from different tax rates gives the arrowed curves shown in Figures 3.6 and 3.7 which may be called 'equilibrium lines'. A movement along an equilibrium line following the arrows indicates an increase in the tax rate. The optimal tax rate is reached in a point like Z' where the equilibrium line is tangent to an indifference curve.

A continued increase in the tax rate τ implies that the pre-tax distribution changes as described by a rightward movement along the self-insurance line, while the post-tax distribution changes as described by the equilibrium line. In Figure 3.6, the optimal pre-tax distribution is charac-

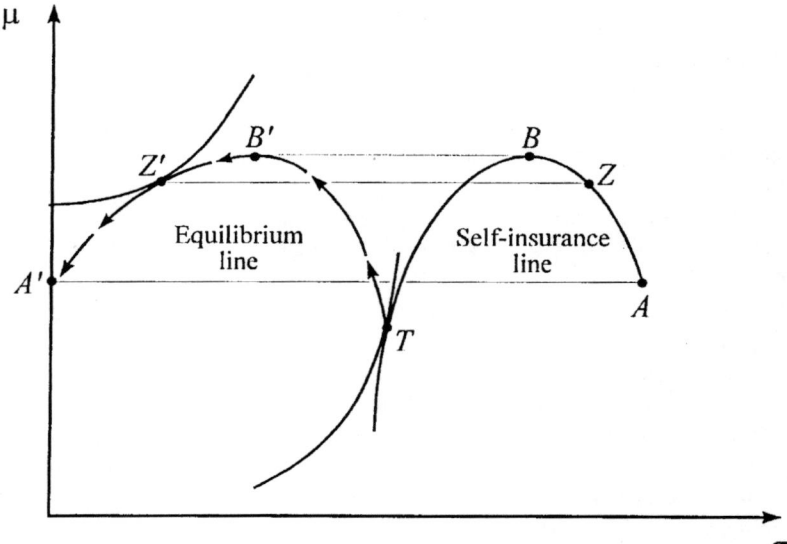

Figure 3.6   The optimal tax problem

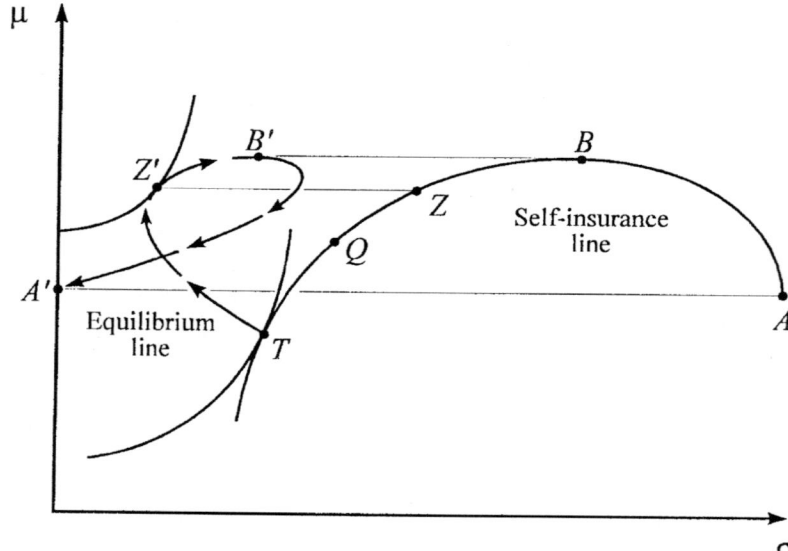

Figure 3.7   Optimal taxation and the redistribution paradox

terized by a point like Z which is to the right of the maximum. In the optimum, a small tax increase reduces average income, increases pre-tax inequality and reduces post-tax inequality.

In Figure 3.7, the optimum is to the left of the maximum of the self-insurance line, because the equilibrium line performs a loop. Such a loop is possible if the self-insurance line is, in parts, fairly straight so that the conditions for the taxation paradox apply. By definition, the taxation paradox characterizes a situation where the arrowed equilibrium line bends to the right. In an optimum like that shown in Figure 3.7, a small tax increase will increase average income as well as pre-tax and post-tax inequality.

It is unclear which of these two constellations will hold in reality. However, whichever does, it is clear that in an optimal redistributive tax system one of two seemingly paradoxical constellations must prevail. Either it is true that the economy operates at a point of its technological efficiency frontier (the self-insurance line) where less inequality results in a larger pie, or it is true that more redistribution makes post-tax incomes more unequal.

VII CONCLUSIONS

This chapter has adopted the view that redistributive taxation can be seen as social insurance that provides protection against the risks of lifetime careers for which, for the reasons given in Section II, no private insurance is available. Social insurance is a mutual assistance that involves a resource transfer from the lucky rich to the unlucky poor which is welcomed by parents before the veil of ignorance covering the destiny of their children has been lifted. It cannot be provided privately unless the fundamentals of western civil law are called into question.

While much is known about a myriad of negative incentive effects created by the welfare state, it seems that its more beneficial risk-taking effects have not been well understood. This chapter has tried to shed some light on the issue. At a time when the welfare state is being rolled back in many countries, this may be an effort worth undertaking.

Notes

1. Sandmo (1991) shows that because of the distortions created by income transfers an efficient redistribution system will always include the free provision of public goods. The question of whether income distribution should or will be carried out in the form of cash, in-kind transfers or genuine public goods is not treated in this chapter.
2. The chapter is a broadened and non-technical discussion that partly draws on previous writings by the author on the subject. See in particular Sinn (1981 and 1995).
3. The t-value for the latter regression is 1.94 while it is only 0.6 for the former. The crowding-out effect in the former (non-significant) case is only 7 per cent. When only private health, accident and life insurance are considered, the regression coefficient with regard to total government outlays is more significant ($t = 2.2$), but has only a value of 0.11.
4. Atkinson (1991) denies this argument pointing to the fact that often bad risks are rejected by the insurance companies. This observation is probably due to pooling contracts enforced by the government and regulating agencies. It does not contradict the fact that adverse selection is a major reason for the non-existence of risk markets. For an explicit treatment of adverse selection in a two-stage lifetime-risk model see Sinn (1996).
5. A related argument has been made by Christiansen (1990).
6. A more detailed discussion of the role of insurance for the Venetian development can be found in Sinn (1988).
7. See, for example., Ehrlich and Becker (1972), Shavell (1979) and Sinn (1978).
8. The probability distributions among which an individual can choose form a linear redistribution class if they are all similar in the sense that they can be

transformed into one another by shifts of, and proportional expansions around, the mean. More technically speaking y' and y'' belong to the same linear class if $y' = \mu' + \sigma'z$ and $y'' = \mu'' + \sigma''z$ where z is a common standarized distribution and the μ's and σ's represent the respective means and standard deviations. Most theoretical decision problems under uncertainty analysed in the literature using the expected utility approach are confined to linear distribution classes. See Meyer (1987) and Sinn (1983, 1990) for the details.

9. Throughout the chapter E is the expectation and R the standard deviation operator.
10. For further discussions of this theme see Konrad (1992) and Sinn (1986).
11. The proof allows for declining, constant, and increasing absolute risk aversion provided that the increase is not 'faster' than with the 'fastest' quadratic utility function compatible with the assumption of increasing marginal utility in the relative range. Since no one ever has found, proposed, or used a utility function whose absolute risk aversion increases faster than with a quadratic utility function nearly perfect generality of the proof can be claimed.
12. This is a general property holding for all von Neumann-Morgenstern functions. See Sinn (1983).
13. See Sinn (1983, p. 116n.).
14. Note that inequality is here defined in absolute rather than relative terms. If inequality is measured by the coefficient of variation, m/s, the borderline case where m/s stays constant despite an increase in redistributive taxation is characterized by constant relative risk aversion which implies a homothetic indifference curve system.
15. See, for example, Shavell (1979).

References

Ahsan, S.M. (1974) 'Progression and Risk-Taking', *Oxford Economic Papers*, vol. 26, pp. 318–28.

—— (1976) 'Taxation in a Two-Period Temporal Model of Consumption and Portfolio Allocation', *Journal of Public Economics*, vol. 5, pp. 337–52.

Alesina, A. and D. Rodrik (1994) 'Distributive Politics and Economic Growth', *Quarterly Journal of Economics*, vol. 109, pp. 465–90.

Allingham, M.G. (1972) 'Risk-Taking and Taxation', *Zeitschrift für Nationalökonomie*, vol. 32, pp. 203–24.

Atkinson, A.B. (1970): 'On the Measurement of Inequality,' *Journal of Economic Theory* 2, 244–63.

—— (1991) 'Social Insurance', The Fifteenth Annual Lecture of the Geneva Association, *Geneva Papers on Risk and Insurance Theory*, vol. 16, pp. 113–31.

—— (1995) *The Economic Consequences of Rolling Back the Welfare State*, Munich Lectures in Economics (Cambridge, Mass: MIT Press, forthcoming).

Atkinson, A.B. and J. Stiglitz (1980) *Lectures on Public Economics* (New York: McGraw-Hill).

Bamberg, G. and W.F. Richter (1984) 'The Effects of Progressive Taxation on Risk-Taking', *Zeitschrift für Nationalökonomie*, vol. 44, pp. 93–102.

Barr, N. (1992) 'Economic Theory and the Welfare State: A Survey and Interpretation', *Journal of Economic Literature*, vol. 30, pp. 741–803.

Boadway, R.W. and D. Wildasin (1990) 'Optimal Tax-subsidy Policies for Industrial Adjustment to Uncertain Shocks', *Oxford Economic Papers*, vol. 42, pp. 105–34.

Böhm-Bawerk, E. von (1889) *Kapital und Kapitalzins, Zweite Abteilung: Positive Theorie des Kapitals* (Innsbruck: Verlag der Wagner'schen Universitäts-Buchhandlung).

Buchanan, J.M. and G. Tullock (1962) *The Calculus of Consent* (Ann Arbor: University of Michigan Press).

Bucholz, W. (1987) *'Risikoeffekte der Besteuerung'*, unpublished habilitation thesis, University of Tübingen.

Bulow, J.I. and L.H. Summers (1984) 'The Taxation of Risky Assets', *Journal of Political Economy*, vol. 92, pp. 20–39.

Christiansen, V. (1990) 'Subsidization of Risky Investment under Income Taxation and Moral Hazard', *Warwick Economic Research Paper* No. 357, Dept. of Economics, University of Warwick.

Cruciger, G. (1921) *Transportversicherung* (München: Steinebach).

Diamond, P.H., L.J. Helms and J.A. Mirrlees (1980) 'Optimal Taxation in a Stochastic Economy', *Journal of Public Economics*, vol. 14, pp. 1–29.

Domar, E. and R.A. Musgrave (1994) 'Proportional Income Taxation and Risk-Taking', *Quarterly Journal of Economics*, vol. 58, pp. 388–422.

Eaton, J. and H.S. Rosen (1980) 'Taxation, Human Capital, and Uncertainty', *American Economic Review*, vol. 70, pp. 705–15.

Ehrlich, I. and G.S. Becker (1972) 'Market Insurance, Self-Insurance, and Self-Protection', *Journal of Political Economy*, vol. 80, pp. 623–48.

Feldstein, M. (1969) 'The Effects of Taxation on Risk-Taking', *Journal of Political Economy*, vol. 77, pp. 755–64.

Fisher, I. (1907) *The Rate of Interest* (New York: Macmillan).

Friedman, M. (1953) 'Choice, Chance, and the Personal Distribution of Income', *Journal of Political Economy*, vol. 61, pp. 277–90.

Gordon, R.H. (1985) 'Taxation of Corporate Capital Income: Tax Revenues versus Tax Distortions', *Quarterly Journal of Economics*, vol. 100, pp. 1–27.

Harsanyi, J.C. (1953) 'Cardinal Utility in Welfare Economics and the Theory of Risk-Taking', *Journal of Political Economy*, vol. 61, pp. 434–5.

Harsanyi (1955) 'Cardinal Welfare, Individualistic Ethics and Interpersonal Comparisons of Utility', *Journal of Political Economy*, vol. 63, pp. 309–21.

Kanbur, R. (1979) 'Of Risk-Taking and the Personal Distribution of Income', *Journal of Political Economy*, vol. 87, 769–97.

Kant, I. (1785) *Grundlegung zur Metaphysik der Sitten* (Riga).

Kaplow, L. (1991) 'A Note on Taxation as Social Insurance for Uncertain Labor Income', NBER Working Paper No. 3708.

Kaplow (1992) 'Income Tax Deductions for Losses as Insurance', *American Economic Review*, vol. 82, pp. 1013–17.

Konrad, K. (1991) 'Risk-taking and Taxation in Complete Capital Markets', *The Geneva Papers on Risk and Insurance Theory*, vol. 16, pp. 167–77.

Konrad, K. (1992) *Risikoproduktivität* (Berlin, Heidelberg and New York: Springer-Verlag).

Meyer, S. (1987) 'Two-Moment Decision Models and Expected Utility Maximization', *American Economic Review*, vol. 77, pp. 421–30.

Mirrlees, J.A. (1995) 'Private Risk and Public Action: The Economics of the Welfare State', *European Economic Review*, vol. 39, pp. 383–97.

Perotti, R. (1992) 'Income Distribution, Politics, and Growth', *American Economic Review*, vol. 82, Papers and Proceedings, pp. 311–16.

Persson, T. and G. Tabellini (1994) 'Is Inequality Harmful for Growth?', *American Economic Review*, vol. 84, pp. 600–20.

Pigou, A.C. (1932) *The Economics of Welfare* (London: Macmillan).

Rawls, J.A. (1971) *A Theory of Justice* (Cambridge, Mass.: Harvard University Press).

Rochet, J. Ch. (1991) 'Incentives, Redistribution and Social Insurance', *Geneva Papers on Risk and Insurance Theory*, vol. 16, 143–65.

Sandmo, A. (1977) 'Portfolio Choice, Asset Demand and Taxation', *Review of Economic Studies*, vol. 44, pp. 369–79.

Sandmo, A. (1991) 'Economists and the Welfare State', *European Economic Review*, vol. 35, pp. 213–39.

Shavell, S. (1979) 'On Moral Hazard and Insurance', *Quarterly Journal of Economics*, vol. 93, pp. 541–62.

Sinn, H.-W. (1978) 'The Efficiency of Insurance Markets', *European Economic Review*, vol. 11, pp. 321–41.

—— (1981) 'Die Grenzen des Versicherungsstaates. Theoretische Bemerkungen zum Thema Einkommensumverteilung, Versicherung und Wohlfahrt', in H. Göppl and R. Henn (eds), *Geld, Banken und Versicherungen* (Königstein: Athenäum) pp. 907–28. Reprinted in G. Rolf, P.B. Spahn and G. Wagner (eds) (1988) *Sozialvertrag und Sicherung – zur ökonomischen Theorie: staatlicher Versicherungs- und Umverteilungssysteme* (Frankfurt and New York: Campus) pp. 65–84.

—— (1983) *Economic Decisions under Uncertainty* (Amsterdam, New York and Oxford: North Holland) (2nd edn, Heidelberg: Physica, 1989).

—— (1986) 'Risiko als Produktionsfaktor', *Jahrbücher für Nationalökonomie und Statistik*, vol. 201, pp. 557–71.

—— (1988) 'Gedanken zur volkswirtschaftlichen Bedeutung des Versicherungswesens', *Zeitschrift für die gesamte Versicherungswissenschaft*, vol. 77, pp. 1–27.

—— (1990) 'Expected Utility, μ, σ Preferences, and Linear Distribution Classes: A Further Result', *Journal of Risk and Uncertainty*, vol. 3, pp. 277–81.

—— (1995) 'A Theory of the Welfare State', *Scandinavian Journal of Economics*, vol. 97, pp. 495–526.

—— (1996) 'The Subsidiarity Principle and Market Failure in Systems Competition' CES Working Paper No. 103.

Stiglitz, J.E. (1969) 'The Effects of Income, Wealth, and Capital Gains Taxation on Risk-Taking', *Quarterly Journal of Economics*, vol. 83, pp. 263–83.

Timm, H. (1961) 'Das Gesetz der wachsenden Staatsausgaben', *Finanzarchiv*, vol. 21, pp. 201–47.

Varian, H.R. (1980) 'Redistributive Taxation as Social Insurance', *Journal of Public Economics*, vol. 14, pp. 49–68.

Wagner, A. (1876) *Allgemeine oder Theoretische Volkswirtschaftslehre: Erster Theil, Grundlegung* (Leipzig and Heidelberg: Winter'sche Verlagshandlung).

4 Unemployment in the United States: The Problem and a Proposal

Robert Haveman

The problem of unemployment among industrialized nations has important implications for the efficiency with which these economies are performing, and hence for economic growth and the well-being of citizens. It also contains the seeds of social instability. A recent volume addressing this issue described the problem and its implications as follows:

> While unemployment will ebb somewhat as countries recover from the recent global recession, millions are likely to remain jobless for a variety of structural reasons. Moreover, there is a disturbing trend in many industrialized countries toward long-term unemployment, especially among low-skilled workers. This trend has had less effect on measured unemployment in the United States than in Europe in part because U.S. workers have greater incentives to accept low-wage jobs. Nonetheless, virtually all industrial countries face a jobs problem that impairs living standards and threatens a breakdown in social cohesion.[1]

This description contains two key points. The first is the emphasis on structural barriers to the reduction of unemployment in all industrialized countries; the second is the contrast between the United States and Europe. While the reduction in the relative demand for low-skilled workers has affected labour markets in all of these economies, they have responded in quite different ways. In Europe, wage rates at the bottom end have been maintained by a variety of measures including policies that set the minimum wage at a high level relative to the average wage; as a result, the declining relative demand has been revealed in high unemployment levels and in the increasing prevalence of long-term unemployment. In the United States, a lower minimum wage and fewer other barriers to employment creation have enabled job growth for low-skilled workers; as a result, a relatively high percentage of all American workers occupy minimum-wage, low-earnings jobs. Predictably, earnings inequality in the United States has increased substantially, as has the incidence of poverty.

In Section I, I describe the employment, earnings and poverty situation in the United States, and compare it briefly with that in Europe. Section II outlines the policy options that have been undertaken in the United States, and describes and assesses the trade-offs that these choices reveal. Finally, in Section III, I outline a policy response that involves direct intervention into the low-wage labour market in the interests of increasing the employment of working-age people with few skills and low productivity. This proposal rests on a pair of policy measures designed to offset serious efficiency problems in the low-wage labour market, and hence holds some promise of contributing to both efficiency and equity goals. Section IV concludes.

I   EMPLOYMENT, EARNINGS AND POVERTY TRENDS IN THE UNITED STATES

Employment Growth

Relative to its industrialized neighbours, the United States has been a 'job creation machine'.[2] As Table 4.1 shows, from 1979 to 1993 the total

Table 4.1   Net new jobs created in ten countries, 1979–93

Country	Total created 1979–93 (000)	New jobs as percentage of 1979 employment
Australia	1 569	25.7
Canada	2 620	25.2
France	480	2.3
Germany	2 750	10.8
Italy	310	1.6
Japan	9 770	18.1
Netherlands	1 110	20.8
Sweden	−146	−3.5
United Kingdom	400	1.6
United States	20 482	20.7

Source: Data from the US Bureau of Labor Statistics.

number of jobs created in the United States exceeded that of the other nine major economies taken together. Over this period, the number of net new jobs created exceeded 20 million, or nearly 21 per cent of the 1979 employment level. This percentage-increase figure was equalled by The Netherlands and exceeded only by Australia and Canada. The median percentage for the economies other than the United States is 10.8 per cent.

With the exception of Germany and The Netherlands, the performance of the other Western European countries is dismal. The percentage increase for France, Italy, Sweden and the United Kingdom ranges from –3.5 to 2.3, and fewer net new jobs were created in these countries than in The Netherlands or Australia. Over the slow-growth period from 1989 to 1994, all four of these economies experienced a net loss of jobs; the total number of net jobs lost over this period exceeded 2.2 million.

Unemployment Trends

This differential pattern of job growth among these industrialized nations is also reflected in the differing unemployment experiences among them. In the United States, the standardized unemployment rate in the 1990s (1990–93) was 6.5 per cent, slightly lower than its average over the 1970–90 period. By contrast, the unemployment rate in the 1990s in the European Community (9.0 per cent) was equal to its value in the 1980s, but more than three times its level during the 1960s and 1970s.[3]

While unemployment in all of these countries tends to be concentrated among particular age, education, and ethnic/racial groups, the pattern in the United States is particularly severe. As Table 4.2 reveals, since 1960 the unemployment rate of youths has been at least three times the level of that of older workers, irrespective of race, and until the early 1990's, the gap between the two has been increasing. The difference in the youth–older worker unemployment rate averaged about 10 percentage points in the 1960 to 1980 period for whites; the difference has exceeded 11 points since 1980. For blacks, the youth–older worker rate difference was about 16 points in the 1960s, increasing to about 25 points since 1970.

Similarly, the difference in black–white unemployment rates has increased since the 1960s. For youths, the percentage-point gap between black and white unemployment rates has risen from about 11 points in the 1960s to over 18 points in the 1970s and to over 21 points since 1980. A similar trend in the racial gap for older workers has occurred.

Table 4.2   Unemployment rates in the United States, by age and race
(percentages)

	1960s	*1970s*	*1980s*	*1990s*[a]
All civilian workers	4.8	6.2	7.3	6.5
White males, age 16–19	12.8	14.7	16.9	16.7
White males, age 20+	3.2	4.1	5.6	5.4
Gap: age 16–19 less age 20+	9.6	10.6	11.3	11.3
Black males, age 16–19	23.6	33.2	39.8	36.9
Black males, age 20+	7.1	8.6	13.3	11.8
Gap: age 16–19 less age 20+	16.5	24.6	26.5	25.1
Gap: black, 16–19 less white, 16–19	10.8	18.5	22.9	20.2
Gap: black, 20+ less white, 20+	3.9	4.5	7.7	6.4

[a] Covers years 1990–93.
Source: Data from *Statistical Abstract of the United States*, various years.

Changes in Male Work Patterns and Joblessness

Table 4.3 presents the allocation of working-age males in the United
States among work-pattern categories from the early 1970s until the

Table 4.3   Percentage allocation of males aged 18–64 across work-pattern
categories, 1973–92

	FTYR[a]	*FTPY*[b]	*PTFY*[c]	*PTPY*[d]	*No work*	*Total*
1973 (peak)	66.8	18.4	2.7	4.7	7.4	100.0
1975 (trough)	59.9	22.2	2.7	4.7	10.5	100.0
1988 (peak)	64.7	15.8	3.1	5.4	11.0	100.0
1991 (trough)	60.5	17.5	3.6	5.7	12.7	100.0

Note: Self-employed workers excluded from this sample.
[a] Full-time, year-round.
[b] Full-time, part-year.
[c] Part-time, year-round.
[d] Part-time, part-year.
Source: Calculations by author from March Current Population Surveys from
1974, 1976, 1989, and 1992.

1990s.[4] Two important changes are revealed. First, there has been a substantial increase in male joblessness – from 7.4 per cent to nearly 13 per cent.[5] In 1973, there were about 3.5 million jobless working-age males, but by 1991 the number had grown to 8.4 million. About 50 per cent of out-of-school American youths aged 16–24 who lack a high school degree are currently jobless. Second, there has been an increase in the prevalence of part-time work, both among year-round and part-year workers. Whereas in 1973 about 13 per cent of all working-age males were either not working or working part-time (7.1 million persons), by the early 1990s working-age people in these categories had increased to over 22 per cent of the group, and about 15 million males were either jobless or working part-time. Most of this increase is in the number of jobless working-age males.

Earnings Trends

In a quite distinct break from the early postwar period in the United States, when the real hourly earnings growth of the average production worker was about 2.1 per cent per year, the real hourly earnings of the average worker have remained nearly constant since the early 1970s. The median real hourly wage fell by 6 per cent from 1973 to 1993.[6]

The basic cause of the sharp decline in average earnings growth is the fall in the rate of productivity growth, to which gains in average compensation are ultimately tied. From 1948 to 1973, output per worker in the US business sector increased nearly 2.9 per cent per year; since 1973, the average gain has been less than 1 per cent per year. Although this pattern explains why average earnings growth has been so low, it leaves aside the question of why the rate of productivity growth has stagnated since the early 1970s. A number of studies have attempted to determine the causes of the productivity slowdown; there is little general agreement among them.[7]

Trends in Wage and Earnings Inequality

The stagnation of average real wages has been accompanied by a substantial increase in wage inequality among male workers; inequality of wages among female workers has increased as well, but substantially less than for males.

Figure 4.1 shows the change in real earnings for full-time male workers at various points in the earnings distribution. Real earnings have declined for all males save for the most highly paid workers. The lowest-

Males

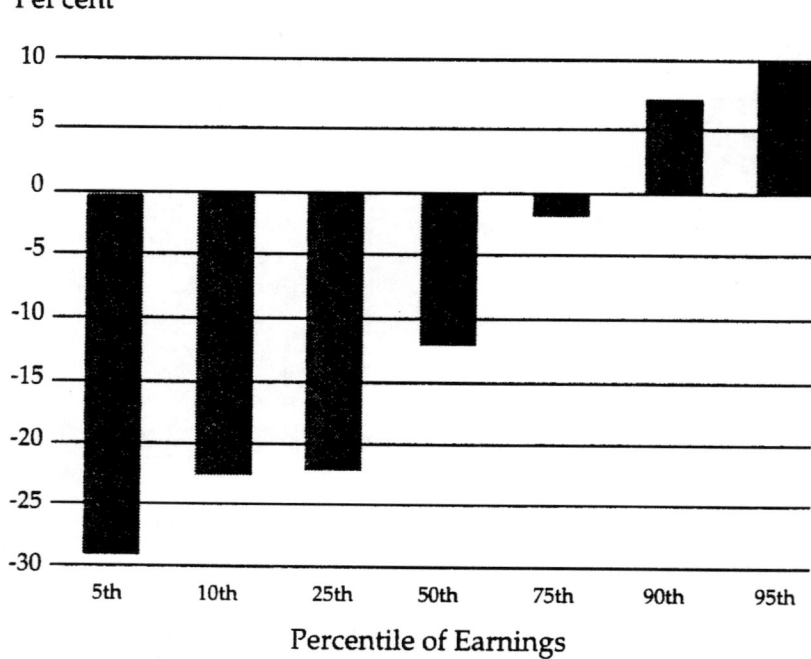

Per cent

Percentile of Earnings

Figure 4.1   Changes in earnings across the earnings distribution, year-round, full-time male workers aged 25–64, 1973–93.

Source: Committee for Economic Development (1996) *American Workers and Economic Change* (New York: CED) p. 8. Calculations by Gary Burtless from Current Population Survey.

paid workers have experienced the largest relative decreases. For example, male workers at the 10th percentile of earnings experienced a 23 per cent reduction in real earnings over the 1973–93 period. As a result, earnings gaps between well-paid and moderately paid, and between moderately paid and low-paid, workers have increased over time; more detailed analysis reveals that this trend has been most intense since about 1980.

Table 4.4 summarizes the trend in male worker earnings inequality from 1973 to 1991, using the variance in the natural logarithm (VLN) of earnings as the indicator of inequality. Throughout the period, and over expansions and recessions, earnings inequality rose; over the entire period, the

Table 4.4   Variance of logarithm (VLN) of earnings,
1973–91, male workers aged 18–64

1973 (peak)	1.11
1975 (trough)	1.18
1988 (peak)	1.29
1991 (trough)	1.30

Notes: Sample includes all civilian males aged 18–64 with positive earnings. Data are from March Current Population Surveys from 1974, 1976, 1989 and 1992. Earnings top-coded at $99 999 in 1991 dollars.
Source: Calculations by author.

Females

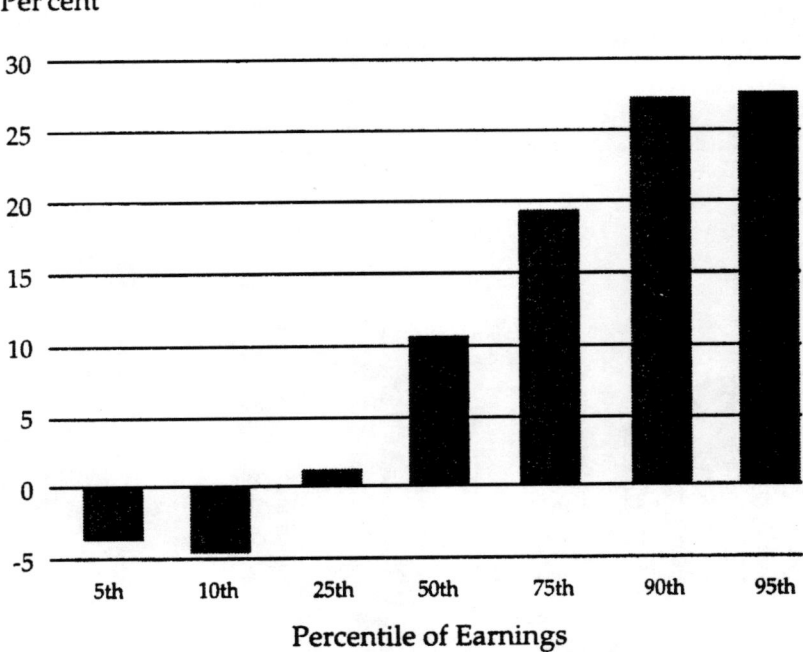

Figure 4.2   Changes in earnings across the earnings distribution, year-round, full-time female workers aged 25–64, 1973–93.

Source: Committee for Economic Development (1996) *American Workers and Economic Change* (New York: CED) p. 8. Calculations by Gary Burtless from Current Population Survey.

VLN measure increased by 17 per cent; the increase over the trough-to-trough period from 1975 to 1991 was over 10 per cent.

Figure 4.2 shows a quite different pattern of earnings change for full-time female workers. Over the two-decade period, earnings gains were experienced over most of the distribution. At the median, for example, real earnings rose by over 10 per cent over the period. However, the largest gains are concentrated at the top of the distribution. For women as well, earnings inequality has increased, but by a smaller amount than for men.

Figure 4.3 presents information on the change in wage inequality among full-time male workers with different levels of education. Whereas real hourly wages of the most highly schooled workers remained roughly constant over the period, the hourly wages of workers with less education fell dramatically. The average real wage of male high school graduates fell by 20 per cent over the 1973–93 period; for men without a high school degree, the reduction is even larger. Taking into account all male workers (including part-time and part-year workers), the earnings premium received by a college graduate, relative to a worker with a high school

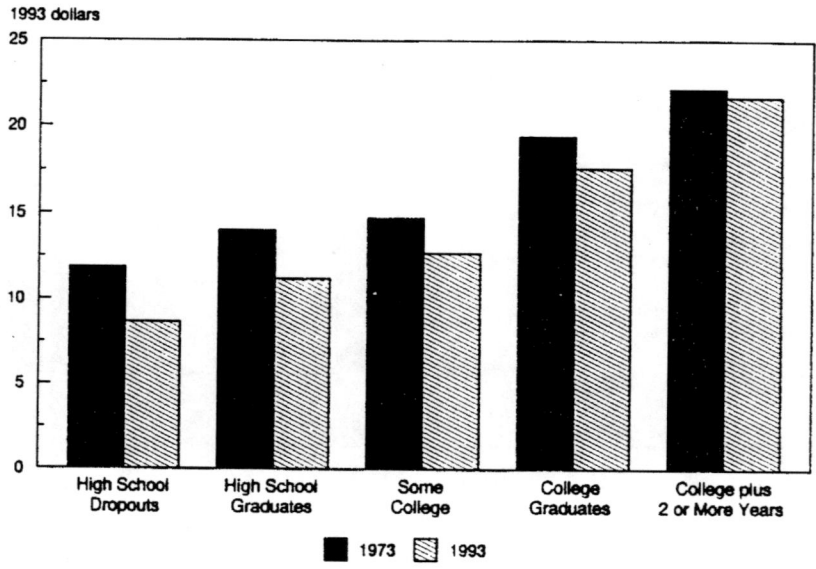

Figure 4.3   Real hourly wages for men, by level of education, 1973 and 1993

Source: *Economic Report of the President* (Washington, DC: GPO, February 1995) p. 175.

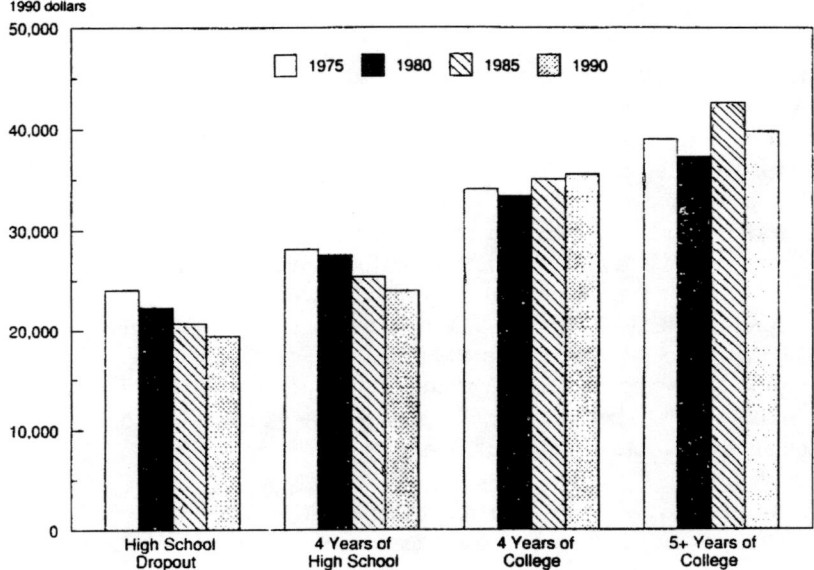

1990 dollars

| | 1975 | 1980 | 1985 | 1990 |

Figure 4.4   Earnings of cohorts of men aged 25–34 years, by education, 1975–90.

Note: Data based on full-time, year-round workers.
Source: *Economic Report of the President* (Washington, DC: GPO, February
1995) p. 99.

degree or less, increased from about 30 per cent in 1979 to over 70 per
cent by the early 1990s. These patterns suggest a dramatic shift in labour
market rewards away from male workers save those with the highest
levels of schooling and, presumably, skills. For women, wage inequality
by education level also increased, but by a much smaller amount.

In addition to the overall increase in earnings inequality, the gap
between younger and older workers has also increased over the entire
period since 1973. This was the period when the baby boom generation
entered the workforce, and as it did older workers prospered while
younger workers saw their relative earnings fall. Figure 4.4 illustrates this
deteriorating economic position among younger workers at all education
levels, with the exception of college graduates. It shows the average real
earnings of cohorts of young male workers (aged 25–34) measured in
1975 and in each of three subsequent years spaced five years apart. Over
the 20-year period, these younger, less-educated men experienced a substantial absolute deterioration in earnings.

The Trend in Poverty

In the late 1960s, the nation declared a War on Poverty and stated a commitment to a Great Society. A poverty line was set and made official, and the federal government made the elimination of poverty a national goal. The effort started fast, and progress was made. Between the time of the declaration in 1965 and the year 1973, the nation's official poverty rate fell from 17.3 per cent to 11.1 per cent. Since the early 1970s, however, the nation's record of progress against poverty and insecurity has been far less bright. As Figure 4.5 shows, the poverty rate has increased substantially since that time, from 11.1 per cent of the nation's population to 14.5 per cent in 1994. With the exception of the economic growth following the deep recession of the early 1980s, the time trend in the poverty rate has been largely positive. Between 1973 and 1994, the number of people officially classified as poor increased from 23 million to 38 million.

Since the early 1970s, then, aggregate employment in the United States has risen rapidly, although the average quality of the jobs (as reflected in the average wage rate) has fallen, especially for males. While the overall unemployment rate has not shown an upward trend – unlike that in Europe – unemployment has become increasingly concentrated among young and minority males, especially minority youths. Moreover, the performance of the overall unemployment rate masks other important aspects of the performance of the US economy. The incidence of joblessness and part-time work (especially for younger and minority male workers) has increased substantially in the United States since 1973, and because of shifts in both the supply of and demand for lower-skilled workers, the bottom has dropped out of the labour market. Wage rates and earnings have fallen substantially for low-skilled, low-education, young and minority workers, and as a result inequality of wage rates and earnings has grown substantially. This, among other factors, has led to a rapid increase in the poverty rate in the United States of over 30 per cent, and an increase in the number of poor people by more than 60 per cent.

II   POLICY RESPONSE TO THE EARNINGS INEQUALITY PROBLEMS IN THE UNITED STATES

The differences in the employment experiences between the United States and Europe suggest a trade-off between an American-style package consisting of:

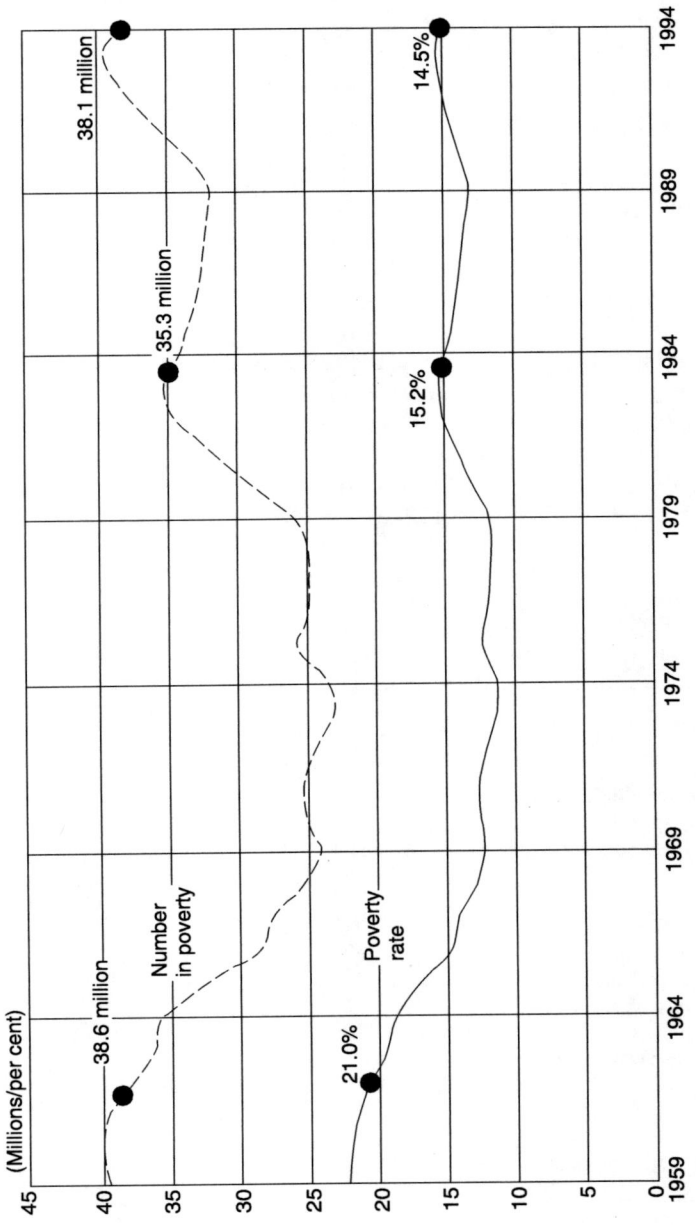

Figure 4.5 Poverty in the United States, 1959–94.

Source: US Bureau of the Census, 'Income, Poverty, and Valuation of Noncash Benefits: 1994', *Current Population Reports (Consumer Income)*, Series P60–189, April 1996, p. xv.

- rapid employment growth
- high and rising wage inequality
- slow wage growth

and a European-style package of:

- slow employment growth
- low and steady wage inequality
- higher wage growth
- high unemployment

Whether or not such an explicit trade-off exists, the situation in the United States would seem to call for a set of policies that could simultaneously address the problems of stagnant average wages, increasing inequality and poverty, and declining wages and high unemployment among low-skilled workers. This nexus of problems suggests a combination of active policies designed to increase investments in education and

Table 4.5   Expenditures by government on education, training and employment, and social services/other, United States, 1970–92 (billions of current $)

	1970	*1975*	*1980*	*1985*	*1990*	*1992*
Federal spending on training and employment	4.3	9.3	17.6	12.8	16.7	21.0
All spending on education	44.6	74.1	112.4	167.5	252.2	–
Total	48.9	83.4	129.0	180.3	268.9	–
Federal spending on training and employment as percentage of total federal spending	2.2	3.3	3.0	1.4	1.3	1.4
Total spending on training and employment plus education spending as percentage of all public spending	16.1	16.1	15.0	12.4	13.1	–
Federal spending on training and employment as percentage of total public spending	1.3	1.7	1.8	0.8	0.7	–

Source: Data are from *Statistical Abstract of the United States*, various years.

training (supply-side policies), stimulate employment opportunities through direct job creation (demand-side policies), and increase the speed and quality of job matches.

Has the nation pursued a strategy designed to address these problems? Table 4.5 shows US expenditures by the federal and other levels of government on education, training and employment, and social services since 1970. Public expenditures on employment and training are primarily undertaken by the federal government. As a percentage of federal spending, these expenditures grew until the late 1970s, after which time the growth slowed notably. During the early 1980s, major cuts in these programmes occurred, in particular federal public service employment for low-skilled workers. From 1980 to 1985, the absolute amount of employment and training expenditures fell, and as a percentage of federal spending, employment and training spending decreased from 3 per cent to 1.4 per cent. During this same period, these expenditures fell from 1.8 per cent of total public spending to 0.8 per cent. This reduction of federal employment and training expenditures as a share of federal spending continued until 1990; only in the past few years has it again begun to drift up. In 1996, as a percentage of total federal expenditures, employment and training spending was less that half its level in the mid-1970s (1.4 per cent compared to 3.3 per cent).

Figure 4.6 shows public expenditures on all labour market programmes for the United States and the other OECD countries in 1985 and 1993. The United States ranks nearly at the bottom of the countries in both years; these expenditures as a percentage of GDP are lower in 1993 than in the mid-1980s. The downward trend for the United States has occurred at the same time as the average OECD percentage has increased from 2 per cent to nearly 3 per cent. The US pattern contrasts with Canada, which maintained labour market expenditures as a percentage of GDP at or above the OECD average for both years.[8]

These statistics give a discouraging answer to the question of the response of United States policy-makers to the labour market problems that have confronted the nation since the mid-1970s. Indeed, precisely during the period when wages were stagnating, earnings inequality increasing, the unemployment of low-skilled and minority workers increasing, and poverty rising, the public sector – primarily the federal government – was withdrawing its support from policies aimed at increasing the capabilities of low-skilled workers, the demand for their services, or the quality of the matches between the supply of and demand for such workers.

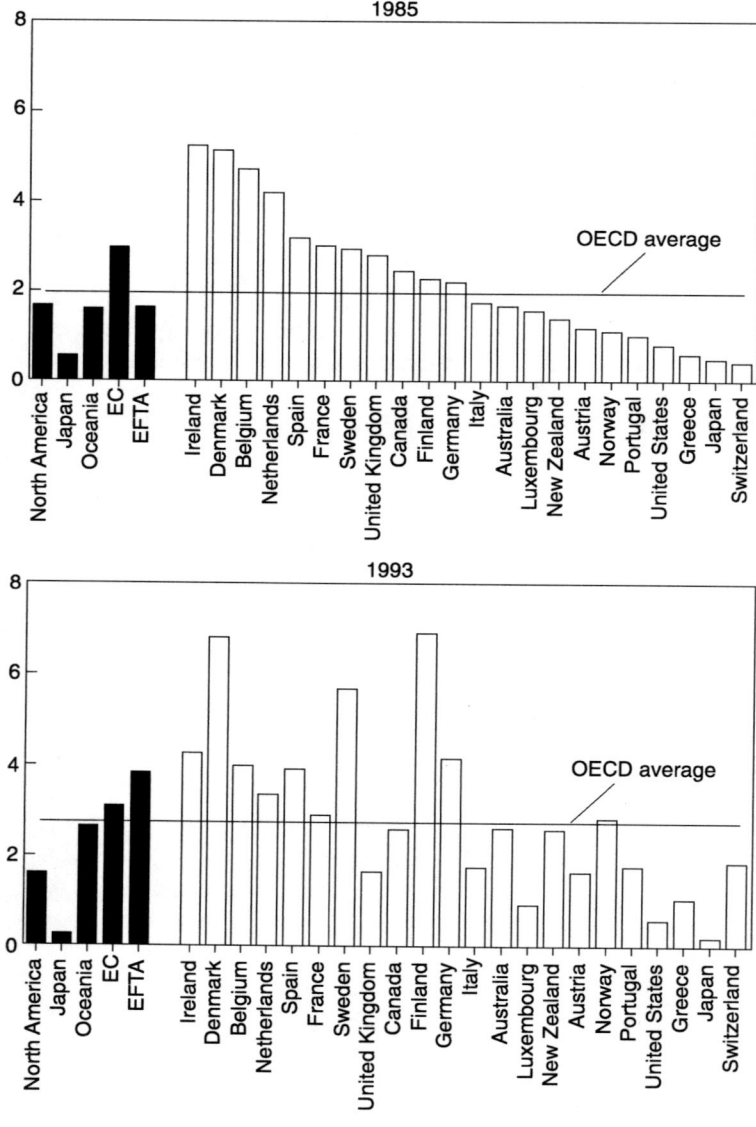

Figure 4.6   Public expenditures on labour market programmes, as a percentage of GDP

Source: Organization for Economic Cooperation and Development, *Employment Outlook* (Paris: OECD, 1994).

III DESIGNING POLICY TO MEET THE PROBLEM: A TWO-PRONGED PROPOSAL

The political environment of the later 1990s is not a propitious one for policy proposals that require increased spending or reduced revenue. The drive to eliminate the large US budget deficit by the year 2000 has assigned a low priority to public sector initiatives designed to meet pressing problems.

Consider, for example, labour market policy. The collapse of the bottom end of the market might be expected to bring forth proposals for stimulating the demand for low-skilled workers, for experimenting with public service employment, or for cushioning the income declines experienced by these workers. However, no such policy proposals are currently being given serious consideration.[9] Instead, cuts in both the eligibility for and the benefits provided by the nation's safety net programmes are being legislated, justified as programme changes yielding both reduced public spending and increased work effort by low-skilled workers (primarily women). With explicit time limits being placed on eligibility for cash benefits, the goal is to achieve independence and self-sufficiency for these low-skilled workers through employment.

When these measures are fully in effect in about the year 2000, from 200 000 to 300 000 low-skilled benefit recipients per year could be required to rely on work, rather than benefits, for their livelihood. These people – primarily women with extensive child-care responsibilities, low levels of schooling and skill, and little history of having or keeping a job – would be required to compete for jobs with other new labour market entrants in the eroded low-skill labour market. While the US economy will probably have no trouble absorbing these people into the workforce, they will be earning a minimum wage rate of less than $5.00 per hour, which is in real terms only about 75 per cent of its level in 1981. Even ignoring the need for child-care services, working full-time, year-round at this rate of pay would not lift these women and their families above the official poverty line.[10] Moreover, this policy will further depress the bottom end of the market.[11]

This 'welfare reform' labour market strategy fails to consider the employment and earnings problems which have come to characterize the United States in the mid-1990s: declining wages and earnings for workers with below-average skills (especially young workers), growing joblessness, and shockingly high unemployment rates among racial minorities and youths. The very nature of these problems suggests the need for policy measures designed to buttress the low end of the labour market, especially as a complement to this current 'welfare to work' strategy.

In this section, I suggest a labour market strategy designed both to increase the demand for low-skilled workers and to increase the reward for taking and accepting a low-wage job. It is a two-pronged approach, targeted both at disadvantaged workers and those who employ them. Its effect would be to alter the terms on which workers would be hired, in effect to make employment of them a more profitable and attractive proposition than it is now.

An Employer-based Marginal Employment Subsidy

An employer-based employment subsidy is designed to increase the contribution of employment and earnings to the economic support of individual workers and their families. An employment subsidy offered to enterprises operates on the demand side of the market. To be effective, such a supplement must affect the choices of employers as they are deciding how much labour and capital to purchase; the subsidies must be marginal in nature.

A feasible form of marginal employment subsidy targeted on enterprises would work as follows. The government would provide a tax credit (or other financial subsidy) to any enterprise equal to (say) 50 per cent of the first (say) $10 000 of wages paid to the (say) 50 workers hired in a firm above (say) 102 per cent of the firm's previous year's employment. Such a programme would be similar in structure to the New Jobs Tax Credit (NJTC) programme that was in place in the United States during the late 1970s. Although that programme did not distinguish among workers by their skill or unemployment status, the subsidy – and hence the incentive for firms to hire low-skilled workers – was a higher percentage of their total wages than it was for more highly paid workers.[12]

The design of such a programme could modify these provisions on several dimensions. The subsidy rate could be increased to more than 50 per cent, which would provide a greater incentive for hiring labour relative to other inputs (while of course increasing programme costs). The base level of wages that is subsidized could also be increased, again increasing the level of the employment subsidy provided, but also decreasing the targeting of the subsidy on the lowest-wage workers. Finally, the 'cut-in hiring level' at which the programme takes effect (the 102 per cent of the previous year's employment in the above example) could be reduced to, say, 100 per cent, providing employers with a subsidy on any workers hired beyond the previous year's level. Receipt of the subsidy could also be conditional on employer measures to provide on-the-job training or to promote long-term employer–employee relationships.

Such an employer-based subsidy does not directly increase the earnings and income of low-wage workers and their families. Rather, such a subsidy exerts its impact indirectly by altering the relative market demands of employers for inputs in favour of low-skilled workers. As a result, the wage rates of lower-skilled workers tend to be bid up, and more low-skilled workers are able to find work. By operating on the demand side of the labour market, such subsidies tend to offset the adverse employment effects of the minimum wage, thereby reducing the effect of existing income support programmes in creating a poverty trap.

As indicated above, the New Jobs Tax Credit programme is an example of such a marginal employer-based jobs subsidy plan. Both empirical studies of the employment effects of the New Jobs Tax Credit and simulation analyses of marginal employment subsidies suggest that such a strategy is effective in simulating employment at reasonable public cost relative to alternative job-creation measures.[13]

These conclusions notwithstanding, several issues need to be carefully considered prior to implementation of a national plan, including:

- the need to attend carefully to design factors in developing an employer-based employment subsidy programme which is marginal in its impact. Many existing employer-based job subsidies (the Targeted Jobs Tax Credit is an example) tend not to be targeted on the marginal employment decision;[14]
- the target effectiveness of an employer-based subsidy needs to be carefully considered in its design. The programme needs to be designed so as to create an incentive to employers to hire low-wage workers, as opposed to simply hiring more workers;
- the incentives implicit in such a system could induce employers to 'cycle' their production decisions, or to 'churn' their labour force, in order to maximize the amount of the subsidy that they receive.[15] This problem could be mitigated by designing the programme with a moving average of the previous year's employment as the base;
- the employer-based credit would provide a windfall to employers who would be expanding jobs in any case. Moreover, to the extent that subsidies lead to hiring that displaces other workers, it is the net effect of the programme that must be considered. While some amount of windfall will result, its magnitude can be constrained through adjustment of the employment base on which the subsidy rests.[16]

It should be emphasized that an employer-based marginal employment subsidy programme cannot provide the basis for safety-net coverage of the population and for effective poverty reduction. However, as a component of a more general restructuring of the low-wage end of the labour market, such a subsidy can contribute to increased employment of low-skilled workers and hence mitigate any existing unemployment or poverty trap created by existing income support policies.

A Wage Rate Subsidy

A wage rate subsidy is a work-conditioned income support programme in which the government supplements a worker's hourly wage. Hence, it rests on the establishment of a target wage rate which is socially determined. For any worker earning a wage rate below the target amount, a per hour subsidy is paid equal to some percentage (the subsidy rate) of the difference between the target wage rate and the actual wage rate.[17] For example, if the target wage rate were set at $8.00 per hour and the subsidy rate was 0.5, a worker earning $5.00 per hour would receive a subsidy of $1.50 per hour worked ($1.50 is 0.5 of the difference between the target wage rate of $8.00 per hour and the actual $5.00 per hour wage). The 'take-home' wage rate of that person would then be $6.50 per hour. A wage rate subsidy cannot be a substitute for existing programmes designed to place a safety net under family income; it supplements earnings for those who work, but it does not provide income to non-workers.[18]

By augmenting the hourly wage of low-wage workers, the wage rate subsidy provides an incentive for additional labour supply, offsetting the tendency of standard income support programmes to create a 'poverty trap'. Simultaneously, it contributes to poverty reduction among this population. Further, in an economy with a distortionary minimum wage policy, the adverse employment effects of the minimum wage tend to be countered and offset by a wage rate subsidy.[19] These three unambiguous effects are its primary merits.

In addition, from the perspective of the low-skilled worker, relative to the pre-subsidy arrangement, this programme would offer an advantage to accepting a job as compared to the receipt of income transfers. This programme would encourage low-skilled workers to exercise job-seeking initiative on their own behalf; it would tend to 'make work pay'. At the same time, however, employers, knowing of the existence of a wage rate subsidy programme, have an incentive to seek out disadvantaged, low-skilled workers and to favour them in hiring decisions – realizing that the low market wage of the job they have available is appraised by the worker as paying a higher-than-market wage rate. The advantage of such an employee-based plan, then, stems from the increased incentives to both workers to search for jobs and employers to hire them. Moreover, firms would not have to significantly alter their personnel practices, there would be no inequities across firms with some qualifying and others not, and there would be no firm 'threshold' problems.

However, perhaps more than other labour market measures, the wage rate subsidy creates a variety of economic impacts that need to be taken into account in an evaluation of it. In particular, wage rate subsidy programmes:

- tend to erode the market wage of low-wage workers by inducing an increase in the supply of labour in response to the higher 'take-home pay'. In part, this bidding down of market wage rates is what gives this policy its potentially large effect on employment. With lower market wages, low-skilled workers become more attractive to many employers.[20] However, with a design that considered the existing minimum wage as a floor, little such erosion would be expected;
- simultaneously reduce the benefits to a low-skilled worker of investments (such as education, training or job search) designed to increase the wage rate. If additional skills and training result in a higher market wage, the per-hour subsidy would fall, and the take-home wage would not rise as much as the market wage. In essence, an effective marginal tax rate is imposed on increases in wage rates, as opposed to providing incentive for increased labour supply and hours worked;[21]
- require employers to keep records on both the wage rate paid to low-wage employees and the hours that they work, and to report both of these. It would also create an incentive for collusion between employer and employee, whereby employers would report a lower than actual wage rate to the fiscal authority, which would result in a larger subsidy payment that would then be shared by employer and employee;[22]
- provide work-related income supplementation to low-wage workers as opposed to low-income workers and their families. To the extent that many low-wage workers are secondary workers (for example, children and spouses) in high- and middle-income families, the 'target efficiency' of a wage rate subsidy may be relatively low.

IV CONCLUSION

The unemployment situation in the United States differs substantially from that in much of the rest of the industrialized world. Joblessness and unemployment are concentrated among those with the lowest skills and schooling, who in turn face a labour market which has created plentiful jobs for them, but at declining real wage rates. Earnings inequality has increased, and along with it income poverty.

The collapse of the bottom end of the labour market has not been a part of the nation's political discourse, and policies designed to reverse this pattern have not been undertaken or seriously proposed. Instead, the emphasis has been placed on making non-work and joblessness less viable through reductions in the generosity of public support and restrictions on access to it.

The nature of the employment problem would seem to call for a reconsideration of this strategy, and a renewed focus on increasing the demand for workers with low skills and making low-paying jobs more attractive relative to non-work, joblessness, or quasi-legal or illegal activities. Two such measures – a marginal employment subsidy and a wage rate subsidy – are suggested as complementary policies designed to improve the performance of the market for the services of low-skilled workers.

The primary economic rationale for this two-pronged demand- and supply-side strategy is that both of the proposed subsidies work largely to offset the distortions (in the form of wedges between demand and supply prices) and the output-reducing effects of minimum wage legislation, labour union practices, payroll and other labour income taxes (relative to the taxation of capital), the labour supply effects of income transfers, and economic discrimination.[23] The subsidies offered slice through these wedges and boost deficient sector demand in ways which would bring workers whose marginal product exceeds the opportunity cost of their leisure into gainful employment.

The new environment at the bottom end of the labour market created by these programmes will tend to generate ongoing demand- and supply-side pressure for the creation of jobs for low-skilled workers at reasonable taxpayer cost. As such, it will equalize employment opportunities. By targeting the additional employment on segments of the labour market with substantial slack (see above), GNP could be increased without significant inflationary pressure. This strategy will fundamentally alter the wage structure in private labour markets, raising the take-home pay of low-skilled workers relative to those with more secure positions in the labour market.

However, both of the employment-related subsidies mentioned involve demands on the public sector budget. A rough estimate of the fiscal costs of this approach depends on the specific design of the programmes, but suggests that these costs are substantially less than the cost of increasing the employment of low-skilled workers via general increases in aggregate demand or the implementation of public service employment programmes.[24] Moreover, if in fact the programmes were effective in increasing employment, reduced joblessness and better pay would both increase tax revenues and reduce the demands on public transfer programmes.

Notes

1. See Higgins (1994).
2. A good summary of recent trends in the US labour market is found in Auer (1995).
3. These figures are from Martin (1994).
4. Labour force participation and employment patterns for women are substantially different than those for men. Female labour force participation has grown substantially since 1970, from a rate of about 43 per cent to a rate of nearly 58 per cent in 1993. Moreover, while the real wage rate for men fell between 1979 and 1992, the real wages of women in full-time employment rose by about 15 per cent.
5. To the extent that this growth in joblessness reflects the voluntary choice of working-age people to, say, accept early retirement, it could be viewed as a natural accompaniment of an increasingly affluent society. Some non-trivial share of this substantial increase is attributable to this source.
6. Hourly compensation, including fringe benefits, has grown over this period, but by about 0.5 per cent per year.
7. The factors identified range from aggregate economic conditions to structural considerations, such as the two oil crises in the 1970s; the changing demographic composition of the labour force; changes in education, training and R&D expenditures; changes in international trade patterns; and the increased costs imposed on private activities because of public regulations, especially in the environmental area. They are summarized in Haveman and Christainsen (1981).
8. Although not shown in the figure, for both 1985 and 1993 'active' labour market expenditures in the United States were about 35–37 per cent of total public labour market programmes.
9. In 1994, the Clinton administration did submit a reform package, the Reemployment Act of 1994, that addressed the problems at the bottom end of the labour market. The proposal identified a number of structural problems in the US economy and proposed a variety of policies addressed to them, including the use of unemployment insurance funds for training purposes, consolidation of labour market services, improved labour market information, and a reemployment bonus for unemployed workers who quickly find employment. The proposal is not currently being considered.
10. The United States does have an Earned Income Tax Credit programme that supplements the earnings of low-wage workers. Over time, this earnings supplement has become increasingly generous, such that for some workers earning the minimum wage the credit would raise the effective wage rate to about $6 per hour. This policy has become an important component of the nation's safety net, though it too is criticized by some as being too generous and for having adverse work incentives.

11. For a discussion of the effect of this policy option on the labour market and the lives and living conditions of those recipients who would be subject to it, see Nightingale and Haveman (1995).

12. This incentive would exist because only the first $10 000 of annual earnings is eligible for subsidization. In the context of the previous example, an employer would receive a subsidy of $5 000 (0.5 × $10 000) for a worker paid $10 000 or $15 000 or $50 000 per year. While 50 per cent of the wages of the $10 000 worker would be covered by the subsidy, only 33 per cent of the wages of the $15 000 worker and 10 per cent of the wages of the $50 000 worker would be covered.

13. Studies of the employment effects of the NJTC indicate that up to 30 per cent of the 1977–78 employment growth in the studied industries was attributable to the programme – that it was a potent job creation device. For evidence on the effect of the New Jobs Tax Credit on employment levels, see Haveman and Bishop (1979) and Perloff and Wachter (1979). Dale Mortenson has undertaken a simulation experiment using a calibrated model of job creation and job destruction to analyse the effects of a New Jobs Tax Credit-type programme. He finds very substantial employment and aggregate income effects, and concludes that this policy is far more cost-effective than alternatives to it. See Mortenson (1994).

14. Several assessments of employer-based employment subsidy programmes instituted in various OECD countries have concluded that they have not been cost-effective policy instruments for generating employment. See, for example, OECD (1993, 1994). It should be emphasized that none of the programmes reviewed were *marginal* subsidy arrangements, which is a key element in the plan discussed here. Without concentrating the subsidy on the marginal employment decision of the firm, the problems of displacement, substitution and deadweight costs discussed in these assessments are likely to be important.

15. For example, an artificially low employment level this period would make it easy for the firm to attain the cut-in hiring level next period, and hence be eligible for a large subsidy on the added workers hired. See the paper by Charles Wilson in Haveman and Palmer (1982).

16. See Bishop and Haveman (1978).

17. The per hour payment is equal to a percentage (the subsidy rate, r) of the difference between some target wage (TW) and the worker's actual wage (W). The total payment would then be subsidy + $r(TW - W)$ × hours worked. If desired, a higher target wage can be set for the heads of large families or in high cost-of-living locations.

18. Theoretical analysis of a wage rate subsidy has established that it creates stronger work incentives than such income support programmes as a negative income tax (Kesselman, 1969), and that it is a preferred mechanism of support if the income (not the utility) of low-wage workers is the subject of social concern (Zeckhauser, 1971) Jonathan Kesselman (1976) has shown that where the utility of low-wage persons is the subject of social concern (that is, an optimal taxation model with an individualistic social welfare function), a wage rate subsidy combined with positive taxation according to wage rates achieves any given degree of equality more efficiently than an income tax with negative components. A wage rate subsidy should also

reduce the level of search or frictional unemployment, as it raises the costs of searching for another job while it simultaneously reduces the pay-off to search by lowering wage differentials. For more recent discussions of the analytic underpinnings of wage rate subsidy proposals, see Palmer (1978), and Haveman and Palmer (1982), especially the papers by Robert Lerman and by David Betson and John Bishop.

19. Analytically, in a competitive labour market, an important effect of a minimum wage policy is to reduce the quantity of services of workers whose productivity is at or below the minimum required wage demanded by employers. As a result, while some low-skilled workers benefit from a minimum wage policy, others find their employment prospects eroded. Higher unemployment of low-skilled workers is a direct result of the minimum wage. When introduced into an economy with a relatively high minimum wage policy, a wage rate subsidy tends to offset the employer response to the minimum wage, expanding the demand for low-skilled workers that has been reduced by the minimum wage.

20. Some view this effect as an important disadvantage of a wage rate subsidy, arguing that the reduced market wage serves as an implicit subsidy to employers. However, if goods markets are competitive, reduced costs to employers tend to be passed along in lower prices for goods and services. With non-competitive markets for goods and services, however, there could be some financial windfall accruing to employers. Indeed, analysts who view such windfalls to be a natural accompaniment of wage rate subsidies often call for wage rate subsidies and minimum wages to be introduced simultaneously, or for changes in wage rate subsides to be accompanied by offsetting changes in minimum wages.

21. The importance of this incentive effect depends on the price elasticity of demand for education and training by those with low skills; there are important reasons to expect that the available subsidies to education and training for those at the bottom of the skill distribution would tend to reduce the expected impact on skill accumulation by those at the bottom of the distribution.

22. While the need for record-keeping would increase somewhat, it should be noted that employers must already keep these records and report them, in association with the unemployment compensation programme and the tax that finances it. The potential for abuse does exist and, as in every fiscal measure, auditing and penalties for non-compliance would be required. There are a wide variety of other administrative issues that would need to be confronted in implementing a national wage rate subsidy programme. For example, how would tips received or fringe benefits be handled in calculating the subsidy? How could benefits be related to family needs? Should benefits be paid directly to the worker, or paid to the worker through the employer? Discussion of design options for accommodating these administrative issues is found in Bishop (1977).

23. Edmund Phelps has analysed the effect of these distortions in the framework of 'natural unemployment rate' theory, concluding that their impact is to drive up the natural rate. The patterns of joblessness and increasing inequality shown above are consistent with this effect. See Phelps (1994a). The theoretical underpinnings of Phelps's natural rate model have been

challenged by a number of reviewers; these challenges are alluded to in Phelps (1995).
24. See Haveman (1988). See also Betson and Bishop (1982) and Phelps (1994b).

References

Auer, Peter (1995) 'The American Employment Miracle', *inforMISEP*, published by the European Commission, Directorate-General for Employment, Industrial Relations, and Social Affairs, no. 49, pp. 18–27.

Betson, David and John Bishop (1982) 'Wage Incentive and Distributional Effects', in Robert Haveman and John Palmer (eds), *Jobs for Disadvantaged Workers: The Economics of Employment Subsidies* (Washington, DC: Brookings Institution).

Bishop, John (1977) 'The Administration of a Wage Rate Subsidy', Special Report 16A, Institute for Research on Poverty, University of Wisconsin – Madison.

Bishop, John and Robert Haveman (1978) 'Targeted Employment Subsidies: Issues of Structure and Design', Special Report 24, Institute for Research on Poverty, University of Wisconsin–Madison.

Haveman, Robert (1988) *Starting Even: An Equal Opportunity Program to Combat the Nation's New Poverty* (New York: Simon & Schuster) Appendix to Chapter 7.

Haveman, Robert and John Bishop (1979) 'Selective Employment Subsidies: Can Okun's Law Be Repealed?', *American Economic Review*, vol. 69, pp. 124–30.

Haveman, Robert and Gregory Christainsen (1981) 'The Contribution of Environmental Regulations to the Slowdown in Productivity Growth', *Journal of Environmental Economics and Management*, vol. 8, pp. 381–90.

Haveman, Robert and John Palmer (eds) (1982) *Jobs for Disadvantaged Workers: The Economics of Employment Subsidies* (Washington, DC: Brookings Institution).

Higgins, Bryon (1994) 'Symposium Summary', in *Reducing Unemployment: Current Issues and Policy Options* (Kansas City, Kan.: Federal Reserve Bank of Kansas City).

Kesselman, Jonathan (1969) 'Labor-Supply Effects of Income, Income-Work and Wage Subsidies', *Journal of Human Resources*, vol. 4, pp. 275–92.

—— (1976) 'Egalitarianism of Earnings and Income Taxes', *Journal of Public Economics*, vol. 5, pp. 285–301.

Martin, John P. (1994) 'The Extent of High Unemployment in OECD Countries', in *Reducing Unemployment: Current Issues and Policy Options* (Kansas City, Kan.: Federal Reserve Bank of Kansas City).

Mortenson, Dale (1994) 'Reducing Supply-Side Disincentives to Job Creation', in *Reducing Unemployment: Current Issues and Policy Options* (Kansas City, Kan.: Federal Reserve Bank of Kansas City).

Nightingale, Demetra and Robert Haveman (eds) (1995) *The Work Alternative: Welfare Reform and the Realities of the Job Market* (Washington, DC: Urban Institute Press). OECD (1993) *Employment Outlook 1993* (Paris: OECD) ch. 2.

—— (1994) *The OECD Jobs Study: Evidence and Explanations* (Paris: OECD) ch. 6.

Palmer, John (ed.) (1978) *Creating Jobs: Public Employment Programs and Wage Subsidies* (Washington, DC: Brookings Institution).

Perloff, Jeffrey M. and Michael Wachter (1979) 'The New Jobs Tax Credit: An Evaluation of the 1977–78 Wage Subsidy Program', *American Economic Review*, vol. 69, pp. 173–9.

Phelps, Edmund S. (1994a) *Structural Slumps: The Modern Equilibrium Theory of Unemployment, Interest, and Assets* (Cambridge, Mass.: Harvard University Press).

—— (1994b) 'Low-Wage Employment Subsidies versus the Welfare State', *American Economic Review, Papers and Proceedings*, vol. 84, pp. 54–8.

—— (1995) 'The Structuralist Theory of Employment', *American Economic Review, Papers and Proceedings*, vol. 85, pp. 226–31.

Zeckhauser, Richard (1971) 'Optimal Mechanisms for Income Transfer', *American Economic Review*, vol. 68, pp. 324–34.

5 Unemployment and Public Finance in Europe[*]

Frederick van der Ploeg

Europe faces high levels of persistent unemployment. Many countries are reforming their tax and benefit systems and trimming back the size of the public sector in order to fight unemployment. This chapter tries to shed some light on these issues.

Section I provides an anatomy of unemployment. Europe has, compared with other OECD countries, relatively high unemployment rates, especially among people with few skills and little education, youth and women. Also, Europe has a hiring problem in the sense that the unemployed have little chance of finding a job. Section II shows that in an economy with competitive labour markets a more progressive tax system or a bigger tax wedge reduces hours worked and production. Due to tax shifting, it does not matter in practice whether consumers, employers or employees pay the tax. Section III shows that these conventional insights do not hold in non-competitive labour markets. In particular, a more progressive tax system induces wage moderation and shorter working hours, thus providing a double boost to employment. A progressive tax system alleviates wage pressure, caused by search frictions and/or monopoly power of trade unions or firms, and thus reduces unemployment. Also, cutting average tax rates on labour or on energy use boosts employment, especially if unemployment benefits are not strongly indexed to after-tax consumer wages. Section III considers tax policy in Europe and the rest of the OECD in the light of these policy conclusions.

Section IV suggests that Europe faces an unpleasant trade-off. Cutting the duration or the level of unemployment benefits and tightening control on informal activities lowers unemployment. Also, cutting the tax wedge lowers unemployment particularly if indexation of benefits to after-tax

* This paper was presented at plenary session IV on 'Changing Public Sector Attitudes to the Unemployment Problem' of the 51st Congress of the International institute of Public Finance on 'The Changing Role of the Public Sector: Transitions in the 1990s', Lisbon, Portugal, 21–24 August 1995. Comments from Peter Sørensen and two anonymous referees are gratefully acknowledged.

market wages is weak and the informal economy is substantial. Section IV also makes a case for an Earned Income Tax Credit, since earlier sections argue that making the after-tax income distribution among workers more equitable while making the gap between unemployment income and employment income bigger is a good recipe for stimulating employment. Section V argues that fiscal consolidation may boost employment in Europe if unemployment benefits are not fully indexed to after-tax wages or the informal economy is significant. Crucial is that room for tax cuts is created by making the welfare state more efficient and making sure that government transfers only go to those people who really need them. However, fiscal consolidation may be harmful if public investment in training and schooling programmes, infrastructure and research and development is cut back. Section V also argues that there is a case for coordinated environmental tax reform in Europe as energy tax rates are on the whole relatively low while labour tax and premium rates on labour are relatively high. The reward may be a boost to environmental quality and employment even though there may be some capital flight.

Section VI makes a case for market-oriented training, schooling and apprenticeship schemes for improving the hiring chances of Europe's unemployed. Section VII stresses that fiscal incentives for new entrepreneurs may provide a bigger boost to employment than the wide variety of workfare programmes. Section VIII ends the chapter with a package of policy recommendations designed to improve the lot of Europe's unemployed.

I ANATOMY OF UNEMPLOYMENT

There are in 1997 around 35 million people unemployed in the OECD. This is more than ever before – 10 million more than in 1990 and 5 million more than the previous peak of 30 million in 1983. For the first two postwar decades OECD unemployment averaged less than 10 million, but tripled between 1972 and 1982 after the two oil price shocks. The roughly 8.5 per cent of the labour force that is hit by unemployment represents a huge waste of resources and human distress. In fact, the official figure of 35 million unemployed is an underestimate because many unemployed do not count as they have given up looking for a job. Furthermore, in some European countries there is a substantial practice of part-time work, shorter working hours, and hidden unemployment financed by unemployment benefit or disability pension schemes. These elements of underemployment might swell the ranks of the unemployed with another 14 to 18 million – offsetting this there is some concealed employment in the informal economy. (Obviously, one should be very careful with these numbers as there are also full-time workers who prefer to work part-time but cannot do so. Should these then in part be deducted from the broad measure of unemployment? It is not clear whether the net effect on the broad measure of unemployment is positive or negative, because even though these people are a lower proportion of full-time workers than would-be full-timers are a proportion of part-time workers there are more full-time than part-time workers.)

The unemployment rate in Europe, 10.6 per cent in 1993, is higher than in the USA, 7.2 per cent, and much higher than in Japan, 2.5 per cent. With the exception of the UK, women face higher unemployment rates in Europe than men, whereas in most other OECD countries unemployment rates are higher for men (especially blue-collar workers). Unemployment in Europe seems, after every adverse shock, to get stuck at a higher level. The two oil price shocks have led to a sharp and persistent rise in European unemployment rates since the mid-1970s. The USA has seen only a modest rise, albeit with more cyclical fluctuations. In the USA there is a greater risk of becoming unemployed than in Europe, but once unemployed it is relatively easy to find another job. Conversely, workers in Europe enjoy a lower risk of becoming unemployed compared to other OECD countries but once unemployed a worker has little chance of quickly finding a new job. This points to badly functioning labour markets and benefit systems in Europe.

The share of long-term unemployed in Europe ratcheted up during the recession in the early 1980s, declining only a bit during the subsequent upswing, and is now almost four times as high as in the USA – see Table 5.1. The phenomenon of hysteresis (for example, Blanchard and Summers, 1987) is thus a typical European problem. It arises if loss of work experience alienates people from the labour market. Long-term unemployment particularly afflicts older workers in Europe, but in Greece, Ireland, Italy and Spain the share of long-term unemployment among youths ranges from 50 to 70 per cent. The USA has more flexible labour markets and less generous benefit systems, hence the USA enjoys lower unemployment rates and less long-term unemployment but suffers from the problem of the working poor especially for those with family responsibilities.

Unemployment particularly hits people with little education and few marketable skills. Youth unemployment rates are double the average unemployment rate in Europe. Notable exceptions are Germany and Austria with their traditionally strong apprenticeships – around 5 per cent compared with 20.6 per cent for Europe as a whole! Without solid apprenticeships many youths in Europe face the danger of becoming unemployed

Table 5.1   OECD unemployment rates, 1993 (%)

	North America	Japan	European Community	EFTA	Australia
All persons	7.2	2.5	10.6	7.4	10.8
Youths	13.8	5.1	20.6	12.6	18.7
Women	6.9	2.6	12.2	7.0	10.1
Share of long-term unemployment in total employment	11.2	15.4	42.2	13.1	34.5

Source: OECD (1994) table 1.

for years after leaving school. The less productive people of Europe are condemned to long spells of unemployment (or disability) unless good training and schooling schemes are available.

During the 1980s Australia, North America, Japan and EFTA experienced employment growth rates of, respectively, 2.3, 1.6, 1.1 and 0.7 per cent per annum. Europe, in contrast, experienced a miserable employment growth rate of 0.5 per cent per annum. Spain fared particularly badly, while The Netherlands with its emphasis on wage moderation, part-time work and temporary work enjoyed rapid employment growth – see Haveman (1995, Table 1). Two-thirds of the ten million jobs created in the EC and EFTA since the early 1970s have been in the public sector. During the 1980s public sector job growth slowed down in Europe while private sector employment started growing again. This is in sharp contrast with the USA and Japan where job growth has largely taken place in the private sector. During the 1980s and 1990s Europe and EFTA generated nearly 7 million jobs in the public sector compared to only 4 million in the private sector; in North America more than 30 million private sector jobs were created and only about 5 million public sector jobs.

Europe suffered relatively large drops in industrial and agricultural employment and to a lesser extent in construction employment – see Table 5.2. However, Europe's job growth in services and government have not been too bad: 2.1 and 1.3 per cent per annum. Although 70 to 80 per cent of international trade for Europe is intra-industry trade, part of the shift in the sectoral composition of jobs is accounted for by the rise in the imports of labour-intensive manufactured products (textiles, clothing and footwear, but more recently also more skill-intensive products as office

Table 5.2   OECD sectoral trends in employment growth, 1979–90 (annual per cent change)

	North America	*Japan*	*European Community*	*EFTA*	*Australia*
Agriculture	−0.6	−2.5	−3.3	−2.8	−0.6
Manufacturing	−0.5	1.0	−1.1	−1.0	−0.2
Construction	1.6	0.3	−0.4	0.7	2.0
Services	2.7	2.3	2.1	1.4	3.4
Government	1.2	0.2	1.3	1.8	2.2
Total	1.6	1.1	0.5	0.7	2.3

Source: OECD (1994) table 1.1, part I.

equipment and telecommunications) from non-OECD countries. Globalization hurts people with few skills and little education in Europe most. Emerging markets in China and elsewhere provide, however, very good opportunities for exports with a high skill content. But the larger countries of Europe have to face up to the fact that the rapidly growing worldwide market for new technology products makes high-tech production even feasible for small countries. Apart from a few countries such as Ireland, Finland and Norway, Europe has been slow to shift to high-tech exports. Germany, The Netherlands and Italy have during the 1980s and 1990s even seen a fall in the relative share of high-tech in total manufacturing exports.

The share of services in total employment has been rising since the beginning of the twentieth century. Now services account for two out of every three jobs in the OECD. The share of services in North America and Australia is more than 70 per cent, roughly ten percentage points higher than in Europe. North America does not only have a bigger share of low-skilled 'hamburger-flipping' jobs, but also a bigger share of highly-skilled and highly-paid jobs in the finance, real estate and business services sectors. The 1980s saw a growing importance of self-employment (particularly in Iceland, Portugal and the UK), part-time work (especially in Belgium, France, Ireland, The Netherlands and the UK) and temporary employment (strongly so in France and Spain). These developments may be due, on the one hand, to a greater tendency of firms and government to contract out work, and, on the other hand, the need for more flexible working arrangements.

Different concerns about the *type* of jobs that are being generated are voiced. On the one hand, the shake-outs in industry and the emergence of low-paid jobs in services leads to *deskilling* of the workforce. On the other hand, technical progress biased in favour of highly-skilled workers has led to an *upskilling* of the workforce and an underclass of low-skilled workers who are either poorly paid (witness the working poor in the USA) or without a job (for example, many of the unemployed in Europe). During the 1980s unemployment rates for the least educated have increased relative to the rates for the more highly educated suggesting that upskilling has led to an underclass of unemployed low-skilled persons.

Unemployment rises if the generation of new jobs is insufficient to cover the increase in labour supply. In the early 1990s the OECD working-age population grew much more slowly (0.5 per cent per year) than in the 1970s (more than 1 per cent per year). Although North America showed a sharp slowdown, it still has a faster population growth than Europe, EFTA and Japan. At the beginning of the twenty-first century Europe in particular will face a sharp rise in the share of older workers and pensioners in the population. Since many of Europe's pension schemes are unfunded, this will lead to a bigger wedge between producer and consumer wages and threaten employment prospects. The negative effects of the greying of the population on labour supply is partially offset by an increase in net migration into Europe following the opening of borders in Central and Eastern Europe and the former Soviet Union. Only two-thirds of Europe's working-age population participate in the labour force, which is lower than the three-quarters that participate in the labour markets of North America and Japan.

A marked difference between Europe and the USA is that Europe has achieved rapid productivity growth, mainly by shedding labour in traditional sectors rather than through shifts to high-tech and skill-intensive activities, whereas the USA has suffered a marked slowdown in productivity growth. The unemployment rate for low-skilled relative to high-skilled workers rose during the 1980s in Europe, but changed little in North America. People with few skills and little education in Europe have been dumped into unemployment and disability schemes, thus paying the price for the substantial productivity improvements. Nevertheless, real wage growth in Europe has outstripped productivity growth thereby further contributing to unemployment. Wage differentials in the USA have widened and real wages for the low-paid (especially low-skilled male workers) fell during the 1980s, thereby contributing to the phenomenon of the working poor. In contrast, Europe has not allowed a lot of wage differentiation so many of the least productive people have been dumped into unemployment or disability schemes.

II   TAX DISTORTIONS IN COMPETITIVE LABOUR MARKETS

We now briefly consider the harmful effects of tax distortions in competitive labour markets. We assume that there is only one source of income: labour income. All variables are denoted as percentage deviations from initial equilibrium values. Percentage changes in labour supply l_s depend on percentage changes in the consumer wage $w - t_C$, that is percentage changes in the producer wage w minus changes in the consumption tax t_C, and on changes in the average and marginal labour income tax (including social premium) rates, t_A and t_M. A higher consumer wage makes leisure more expensive and thus boosts labour supply (that is, the substitution effect, measured by the compensated wage elasticity $\varepsilon_{CL} > 0$), but it also raises income and thus boosts consumption of leisure and depresses labour supply (that is, the income effect, measured by the income elasticity $\varepsilon_{IL} < 0$). Hence, labour supply only rises with the consumer wage if the substitution effect dominates the income effect, that is, if the uncompensated wage elasticity $\varepsilon_{UL} \equiv \varepsilon_{CL} + \varepsilon_{IL}$ is positive.

A higher marginal labour income tax rate lowers, for a given average rate t_A, the opportunity cost of leisure at the margin. Hence, households substitute leisure for consumption and work less hours ($-\varepsilon_{CL} t_M < 0$). For example, raising both tax allowances and the marginal tax rate in a budgetary neutral fashion depresses labour supply. However, for a given marginal rate t_M, a higher average labour income tax rate makes workers poorer and increases the incentive to work. Conversely, cutting the average tax through raising tax allowances reduces labour supply.

A measure of the progressivity of the tax system is the coefficient of residual income progression (the $RIP = Z$), that is, the elasticity of after-tax income with respect to pre-tax income Z. A progressive tax system has an RIP less than unity. Percentage changes in labour supply can now be written in terms of the various income and substitution effects:

$$l_S = \varepsilon_{UL} (w - t_C) - \varepsilon_{CL} t_M - \varepsilon_{IL} t_A = \varepsilon_{UL} (w - t_A - t_C) + \varepsilon_{CL} z$$

where $z \equiv t_A - t_M$ is the percentage change in the RIP. More progressivity (that is, $z < 0$) thus depresses labour supply. Labour demand, l_D, falls if the producer wage rises:

$$l_D = - \varepsilon_D (w + t_L), \quad \varepsilon_D > 0$$

where t_L stands for the change in the payroll tax (including employers' contributions) rate and $w + t_L$ shows the percentage change in the producer wage. Labour market equilibrium yields:

$$l \equiv l_D = l_S = \varepsilon_D(\varepsilon_D + \varepsilon_{UL})^{-1} \, (\varepsilon_{CL} \, z - \varepsilon_{UL} t)$$
$$w - t_A - t_C = - (\varepsilon_D + \varepsilon_{UL})^{-1} \, (\varepsilon_D \, t + \varepsilon_{CL} \, z)$$

where $t \equiv t_A + t_L + t_C$ denotes the change in the total average tax (and premium) wedge.

A more progressive tax system (that is $z < 0$) lowers hours worked and production, but boosts wages. A higher average tax wedge lowers the after-tax wage and, generally, depresses hours worked and employment. It does not matter whether firms, workers or consumers pay the tax. If the wage elasticity of labour supply is large and positive while that of labour demand is small, most of the tax burden is borne by firms. For example, a higher average income tax rate induces a higher wage and is in that case mostly passed on to firms. However, if the wage elasticity of labour demand is large and that of labour supply small, workers carry most of the tax burden. Firms then shift the burden of the payroll tax to workers. Most empirical evidence suggest a wage elasticity of labour demand between 0.5 and 1.0 and, for males, a very small labour supply elasticity. This suggest that cuts in the (average) tax wedge translate mainly into an increase in consumer wages, not an increase in employment. It is fairly straightforward to extend the above results to situations in which wage-setters and firms operate under monopolistic competition by inverting the labour supply schedule and reinterpreting it as a wage schedule (see Layard, Nickell and Jackman, 1991).

III   SETTING TAXES IN ORDER TO FIGHT STRUCTURAL SLUMPS

In a competitive labour market hours worked and production are high if tax rates and tax progressivity are small. We now show that such first-best results are not robust, since they do not hold in labour markets with structural unemployment arising from hiring costs. We assume a small open economy where the interest rate is determined on the global capital market.

Matching Jobs and Vacancies

We focus on trade between employers with vacant jobs and unemployed workers where search frictions cause structural slumps (for example,

Pissarides, 1990; Phelps, 1994). We ignore on-the-job search. Tightness of the labour market is proxied by the ratio of the vacancy rate V to the unemployment rate U, that is $X \equiv V/U$. The Poisson matching probability $Q(X)$ of a vacant job is small if the labour market is tight (that is, $Q'(X) < 0$). The flow into the pool of unemployed (that is, $S(1 - U)$ where S stands for the exogenous separation rate) must equal the outflow (that is, QUX where QU is the probability of an unemployed person finding a job). Hence, the equilibrium unemployment rate rises as the separation rate rises, labour market tightness falls and matching technology worsens: $U = S[S + XQ(X)]^{-1}$. In percentage changes we obtain the *Beveridge curve*:

$$l = U(1 - \mu)x \text{ or } u = -L(1 - \mu)x, \text{ where } 0 < \mu \equiv -d\log Q/d\log X < 1 \tag{5.1}$$

L stands for the level of employment and l denotes the percentage change in the level of employment.

Hiring

The economy consists of many small firms, each one of which has one job which is either vacant or occupied. Each operating firm thus employs one unit of labour and produces output $Y = F(K,E)$, where capital is rented at the world rate of interest R and energy E is imported at the world price P_E and faces an *ad valorem* tax rate T_E. Matching workers and jobs is a time-consuming, costly and uncoordinated activity. We capture this by postulating that hiring costs are a fraction γ of the economy-wide producer wage. In equilibrium each firm sets the discounted net productivity of labour (that is, after separation is taken into account) equal to the expected capitalized wage costs plus hiring costs. This optimum condition can be rewritten as:

$$A(R,P_E,T_E) \equiv F(K,E) - RK - P_E(1 + T_E)E =$$
$$(1 + T_L) W [1 + \gamma(R + S)/Q(X)]$$

We can write this (suppressing the effects of R and P_E) in percentage terms as a *hiring schedule*:

$$x = -\varepsilon_D(w + t_L + \omega t_E) \text{ with } \varepsilon_D \equiv [(R + S)\gamma + Q]/(R + S)\gamma\mu > 1 \text{ and}$$
$$\omega \equiv P_E(1+T_E)E/A \tag{5.2}$$

A tight labour market means that vacancies take long to fill and the capitalized value of expected hiring costs are high, hence firms are less willing to pay a high wage. A lower productivity of labour (for example, due to a higher world interest rate or cost of energy) depresses hiring.

Sharing the Surplus

A job match involves a rent, which is the sum of expected search costs for the firm and the worker (including forgone profits and wages). Splitting up means that both the firm and the worker have to engage in costly search activities. A more progressive tax system (lower Z) induces wage moderation as the worker and the firm realize that the government gets a larger slice of wage increases. Consequently, the firm gets a larger share of the rent and the wage mark-up M falls. A bigger separation rate S or interest rate R and a tighter labour market (higher X) raise the capitalized value of hiring costs and thus boost the wage mark-up. In addition, a tighter labour market improves the chances of an unemployed person finding a job and boosts the bargaining power of the worker thereby further pushing up the wage mark-up. This discussion of the factors determining the wage mark-up can be formalized with deriving a Nash bargain for sharing the rent that arises from frictions in the labour market. Indeed, this leads to the following expression for the wage mark-up (see Bovenberg and van der Ploeg, 1994a):

$$M \equiv (C_E - C_U - \delta)/C_E = \gamma\beta\, Z[X + (R + S)/Q(X)]$$

where C_U denotes consumption when unemployed, $C_E \equiv (1 - T_A)\, W/(1 + T_C)$ is the consumer wage, δ stands for the disutility of work and β is the bargaining power of the worker relative to that of the firm. If hiring costs are zero ($\gamma = 0$), workers are indifferent between being employed and unemployed (that is $M = 0$). Hiring costs drive a wedge between the utility of employment and that of unemployment (that is $M > 0$).

Percentage changes in the consumer wage can, for constant ε_D, be written as:

$$c_E = w - t_A - t_C = c_U + M\,(z + \kappa\, x) \tag{5.3}$$

where $0 < \kappa \equiv 1 - (R + S)(R + S + XQ)^{-1}\,(1 - \mu) < 1$. This *wage schedule* clearly shows a bigger gap between income under employment and unemployment if the tax system becomes less progressive or the labour market tighter.

Policy Implications

The hiring schedule (5.2) and the wage schedule (5.3) jointly determine the effects of taxation and benefits on labour market tightness and wages. The Beveridge curve (5.1) then gives the effects on employment and the unemployment rate. For example, a higher energy tax induces a lower productivity of labour, a lower wage, a looser labour market and a higher unemployment rate. In contrast to what happens in a competitive labour market, a less progressive tax system pushes up wages and boosts the unemployment rate. Conversely, Robin Hood is good for getting the unemployed into a job. The precise effects of taxation depend on how benefits are set.

If unemployment benefits are indexed to after-tax consumer wages ($c_U = c_E$), we have a constant replacement rate. Hence, $u = L (1 - \mu) \kappa^{-1} z$ and $c_E = c_U = (M\varepsilon_D)^{-1} z - t - \omega t_E$. An increase in the average labour tax rate is entirely borne by both employed and unemployed consumers, so that the producer wage and the unemployment rate are unaffected. Conversely, lowering the average labour income tax rate does not affect the unemployment rate either. A fall in labour productivity (for example, caused by a rise in the energy tax) induces a one-for-one cut in the consumer wage and no change in the unemployment rate. The substantial productivity improvements over the centuries have indeed not affected the unemployment rate. This suggests that changes in the average labour tax rate might not affect the unemployment rate in the long run either.

If unemployment benefits merely keep up with consumer prices (that is, $c_U = 0$), we have $u = L (1 - \mu) \varepsilon_D (1 + \kappa\varepsilon_D M)^{-1} (Mz + t + \omega t_E)$ and $c_E = M (1 + \kappa\varepsilon_D M)^{-1} [z - \kappa\varepsilon_D (t + \omega t_E)]$. Indexing to prices rather than after-tax wages implies that less progressive taxes (that is, $z < 0$) induce a smaller rise in wages and thus a smaller increase in the unemployment rate. As wages rise, the unemployment benefit does not rise which weakens the bargaining position of workers and induces them to accept a lower wage. Similarly, a higher labour tax rate or adverse shocks to productivity (such as a higher energy tax rate) induce a smaller drop in wages and thus a rise in the unemployment rate. Effectively, the unemployed escape the tax burden so that unemployment becomes less unattractive for the employed, who do face a higher tax burden. The resulting wage pressure boosts after-tax wages at the expense of more unemployment. Tax policy thus has real effects. Payroll and consumer taxes are not fully shifted to consumers while labour income taxes are to some extent shifted to firms, thereby harming employment.

We have learned two lessons on how to fight unemployment in structural slumps. The first lesson is, in contrast to what the competitive labour market story tells us, that a progressive tax system induces wage moderation and boosts employment. Lockwood and Manning (1993) present evidence for the UK. In a second-best world the distortions arising from non-competitive labour markets are partially offset by the distortions arising from progressive taxes. In fact, a more progressive tax system also reduces hours worked per person which boosts the number of people in a job as well. Another way of putting the same thing is that progressive taxes induce work-sharing and thus boost employment. More flexible arrangements for daily, weekly, annual and lifetime working hours are good for a more dynamic economy (for example, more intensive use of intensive machinery or a better match of demand and production) and for emancipation of the workforce. Most economic models predict that shorter working hours and other methods of reducing labour supply are likely to exert upward wage pressure and have negative effects on employment (for example, Layard, Nickell and Jackman, 1991; Booth and Schiantarelli, 1987). However, this presumes a fixed number of shifts and ignores that shorter working hours are usually traded off for a change to more flexible, productivity-enhancing production methods which permit a fuller utilization of capacity. Even so, shorter working hours may boost unemployment and possibly lower welfare. For example, within the context of a search model with a constant return to scale matching technology, shorter working hours lower the value of a vacancy, increase the cost of a vacancy per unit of labour, and thus raise unemployment. Also, incentives for job search may be lowered as a result of shorter working hours. A similar story can be told within the context of an efficiency wage model.

Although we argue that higher tax progression induces wage moderation and expands employment, a few critical remarks can be made. First, tax progression makes it less attractive to accumulate wealth and at a later stage become capitalists. This may harm the future creation of new firms. Second, tax progression reduces the incentives and possibilities for investing in human capital which may harm long-term growth and employment prospects. Third, the empirical results should be treated with a lot of caution as the marginal tax rate is extremely difficult to measure.

The second lesson is that cutting (average) tax rates on labour or on energy use only lower unemployment if benefits are not fully indexed to after-tax consumer wages. This illustrates the cruel trade-off politicians on the left have to face: cutting taxes *either* leads to higher disposable incomes for the employed and the unemployed and no boost to employment *or* to more employment if one is willing to accept more inequality between the employed and the unemployed. These important lessons also hold in labour markets with trade unions or efficiency wages (see Bovenberg and van der Ploeg, 1994a).

IV   CONSEQUENCES OF UNEMPLOYMENT BENEFITS AND THE EITC FOR EMPLOYMENT

Analysis

We now investigate the effects of the replacement ratio $B \equiv C_U/C_E$ and the informal economy on unemployment. We suppose that unemployment benefits are fully indexed to after-tax consumer wages. However, income from the informal sector follows labour productivity in the formal economy. Hence, the change in consumption of an unemployed person can be written as:

$$c_U = \eta(b + c_E) + (1 - \eta)(i + c_E + t), \quad 0 < \eta < 1$$

where b stands for the autonomous percentage change in the replacement ratio, $i < 0$ indicates a tighter control on informal activities and η represents the share of the unemployment benefit in total unemployment income. Combining this relationship with the wage and hiring schedules and the Beveridge curve, we obtain the relative change in the unemployment rate:

$$u = L(1 - \mu)(M\kappa)^{-1} [Mz + \eta b + (1 - \eta) (i + t)]$$

Clearly, reducing the replacement ratio or tightening the control on informal activities (that is, $b < 0$ or $i < 0$) results in a lower unemployment rate. Workers bear the entire burden of a decline in labour productivity (arising from, say, a higher energy tax rate). Energy taxes do not affect wage costs or employment; they just lower the purchasing power of the employed and the unemployed. If the unemployed engage in informal activities (that is, $\eta < 1$), they escape some of the burden of a higher tax wedge so wage costs rise and employment falls.

Two further lessons can be drawn from this analysis. First, cutting the replacement ratio or reducing the level and duration of unemployment benefits and tightening control on informal activities reduces unemployment at the expense of more inequity. Second, even if unemployment benefits are indexed to after-tax consumer wages, cutting the (average) tax

Table 5.3   Unemployment benefit replacement rates by duration, 1991 (%)

	First year	Second and third year	Fourth and fifth year	Overall average
Austria	45	43	43	31
Belgium	52	52	52	43
Denmark	74	67	43	52
Finland	58	44	30	38
France	58	37	28	37
Germany	41	36	36	28
Greece	53	4	0	17
Ireland	52	41	39	29
Italy	8	0	0	3
Netherlands	70	56	48	51
Norway	62	41	14	39
Portugal	65	40	0	34
Spain	70	30	0	33
Sweden	80	6	0	29
Switzerland	72	0	0	22
United Kingdom	31	27	27	18
Australia	50	51	51	26
Canada	58	25	25	28
Japan	25	0	0	8
United States	26	10	10	11

Note: Benefit entitlements for an unemployed with a dependent spouse before tax as a percentage of previous earnings before tax (calculated as average of average earnings and two-thirds of average earnings). Overall average includes other family circumstances (single, spouse in work).

Source: OECD (1994) table 8.1, part II.

wedge helps in the fight against unemployment as the informal economy does not benefit from the tax cut. This is not true for cutting the energy tax rate, which raises productivity in the informal sector and thus boosts the incomes of unemployed people working in the informal economy.

Level, Duration and Administration of Unemployment Benefits in Europe

The relative generosity of unemployment benefits, as measured by the replacement rate, is generally bigger in Europe than in other OECD countries – see Table 5.3. Denmark, The Netherlands and Belgium top the bill as far as the level of the replacement rate is concerned. The unemployed of

Greece, Sweden and Switzerland have to put up, after two or three years out of a job, with a sharp drop in the replacement ratio. However, most other countries in Europe cut the replacement rate only gradually as people become longer unemployed. Norway, Portugal and Spain cut benefits significantly after three years of unemployment. The big European countries do not cut replacement rates with duration as much a Japan, the USA and to a lesser extent Canada. Australia differs in the sense that replacement rates do not seem to be cut with duration.

Denmark, Norway, Finland, Portugal, Spain, Ireland, Sweden and Switzerland saw a substantial rise in the replacement rate during the 1970s and 1980s; the UK and to a lesser extent Germany have managed to reverse the rise in the replacement rate. Comparing most countries of Europe with other OECD countries and taking into account the beneficial effects of lower replacement rates on employment, a case might be made for reducing the level and duration of unemployment benefits. However, in a situation in which the number of unemployed far exceeds the number of job vacancies, one could argue that the unemployed do not need a stick in order to be more willing to accept a job. Even if this argument is true, lowering replacement rates exerts downward wage pressure and thus stimulates the demand for labour. Ultimately, whether one is prepared to trim down unemployment benefits depends on whether one is prepared to tolerate a drop in income for those who really are unable to find a job in order to create more jobs for those unemployed who are eventually lucky enough to find a job. In the meantime the countries of Europe should proceed with toughening eligibility requirements (that is, be tough on those who can work in order to ensure a decent benefit for those who cannot) and improving the effectiveness of the administration of benefits. Too often corporatist structures of employers' and employees' organizations have allowed less productive employees to be dumped into unemployment and disability pension schemes.

Table 5.4 shows that the efficiency of employment offices and related services varies widely among countries in Europe. (Of course, these data are extremely sensitive to the unemployment rate itself. For example, in Sweden the numbers soared in recent years). The Netherlands and Sweden need a lot of people monitoring the unemployed, but at least in Sweden most of them are devoted to actively seeking jobs for their clients. France, Ireland, Greece and Spain, in contrast, do not have many people monitoring the unemployed. They could do with more people, not for administering benefits but for actively helping to match the unemployed to jobs. In some countries there may be room to make benefit administration schemes more efficient, so that social insurance contributions can fall thereby

Table 5.4   Number of unemployed per staff member in employment offices and related services, 1992

	Employment offices only	Plus network and programme management	Plus unemployment benefit administration
Sweden	38	28	27
Netherlands	103	80	32
Austria	70	49	34
Germany	70	60	39
Norway	56	41	40
Belgium	118	76	44
Switzerland	65	65	50
Portugal	169	51	51
Denmark	134	102	–
Finland	136	105	–
Canada	199	119	68
United Kingdom	82	72	72
New Zealand	176	80	76
France	276	124	79
Australia	173	142	89
Japan	111	93	93
Ireland	788	–	100
Greece	994	497	172
Spain	350	191	191
Turkey	1061	1061	771

Source: OECD (1994) table 6.16, part II.

boosting employment. Non-wage labour costs must be cut in Europe, not so much through cutting benefits as through a more efficient benefit administration, as they represent a relatively large proportion of total labour costs.

Plea for an Earned Income Tax Credit in Europe

One way out of the cruel trade-off between more jobs and poverty is to introduce a special tax credit for low-paid workers – the Earned Income Tax Credit. We have seen from the analysis in Section III and in this section that the best way to stimulate job growth is, on the one hand, to make the tax system for those in work more progressive (Robin Hood), and, on the other hand, to widen the gap between employment income and unemployment income. Instead of pursuing the unpopular policy of cutting unemployment benefits, it is easier to gain political support for a policy of giving a tax credit for those working at and just above the minimum wage. One should be careful, of course, to avoid high marginal tax rates for the low-paid and the associated poverty traps by *gradually* reducing the EITC as people earn more. Means-tested subsidies (for example, for housing and legal assistance) also contribute to poverty traps. In practice, the poverty traps are a major obstacle but only a few people are confronted with them. A potential problem with an EITC which is directed without a sliding scale at the lowest-paid workers is that incentives to train, school and move up the earnings scales are destroyed. The EITC carries the danger of creating segmented labour markets; even so it is better for people with few skills to get work experience rather than stay on the dole for year after year. Of course, even though the EITC clearly reduces unemployment, it should not be so large as to harm schooling, capital accumulation and innovation too much. Hence, there is an optimum level of the EITC.

V FISCAL CONSOLIDATION AND ENVIRONMENTAL TAX REFORM

Many governments in Europe have been wrestling to get their public finances in order. Mostly this has been attempted by trimming back the size of the public sector. Unfortunately, politicians have found it easier cutting essential investment in infrastructure, research and development, training and schooling rather than cutting public consumption, subsidies to the rich and other unnecessary transfer incomes. Clearly, this practice has damaged employment and long-term growth prospects. Given the high levels of unemployment governments in Europe have also tried to reduce the size of the public sector in order to make room for cuts in the tax rate on labour and improve employment – *fiscal consolidation*. Governments have also been talking about *environmental tax reform* which amounts to using the revenue from a higher energy (dirt) tax to lower the labour tax in the hope that this boosts both environmental quality and employment. Rather than taxing virtues (work) heavily while not taxing or even subsidizing energy use (for example, in agriculture), we should do the opposite in order to obtain a double dividend.

We assume that the revenues from labour and energy taxes must cover public consumption and the funds required to pay for unemployment benefits (see Bovenberg and van der Ploeg, 1994b). Apart from the direct positive effects of a higher labour or energy tax rate on public revenue, we take account of the indirect negative effects due to erosion of the labour tax base (for the energy tax through the fall in labour productivity). We also take account of the consequences of the erosion of the energy tax base for public revenue.

Using the revenue from a cut in public consumption to lower the labour tax rate lowers wage costs and boosts employment if unemployment benefits are not fully indexed to after-tax market wages or if the unemployed receive income from the informal economy. Otherwise, the unemployed benefit from the lower tax burden as well. Workers thus absorb the entire benefit of a lower tax burden and enjoy higher after-tax wages while employment does not rise very much.

A less popular form of fiscal consolidation is to cut unemployment benefits in order to make room for a cut in the tax wedge. Making the unemployed worse off in this manner boosts employment in two ways: lower wage costs and a less attractive outside option. This is just one way in which the trade-off between equality and efficiency raises its unpalatable head.

The mid-1970s saw a sharp drop in saving and investment rates in OECD countries, especially in Europe. The fall in saving was mostly due to the public sector. Clearly, public consumption and transfer payments have crowded out public investment while growing public sector deficits have pushed up real interest rates and crowded out private investment.

Now consider environmental tax reform in an economy with mobile capital. If the initial energy tax rate is small and the informal economy is insignificant, the reform leaves the labour market unaffected and there is no double dividend. The point is that an energy tax lowers labour productivity, which amounts to an implicit tax on labour. Accordingly, in the special case of an economy with a neglible energy tax rate and a very small informal economy, environmental tax reform replaces an *explicit* labour tax with an *implicit* labour tax without affecting the overall tax burden.

Now consider the case of a small initial energy tax and a substantial informal economy. By making the outside option for workers in the formal sector relatively less attractive, the reform moderates wages and boosts employment. Energy taxes are more difficult to evade than labour taxes. Alternatively, people working in the informal economy escape the income tax, but not the energy tax as informal incomes are linked to labour productivity. Due to this *tax shifting* effect, environmental tax reform produces a double dividend at the expense of lower after-tax incomes.

With a sizeable initial energy tax and no informal incomes environmental tax reform pushes up the aggregate tax burden. Since the initial energy tax drives a wedge between the social benefits and costs of energy use, the fall in energy demand imposes costs and thus a cleaner environment is no longer a free good. There is now a *tax level* effect, but no *tax shifting* effect. Effectively, an explicit labour tax is replaced by a higher implicit labour tax. The reform thus boosts unemployment unless unemployment benefits are indexed to after-tax wages. In general, the costs of a cleaner environment amount to lower after-tax incomes and less employment. With a sizeable energy tax and a big informal economy, a double dividend only occurs if the *tax shifting* effect dominates the *tax level* effect. This is the case if there is a large informal economy, tax shifting is substantial, the initial energy tax is small, and the price elasticity of energy demand is modest. In that case, the costs of a cleaner environment are small and shifted to the unemployed rather than to those employed in the formal sector. Hence, under these conditions, environmental tax reform leads to wage moderation and more jobs as well as less energy use (double dividend).

Three further lessons can be distilled from the above. First, fiscal consolidation through cutting public spending only boosts employment if unemployment benefits are not fully indexed to after-tax wages or the informal economy is sizeable. Second, fiscal consolidation through cutting unemployment benefits always boosts employment at the expense of inequity. Third, environmental tax reform boosts employment if the unemployed earn substantial incomes in the informal economy and the initial tax rates on energy use are small. This double dividend occurs even though capital flight is possible and the tax burden cannot be shifted to fixed production factors. Nevertheless, environmental tax reform is more effective if many countries do it together.

VI SCHOOLING, TRAINING AND ACTIVE LABOUR MARKET POLICIES

We have seen that in non-competitive labour markets more progressive taxes punish wage increases and boost employment. In fact, more progressive taxes also stimulate shorter working hours. Both boost employment. A disadvantage of progressive taxes, however, is that they diminish the incentive to school, train and acquire skills, and thus harm productivity and economic growth. They also reduce the intensity of job search. The same is true for an EITC. Targeting tax and premium exemptions on the lowest-paid makes it difficult for these people to move up. However, in many European countries there is a significant gap between the minimum wage and the first wage scales. Targeting the EITC at that segment gives people out of work a chance of a new type of low-skill job, especially in labour-intensive services, without jeopardizing the jobs of those in work too much. It seems sensible to integrate the EITC with existing wage subsidies for the long-term unemployed. The challenge is to avoid displacement and deadweight losses by opening up new markets and new jobs for the long-term unemployed. Deregulation of markets for goods and services and innovative ways of pursuing active labour market policies are essential for giving unemployed people with few skills a chance. Wage and labour costs in Europe should be made more flexible and more in line with local conditions and individual skill levels, particularly for young employees. There is a big potential for new simple jobs in personal services (gardening, shopping, child care, painting, cleaning, and so on). Since trade unions typically are not too enthusiastic about exploring the potential for creating new jobs in personal services, a market-oriented rather than just a corporatist approach should be followed.

Schemes for job vouchers that operate in Belgium (PWA), the UK (Workstart) and Australia (Jobstart) seem very promising. One should avoid displacement (subsidized workers crowding out existing employees) and deadweight (vouchers spent on those who would have found a job anyway), especially as even the best programmes waste about half of the subsidies on these undesirable side-effects. Hence, wage subsidies (that is, vouchers) should be targeted at the long-term unemployed and temporary (see Snower, 1994). By giving the long-term unemployed a better chance to compete with insiders for jobs, wages are bid downwards and the demand for labour rises. The value of vouchers should be higher if there is an on-the-job training component. Training and education subsidies compensate for the adverse effects of progressive taxes and the EITC on investment in human capital. Vouchers may help to bring work from the informal to the formal economy. Being targeted at the long-term unemployed, vouchers do not add inflationary pressure. OECD countries typically spend 2 or 3 per cent, in Europe more, on passive (unemployment benefits) and active labour market policies, but less than 1 per cent on active programmes. Europe may benefit from more active labour market programmes – see also Table 5.4.

New cohorts entering the labour market can no longer expect to serve one employer through their entire working life. People must be able to adjust to multiple careers. Hence, education and (re)schooling is of immense importance. Legislation and fiscal incentives to make schooling and training sabbaticals more attractive are thus desirable. Trade unions and employers face the challenge of integrating reductions in hours worked with new patterns of life-long learning. Such a high-skill, high-wage strategy is essential for Europe. Evidence from France, The Netherlands and the USA suggest that children from disadvantaged backgrounds benefit from pre-primary schooling; once they leave school it is important that youngsters return to school regularly until they find a job. The German, Austrian or Swiss apprenticeship schemes work and are an example for other European countries suffering from excessive youth unemployment rates.

VII   FISCAL INCENTIVES FOR ENTREPRENEURS

Since Europe has created on balance few private sector jobs since the 1980s, it should benefit from promoting entrepreneurship. This can be done by giving starters a better chance. This means fewer bureaucratic headaches by removing unnecessary red tape or by streamlining necessary regulations and controls and possibly creating free-enterprise zones near areas with a high concentration of unemployed and cheap housing, and also tougher anti-cartel regulation. Reliable infrastructure and easy access to centres of technological know-how also help. Since small and medium-sized enterprises can be viewed as the engine for durable job growth, Europe should set aside additional funds for stimulating starters rather than using perhaps too much public funds to create public sector jobs for which there may be no real need. Given the scarcity of seed capital, venture and equity capital for starters and the inherent risk starters take, one could think of tax incentives for citizens who put up equity for starters. Capital market imperfections may be somewhat remedied by making the return on equity and, if the starter goes bankrupt, the equity stake itself exempt from income taxes. To avoid fraud, there should be a limit on the equity stake that is covered by this scheme. Other possibilities are exemption from VAT for the first few years of operation, wage subsidies (especially for personnel that are involved in research and development), facilities for export credit and accelerated schemes for writing investment off for tax purposes.

VIII   POLICY CONCLUSIONS FOR EUROPE

Since unemployment in Europe is persistent and hits people with little or no education, four weapons are suggested to fight unemployment. First, cut taxes for people employed on low pay (an earned income tax credit). Progressive taxes for those who work moderate wages; in a second-best world they boost employment. Progressive taxes also provide incentives for shorter worker hours and thus for work-sharing. Second, introduce wage subsidies for firms that take on long-term unemployed persons. In order to minimize unfair competition with existing employees and dead-weight losses, make sure the subsidy is temporary and targeted at the long-term unemployed. The subsidy should be larger if the employer provides training. These wage subsidies can be introduced in a market-oriented fashion through vouchers. Third, introduce fiscal incentives for apprenticeships and entrepreneurs in order to boost productivity and promote small enterprises. Fourth, given that dirt taxes are currently small and labour taxes large, go for an environmental tax reform.

Europe and the USA may have more in common than most commentators seem to think: on both sides of the Atlantic ethnic minorities and people with little or no education swell the ranks of the unemployed – see Haveman (1995). Hence, policy should be aimed at giving these groups training and work experience before they become entirely alienated from the labour market.

There are no cheap and easy fixes. Fiscal consolidation does not work if it amounts to abolishing training programmes. What is needed in Europe is more efficient job matching and possibly lower replacement rates in order to ensure a reduction in government transfers rather than cutting back on government investment in the immaterial and material infrastructure. This makes room for a cut in tax and premium rates. The resulting cut in the wedge between producer and consumer wages boosts employment. However, cutting back on training programmes and infrastructure in order to make a room for a tax cut is like the dog who bites his own tail. In a second-best world a more progressive tax system induces work-sharing and stimulates employment. In view of the importance of commitment to on-the-job training and long-term relationships between firms and its employees (see MacLeod and Malcolmson, 1993; Teulings, 1994) less weight should be given to those who wish to break down corporatist institutions in European labour markets. However, Europe does need competitive and more flexible goods markets. Modern trade unions should therefore not aim for a general reduction in working hours, but go for a judicious trade-off between more flexible and shorter working hours.

Modern trade unions should resist luddite tendencies and not fight labour-saving technologies. Although technological progress destroys low-wage jobs, it creates new high-skill jobs. History shows that technological progress does not only lead to higher output and productivity but also to more employment. Since imports from low-wage countries constitute only 1 or 2 per cent of OECD expenditures on goods and services, the

sirens of protectionism should be resisted and instead exports to emerging
markets should be seen as an opportunity for growth in employment and
output. General reductions in working hours imposed from above, luddite
movements and protectionism make a country poorer and do not boost
employment in the long run.

References

Blanchard, Olivier J. and Lawrence H. Summers (1987) 'Fiscal Increasing
Returns, Hysteresis, Real Wages, and Unemployment', *European Economic
Review*, vol. 31, pp. 543–60.
Booth, Alison and Fabio Schiantarelli (1987) 'The Employment Effects of a
Shorter Working Week', *Economica*, vol. 54, pp. 237–48.
Bovenberg, A. Lans and Frederick van der Ploeg (1994a) 'Effects of the Tax and
Benefit System on Wage Formation and Unemployment', Tilburg University.
Bovenberg, A. Lans and Frederick van der Ploeg (1994b) 'Tax Reform, Structural
Unemployment and the Environment', *Scandinavian Journal of Economics*
(forthcoming).
Haveman, Robert H. (1995) 'The Unemployment Problem: A United States
Perspective', presented at the 51st Congress of the International Institute of
Public Finance, Lisbon.
Layard, Richard, Stephen Nickell and Richard Jackman (1991) *Unemployment,
Macroeconomic Performance and the Labour Market* (Oxford: Oxford
University Press).
Lockwood, Ben and Alan Manning (1993) 'Wage Setting and the Tax System:
Theory and Evidence for the United Kingdom', *Journal of Public Economics*,
vol. 52, pp. 1–29.
MacLeod, W. Ben and James M. Malcolmson (1993) 'Investment, Holdup, and the
Form of Market Contracts', *American Economic Review*, vol. 83, pp. 811–37.
OECD (1994). *The OECD Jobs Study. Unemployment in the OECD Area,
1950–1995* (Paris: OECD).
Phelps, Edmund (1994) *Structural Slumps* (Cambridge, Mass.: Harvard University
Press).
Pissarides, Christopher A. (1990) *Equilibrium Unemployment Theory* (Oxford:
Basil Blackwell).
Snower, Dennis J. (1994) 'Converting Unemployment Benefits into Employment
Subsidies', *American Economic Review, Papers and Proceedings*, vol 84,
pp. 65–70.
Teulings, Coen A. (1994) 'The Role of Corporatism in Models of Surplus
Sharing', mimeo, University of Amsterdam.

Part III
Public Finance with Many Jurisdictions

6 Factor Mobility and Redistributive Policy: Local and International Perspectives*

David E. Wildasin

I INTRODUCTION

The literature of local public economics, club theory and fiscal federalism has been distinguished by its attention to the problems of fiscal policy in an open-economy setting. The actual or potential movement of goods and services, households, and business activity across jurisdictional boundaries raise a wide variety of issues for public economics. First and most importantly, the openness of jurisdictional boundaries implies the existence of margins of behavioural response to fiscal policy that do not arise in traditional closed-economy public economics. The possibility of cross-border shopping, capital flows, and movements of workers and households across jurisdictional boundaries all affect the allocative and distributional effects of tax and expenditure policies. The openness of the market environment within which local fiscal policies are implemented also naturally raises questions of interjurisdictional fiscal interactions. A taxpayer who leaves one jurisdiction must arrive somewhere else, businesses that are attracted by a favourable fiscal climate in one locality might have been established elsewhere, and local public services that improve environmental quality, reduce crime, or raise the level of health care in one jurisdiction may benefit residents of other localities. These and many other forms of interactions lead one to ask whether the fiscal policies pursued by independent

* Much of the work on this chapter was done while the author was visiting the Public Economics Division of the World Bank's Policy Research Department; some of the work was also done during a visit to the Economic Policy Research Unit of the Copenhagen Business School. I am grateful to PRDPE and to EPRU for their support and hospitality, but bear all responsibility for the content of the chapter, including any errors or omissions. I also thank Peter Birch Sørensen for comments on a previous version of the chapter.

jurisdictions are collectively optimal, in some sense, or whether there are potential gains from coordination of policy. In the latter case, explicit interjurisdictional compacts may provide one mechanism for reaping the gains from policy coordination. Higher-level governments may also discipline and coordinate the policies of lower-level governments, for instance through the use of fiscal inducements such as intergovernmental grants, restrictions on taxing authority, or through regulatory oversight in service delivery. Indeed, issues of policy coordination among jurisdictions lead directly to the question of government structure and jurisdiction formation. If decentralized fiscal policies lead to unfavourable outcomes, perhaps some or all policy-making responsibilities should be shifted to higher-level governments; if those higher-level governments do not exist, to paraphrase Voltaire, then perhaps they need to be invented. Much of the literature of local public finance can be read as an attempt to understand and ultimately to assess the economic performance, in a broad sense, of decentralized public sector units, a necessary step in the development of a thorough appreciation of the comparative advantages and disadvantages of centralized and decentralized fiscal systems.

It is increasingly recognized that these issues, though of long-standing and obvious interest in the context of local public finance, also arise in many other policy contexts. Indeed, the movement of goods, services, people and capital across space, including national boundaries, is a pervasive feature of economic life, and one that appears to be of growing importance over time. It is natural, therefore, to search for general principles of 'open economy public economics' that can be applied in a variety of different policy contexts. In practical applications, however, the analysis of fiscal policy, intergovernmental fiscal relations and jurisdictional structure must be adapted to specific institutional, historical and social contexts. For instance, analyses of the tax treatment of international capital flows and of multinational corporations are likely to take explicitly or implicitly into account the differing accounting and legal traditions of different countries and the problems of tax enforcement on an international scale, issues which recede somewhat in importance when studying capital taxation within a given country. Similarly, the movement of labour across national boundaries is often subject to legal constraints of kinds that do not apply to migration within countries, and these constraints – for instance, involving the eligibility of immigrants for fiscal transfers or social benefits – may be of some importance for fiscal analysis. While there are thus interesting analytical parallels between local public economics and the analysis of fiscal policy at the national and international level, it is important to appreciate that insights of great relevance in one context are not necessarily of universal validity.

The relationship between factor mobility and income redistribution is one which is of considerable importance at all levels of government, both within countries and at the international level. Capital and labour movements directly affect factor markets and the determination of income levels and thus interact directly with income redistribution policies. Governments at all levels engage in redistribution, sometimes very explicitly through cash tax-transfer mechanisms and sometimes less explicitly by distributing in-kind benefits (or imposing in-kind costs) through public good provision or regulatory policies; indeed, there are few if any spheres of government activity in which actual or potential distributional effects are not of importance to policy-makers, voters and other participants in public sector decision-making. Thus, factor mobility impinges, directly or indirectly, on an extremely wide range of government policies. This chapter discusses a number of the important issues for fiscal policy that arise in the presence of factor mobility. Since these issues are so multi-faceted, it is impossible to discuss particular policy issues in the detail that they might otherwise warrant, or to refer to all relevant literature. The goal, instead, is to focus on a few central issues, to summarize and synthesize, as informally as possible, some broad findings from selected branches of literature, and to identify areas that seem to warrant additional research attention.[1]

The chapter begins, in Section II, with a brief recapitulation of some of the basic economic implications of factor mobility without specific reference to government redistributive or other policies; this provides a background to the main discussion in Section III. One basic theme of this discussion is that both the benefits and the costs of redistributive policies can be significantly affected by factor mobility. Mobility of capital and labour may, indeed, pose significant challenges to the ability of governments to engage in redistribution, and it is possible that increases in factor mobility may thus result in substantial restructuring, if not dismantling, of government redistributive programmes. However, factor mobility also requires a reconsideration of the goals of redistributive policies; at least to some extent and in some cases, factor mobility may obviate the need for redistributive interventions. These considerations are important when considering the reorganization of fiscal activities among jurisdictions, including the formation or dissolution of jurisdictions themselves: on the one hand, as emphasized strongly in the Hecksher–Ohlin tradition in trade theory, factor mobility may be significantly altered by the redrawing of jurisdictional boundaries or through interjurisdictional compacts, while, on the other hand, changes in jurisdictional structure and function alter the very political mechanisms of the public sector through which redistributive fiscal policies are undertaken. In short, factor mobility can interact with redistributive fiscal policies in surprisingly complicated ways, and these interactions are important in a surprisingly wide variety of contexts.

Many of the principles and insights concerning the fiscal implications of factor mobility that are discussed in Sections II and III are equally applicable to both capital and labour. No doubt the relative importance of capital and labour mobility varies from circumstance to circumstance; one might indeed argue that one crucial distinction between the 'local' and 'international' public finance contexts revolves around whether labour is or is not considered to be mobile. However, the Hecksher and Ohlin tradition notwithstanding, it seems debatable whether labour should really be treated as immobile among nations, and, if so, whether this immobility is economically intrinsic to labour itself or whether it is simply the result of policies which, if altered, would reveal labour to be mobile after all. In part because the literature on capital mobility is better-developed, in part because the distribution of income among households is really the main focus of redistributive policy and politics, and in part to be a bit provocative, the discussion in Sections II and III places a somewhat unusually heavy emphasis (at least by way of illustrations) on the importance of labour mobility in an international setting as well as within countries. Section IV returns more specifically to the question of labour mobility, attempting to identify more clearly the empirical issues that arise in assessing its potential importance for fiscal analysis. Section V offers some brief concluding remarks.

II   THE EFFECTS OF FACTOR MOBILITY ON EFFICIENCY AND EQUITY

The potential fiscal implications of factor mobility are quite far-reaching. However, in this as in other contexts, analysis of fiscal policy cannot proceed very meaningfully without an appreciation of the underlying economic environment within which policies are implemented and through which their impacts are transmitted. In the present context, it is necessary to have some theory of spatial factor allocation and pricing before proceeding to an analysis of the allocative and distributional consequences of fiscal policy in the presence of factor mobility. Indeed, factor mobility has important implications in itself for economic efficiency and for the distribution of income, even in the absence of fiscal policies. These most basic economic effects of factor mobility form the fundamental backdrop against which government redistributive interventions should be assessed.

Factor Market Integration can Improve the Efficiency of Factor Allocations

To the extent that factor markets generate price signals that are indicative of the economic productivity of labour, capital and other productive inputs, and to the extent that factor owners are able to respond to these signals in deciding on the locations and sectors in which factors of production are employed, greater intersectoral and interregional mobility of factors can contribute to more efficient resource allocations. Of course, the extent of spatial and intersectoral factor mobility is a matter of degree, as discussed in more detail in Section IV below. On sufficiently small geographical scales, however, it is obvious that there are very few (if any) places in the world where the uses of labour and capital goods, including their places of employment, are completely inflexible. For instance, in virtually all market-oriented economies, it is common for workers within a country to be able to move from one region to another without legal prejudice; even more is it possible for workers to change their places of employment within urban agglomerations. Factor markets may in practice fall far short of the ideal assumptions of perfect competition – indeed, much of the following discussion deals with the implications of fiscal distortions for the efficient allocation of mobile resources. Nevertheless, only brief and casual consideration is necessary to realize that devastating economic consequences would result if no workers were able to move from very narrowly defined neighbourhoods over the course of their lifetimes, and that the efficiency gains from labour mobility within countries must be immense.

There are of course examples of countries where restrictions on internal labour mobility are or have been quite important. For instance, under the *apartheid* system, South Africa imposed significant race-based restrictions on the (spatial and sectoral) mobility of labour. In China, a household registration (*hukou*) system has been in effect throughout the postwar era, the purpose of which has been to provide government control over the assignment of households to residential and employment opportunities. In both of these cases, economic and political reforms have eliminated or weakened the constraints on internal migration, although China has much further to go in this direction than South Africa, where the *apartheid* system no longer exists. In both of these countries, there would appear to be significant potential productivity gains from liberalization of factor markets.[2]

On a more global scale, international movements of labour and capital have undoubtedly played major roles, in historical terms, in raising incomes. For example, Hatton and Williamson (1994) (and references therein) discuss recent research on nineteenth-century flows of both capital and labour from the Old World to the New. It is clear from data on factor returns that this was a move from a region of low to one of high productivity, resulting in increases in aggregate income. The opportunities for productive spatial reallocations of labour and capital are recurring ones, as fertility, mortality, education, savings rates, the state of the productive arts, climate, natural resource availability and institutional structures vary over time in ways that give rise to spatial divergences in factor productivity, and these effects are surely operative at the international level as well as within countries.[3]

Factor Market Integration May Affect the Distribution of Income

When labour and capital flow across jurisdictional boundaries, they alter factor supplies. In doing so they can affect equilibrium factor prices; there may also be 'short-run' impacts on unemployment rates. Since so much of fiscal policy is concerned with income distribution issues, the distributional effects of factor mobility are of critical importance for public policy.

Of course, it is obviously necessary to go beyond the most aggregative representative-agent models if one hopes to address the distributional effects of factor mobility. Indeed, the general equilibrium impacts of factor mobility are potentially quite intricate; the classic Harberger (1962) analysis of the incidence of a corporation income tax in a two-sector economy, the study of the effects of changes in factor endowments in neo-classical models of international trade, and analyses of related issues in more complex multi-sectoral computable general equilibrium models have highlighted many of these intricacies. However, even very simple and minimally disaggregated models, through varied interpretations, can yield surprisingly rich insights. Perhaps the simplest model of the effect of factor mobility on income distribution is one in which the perfectly competitive economy of each jurisdiction is assumed to employ two factors of production to produce a single homogeneous output. One of these factors of production is assumed to be immobile and the other is assumed to be mobile. Assuming further that production exhibits diminishing returns to the fixed or immobile factor, at least in the relevant range, it follows immediately that inflows of the mobile factor will depress its equilibrium price and raise the return to the immobile factor. In the absence of compensatory transfers, the owners of resources that are identical to or highly substitutable with 'immigrant' factors are harmed by factor inflows and those who own complementary factors – the immobile factor owners, in the simple model – gain. In short, this simplest of models reveals the important point that factor market integration may not be Pareto-improving, however great the efficiency gains associated with it. To apply this insight in practice requires a determination of the extent of sub-stitutability or complementarity of different factors and the identity of the immobile factors. Some illustrations will indicate the rather subtle empirical questions involved in these determinations.

As one important example where the potential distributional effects of migration are often cited, consider 'South–North' labour migration, that is, migration from poor to rich countries. Does such migration tend to reduce the earnings of workers in rich countries? The answer, plausibly, is that it does, especially for workers in rich countries with skills and other attrib-utes that make them very substitutable with immigrants. When considered in detail, of course, not all labour in origin and destination countries is economically homogeneous. For example, workers in rich countries gener-ally possess high levels of human capital relative to those from poor coun-tries. One view of human capital is that it raises the effective labour supply of a worker: an educated worker might be able to provide, say, twice as many units per year of labour services as an uneducated worker. An alter-native view is that workers with high levels of human capital are different in kind from low-skilled workers and complementary in production with them. In the former case, inflows of workers from poor countries would be expected to *depress* earnings for all workers in rich countries whereas, in the latter case, they would *raise* the earnings of highly-educated workers in rich countries. The issue is one of aggregation: which factors (high-skilled labour, low-skilled labour, capital, natural resources) can appropri-ately be aggregated and treated as having a common price? This is a well-known problem in empirical analysis, and one which cannot be answered on an *a priori* basis. Among other complications, the appropriate aggregation depends on the time frame of the analysis, as discussed in Section IV.[4]

Likewise, the mobility of different factors of production cannot usually be settled on an *a priori* basis. It is certainly reasonable to argue that land and many natural resources are immobile. These are also resources, however, for which asset markets are in some cases rather well-developed and that can therefore be owned at a distance, for instance through invest-ment in (perhaps multinational) corporations and financial institutions. Changes in the returns on such immobile resources resulting from migra-tion thus need not carry very obvious implications for the distribution of income in the jurisdiction experiencing migration. Labour and capital are plausibly mobile in the 'long run', but the horizon over which mobility is important for these resources is variable. Old workers, for instance, are less mobile than young workers, and better-educated workers are more mobile than the unskilled. Capital embodied in public infrastructure may be extremely immobile; for instance, although road surfaces deteriorate with use, the establishment of rights of way, network connections, and basic grading associated with the establishment of a highway system cannot easily be physically removed and can constitute extremely durable investments. Other types of physical and financial capital can be extremely mobile. Depending on the intended application, it is appropriate to aggregate different types of labour and capital in different ways.

These observations suggest several interesting distributional issues associated with factor mobility. For instance, in the context of German unification, it is fairly clear that substantial numbers of workers, especially young workers, might in the short run flow into the labour market of western Germany, especially in the absence of policies that provide incentives to remain in the east. This migration, if unchecked, would depress wages in the west for those who compete in the labour (and housing) market with the migrants from the east. In Figure 6.1 (drawn from Wildasin (1994), let X, measured along the horizontal axis, denote the aggregate earnings of workers initially located in western Germany and let Y, measured along the vertical axis, represent the incomes of other factor owners initially situated in the west (for instance, owners of land, capital, and perhaps specialized labour resources). Let the point A represent the gross or before-tax incomes received by each of these groups before unification. The 45-degree line PQ represents alternative distributions of the total income of pre-unification western Germany that could be achieved through lump-redistributive transfers.[5] Assuming for the present that no redistribution takes place, so that the distribution of income in the west is initially given by the *laissez-faire* point A, consider the distributional impact of unification. Provided that western wages exceed those in the east, workers will flow from the latter to the former, with the result that the aggregate income of those workers initially situated in the west will fall from X_0 to X_1 and the aggregate income of immobile factors in the west will rise from from Y_0 to Y_1. (It can be shown that the aggregate of $X + Y$ does indeed rise, as shown in the figure.) Of course, as already indicated above, factor mobility can generate efficiency gains, and the combined economies of eastern and western Germany could certainly be more productive, with free mobility, in the post-unification situation. However, even a first-pass disaggregation of factors in this very simple framework

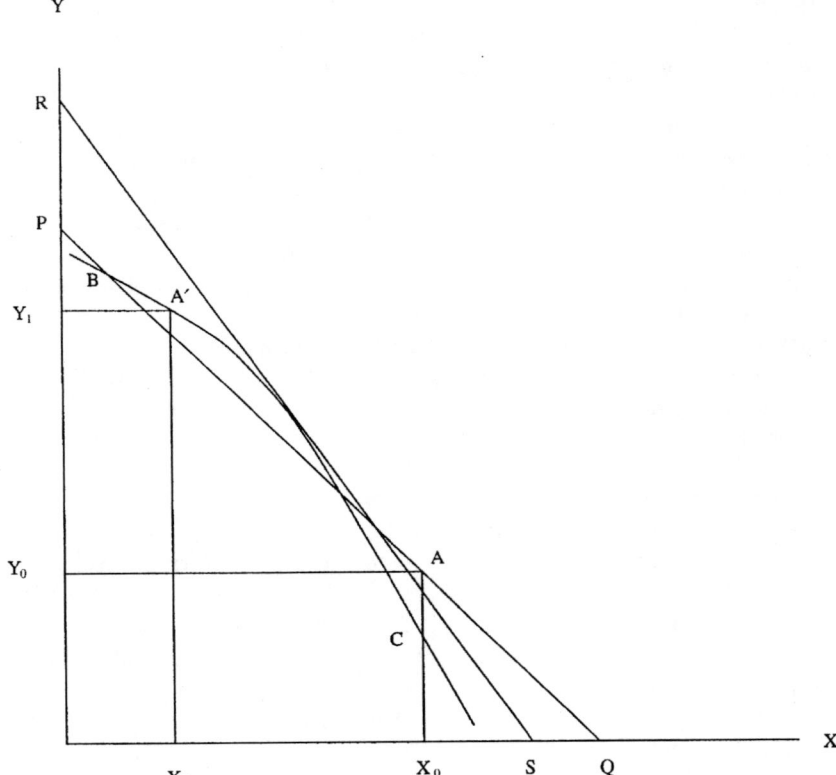

Figure 6.1   Attainable distributions of income with migration

suffices to show that not all relevant groups in society necessarily share in these productivity gains. From the viewpoint of political economy, the identification of gainers and losers is a crucial first step not only in determining who might gain or lose from factor mobility, but also in suggesting what sorts of policy responses might emerge as a result of (or in anticipation of) these distributional impacts. This point is taken up again below.

Factor Mobility May Insure Against Income Risk

Economic theories of migration and capital flows are essentially based on spatial arbitrage arguments. Differences in factor returns are indicative of relative local scarcities of factors. Factor owners – those who hold capital or workers who embody their productive labour – have incentives to move their productive resources from locations where their returns are low to where they are high. Under the standard neoclassical assumption of diminishing returns to mobile factors, this is a self-limiting equilibrating adjustment that erodes wage or rate-of-return differentials. As with most arbitrage mechanisms, interjurisdictional labour migration and capital flows perform a useful economic function by directing resources to productive uses, but they also have distributional consequences because the process of arbitrage itself affects the equilibrium prices of the arbitraged commodity and of related commodities. Although factor mobility may be harmful to those who compete with immigrants and industry entrants, it is natural, when taking a system-wide view of factor mobility as an arbitrage mechanism, to suggest that it can be equalizing and risk-reducing as well as efficiency-enhancing. Viewed from an *ex ante* perspective, the prospect of equalization of factor returns implies a reduction of income dispersion or risk (Wildasin, 1995).

To illustrate how factor movements can help to equalize incomes, it is instructive to consider the evolution of per capita incomes in major regions of the USA over the course of the twentieth century. In 1900, per capita incomes in the South were less than half the national average, while incomes in the West were twice as high as the national average. Unsurprisingly, workers tended to migrate out of the South and into the West during most of the century; meanwhile, per capita incomes gradually but steadily converged. By 1980, per capita incomes in the South stood at over 90 per cent of the national average, while those in the West had fallen to less than 15 per cent above the national average. These crude figures are not adjusted for regional cost-of-living differentials, nor do they reflect regional amenities or disamenities; furthermore, they represent income from all sources and thus do not measure the returns to particular factors of production. However, the broad message is clear: poor southerners benefited from access to nationally integrated labour markets. Some southerners left for more prosperous regions, which not only enabled them to earn higher incomes but tightened the labour market in the South and thus raised incomes for those who remained behind. Conversely, the high-income West has consistently drawn immigrants from the rest of the country, gradually eroding the income premium of those who reside there.[6]

Now consider these trends from the perspective of an individual young worker. At the beginning of the life cycle, this worker enters the labour force with a first job. This job requires an attachment to a particular occupation, a particular firm and a particular location. Even if this initial employment match is a very good one, a worker who had no opportunity, over the entire life cycle, to change occupations, employers or locations would face considerable earnings risk, including the possibility of zero earnings in the event of job termination as a result of a lay-off or of the failure of the firm. Mobility across occupations, employers and locations provides workers with options, and one need only observe that many of these options are in fact exercised over the course of a typical worker's life cycle to see that they have significant value.[7]

Krugman (1991) has emphasized that large metropolitan areas provide dense labour markets that attract risk-averse workers because they are places where workers can switch from unfavourable to favourable job matches at low cost. The large city, in other words, provides an integrated labour market where income risk is reduced and expected utility is thereby increased. By the same token, a representative US worker benefits, in an *ex ante* sense, from being able to participate in the national labour market. Standing behind a veil of ignorance, a worker who might be randomly assigned an initial residence in any US region (looking back, say, to the situation of a young worker in 1930, or, looking forward from the present time, in 1996) would view the ability to migrate from one region to another as a kind of insurance against certain types of lifetime earnings risk. The 'premium' for this insurance is the erosion of earnings suffered by workers initially situated in high-wage regions when they face intensified labour market competition from migrants, but in exchange for this premium they are protected (to some extent) from low earnings if they happen to be assigned initially to a low-wage region. To the extent that migration is efficiency-enhancing, this market insurance mechanism may be better than actuarially fair, though this depends on the distribution of ownership claims to immobile as well as mobile factors and on the distribution of the efficiency gains from migration between mobile and immobile factors (see Wildasin (1995) for further details). In any case, however, the spatial competition that results from factor mobility does tend to equalize returns for the mobile factors themselves, and thus tends to reduce the income risk that they face.[8] This is of importance when assessing the implications of factor mobility for redistributive fiscal policies whose objectives are also to reduce income variations.

III FISCAL ASPECTS OF FACTOR MOBILITY

Having reviewed the most basic economic effects of factor mobility, let us now consider some of its fiscal dimensions.

Factor Mobility May Raise the Cost of Income Redistribution and Limit Its Effectiveness

Early contributors to the literature on fiscal decentralization recognized that the economic impact of redistribution is very different when undertaken by small open jurisdictions rather than large closed ones (although they did not use this terminology, borrowed from international economics). Stigler (1957), for example, explains clearly that redistribution from rich to poor within a small locality can lead to an exit of the rich and an influx of the poor.[9] Since migration of this sort is a response to artificial fiscal incentives rather than to fundamental economic productivity and locational preference considerations, it is fairly obvious that this type of migration tends to detract from efficient locational choice. There is, therefore, a real economic cost associated with local redistribution.

It is also clear that factor mobility can greatly limit the ability of a government to alter the distribution of income among households within its boundaries. In the simplest formulation, following the international trade tradition of 'small open economy' analysis, one might regard the net return to mobile factors of production as exogenously fixed on external markets. In this case, it is impossible, by construction, for local redistributive policy to be effective: there is simply no way to alter net factor returns. This does not mean that local redistributive policies cannot be undertaken, of course. But, under the assumption of smallness and openness in the external factor markets, the effect of these policies must be, fundamentally, to generate deadweight losses that are borne by immobile factors of production (Wildasin, 1992). As a predictive matter, one might expect that the ineffectiveness of local redistributive policy in small open economies might lead political actors, or the populations to whose demands they are more or less responsible, to limit the amount of income redistribution they undertake. That is, the small open model suggests that factor mobility affects the *political economy* of redistribution, a point that is taken up further below.

While the theoretical paradigm of the small open jurisdiction is very useful and suggestive, its limitations – particularly, its partial equilibrium character – should be borne in mind. The importance of the general equilibrium effects of local property taxes is explicitly recognized in the work of Mieszkowski (1972) and in numerous subsequent analyses of the incidence of local capital taxes and of tax competition. This is well-illustrated by the analysis of the incidence of local property taxation in Bradford (1978). In this analysis, a single locality's tax on a mobile factor of production (capital, in the property tax context) causes an outflow of that factor to the external market; under conventional assumptions, this outflow reduces the equilibrium price of the factor on the external market. If the locality is very small, the economy-wide equilibrium return to the taxed factor will fall by a very small amount. However, this 'very small' reduction in the equilibrium return to the taxed factor is borne by the 'very large' world supply of the factor. The incidence of the local tax, therefore, which is the reduction in the total return to the factor in the world as a whole, is thus the product of a small number (the reduction in the world price of the factor) and a large number (the world supply of the factor). Bradford's analysis shows that this product is likely to be of the same order of magnitude as the amount of tax collected by the locality that imposes it. In other words, the tax levied by a single small jurisdiction on a mobile factor of production reduces the global net return to that factor by (approximately) the amount of the tax collected. In this sense, factor mobility does not allow factor owners to escape the burden of local taxes; it does, however, mean that the burden of local taxes (or the benefits of local expenditures) are transmitted to factor owners outside as well as inside the taxing (and spending) jurisdiction. This fact is important to bear in mind when analysing the effects of decentralized fiscal policies of a group of small jurisdictions: what appears to be true from the viewpoint of any one small jurisdiction considered in isolation (that is, that local fiscal policy has no impact on the net returns to mobile factors) is not true from the viewpoint of the collectivity.

If local redistribution is costly in efficiency terms and is unlikely to be very effective in altering net factor returns, it may still be very difficult, as a practical matter, to avoid at least some redistributive impact from local fiscal policy. For example, consider primary and secondary education, public services that have been major functions of local governments in the USA throughout the twentieth century. If provided publicly, how could this service be financed so as to avoid redistributive impacts, assuming that this were desired? In the USA, local property taxes have historically been used as the major source of own revenues for school finance. This system of finance, though perhaps not strongly redistributive, is nevertheless likely to entail net fiscal transfers from households that pay heavy property tax burdens but do not value public schools very much (for example, households with large expensive dwellings and few or no children in public schools) to households with opposite characteristics (for example, those with many children in public schools and those with small inexpensive dwellings). According to the principles of local redistribution just discussed, one would expect that this system of school finance would give rise to incentives for spatial stratification of households that limits the extent of local redistribution. The theory thus appears to be broadly consistent with the observed development of high-income suburbs around low-income central cities. Of course, some exclusion mechanism is needed to prevent net fiscal beneficiaries from following net fiscal contributors into high-income suburbs. In the USA, local government regulations in the form of land-use controls appear to play a particularly important role in restricting residential developments that would allow cross-subsidization of local public service provision between high- and low-income consumers (Hamilton, 1975).[10]

Factor Mobility May Curtail Redistributive Policy

Does factor mobility imply that a government cannot or will not undertake income redistribution? If so, does this mean that factor mobility is harmful to equity? The first of these questions is really a problem of public choice or political economy, and its answer depends on the way that the political process works. The second question is partly normative in nature. To answer it requires a predictive judgement about how factor mobility may affect government policy-making (the first question, again) and a normative criterion with which to evaluate whatever changes in redistributive policy result from factor mobility.

Without attempting to provide a thorough analysis of redistributive politics, various conjectures about the effect of factor mobility on redistribution are possible. It seems plausible that the economic costs of redistribution in a world of factor mobility are likely to make themselves felt in ways that do, in fact, reduce the extent of income redistribution; in effect, by raising the the marginal welfare cost of redistribution, factor mobility would appear to have a relative price effect that would induce substitution away from redistributive policies. For this reason, Brennan and Buchanan (1980) argue that a federalized fiscal structure provides a useful mechanism through which limits on redistributive interventions can be established at a constitutional level.[11]

Do limits on redistribution harm or promote equity? This is a very contentious issue. 'Redistribution', to some, means 'redistribution in favour of those who are ethically deserving, especially the poor'. Redistribution in this sense can clearly be a public sector activity that many value and factor mobility may thus pose a threat to equitable fiscal policy. It is possible to take a less benign view of government redistribution, however. Rent-seeking behaviour, the objective of which is to achieve redistributive transfers in favour of politically influential groups, clearly pervades many important areas of government policy formulation, ranging from corporate income tax policy to the regulation of industry to international trade policy. Social services programmes, though ostensibly designed to benefit the poor or disadvantaged, may be captured by service providers who exploit them for high wages, protected employment, or simple corruption. Greater mobility of capital and labour can limit the ability of government officials to exploit their regulatory and other powers to extract rents and can help force government resources to be employed in economically productive uses. From this perspective, factor mobility helps to discipline the public sector, forcing it not only to be more efficient but to forgo redistributive policies which, being arbitrary in nature, may be viewed *ipso facto* as inequitable, and which may also violate distributive equity norms by transferring resources from the poor and disadvantaged to the rich and powerful.

In general, jurisdictions of small geographic scope are more open to factor movements than large ones, and this may be an important reason why extensive redistributive activities tend to be undertaken by national governments rather than by lower-level governments. For instance, in modern welfare states, income support for the poor, the elderly and the unemployed are frequently financed by central governments, an observation that is consistent with the notion that factor mobility is indeed effective in limiting the redistributive activities of the public sector. It should be noted, however, that even if factor mobility raises the welfare cost of local redistributive policies, that is not the entire story. To the extent that factor mobility contributes to greater economic efficiency, it raises incomes in general, and if income redistribution is a normal good, these efficiency gains may generate demands for increased rather than reduced levels of redistribution (as illustrated in Wildasin, 1997). In general, highly developed welfare states are found in high-income societies, and it is not implausible to suggest that efficiency-improving institutions, which could certainly include relatively freely functioning factor markets, may thus be conducive to some forms of public sector redistribution.

Factor Mobility May Reduce the Benefits of Redistributive Policy

Although factor mobility may raise the costs of local redistribution, it may also reduce its benefits (Wildasin, 1995). As noted in Section II, the standard economic theory of factor movement is a theory of spatial arbitrage, and arbitrage tends to equalize factor returns and to reduce income risk. As many analysts have observed (see, for example, Varian, 1980; Atkinson, 1987; Sinn, 1995, this volume, and references therein), much of income distribution policy can be interpreted as a form of insurance. The income inequalities that redistribution policies attempt to redress result in part from fundamental inequalities in underlying endowments and from fundamental risks, including many personal attributes such as physical endowments (for example, birth defects), behaviour-independent health risks (for example, multiple sclerosis) and 'deep' personal differences in aptitude and motivation (resulting, for example, from mental disabilities and illnesses). However, economic inequalities also result from attributes of places and sectors. Some regions are technologically advanced, some have abundant fertile land or rich mineral deposits, and some have well-ordered legal and political institutions conducive to efficient resource allocation. Similarly, some 'sectors' – which in this context should probably be thought of in terms of 'occupations' rather than in terms of product types, though the two are obviously related – may be characterized by technologies or (derived) demand conditions that contribute to higher or lower factor returns. Factors of production that are location- or sector-specific thus experience returns that reflect location- or sector-specific conditions. Greater mobility of factors across space or sectors reduces factor specificity and thus some causes of economic inequality.[12] Therefore, although increased integration of factor markets may raise the costs of local redistributive policies and thus limit the extent of redistribution that is undertaken, it does not necessarily follow that factor mobility results in a less equal distribution of income. Referring once again to the twentieth-century experience of migration among regions in the USA and Canada or the nineteenth-century experience of migration between Europe and North America, it is arguable that the net effect of labour (and capital) mobility may have been to reduce overall economic inequality. Moreover, even if factor mobility did not reduce the dispersion of the size distribution of income, it may nonetheless have generated efficiency gains large enough to raise the incomes of both the poor and the rich. There is scope for valuable empirical research on this question which, so far, seems to have been only incompletely investigated.

Although factor mobility may reduce some income risks, it must be noted that it does not really pool regional income risks and thereby reduce the riskiness of returns for all factors.[13] Underlying differences in technologies, demand conditions and endowments can still give rise to inequalities among regions in the returns to certain factors of production. What factor mobility does is to shift the incidence of these risks away from mobile to immobile factors of production. In principle, this may either increase or decrease the social cost of income risk. Some income risks – for example, those accruing to tradable non-human assets such as land – can be effectively pooled through financial markets; other risks, particularly those accruing to labour, generally cannot be. Integration of labour markets can shift income risk away from labour towards non-human assets and thus from an uninsurable to an insurable form, perhaps leading to new roles for financial institutions. Conversely, integration of capital markets (specifically referring here to increases in opportunities for direct investment) may lead to reduced reliance on financial markets to pool risks among regions, and to an increase in the relatively uninsurable income risks borne by workers. The relationship between labour mobility, capital mobility and financial markets warrants attention in future research.

Factor Mobility May Increase the Scope for Central Government Transfers

Consider a collection of subnational governments, such as localities within a state or province, or states or provinces within a nation, among which factors of production are relatively mobile. Factor mobility may induce these lower-level governments to limit their redistributive interventions. In practice, however, very few government functions are free of redistributive impacts. Even in cases where market failures may warrant public sector interventions for allocative reasons (for example, provision of highways), it can be difficult if not impossible to avoid redistribution, short of government withdrawal from the sector altogether. Furthermore, lower-level governments may have some comparative advantage, relative to higher-level governments, in providing in-kind redistribution through health, education, and other public goods and services. If desirable lower-level government activities do entail some redistribution, therefore, factor mobility may limit these activities to an undesirable extent.

These considerations can provide a rationale for fiscal transfers from higher- to lower-level governments.[14] Fiscal equalization is one possible goal for such transfers. As argued by Buchanan (1950, 1952) and elaborated by Boadway and Flatters (1982), transfers from rich to poor jurisdictions within a federation may reduce the incentives for inefficient migration of labour in response to fiscal differentials among lower-level governments. Furthermore, transfers which are based at least in part on population size (or other demographic indicators of the number of beneficiaries) can compensate jurisdictions for inflows of households who would otherwise impose net fiscal burdens, and thus can reduce the incentive for these jurisdictions to curtail public services in order to limit these inflows. Alternatively, a central government may use matching grants (or, as in the US case, implicit subsidies through federal income tax deductibility of state and local taxes) to provide direct support for the redistributive programme of lower-level governments. As noted above, any single open jurisdiction's redistributive policies can affect economy-wide factor returns, even if only to a slight degree. Factor mobility thus implies that the effects of local redistribution spill out to the rest of the economy, and, in the absence of Coasian bargains, intergovernmental grants may be needed to internalize these interjurisdictional externalities.[15]

Factor Mobility, Economic Unions and Jurisdiction Formation

The spatial mobility of factors of production, particularly labour, is often closely linked to the definition of jurisdictional boundaries. Freedom to reside, work, or establish an enterprise in different locations within a country is one of the most important economic attributes of citizenship, even if it is not a guaranteed right in every country. Changes in national boundaries through accessions of territory (as in the case of German unification, or as seems likely to occur in the medium term in Korea) create larger effective market areas for factors of production and increase factor mobility. Free mobility of labour and capital was one of the founding principles of the European Union, which can be viewed from this perspective as a new jurisdiction whose spatial extent encompasses all of its member states. Indeed, a practical current question facing the European Union is which, if any, of numerous applicants for membership should be admitted to the EU, and the prospect of increased mobility of labour and capital that membership entails may be one of the more important factors to be taken into account in evaluating membership applications. It is perhaps noteworthy that Turkey applied for membership many years ago but that its application was held in abeyance for many years before being rejected, while the more recent applications for membership by countries such as Finland, Sweden and Norway were acted upon favourably in rather short order (even though a Norwegian referendum subsequently rejected EU membership). Have fiscal considerations and factor mobility played any role in this process? What, in any case, would be some of the fiscal implications of the accession of new countries (for instance, recent applicants like Poland, the Baltic republics, Hungary, Romania, or Bulgaria) to an entity like the EU? Conversely, what would be the fiscal effects of the break-up of existing jurisdictions? The dissolution of the Soviet Union may be the most conspicuous recent example of such an event, but movements toward increased regional autonomy or outright secession are under way in many other countries at the end of the 1990s.

To begin with, the formation of a new market area from smaller constituent jurisdictions offers the opportunity to reap the efficiency gains from integration of markets for goods, services and factors of production, and perhaps to reduce the social cost of some types of factor-price risk, as discussed above. On the other hand, if no strong central government structure emerges that can implement fiscal policies over the more extensive market area, that may mean that the redistributive functions of the public sector will become more constrained for the reasons already described.

A further issue of some interest concerns the implications of asymmetries among regions which are potential members of an economic union or unified political jurisdiction. As discussed in Wellisch and Wildasin (1996) in the context of EU membership, the welfare impact on existing EU member states of the entry of a new country depends on the net fiscal burden (or net fiscal contribution) of immigrants from the new country. This net fiscal impact of immigrants depends both on the attributes of the immigrants themselves as well as on the fiscal policy of the existing countries. Large international migrations prior to the second World War antedate the modern welfare state with its extensive programmes of redistribution, and the net fiscal impact of migrants was therefore comparatively modest. In modern EU countries, however, where the growth of redistributive policies has resulted in government expenditures that commonly amount to roughly half of national income, the fiscal impact of migrants is of great potential importance and suggests the undesirability of allowing comparatively free entry of immigrants who impose net fiscal burdens. The rapid acceptance of the applications of the Nordic countries for EU membership, hesitation over the applications of applicants from Eastern Europe, and the denial of the application from Turkey, can perhaps be partly explained in these terms.

Asymmetries among jurisdictions suggest that greater factor mobility between rich and poor regions can work to the fiscal disadvantage of the rich; this might make the rich reluctant to form economic and political unions with the poor. On the other hand, economic disparities can create very powerful incentives for factor movements which may not be easily resisted; in particular, the high-wage, low-birth-rate regions of Western Europe and North America will find it difficult to limit immigration from the neighbouring low-wage regions of Eastern Europe, North Africa, and Latin America, the latter two also being regions with high fertility rates. The degree of economic integration of the labour markets of these regions can obviously be influenced by government policy (decisions about EU membership, for instance), but it is costly, and perhaps ultimately infeasible, to halt labour flows between these regions. As indicated already with reference to Figure 6.1, immigration from poor to rich countries can depress labour earnings in the latter, at least in the absence of offsetting compensatory mechanisms. It is natural to ask whether fiscal policies could perform this function.

The extent to which fiscal policies can compensate existing workers from erosion of income due to immigration depends on the precise instruments that are available to the fiscal authorities, and, in particular, on the ability of these instruments to discriminate between native and migrant workers. If it is possible to increase the net fiscal burden imposed on immigrants, for instance on the basis of rules for taxation and access to social benefits based on citizenship status, the gains in aggregate income to original factor owners in an immigrant-receiving country, as represented in Figure 6.1 by the attainability of point A when immigration occurs, can be partially redistributed to initial workers in such a way that they are better off as a result of immigration.[16] In practice, however, it is often quite costly to exclude immigrants from the benefits of public goods or to subject them to different tax treatment, and the existence of binding immigration quotas in at least some countries indicates that discriminatory fiscal treatment of immigrants, to the extent that it occurs at all, has not been carried sufficiently far to discourage entry to the level of the quota limits. To the extent that immigrants enjoy the same fiscal standing as existing residents, however, the ability of a government to use fiscal instruments to compensate native residents from the distributional impact of migration is compromised. In Figure 6.1, the curve PQ shows possible distributions of net income that can be attained, in the absence of migration, through redistributive transfers between owners of potentially mobile labour and owners of immobile factors of production. The curve $BA'C$ illustrates the set of net income distributions that are attainable in a given jurisdiction when it is open to immigrant workers who are subject to the same fiscal treatment as native residents. Note, in particular, that this curve cuts below the *laissez-faire* point A on the original income distribution frontier PQ. Since the *laissez-faire* point with immigration, A', lies above PQ, this means that if the workers who compete with immigrants initially are net fiscal beneficiaries, that is, if the pre-immigration distribution of net income lies on the segment AQ, then either those workers, the owners of immobile factors of production, or both, must be worse off after immigration, no matter what redistributive policy the government follows.[17]

Since immigration can be harmful, even Pareto-harmful, when the government is unable to discriminate in its fiscal treatment of immigrants, the question arises whether it could be advantageous to attempt to use fiscal instruments to forestall immigration. Indeed, if a destination jurisdiction (EU countries, the USA) can transfer resources to an origin jurisdiction (Eastern Europe, Latin America) in such a way that the benefits of those transfers accrue to workers who remain in the origin jurisdiction, it is possible that welfare in the donor (destination) jurisdiction may rise. In Figure 6.1, the line *RS*, which just touches the schedule *BA'C* at one point and lies strictly above it everywhere else, shows the set of net income distributions that can be attained by the original owners of mobile and immobile factors in the destination jurisdiction if they can make transfers to workers in the origin jurisdiction who do not migrate.

The fact that a jurisdiction's residents can gain from transfers to another jurisdiction raises the question of how such transfers might be effectuated. One possibility is through mechanisms such as foreign aid. For such aid to forestall migration, it is important that its benefits accrue to potential migrants in the origin jurisdiction. From this viewpoint, donor jurisdictions might seek to promote infrastructure investment and other developmental programmes that raise labour productivity in the origin jurisdiction, though the recipient governments might take advantage of the fungibility of aid to channel these resources into other expenditures. But the origin and destination jurisdictions need not be interpreted as countries; they could, instead, be viewed as regions within a country, and fiscal transfers from rich to poor regions could be brought about through intergovernmental grants or, indeed, through central government redistributive or developmental programmes (for example, development of a national highway or waterway system that is disproportionately financed by rich regions). If rich regions wish to direct resources to potential migrants in poor regions, the formation of a political union with a central government that engages in systematic interregional transfers might provide donor regions with a better framework for monitoring and control of transfers than could be achieved by international transfers. Central governments, from this perspective, may be viewed as the outcome of a kind of Coasian bargaining in which donor and recipient jurisdictions attempt to find an efficient institutional mechanism through which to make interjurisdictional transfers. Thus, even jurisdictions that are asymmetrically situated may find it advantageous to form or to maintain political unions, despite the fact – indeed, because of the fact – that the political union entails net fiscal transfers from one jurisdiction to another.[18]

IV   HOW IMPORTANT ARE THE FISCAL IMPACTS OF LABOUR MOBILITY? ISSUES FOR EMPIRICAL RESEARCH

Labour market integration is potentially of great importance for fiscal analysis, and for public policy, because such a large fraction of both the revenue and expenditure sides of the government budget depend on earnings and household demographics. A large share of national income in every economy derives from the return to labour services. Tax systems in developed countries (and to a lesser extent in developing countries) generate revenue either from direct taxation of wage income through personal income taxes and wage-based social insurance contributions or indirectly (if not quite equivalently) from broad-based taxation of consumption via value-added taxes or retail sales taxes. On the expenditure side of the fiscal account, programmes dealing with education, health and transfer payments to the elderly, poor and young are responsible for a very large share of public expenditures. As a consequence, changes in the demographic composition of a jurisdiction can affect both the demands for public services and the revenues with which these services are financed. Much of the preceding discussion has referred to some of the possible fiscal impacts of labour mobility. However, whether within countries or at the international level, the empirical importance of labour mobility may be open to question. And, if labour is mobile, how important really are the fiscal consequences of the spatial allocation of labour? These are large and difficult empirical questions, on which significant amounts of research have already been undertaken. The proper formulation and analysis of these empirical questions, however, is not altogether obvious. The present section raises, though it does not resolve, some of the important conceptual issues which empirical analyses must address, explicitly or implicitly.

Costly Migration

Does labour mobility 'matter' for fiscal policy? Some might be inclined to answer this question on an *a priori* basis, perhaps with a definitive 'yes' or perhaps with a definitive 'no'. A more cautious response would be to say that this is an 'empirical question'. While unexceptionable, this cautious response is not in itself enlightening nor does it reflect the fact that the analysis of labour mobility for the purposes of fiscal policy actually presents many distinct 'empirical questions'. In order to progress beyond conflicting *a priori* assertions about mobility or vague appeals to empirical analysis, a clear conceptual framework is necessary. The following paragraphs attempt to sort out some of the conceptual issues and to outline some important directions for empirical research.

First, one might think that a high level of migration would be the crucial indicator of the importance of labour mobility and the extent of labour market integration over space. One might also suspect that erosion of wage or income differentials provides crucial information about the extent

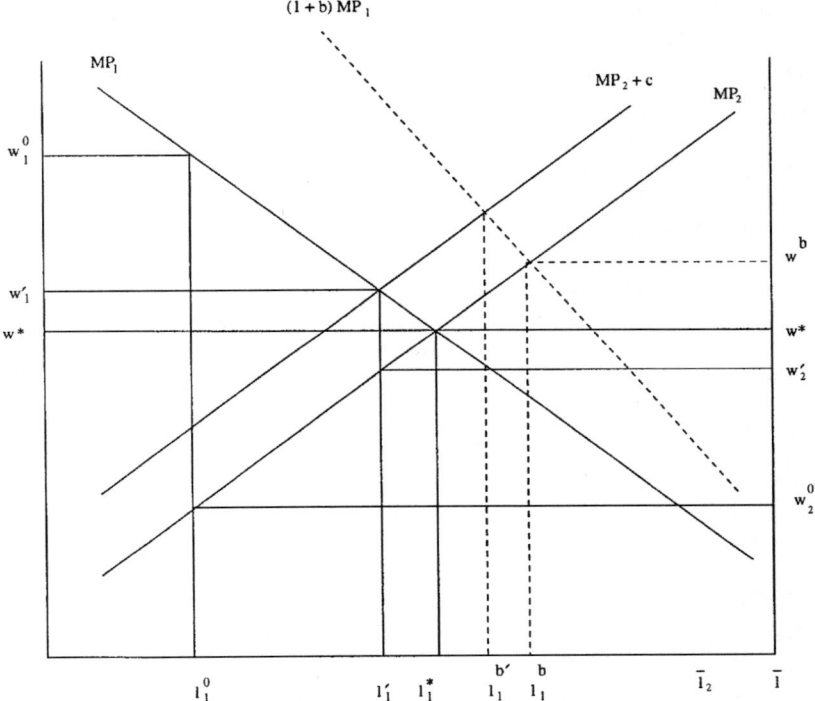

Figure 6.2   Fiscal transfers and migration with and without mobility costs

to which labour markets are linked. In fact, however, neither observed migration flows nor income differentials necessarily carry obvious implications for the extent of labour market integration. In this respect, migration flows are analogous to net flows of investment in non-human capital: migration is a stock-adjustment mechanism, and low levels of migration may simply indicate that sufficient equilibrating adjustments have already taken place so that further spatial reallocation of labour is unwarranted. A simple static model illustrates these points effectively and provides a basis for deeper discussion.

Figure 6.2 provider a standard representation of the allocation of a fixed amount of a factor of production, such as a fixed population of identical workers, $\bar{l}$, between two locations, 1 and 2. Any point along the horizontal axis of the figure portrays a division of the total workforce between the two locations. In each location, suppose that there is a production function in which labour enters as a variable input and that there is at least one factor of production that is locationally fixed. The curves MP_1 and MP_2 show the marginal productivity of labour in each location, denominated in units of some numéraire commodity, as a function of the level of employment there. Assume, first, that these two locations are completely isolated from one another, so that it is physically impossible for labour to migrate between them. If by chance the number of workers in location 1 is l_1^*, the marginal productivity of labour in each location will be the same, and, if labour markets are competitive, wage rates will also take the same value w^* in both locations. The absence of a wage differential does not indicate that labour is mobile between them.

Next, suppose that labour is costlessly mobile between the two locations. Assuming again that there are l_1^* workers initially situated in location 1, wage rates in both regions will be equal if labour markets are competitive and, assuming that workers seek only to maximize their wages, no workers will have any incentive to migrate. Thus, labour markets can be perfectly integrated in the complete absence of observed migration.

More generally, suppose that the initial assignment of workers differs from l_1^*. For instance, suppose that l_1^0 workers start out in location 1. If migration is costless, markets are competitive, and workers seek to maximize earnings, then $l_1^*-l_1^0$ workers will migrate from location 2 to location 1, eliminating the initial wage differential of $w_1^0 - w_2^0$ between the two locations. Comparing this case with the preceding one, it is apparent that the level of migration may be an indicator not of the extent to which labour markets are integrated but of the extent to which the initial distribution of labour across locations differs from the equilibrium distribution.

Now consider the costs of migration. Note first that these costs may be 'intrinsic', that is, they may represent real economic costs, or they may be determined by deliberate policy choices, for instance through legal restrictions on migration. The real costs of migration, and perhaps the legal impediments to migration, are unlikely to be the same for all workers. What matters for many analytical purposes is the level of migration costs for the 'marginal' household or worker. For example, workers who have strong locational preferences, who have dependent family members to care for, or who are old, sick, poor, or poorly educated are likely to be relatively immobile. The distribution of these attributes among workers may affect the *composition* of any migration flow but need not necessarily affect its *level* or its allocative or distributional implications. In Figure 6.2, it is obvious that if $\bar{l}_2$ workers are unwilling or unable to leave location 2, this has no effect at all on the level of migration or on its allocative or distributional consequences.

It could be argued, of course, that migration is not costless for *any* workers. Suppose, for example, that every worker moving from location 2 to 1 must bear a cost of c. This cost could be interpreted narrowly to include only out-of-pocket pecuniary outlays associated with moving, but it could also be interpreted very broadly as the monetized value of all non-pecuniary as well as pecuniary costs of migration, such as the disruption of social ties, learning a new language, or acquiring information about different market and legal institutions in a new environment. Under either interpretation, these are real economic costs, and in their presence, earnings in location 1 must exceed earnings in location 2 by at least c if workers are to migrate. In Figure 6.2, if l_1^0 workers are initially assigned to location 1, $(l_1'-l_1^0)$ workers would have to move from 2 to 1 before the higher wage in 1 would no longer be sufficiently high to compensate workers for the cost of moving plus lost earnings in location 2. Note that earnings levels would not in general be completely equalized in equilibrium due to mobility costs; arbitrage (or labour market integration) only implies that equilibrium earnings differentials cannot exceed the level of migration costs. Moreover, if the number of workers in location 1 exceeds l_1' – for instance, if this number lies between l_1' and l_1^* – migration would not be observed, even though workers are potentially mobile.

We have so far considered the cases where (i) all workers face prohibitive migration costs, (ii) no workers face any migration costs, and (iii) all workers face a fixed cost of migration c. More complex cases amount essentially to combinations of these simple ones. For instance, suppose that the costs of migration are 0 for some workers, c for others, and prohibitive for still others. The first group would migrate even if wage differentials are very small, the last group would never migrate, and the middle group will migrate if earnings differentials are sufficiently large. One or the other of these groups might constitute the pool of 'marginal' workers, depending on technologies in each location, the initial distribution of workers, and the size of each group. With reference to Figure 6.2, suppose that the initial division of workers between locations 1 and 2 is given by l_1^0. Then, if more than $\bar{l} - l_1^0$ workers in location 2 face prohibitive migration costs, the analysis of case (i) applies. If more than $l_1^* - l_1^0$ workers in location 2 can migrate at zero cost, then the analysis of case (ii) is applicable. If the number of workers facing a migration cost of c exceeds $l_1^* - l_1^0$, then case (iii) applies. More generally, migration costs might vary continuously over the population from a zero or negligible level to a prohibitively high level. Then, in equilibrium, there will be some critical level of migration costs c^* such that workers with migration costs less than c^* do migrate, those with migration costs greater than c^*

do not migrate, and the equilibrium earnings differential is $c*$. Practically speaking, this amounts to case (iii) except that c is now understood to vary over the population.

Realistically, non-zero migration costs are likely to be the rule rather than the exception for most or all migrants, and for some analytical purposes these costs can be quite important. Migration costs drive wedges between the equilibrium returns to labour in different locations, implying that complete spatial wage convergence is unlikely to be observed in practice.[19] Indeed, the spatial wage inequalities created by migration costs may be sufficiently large to contribute significantly to overall income inequality and may warrant policy attention in some cases.[20] However, from the viewpoint of the analysis of fiscal policy, and particularly redistributive policy, they need not change the qualitative implications of factor mobility itself. To illustrate this point with reference to Figure 6.2, suppose that location 1, which might be interpreted as the USA or Western Europe, offers social benefits to workers that raise their net incomes by the proportional amount b, illustrated by the schedule $(1 + b) MP_1$. Assume that location 1 offers these benefits on a non-discriminatory basis to immigrant workers from location 2, which might be interpreted as Mexico, Eastern Europe, or North Africa, either because fiscal discrimination is infeasible or because non-discrimination is chosen as a matter of policy. If there are no migration costs, then l_1^b rather than $l*$ is now the equilibrium allocation of labour. Note that the social benefits offered in location 1 raise equilibrium real incomes in location 2, cause an inefficient allocation of labour, and induce more migration from 2 to 1 than would otherwise be the case. Now suppose that each migrant must bear a migration cost of c. With social benefits to workers in location 1, the intersection of the $(1 + b) MP_1$ curve with the $MP_2 + c$ schedule determines the equilibrium net incomes, gross wages, and levels of employment and migration in both locations. Exactly as with costless migration, fiscal benefits in location 1 spill out to region 2 via higher levels of migration from 2 to 1, resulting in higher incomes in region 2 and excessive employment in location 1 (the equilibrium level of employment in location 1 is $l_1^{b'}$ while the efficient level is l_1'). In fact, in the costless migration case, the MP_2 curve in effect is a supply curve of labour to location 1 from the rest of the world; with costly migration, the $MP_2 + c$ curve is the supply curve from the rest of the world. The qualitative analysis of fiscal policies in location 1 is essentially unaffected by the fact that migration costs shift this supply curve upwards, provided only that migration costs are sufficiently low (or original labour assignments are sufficiently far from equilibrium) that there is a non-zero level of migration. What matters most for fiscal analysis is not whether migration costs are 'negligible' but whether they are sufficiently small that policies undertaken in one geographic location can potentially give rise to factor movements into or out of another location.

The Dynamics of Migration: Market Integration and Factor Aggregation

Migration is a process that occurs in time, at one or more points in the life cycle of the (potential) migrant. Given that migration is costly, migration decisions are not costlessly irreversible. Given imperfect information about (and imperfect insurability of) present and future local labour market conditions, the prices and quantities of local non-traded goods, services and amenities and other relevant local conditions, migration choices should be viewed as investment decisions made under conditions of uncertainty. The opportunity to migrate is thus an option which particular households may choose to exercise at any particular point in time (Dixit and Pindyck, 1994). The benefits and costs of migration vary over the life cycle, depending among other things on the evolution of (planned) labour force participation, family formation, anticipated mortality, and the like. To the extent that parents and children are linked, altruistically or otherwise, the private benefits and costs of migration can extend across generations.

Explicit recognition of the intertemporal setting of migration suggest that the extent of labour market integration over *space* depends on the amount of *time* over which market integration is to be assessed. The least costly job switches for workers are probably those that involve task reassignments within a given workplace; somewhat more costly is a switch in job locations within a firm, or a switch in employers, within those parts of a metropolitan area in close proximity to a worker's current residence. Moves among metropolitan areas, larger regions such as states or provinces, or among countries, are likely to be more costly still. It is to be expected, then, that the magnitude and anticipated durability of the benefits of these types of moves must be successively greater, as well, if they are to occur. Particularly under conditions of uncertainty, signals of persistently higher returns in other locations may be necessary to induce very costly migration.[21] The migration-adjustment process is thus likely to be attenuated in time, as succeeding waves of workers with the best information about market opportunities and the lowest costs of migration gradually flow from low- to high-return locations. If distances and information costs are low, legal impediments to migration are absent, and labour market institutions are flexible, the speed of adjustment may be relatively fast, whereas in other cases it may be substantially slower. In any case, the issue of labour mobility is not binary in nature: the empirical question, in general, is not whether labour is mobile or immobile, but rather the *speed* with which the spatial allocation of labour adjusts to wage variations or, of particular concern here, to changes in fiscal policy.[22] The migration response to redistributive and other fiscal policies is unlikely to be instantaneous, and it may well be appropriate for some analytical purposes to treat labour as immobile in the 'short run'. At the same time, slow migration responses to fiscal policy are likely to be relatively costly to reverse and their consequences may therefore be quite durable.

For some purposes, it may be helpful to think of spatial labour market integration as an aggregation problem, in which the essential question is whether workers in two different locations can be viewed as 'sufficiently substitutable' that it makes sense to 'add them up' for analytical purposes. Analyses of labour market conditions that refer to 'the' US, German, or Mexican wage or unemployment rates implicitly or explicitly assume that labour can meaningfully be aggregated at the country level. This involves an aggregation across workers of different educational levels, occupations, skill types, ethnic, religious, or age groups, and, of course, geographical sub-units within the country. Sometimes these subgroups can be broken down and analysed separately, which is of interest to the extent that they do not constitute a homogeneous aggregate. For example, the differential incidence of macroeconomic shocks on subgroups within the labour market (for instance, white-collar versus blue-collar workers) has been a topic of some interest for empirical researchers, and generally indicates that identifiable subgroups have labour market experiences that are distinguishable to some extent. The same is true for subgroups that are spatially separated. When data permit, it is possible to investigate the degree of substitutability between workers in different locations, as measured for example by the degree to which relative wages are fixed over space; to the extent that this is so, it is acceptable to view labour in different locations as a Hicksian composite commodity. We may think of the distribution of labour over space at a particular moment as rather like the distribution of labour over occupational groups, that is, as location- or occupation-specific stocks (as the case may be) that adjust gradually over time as old workers exit the labour force through retirement or death, while young or middle-aged workers establish themselves in particular locations or occupations through migration or through education and training. In the 'short run', location- or occupation-specific wage differentials (quasi-rents) may arise, and are evidence of imperfect short-run substitutability, but these differentials are expected to be eroded over time, implying greater substitutability in the long run. To say that labour is mobile across locations is thus essentially equivalent to saying that labour can be spatially aggregated; broader aggregates are in general more appropriate, the longer the time horizon of the analysis.[23]

Indeed, the parallels between aggregation of labour over space and over sectors or occupational categories can and for some purposes should be pursued still further. Immigrants, and their families, typically undergo a complex process of adjustment to their new locations in which they become increasingly functional in local language, markets and social institutions, a process commonly called 'assimilation'. Over time – perhaps over generations – assimilation can become so complete that the immigrants – or their descendants – become economically indistinguishable from 'natives'. Immigrants may initially differ from the indigenous population in terms of education levels or sectoral or occupational concentrations, but these differences may disappear over time. This process of economic assimilation of immigrants is also normally part of the process by which labour is reallocated among sectors and locations within the economy, for instance as internal migration carries immigrant groups away from 'gateway' cities. This dynamic process complicates the empirical assessment of the impact of immigrants on domestic labour markets, a much-researched topic. Borjas *et al.* (1996) find that recent immigrants to the USA appear to depress earnings relatively little in the particular metropolitan areas where they are concentrated but relatively much for domestic workers with comparable (low) levels of educational attainment. In this case, it appears that workers in US labour markets can more appropriately be aggregated over space than across skill levels. But, of course, the educational status of these immigrants, and their offspring, may well change over time, so that those who are not now readily substitutable with immigrant workers may become so, perhaps in a generation or two. In other words, the extent of spatial and sectoral labour market integration is critically dependent on the time horizon over which it is assessed.

The Dynamic Fiscal Impact of Migration

The preceding subsections have emphasized that labour mobility does depend on migration costs, but that the importance of these costs, and the extent of spatial integration of labour markets, must be seen within a dynamic context, possibly extending over several generations. It follows that the implications of factor mobility for redistribution policy should also be assessed within a dynamic setting. This presents significant challenges for empirical research.

Consider, for instance, the question of whether migrants impose net fiscal burdens, or make net fiscal contributions, to origin or destination jurisdictions, an important and contentious public policy issue. A first question to consider is the demographic and socioeconomic composition of the migrant population, for instance with respect to age, sex, family status, and possession of human and non-human wealth. All of these attributes affect the way that households interface with the fiscal system: taxes are typically levied on earnings, non-wage income, wealth and consumption, while access to benefits from income support, education, health, public pension, housing and other public expenditure programmes depends on income, wealth and demographic characteristics.[24] However, migrant attributes change over time, and the fiscal burdens or contributions of migrants therefore change over time as well.

For example, young single males are often an important migrant type. These individuals are likely to be labour force participants; they are not likely to have much labour market experience or previous on-the-job training; they are relatively likely to be involved in criminal activities, to be healthy, and to have completed or nearly completed their primary and secondary education. These initial characteristics all have important fiscal implications for both the origin and destination jurisdictions. Young single males also age, however, and as they do, their job experience and earnings are likely to grow; they are less likely to commit crimes and more likely to become sick or disabled. They are also likely to form families and have children, possibly with women who follow them from origin locations but also possibly with non-immigrant women, and they may be joined by elderly parents or other relatives. Their mates, offspring and relatives may receive fiscal benefits or make fiscal contributions. And, of course, the demographic, economic, social and finally fiscal characteristics of the whole migrant-related group gradually change over time, giving rise to time-streams of consumption of public service benefits and of tax and other fiscal contributions. Eventually, the original migrants, if they remain in the destination jurisdictions, will retire and die, possibly leaving survivors who continue to participate in the economy and the fiscal system of the destination jurisdiction. These impacts may persist over many generations, becoming more diffuse as successive generations produce offspring with members of other family lines.

It would be possible, in principle, to record the economic and fiscal impacts of migrants, their partners, relatives and offspring over time. (In practice, of course, this would be a very difficult undertaking due to basic limitations of data, the fact that many migrants may be illegal and thus not readily observable, and a host of other complicating factors.)

Assuming that such data could be gathered, there is still a basic problem in deciding exactly how to formulate empirical questions. At the conceptual level, to determine 'the' fiscal impact of migrants, it is necessary to define both the demographic 'breadth' of the 'migration event' – that is, the set of individuals whose fiscal benefits and burdens are to be associated with migration – and its temporal 'depth' – that is, the time horizon over which these fiscal effects are counted. From a generational accounting perspective, it may be appealing to limit attention to the fiscal streams that persist during the lifetime of a migrant, perhaps also including a surviving spouse. From a dynastic family perspective, on the other hand, there is no reason to ignore the migrant's offspring and subsequent descendants.

It is not obvious how to settle these conceptual questions, but the stakes are large. After all, as a close approximation, all of the taxes that US residents have ever paid, and the fiscal benefits that they have received, can be attributed to immigration that has taken place during the past several centuries! Consistency with the simple static models sketched above suggests that the planning horizon of the potential migrant determines the period over which (the present value of) the fiscal redistribution associated with streams of taxes and benefits should be calculated. Although this begs the question, it does suggest that the 'instantaneous' or 'initial' fiscal contributions or burdens of migrants are likely to be seriously misleading indicators of their fiscal impacts. Indeed, for some purposes, such as the assessment of the fiscal consequences of jurisdiction formation and dissolution, very long-run perspectives might be quite appropriate. This is well-illustrated by a consideration of the potential effects of migration on public pension programmes. Throughout the developed world, these programmes are enormous mechanisms of redistribution, accounting for a very large fraction of total public revenues and expenditures; because of the intergenerational transfers to which they give rise, they must be analysed in a very long-run setting. They are generally beset by impending funding problems due to population ageing, the resolution of which will constitute one of the chief problems for fiscal policy in these countries during the first half of the twenty-first century. Over this time horizon, actual or potential events such German unification, the admission of Eastern European countries into the EU, the break-up of the Soviet Union, major changes in immigration policy (including the fiscal treatment of immigrants) in North America, and gaps in population and economic growth rates between developed and less-developed countries may well have significant impacts on interjurisdictional flows of labour, and thus on the fiscal stability of public pension programmes and other redistributive policies. The fiscal and other economic impacts of migrants, in this context, should be analysed over quite lengthy periods.[25]

V   CONCLUSION

Public economics has evolved mainly as a 'closed economy' specialization in economics. In viewing factors of production as immobile, to a first approximation, it reflects the tradition in international economics associated with the names of Hecksher and Ohlin. The broad acceptance of factor immobility as a stylized fact has contributed to an intellectual division of labour between public and international economics. Within the context of national economic policy, taxes and expenditures whose primary impact falls directly on labour and capital – the the bulk of all taxes and expenditures – have been viewed essentially as 'domestic' policies, falling within the purview of public economics. International economists have tended to focus on those aspects of policy that directly affect the international flows of goods and services among countries, such as tariffs, while leaving 'domestic' economic policy in the background.

The value of this division of scholarly labour between public and international economics has been amply demonstrated by the important progress made in both fields over the past decades. In the aftermath of the Second World War and throughout the Cold War era, national boundaries among OECD and Warsaw Pact countries were quite stable and the mobility of labour and capital, though certainly not altogether absent, appeared nonetheless to be quite limited. More recently, however, international capital market institutions have become increasingly developed. Immigration to the USA has risen to levels that are relatively high by historical standards and immigration has also increased substantially in Western Europe. The process of economic integration in Europe, including particularly the recent and prospective accession of new member states to the EU, is lowering the barriers to factor movements. Recent or prospective restructuring of national boundaries and of economic unions naturally raises interest in the potential implications of factor mobility and also invites consideration of the fundamental economic determinants of market areas both for factors of production and for goods and services. For these reasons, the boundaries between 'domestic' and 'international' policy have become somewhat blurred, and it is useful to revisit many issues in public economics to see to what extent the potential mobility of factors of production (as well as of goods and services) can affect the economic analysis of fiscal policy.

The mobility of labour and capital has long played a major role in research on public economics issues at the local or state/provincial level (and on related issues in urban and regional economics). While the specific policy questions faced by national governments differ in many important ways from those confronting lower-level governments, there are nevertheless some fundamental economic similarities between them. The preceding discussion has drawn together some of the important insights that have emerged from research on redistributive policy in the presence of factor mobility, insights which in many ways have their roots in the early literature of local public finance and fiscal federalism but which are of potential applicability in much broader contexts. This field remains open to much further development, however, both in its theoretical and empirical dimensions. As emphasized in Section IV, there are many subtle questions involving the simultaneous demarcation of the spatial and temporal dimensions of factor markets which warrant empirical examination. These questions are similarly relevant in defining the time horizon over which the process of redistributive policy takes place and over which factor mobility matters for the purposes of fiscal analysis. These questions probably cannot be satisfactorily settled on an *a priori* basis. Rather, they attest to the complexity of the phenomena under investigation, which cut across the boundaries of many specializations in economics, including not only public and international economics but labour economics, economic history, urban and regional economics, and others. If this means that there are some daunting barriers to research on these problems, it also means that progress can be made on many fronts. The ongoing evolution of economic and political institutions throughout the world seems certain to require analysis of policy issues revolving around redistributive policies and factor market integration for the foreseeable future. There is much scope here for intellectually innovative research that can shed significant light on some of the major issues of our time.

Notes

1. The topics discussed in this chapter stand at the intersection of many distinct but related fields of inquiry, including not only much of public economics but population and labour economics, economic history, political economy, international economics, and urban and regional economics. A comprehensive treatment of these topics, including references to the many valuable and relevant contributions to the literature, is well beyond the scope of this chapter. In order to limit its length, the discussion and references are highly selective and admittedly idiosyncratic. Serious students of these issues can find references to much other useful literature in the works cited here. Other

broad treatments of issues relating to open economy public finance, factor mobility, and related topics, containing many citations to other literature, include Wildasin (1986, 1987), Rubinfeld (1987), Mieszkowski and Zodrow (1989), Tanzi (1995), Frenkel *et al.* (1991), Cremer *et al.* (1995), and Wellisch (1996); see also Cremer and Pestieau (1996a).

2. For example, urban per capita incomes among major regions in China differ by nearly a factor of 2, with even larger variations in rural incomes (World Bank, 1995, pp. 103–4). Income variations of this magnitude, and the associated internal migration flows that are now occurring in China, suggest the existence of important factor productivity differentials across regions, and correspondingly important potential gains from factor reallocations. It should be noted that housing market liberalization can contribute greatly to labour mobility; indeed, restrictions on housing markets played a crucial role in the enforcement of *apartheid* and *hukou* controls on population movements. (Since housing markets are in turn closely linked to capital markets, there are many interesting connections between capital and labour market reform in countries like South Africa and China. Explicit treatment of these connections goes beyond the scope of the present discussion, however.)

3. Using computable general equilibrium methods, Hamilton and Whalley (1984) estimate large productivity gains from the efficient allocation of labour on a worldwide scale.

4. In 'brain drain' models, highly-skilled workers migrate from poor to rich countries (see, for example, Bhagwati and Wilson, 1989). The same issues of factor aggregation arise in this context, as well. Schiff (1996) emphasizes that many studies have found that very low-wage workers are less likely to migrate to high-wage regions than those with somewhat higher incomes. Informational constraints, capital market imperfections, and the fact that workers from low-wage areas with better education may embody greater amounts of labour services and thus may achieve greater income increases from migration than the very poor may all be part of the explanation for this finding. Here again the question of labour aggregation comes to the fore.

5. Such ideal transfers are of course generally unavailable; but labour/leisure, consumption/savings, and other distortions associated with feasible tax and expenditure instruments are suppressed here for simplicity.

6. These basic observations on income convergence and migration appear, for example, in Mieszkowski (1979) and Mills and Hamilton (1984). More recently, work by Barro and Sala-i-Martin (1991) has drawn further attention to the issue of income convergence across space. Carrington *et al.* (1996) discuss the South–North migration of blacks in the USA during the twentieth century, and conclude that it played an important role in income growth for this generally poor part of the population. Helliwell (1996) shows that the Canadian experience is very much similar to that of the USA: incomes among provinces have tended to become more equal over time, and migration has proceeded in the expected direction, that is, from poor to rich provinces. See Asdrubali *et al.* (1996) and Sørensen and Yosha (1996) for discussions of the sharing of risk among US states through capital markets (as well as through central government fiscal policies).

7. As described in Topel (1991) and Topel and Ward (1992), workers in the US economy often change jobs rapidly at the beginning of the life cycle, and in doing so experience rapid earnings growth; as their earnings rise, their attachment to specific jobs tends to increase. These studies address the issue of mobility among jobs rather than among places. However, findings reported in Topel (1986) indicate that young workers are more geographically mobile than old workers. Thus, especially in the early part of the life cycle, workers do in fact exercise their options to switch jobs, and do so in part by switching locations.

8. To the extent that investment in human capital entails the acquisition of durable, specialized skills, it exposes workers to skill-specific risks. If these occupational risks are not perfectly correlated over space, labour mobility can provide some insurance against them and thus provide a more certain environment within which to undertake such investment (Wildasin, 1996).

9. See also Oates (1968) and Musgrave (1971) for early discussions. The term 'welfare magnets' has become a popular expression for this phenomenon; see, for example, Peterson and Rom (1990).

10. A more thorough discussion of the equity and efficiency dimensions of local school finance goes beyond the scope of the present chapter. See, however, Inman and Rubinfeld (1979) for an integrated discussion of the economic and legal dimensions of school finance. One major policy response to the issue of inequality in school finance has been the growth of equalizing state grants to local school authorities, an example of a case where higher-level governments have assumed greater responsibility for redistributive functions of the public sector. See Ladd and Yinger (1994), Oakland (1994), and Reschovsky (1994) for recent discussions of this important topic.

11. See, for example, Cremer et al. (1995). The political economy of redistribution is complex, however; on issues of centralized and decentralized voting, in addition to a long line of contributions in the literature of local public finance (see Epple and Romer, 1991, for one recent example), see Janeba and Raff (1995), Piketty (1996), Crémer and Palfrey (1996), and Cremer and Pestieau (1996b).

12. By the same token, mobility can change the distribution of fundamental personal risks within a jurisdiction. Bureau and Richard (1997) analyse the integration of insurance markets, for example through household mobility, in the presence of asymmetric information. In their model, public insurance systems may or may not break down in the presence of labour mobility depending on the distribution of risks in different countries. It would be interesting to extend this analysis to a model with endogenous wage determination. It should also be noted that the sector specificity of factors – human capital is perhaps the most important example – is endogenously determined. Factor market integration may make investment in more specialized skills more attractive, which may increase productivity but which also partly undoes the risk-reducing impact of more extensive factor markets. Factor mobility may also introduce tax competition among governments, however, possibly limiting their ability to use fiscal instruments that recapture the costs of publicly provided human capital investment (Wildasin, 1996).

13. Many studies have drawn attention to the possibility that the fiscal policies of central governments can pool income risks among households, including

households in different regions, an idea that can be viewed as an application of the insights of Domar and Musgrave (1944) to the context of location-specific income risks. Persson and Tabellini (1996) discuss risk-sharing in political equilibria with various combinations of central government transfers to decentralized local governments as well as central and local government taxes on individuals, abstracting however from interjurisdictional factor mobility.

14. Boadway and Keen (1996) discuss possible justifications for fiscal transfers from lower- to higher-level governments. Their analysis focuses explicitly on the distortionary effects of taxation on factor supplies (for example, through labour/leisure trade-offs) and the fact that these distortions are compounded when multiple levels of government independently attempt to raise revenues from the same tax base. The present discussion abstracts from these types of distortions for simplicity.

15. See, for example, Oates (1972) for a standard treatment of interjurisdictional spillovers and of the rationale for matching grants to correct them. In general, internalization of the external effects associated with decentralized provision of public goods does not imply uniformity of policy across jurisdictions, since local preferences and costs may vary. The application of this idea in the context of local redistribution (see, for example, Pauly, 1973) suggests that diverse preferences for redistribution by heterogeneous taxpayer-donors in different jurisdictions should be accommodated by correspondingly varied local taxes and transfers. However, provided that the beneficiaries of redistributive transfers are mobile, an optimal structure of matching grants would induce lower-level governments to set redistributive policies such that net fiscal burdens or benefits are the same everywhere, even when lower-level jurisdictions differ in their underlying endowments, technologies, or preferences for redistribution (Wildasin, 1991). Uniform fiscal treatment of mobile net fiscal contributors is also necessary for efficiency. See also Goodspeed (1995) and Cremer and Pestieau (1996a) for related discussion.

16. Sandmo and Wildasin (1994) show that it is generally in the interest of the native residents of a jurisdiction to apply fiscal instruments to migrants in a discriminatory fashion, if feasible; for example, it is preferable to raise taxes on immigrants to the point where any immigration quotas become non-binding. Note that effective fiscal discrimination does not necessarily require the application of individual fiscal instruments on a discriminatory basis. For example, Bucovetsky (1995) considers the case where native residents are initially endowed with ownership of all land in their jurisdictions. Even if native residents and immigrants earn identical amounts in labour markets and are taxed identically on these earnings, a locality can discriminate between immigrants and native workers by varying the fiscal treatment of land and labour (or other factors).

17. For example, if the economy begins at the *laissez-faire* point A, a system of taxes on immobile factor owners can be used to finance compensatory transfers to workers that preserve their net incomes at the level X_0. However, this would reduce the net incomes of immobile factor owners to the level corresponding to point C, thus necessarily making them worse off, despite the fact that they would receive higher before-tax incomes due to the increased supply of mobile labour.

18. Friar and Leonard (1995) present estimates of net fiscal flows among US states, taking the effect of a number of federal government fiscal instruments into account. These estimates indicate that some states – for instance, Mississippi, a persistently low-income state – are the recipients of net fiscal transfers from the central government, while others – for instance, New Jersey, a persistently high-income state – are net donors. These patterns of net transfers show considerable stability over the decade 1984–94 for which the estimates are made. Many of the states that are estimated to be net fiscal recipients tend to have low levels of redistributive transfers (as indicated, for example, by levels of AFDC (Aid to Families with Dependent Children) benefits) while those that are net fiscal contributors tend to have more extensive redistributive policies. More detailed empirical investigation to see whether there is indeed a positive relationship between the magnitude of local redistribution and net local fiscal contributions to the central government would be of interest.

19. It should also be borne in mind that if labour market arbitrage is effective, it equalizes the *real*, not nominal, returns to labour. Quite aside from migration costs, spatial nominal wage differentials may reflect differentials in the prices of non-traded goods, most notably housing, or differences in congestion costs and local amenities and disamenities. Many hedonic wage models of environmental and other local amenities (see, for example, Rosen, 1986) are indeed premised on the assumption that money wages are *not* expected to converge, but rather should exhibit compensating differentials that reveal implicit valuations of non-market goods such as air quality, crime rates, and the like.

20. There are strong parallels between inequalities due to imperfect spatial arbitrage in labour markets, for instance due to migration costs, and the inequalities that arise due to sluggish adjustment to sectoral shocks. Protection for workers (or other factor owners) from negative quasi-rents appear to play an important role in the political economy of trade policy, privatization, and economic liberalization and reform in general (see, for example, Boadway and Wildasin, 1990, and references therein). For instance, inequalities attributable to costly intersectoral reallocation of labour play a central role in Diamond (1982); Lawrence and Litan (1986) argue specifically for retraining programmes for displaced workers as a policy for dealing with the adverse distributional consequences of trade liberalization, and thus to defuse political opposition to free trade. Job retraining, and education in general, can be viewed as mechanisms of inter-occupational or intersectoral job switching; the cost of retraining, or of education or skill acquisition more generally, can be viewed as the cost of 'migration' between declining and expanding sectors, or between unskilled and skilled job 'locations'. (Sometimes, as in the case of spatially concentrated declining industries like coal mining in Appalachia, sectoral and geographical job switching become thoroughly intertwined.) Much of measured economic inequality is attributable to these costs.

21. As Topel (1986) and others show, young workers are more likely to migrate in response to spatial wage differentials, both because their migration costs are lower and because they have a longer employment horizon over which to reap the benefits of higher earnings.

22.   Decressin and Fatás (1995) compare the role of migration in adjustment to labour market shocks among regions in Europe and the USA, finding in general that migration plays an important role in both cases but that migration responses in the USA are faster than in Europe – adjustments that take one year in the former might take as long as three years in the latter.

23.   The distribution of non-human capital over space and over industrial sectors also adjusts gradually as old capital depreciates and new capital comes on line; intersectoral differentials in Tobin's q (appropriately adjusted for tax and other factors) reflect quasi-rents arising from the short-run sector specificity of capital. Note that labour and capital adjustments are likely to be linked: employment opportunities for workers are likely to expand more rapidly in a region that is attracting capital inflows, and, similarly, rapidly growing labour resources are likely to attract increased capital investment. The dynamics of migration and capital flows should therefore be analysed simultaneously – as for instance in the historical investigations described in Hatton and Williamson (1994). This interdependency gives rise to interesting connections between the fiscal treatment of labour and capital that deserve analytical attention.

24.   Borjas and Hamilton (1996) show that immigrants to the USA differ from the existing population, and among themselves, in these attributes, which are important determinants of the benefits that they receive from AFDC, SSI (Supplemental Security Income), Food Stamps, and other social welfare programmes.

25.   See Johnson and Zimmermann (1993) for discussion of many of the possible economic and fiscal consequences of long-run demographic trends, including population ageing in Europe and the pull that this may exert on migrants from younger and poorer countries. Wildasin (forthcoming) presents some illustrative calculations of net lifetime social security (public pension) wealth for hypothetical workers moving among a set of EU countries, indicating that the changes in social security wealth resulting from intra-EU migration can be as high as 10 per cent of lifetime earnings, depending on the country pairs under consideration. Calculations of this sort cannot really be undertaken meaningfully without taking earnings growth, retirement age, life expectancy, and other life-cycle factors into account, emphasizing the need for long-run dynamic analysis of the implications of migration for these very important redistributive fiscal policies.

References

Asdrubali, P., B.E. Sørensen and O. Yosha (1996) 'Channels of Interstate Risk Sharing: United States 1963–1990', *Quarterly Journal of Economics* vol. 111, pp. 1081–1110.

Atkinson, A.B. (1987) 'Income Maintenance and Social Insurance', in A.J. Auerbach and M.S. Feldstein (eds), *Handbook of Public Economics* (Amsterdam: North-Holland).

Barro, R.J. and X. Sala-i-Martin (1991) 'Convergence Across States and Regions', *Brookings Papers on Economic Activity*, pp. 107–82.

Bhagwati, J.N. and J.D. Wilson (eds) (1989) *Income Taxation and International Mobility* (Cambridge, Mass: MIT Press).

Boadway, R.W. and F.R. Flatters (1982) 'Efficiency and Equalization Payments in a Federal System of Government: A Synthesis and Extension of Recent Results', *Canadian Journal of Economics*, vol. 15, pp. 613–33.

Boadway, R. and M. Keen (1996) 'Efficiency and the Optimal Direction of Federal-State Transfers', *International Tax and Public Finance*, vol. 3, pp. 137–56.

Boadway, R.W. and D.E. Wildasin (1990) 'Optimal Tax-Subsidy Policies for Industrial Adjustment to Uncertain Shocks', *Oxford Economic Papers*, vol. 42, pp. 105–34; reprinted in P.J.N. Sinclair and M.D.E. Slater (eds), *Taxation, Private Information, and Capital* (Oxford: Clarendon Press, 1991) pp. 105–34.

Borjas, G.J. and L. Hilton (1996) 'Immigration and the Welfare State: Immigrant Participation in Means-Tested Entitlement Programs', *Quarterly Journal of Economics*, vol. 111, pp. 575–604.

Borjas, G., R.B. Freeman and L.F. Katz (1996) 'Searching for the Effects of Immigration on the Labor Market', *American Economic Review, Papers and Proceedings*, vol. 86, pp. 246–51.

Bradford, D.F. (1978) 'Factor Prices May Be Constant but Factor Returns Are Not', *Economics Letters*, vol. 1, pp. 199–203.

Brennan, G. and J. Buchanan (1980) *The Power to Tax: Analytical Foundations of a Fiscal Constitution* (Cambridge: Cambridge University Press).

Buchanan, J.M. (1950) 'Federalism and Fiscal Equity', *American Economic Review*, vol. 40, pp. 583–99.

—— (1952) 'Federal Grants and Resource Allocation', *Journal of Political Economy* vol. 60, pp. 208–17.

Bucovetsky, S. (1995) 'Rent Seeking and Tax Competition', *Journal of Public Economics*, vol. 58, pp. 337–64.

Bureau, D. and C. Richard (1997) 'Public Insurance and Mobility: An Exploratory Analysis in the Context of European Economic Unification', *Annales d'Economie et de Statistique*, vol. 45, pp. 275–90.

Carrington, W.J., E. Detragiache and T. Vishwanath (1996) 'Migration with Endogenous Moving Costs', *American Economic Review*, vol. 86, pp. 909–30.

Cremer, H., V. Fourgeaud, M.L. Monterio, M. Marchand and P. Pestieau (1995) 'Mobility and Redistribution: A Survey', unpublished.

Cremer, H. and P. Pestieau (1996a) 'Distributive Implications of European Integration', *European Economic Review*, vol. 40, pp. 747–57.

Cremer, H. and P. Pestieau (1996b) 'Social Insurance and Labor Mobility: A Political Economy Approach', unpublished.

Crémer, J. and T. Palfrey (1996) 'In or Out? Centralization by Majority Vote', *European Economic Review*, vol. 40, pp. 43–60.

Decressin, J. and A. Fatás (1995) 'Regional Labor Market Dynamics in Europe', *European Economic Review*, vol. 39, pp. 1627–55.

Diamond, P.A. (1982) 'Protection, Trade Adjustment Assistance, and Income Distribution', in J.N. Bhagwati (ed.), *Import Competition and Response* (Chicago, Ill: University of Chicago Press) pp. 123–45.

Dixit, A.K. and R.S. Pindyck (1994) *Investment under Uncertainty* (Princeton, NJ: Princeton University Press).

Domar, E.D. and R.A. Musgrave (1944) 'Proportional Income Taxation and Risk Taking', *Quarterly Journal of Economics*, vol. 58, pp. 387–422.

Epple, D. and T. Romer (1991) 'Mobility and Redistribution', *Journal of Political Economy*, vol. 99, pp. 828–58.

Friar, M.E. and H.B. Leonard (1995) *The Federal Budget and the States: Fiscal Year 1994* (Cambridge, Mass.: Alfred Taubman Center for State and Local Government).

Frenkel, J.A., A. Razin and E. Sadka (1991) *International Taxation in an Integrated World* (Cambridge, Mass.: MIT Press).

Goodspeed, T.J. (1995) 'Local Income Taxation: An Externality, Pigouvian Solution, and Public Policies', *Regional Science and Urban Economics*, vol. 25, pp. 279–96.

Hamilton, B.W. (1975) 'Zoning and Property Taxation in a System of Local Governments', *Urban Studies*, vol. 12, pp. 205–11.

Hamilton, B. and J. Whalley (1984) 'Efficiency and Distributional Implications of Global Restrictions on Labour Mobility: Calculations and Policy Implications', *Journal of Development Economics*, vol. 14, pp. 61–75.

Harberger, A.C. (1962) 'The Incidence of the Corporation Income Tax', *Journal of Political Economy*, vol. 70, pp. 215–40.

Hatton, T.J. and J.G. Williamson (1994) 'International Migration 1850–1939; An Economic Survey', in T.J. Hatton and J.G. Williamson (eds), *Migration and the International Labor Market 1850–1939* (London: Routledge) pp. 3–54.

Helliwell, J.F. (1996) 'Convergence and Migration Among Provinces', *Canadian Journal of Economics*, vol. 29, pp. S324–S330.

Inman, R.P. and D.L. Rubinfeld (1979) 'The Judicial Pursuit of Local Fiscal Equity', *Harvard Law Review*, vol. 92, pp. 1662–1750.

Janeba, E. and H. Raff (1995) 'Voting with Your Hand and Feet', presented at ISPE conference on 'Distributional Aspects of Fiscal Policy: The Implications of Economic Integration', University of Essex.

Johnson, P. and K. Zimmermann (1993) 'Ageing and the European Labor Market: Public Policy Issues', in P. Johnson and K. Zimmermann (eds), *Labour Markets in an Ageing Europe* (New York: Cambridge University Press) pp. 1–25.

Krugman, P. (1991) *Geography and Trade* (Cambridge, Mass.: MIT Press.

Ladd, H.F. and J. Yinger (1994) 'The Case for Equalizing Aid', *National Tax Journal*, vol. 47, pp. 211–24.

Lawrence, R.Z. and R.E. Litan (1986) *Saving Free Trade* (Washington, DC: The Brookings Institution).

Mieszkowski, P. (1972) 'The Property Tax: An Excise Tax or a Profits Tax?' *Journal of Public Economics*, vol. 1, pp. 73–96.

—— (1979) 'Recent Trends in Urban and Regional Development', in P. Miesz Kowski and M. Straszheim (eds), *Current Issues in Urban Economics* (Baltimore, Md: Johns Hopkins University Press).

Mieszkowski, P. and G. Zodrow (1989) 'Taxation and the Tiebout Model', *Journal of Economic Literature*, vol. 27, pp. 1098–1146.

Mills, E.S. and B.W. Hamilton (1984) *Urban Economics*, 3rd edn (Glenview, Illinois: Scott Foresman).

Musgrave, R.A. (1971) 'Economics of Fiscal Federalism', *Nebraska Journal of Economics and Business*, vol. 10, pp. 3–13.

Oakland, W.H. (1994) 'Fiscal Equalization: An Empty Box?' *National Tax Journal*, vol. 47, pp. 199–210.

Oates, W.E. (1968) The Theory of Public Finance in a Federal System', *Canadian Journal of Economics*, vol. 1, pp. 37–54.

—— (1972) *Fiscal Federalism* (New York: Harcourt Brace Jovanovich).

Pauly, Mark V. (1993) 'Income Redistribution as a Local Public Good', *Journal of Public Economics*, vol. 2, pp. 35–58.

Persson, T. and Tabellini, G. (1996) 'Federal Fiscal Constitutions: Part I: Risk Sharing and Moral Hazard', *Econometrica*, vol. 64, pp. 623–46.

Peterson, P.E. and M.C. Rom (1990) *Welfare Magnets: A New Case for a National Standard* (Washington, DC: The Brookings Institution).

Piketty, T. (1996) 'A Federal Voting Mechanism to Solve the Fiscal-Externality Problem', *European Economic Review*, vol. 40, pp. 3–18.

Reschovsky, A. (1994) 'Fiscal Equalization and School Finance', *National Tax Journal*, vol. 47, pp. 185–98.

Rosen, S. (1986) 'The Theory of Equalizing Differences', in O.C. Ashenfelter and R. Layard (eds), *Handbook of Labor Economics*, vol. 1 (Amsterdam: North-Holland) pp. 641–92.

Rubinfeld, D.L. (1987) 'The Economics of the Local Public Sector', in A.J. Auerbach and M. Feldstein (eds), Handbook of Public Economics (Amsterdam: North Holland) pp. 571–645.

Sandmo, A. and D.E. Wildasin (1994) 'Taxation, Migration, and Pollution', Norwegian School of Economics and Business Administration, Institute of Economics Discussion Paper No. 3/94; Vanderbilt University Working Paper No. 94–W02.

Schiff, M. (1996) 'South–North Migration and Trade: A Survey', World Bank, International Economics Department, unpublished.

Shapiro, P. and J. Petchey (1994) 'Secession and the Median Voter', presented at ISPE conference on 'Fiscal Aspects of Evolving Federations', Vanderbilt University.

Sinn, G. and H.-W. Sinn (1992) *Jumpstart: The Economic Unification of Germany* (Cambridge, Mass.: MIT Press).

Sinn, H.-W. (1995) 'A Theory of the Welfare State', *Scandinavian Journal of Economics*, vol. 97, pp. 495–526.

—— 'Social Insurance, Incentives and Risk Taking', this volume.

Sørensen, B. and O. Yosha (1996) 'Income and Consumption Smoothing among US States: Regions or Clubs?' unpublished.

Stigler, G.J. (1957) 'The Tenable Range of Functions of Local Government', Joint Economic Committee, *Federal Expenditure Policy for Economic Growth and Stability*, reprinted in E.S. Phelps (ed.), *Private Wants and Public Needs*, revised edn. (New York: Norton, 1965), pp. 167–76.

Tanzi, V. (1995) *Taxation in an Integrating World* (Washington, DC: The Brookings Institution).

Topel, R.H. (1986) 'Local Labor Markets', *Journal of Political Economy*, vol. 94, Part 2, pp. 111–43.

—— (1991) 'Specific Capital, Mobility, and Wages: Wages Rise with Job Seniority', *Journal of Political Economy*, vol. 99, pp. 145–76.

Topel, R.H. and M.P. Ward (1992) 'Job Mobility and the Careers of Young Men', *Quarterly Journal of Economics*, vol. 107, pp. 439–80.

Varian, H. (1980) 'Redistributive Taxation as Social Insurance', *Journal of Public Economics* vol. 14, pp. 49–68.

Wellisch, D. (1996) 'A Theory of Local and Regional Public Finance', unpublished.

Wellisch, D. and D.E. Wildasin (1996) 'Decentralized Income Redistribution and Immigration', *European Economic Review*, vol. 40, pp. 187–217.

Wildasin, D.E. (1986) *Urban Public Finance* (New York: Harwood Academic Publishers).

—— (1987) 'Theoretical Analysis of Local Public Economics', in E.S. Mills (ed.) *Handbook of Urban and Regional Economics*, vol. 2 (Amsterdam: North Holland) pp. 429–76.

—— (1991) 'Income Redistribution in a Common Labor Market', *American Economic Review*, vol. 81, pp. 757–74.

Wildasin, D.E. (1992) 'Relaxation of Barriers to Factor Mobility and Income Redistribution', in P. Pestieau (ed.), *Public Finance in a World of Transition*, supplement to *Public Finance/Finances Publiques*, vol. 47, pp. 216–30.

Wildasin, D.E. (1994) 'Income Redistribution and Migration', *Canadian Journal of Economics*, vol. 27, pp. 637–56.

Wildasin, D.E. (1995) 'Factor Mobility, Risk, and Redistribution in the Welfare State', *Scandinavian Journal of Economics*, vol. 97, pp. 527–46; an expanded version of this paper is to appear as 'Factor Mobility, Risk, Inequality, and Redistribution', in D. Pines, E. Sadka, and I. Zilcha (eds), *Topics in Public Economics* (Cambridge: Cambridge University Press).

Wildasin, D.E. (1996) 'Labor Market Integration, Investment in Risky Human Capital, and Fiscal Competition', unpublished.

Wildasin, D.E. (1997) 'Income Distribution and Redistribution in Federations', *Annales d'Economie et de Statistique*, vol. 45, pp. 291–313.

Wildasin, D.E. (forthcoming) 'Public Pensions in the EU: Migration Incentives and Impacts', in A. Panagariya, R.R. Portney, and R.M. Schwab (eds), *Environmental Economics and Public Policy: Essays in Honour of Wallace E. Oates* (Cheltenham: Edward Elgar).

World Bank (1995) *China: Macroeconomic Stability in a Decentralizing Economy* (Washington, DC: The World Bank).

7 Theory and Practice of Confederate Finances

Dubravko Mihaljek*

I INTRODUCTION

Recent coalescing and splintering movements in Europe and other parts of the world have highlighted the importance of political and constitutional constraints on the design of interjurisdictional fiscal arrangements, and challenged public finance analysts to understand why it is that nations enter or leave such arrangements. In an attempt to address these important issues, this chapter looks at the historical experiences of confederations – that is, structures in which the 'federal' government is subordinate to 'lower-level' governments – and at the key issues that arise in the design of fiscal arrangements within confederations.

Confederations appeared on the historical scene long before the federations and they usually evolved into federations or disintegrated into independent states. As a result of these historical mutations, confederations have often been described as inherently unstable.[1] A review of historical experiences (Section II) suggests, however, that the financial strains that confederations had experienced in the past had more to do with their weak economic fundamentals and inadequate macroeconomic policies than the confederate structure of intergovernmental relations.

The historical experiences provide a useful framework for discussing how confederations differ from federations (Section III) and clarifying their economic rationale (Section IV). More generally, these experiences provide valuable insights for understanding whether confederations could become a useful model around which countries could build intergovernmental relations in the future. The chapter argues that confederations have two major advantages over federations. First, member states can exercise independent powers in all the key areas of sovereignty – political, legal, and economic. Second, confederations enable member states to reap the

* The views expressed are those of the author and do not necessarily represent those of the IMF. I am grateful to Bev Dahlby and an anonymous referee for insightful comments.

benefits of economic integration without imposing on them the tight policy strictures and institutional requirements that federal-type fiscal structures normally impose.

In discussing the design of confederate fiscal arrangements (Section V), the chapter focuses on the importance of constraints such as reservation of powers over distributional policies to member states. The traditional theory (Musgrave, 1959, 1983; Oates, 1972) has largely ignored such political and constitutional constraints by assuming that the central authority could overrule conflicts over policy between members of a federation, or that the federal constitutions could be easily adapted to fit in with the policy norms derived from economic arguments. The chapter therefore draws on the non-traditional theory (Scott, 1964; Wiseman, 1965; Dafflon, 1977; Breton and Scott, 1978), which has recognized that certain constraints on public policies could not be waived by assuming a centralist structure of intergovernmental relations.

With regard to regional redistribution, the chapter argues that, since regional policy diversity is likely to be considered a virtue of confederations, redistribution functions should be assigned to member states. Nevertheless, it may be necessary (and desirable) to establish a system of interregional transfers to prevent the emergence (or widening) of disruptive differences in regional economic performance.

With regard to stabilization function, the chapter argues that coordination of fiscal policies offers greater advantages to confederate states than either rules-based or centralized fiscal policy. Institutionalized procedures for coordination proposed in the non-traditional fiscal federalism literature are likely to overcome the weaknesses that had led to macroeconomic instability in some historical cases of 'cooperative federalism', and offer greater potential for efficient fiscal stabilization policy than a centralized system of stabilizing fiscal transfers to regional economies.

With main policy functions assigned to member states, and the scope of joint confederate activities being small, issues of expenditure and tax assignment become relatively simple. The chapter argues that flexible forms of expenditure provision, such as regional cooperation agreements covering regions belonging to different states, provide an efficient way of organizing provision of many public goods and services that do not have distributional content. On the issue of tax assignment, it is argued that considerations of benefits and costs of tax competition suggest that, with properly functioning factor and commodity markets, tax competition is likely to bring about a gradual convergence of the tax burdens, so there would be no need for confederations to insist on tax harmonization.

The chapter concludes with a brief summary of the main conclusions (Section VI).

II HISTORICAL EXPERIENCES

As noted above, confederations are historically much older than federations. Among the oldest known confederations were amphictyonies in ancient Greece, the leagues of states united for mutual protection and the worship of a common deity.[2] Modern federations that evolved from confederations often bear the marks of their confederate past. This section briefly describes five historical episodes of confederate finances: the Confederate States of America (1777–89), Switzerland (1815–48), Germany (1871–1919), the former Yugoslavia (1972–90), and China (1988–93). The focus is on the functioning rather than design of confederate finances. The five cases were chosen because they show a variety of possible evolutionary paths: from the rather decentralized federations (Switzerland and the United States) or the relatively centralized (in tax terms) federations (Germany) to independent states (former Yugoslavia) or to a 'recentralized' unitary state (China).[3] Some implications of these experiences for the newly emerging confederations are discussed in the concluding subsection.

Confederate States of America, 1777–89

Under the 1777 Articles of Confederation, the only financial power given to the central government was the printing of paper money, the so-called 'Continentals'. The Congress had not been granted tax powers by which it might meet appropriations or pay off borrowings and bills of credit; instead, the funds to cover Confederation expenditures were to be obtained by requisitions on the states in proportion to the values of their lands and improvements (Schultz and Caine, 1937). This rule was never operative because an appraisal of land values was impracticable during the war of 1775–83, so the Congress tried to make population the standard, basing each state's quota of requisitions on the estimated number of its inhabitants. The Articles of Confederation also failed to provide a mechanism to compel the states to comply with their obligation. As a result, the settlement of accounts gave rise to conflicts of interest in which no state could realize its own advantage without conceding something to the others. Despite the hostility towards central taxation, the pressure of circumstances forced the state representatives to become advocates of a central tax system. But the unanimous consent necessary to effect the proposal for such a system was elusive. Every time, one state or another would jealously fight to protect its financial autonomy.

During this period, the borrowing requirement of the Confederation was sharply increasing and the Congress accumulated substantial arrears of pay owed to the soldiers of the Revolutionary Army. Although the Congress had the power to borrow the funds, there was no one in America who would willingly lend to it (Bullock, 1895). Many creditors, though, had no choice, and were forced to accept the Revolutionary Debt Obligations. When interest on these bonds came due, the holders had to accept *indents*, promises to pay at an uncertain time in the future, when and if the government became solvent. Speculators willing to take the chance that the Congress might eventually pay off its debts fully bought up indents at heavy discount and soon held a large part of the national debt.[4] Besides the Treasury, many individuals were in debt as well. As a result of political unrest, the states had stirred up public discussion of the issuing of paper money, and seven of the states authorized new emissions (Dewey, 1934). In 1786, the national financial system broke down completely. Further borrowing at home or abroad was almost impossible, requisitions were of almost no avail, creditors became alarmed, and when the efforts to secure unanimous consent for a national tax failed, it was agreed that, if a federated republic were to continue, the government, particularly in relation to finance and commerce, must be remodelled. This agreement paved the way for the Convention of 1787, which framed a new Constitution that became effective in March 1789.

Federal powers were greatly enhanced in the new Constitution. The Congress received the power 'to lay and collect taxes, duties, imposts and excises, to pay the debts and provide for the common defense and general welfare of the United States', subject to the proviso that 'all duties, imposts, and excises shall be uniform throughout the United States'. These changes at once began to bring in badly needed revenue and soon the debts of the Confederation were repaid.

Despite these vigorous steps, the divisive forces latent in the new federalism revived during the next sixty years. Geographic expansion had brought into the Union new states with diverse interests. In addition, the old cleavage between the North and the South had deepened with the spread of cotton and slavery. Most statesmen came to believe that national functions should be held to a minimum in order to preserve the Union. The sectional rift deepened until the nation drifted into the Civil War, which settled the issue of national supremacy by force. The victorious side imposed its view that the 'Union was not a compact among the states; the national government was entitled to enforce its constitutional decisions in the face of state objections' (Aronson and Hilley, 1986, p. 12).

Switzerland, 1815–48

Throughout its history, Switzerland has experienced cycles of confederatism and federalism. After the fall of Napoleon in 1815, Switzerland became once again a loose confederacy of sovereign states. The number of cantons was brought to twenty-two; each canton had one deputy and one vote in the Swiss Diet; and the status of head canton rotated biannually between Bern, Lucerne and Zurich. A Federal Chancellery, associated with the head canton, was the only permanent organ of the Confederation. The Diet was granted control of foreign affairs, of cantonal troop contingents, and of the special war fund to which the cantons contributed (Boczek, 1976; Codding, 1961).

The tax system of individual cantons included customs duties, salt monopolies, manorial levies and some indirect taxes of the old Helvetic Republic. Because the cantons were sovereign states, they were divided by customs barriers. The few expenses which the Confederation was required to bear were covered by the customs duties of the border cantons, interest from the war fund and cantonal contributions. The contributions were calculated on the basis of fiscal capacity keys, which included population and simple measures of taxable resources. This system brought about financial consolidation, but internal trade constraints resulting from the sovereignty of cantons in such areas as customs duties and road tolls soon became obstacles to faster economic development; these obstacles were particularly severe given that Switzerland was poor in natural resources.

The weakness of the financial system also manifested itself in the growing feeling of insecurity, both internal and external. Many citizens disliked the constant interference of foreign powers in Swiss internal affairs, but realized that the strength to resist it did not exist. Together with economic stagnation, these events shaped the forces that put in place the new Constitution of 1848, when Switzerland's present system of government was essentially established. The Constitution allocated to the federal government much broader revenue powers, including the interest from the federal war fund, customs duties, post office revenue, gunpowder monopoly revenue, and contributions from cantons, which were collected only once, in 1849. These revenue sources proved quite sufficient to meet the needs of the Confederation until the First World War. The customs duties were especially profitable, accounting for about 75 per cent of total federal revenues, and allowing the federal government to grant subsidies to the cantons, which absorbed 25 per cent of federal revenues in 1913.

Although most of the subsequent changes of the Constitution augmented the powers of the centre, Swiss cantons remained essentially superordinate to the federal government. Centuries-old traditions of cantonal independence, ethnic and cultural diversity, and the practice of direct democracy were too strong to be overcome by the central government.

Germany, 1871–1919

The first step in creating a confederation of German states was taken with the formation of the Customs Union in 1834, when the participating states agreed to abolish interstate customs duties, establish a uniform external tariff, and form a joint tariff-collection authority. The entire amount of tariffs collected was returned to the states on a per capita basis; the few occasional losses were soon offset by the growing foreign trade (Newcomer, 1937). Other uniform taxes were added to the customs duties in later years (on beet sugar, salt and tobacco) and were also distributed to the states on a per capita basis. Gradually, the states had given up their shares in tariffs and excises in return for the Reich's assumption of the cost of national defence.

The Constitution of 1871 envisaged four main revenue sources for the Reich: customs duties, consumption taxes, revenue from the postal and telegraph services, and state contributions (*Matrikularbeiträge*).[5] Article 70 of the 1871 Constitution established under the *Miquel Clause* that 'In so far as the [the Reich's expenditures] cannot be provided by these revenues, they are, as long as Imperial taxes are not introduced, to be met by contributions from the single States of the Confederation, in proportion to their population, which contributions will be assessed by the Chancellor of the Empire' (Putkammer, 1955, p. 145).[6] The financial powers of the Reich were thus greatly enhanced, an implication which did not escape the attention of the states. As the fiscal position of the Reich grew stronger, the states succeeded in putting into the 1879 Tariff Law a provision that 'those proceeds of the tariffs and the tobacco tax, which in any year exceed a certain amount [130 million reichsmarks] are to be assigned to individual States in proportion to their population' (ibid., p. 145). Under this famous *Franckensteinsche Clause*, the Reich had effectively agreed to renounce its latent taxing powers, and, as the Chancellor put it, to 'beg at the doors of the individual States' (Adarkar, 1933, p. 85).

Between 1879 and 1899, the Reich had received a net contribution from the states in six years and had made a net contribution to the states in fourteen years. While this system simplified the balancing of the imperial budget and in the long run benefited the states, the states could never tell beforehand exactly how much was coming into their treasuries. The *Matrikularbeiträge* had to be paid in advance each month, while the surplus assignments were paid out each quarter, so that the set-off was not perfect in point of time. Moreover, there was no constitutional obligation for the payment of the surplus assignments, as there was for the payment of contributions. Such an arrangement quickly developed into a sort of 'market-day higgle-haggling, each side trying to get something for nothing from the other' (Adarkar, 1933, p. 85).

The financial position of the states would still have remained relatively strong were it not for the rapid increase in the Reich's expenditures on armaments in the 1890s. The imperial surpluses distributed to the states gave way to increasing deficits, which were once more met by net requisitions on the states. Public debt grew rapidly, from 218 million reichsmarks in 1880 to 2182 million reichsmarks in 1898, in spite of the very negative perception of deficit financing at that time. The decline in the importance of the *Matrikularbeiträge* after 1903 did not diminish some of their negative effects. The budgetary procedure continued to depend on the amount of transfers, and if they were insufficient, the balance had to be financed by borrowing.

Yugoslavia, 1972–90

Confederate fiscal arrangements in the former Yugoslavia had their origins in the nationalist movements that took place in 1968–72.[7] In 1968, a power vacuum was felt in central organs of the communist party. At the same time, party organizations in individual republics had become virtually autonomous and some of their leaders were eager to be seen as defenders of the interests of their republic against what was perceived as the attempts at exploitation or domination by other republics. There was little possibility of dealing with economic issues at the republic level because key monetary and fiscal instruments, especially turnover and capital taxes, remained in the hands of the immobilized federal administration. The power of regional authorities was thus almost entirely negative: they could veto federal proposals but they could not implement policies of their own. Of the three possible solutions to the stalemate – recentralization, radical decentralization, and decentralization with an inter-republic consensus mechanism – the second temporarily prevailed, thus opening the view towards a loose confederation.

Although central party organs subsequently reasserted strict control over republic parties on the basis of the principle of 'democratic centralism', some of the more radical demands voiced by republic leaderships in the late 1960s ultimately also found their expression in the 1974 Constitution. Because the nationality question was the central constitutional problem and the economic system its most important aspect, the realization of economic sovereignty of nations became the leading principle of the new federal order. This implied control by the republics of all key aspects of economic life, including investment, credit policy, public spending and revenues, and foreign exchange allocation. As a result, it was no longer possible to maintain a model of federation in which the federal government had supremacy over republics in deciding on important economic issues. Instead, the federal government could only perform the 'joint functions' of federation, that is, those functions that had been explicitly delegated to it by sovereign republics. The 1974 Constitution also confirmed the right of republics to secede from the federation, introduced in the first constitution of 1946. Thus, the third constitutional model – decentralization with inter-republic consensus mechanism – had eventually prevailed.

The new concept of federalism implied that the number of fiscal issues about which republics could quarrel at the federal level ought to be minimized. The federal budget only provided for defence, federal administration and supplementary development grants, which together accounted for one-sixth of total public spending.[8] The federal government had only one own revenue source (tariffs); it shared with republics the proceeds of the federal sales tax; and received contributions from the republics. In principle, the apportioning of contributions was determined by the republics' shares in gross social product, and sales tax shares by the republics' shares in total sales. In practice, the allotment of contributions and sales tax shares was decided in annual budget negotiations between republics and the federal government. Republics levied their own sales taxes on the tax base determined by the federal government and controlled excises, enterprise income taxes, social security contributions and part of the wage tax. Local governments also enjoyed considerable taxation powers, including wage and personal income taxes, taxes on property and local sales taxes.

As with contributions of member countries to international organizations, republics viewed their contributions as the payment for services offered by the federation. During protracted budget negotiations, the federal government frequently had to borrow. While republics would eventually transfer the amounts necessary to balance the budget, federal borrowing had crowding-out and inflationary effects. As a result of these difficulties, the composition of federal revenue sources had changed considerably over time. The share of contributions in federal revenue declined from about 40 per cent in 1982 to 6 per cent in 1990. In the same period, the share of tariffs more than doubled, while the share of the sales tax increased by a quarter.

Because of the apparent absence of deficits at the federal level, the reform of public finances was never considered a pressing macroeconomic issue. The system functioned relatively smoothly as long as the dominant position of the communist party ensured the minimum amount of trust between the republics and the federation. Political developments that took place in 1989 and 1990 disproved the expectation that such trust could be established in a post-communist environment. In economic terms, two challenges faced the old federation. First, it was not clear that there was a surplus from the integration of six republics and two autonomous provinces into the Yugoslav economic system. Second, to the extent that this surplus existed, all members of the federation argued that it was not distributed in a way acceptable to them.

China, 1988–93

Although China is a unitary state, during the 1980s a system of intergovernmental contracts with strong confederate overtones had evolved.[9] The central government controlled all tax legislative powers, but tax assignment and revenue-sharing arrangements were to a large extent negotiated with local governments. Revenue from certain taxes was designated as 'central fixed revenue' and a portion of revenue from other taxes as 'local fixed revenue', with the remainder going into a pool of shared revenue. 'Fixed' shared revenue was split according to some fixed proportion, while most shared revenue was split according to formulae stipulated in fiscal contracts between the central and local governments. The contracts typically fixed revenue transfers with respect to a base year, with annual increments agreed upon *ex ante*. The bulk of tax collection was undertaken by local governments, as the central government in China did not have nationwide tax administration until 1994. The central government also devolved considerable expenditure responsibilities to local governments.

The results of fiscal contracting with provinces were mixed. There was a vertical fiscal deficit at the central level of about 2 per cent of GDP in 1985–88, and a small but diminishing vertical surplus during 1989–92. The amounts transferred to the central government from 1989 on were entirely redistributed to the provinces, and the central government made additional transfers from its own resources. The contracting system thus provided a mechanism for redistributing fiscal resources from surplus to deficit provinces. As discussed below, this process proved to be very difficult to manage smoothly, and at times the central or local government finances were disrupted. On balance, given the central government's steadily declining share in total revenue and the generally rapid regional growth and development, it seems that contracting had affected the central fisc more negatively than the local ones.

Given the fiscal-contracting arrangements and the local management of tax administration, local authorities had an incentive to concentrate on the local tax bases and, as far as possible, shift the tax bases from those that had to be shared with the central government to those over which they had greater control. This involved promoting the growth of locally owned enterprises and granting generous tax reductions and exemptions in respect of indirect taxes (which had to be shared with the central government). The resources thus 'saved' could then be retained by local enterprises as extra-budgetary funds that local governments could tap for local projects that they favoured. Thus, although tax policy was nominally set by the central government, local governments effectively controlled the total revenue take. This practically severed the link between tax policy set at the central level and collections at the local level.

Fiscal contracting also exerted a strong expansionary bias. As the multi-year contracts fixed the central government revenue for an extended period, central government revenue responded more quickly. When the local economy expanded, local tax revenue was boosted. As only a relatively small portion of additional revenue had to be shared with the central government, local spending tended to increase in periods of economic expansion, thus increasing the risk of overheating. The threat of macroeconomic instability could not restrain local spending plans because local governments did not have macroeconomic management responsibilities. Also, given the design of fiscal contracts, local governments that accumulated budgetary surpluses could worsen their bargaining position with the central government in negotiations for subsequent contracts.[10] Finally, fiscal contracting may have also contributed to the widening of regional disparities and emergence of regional protectionism.[11]

In response to these developments, in 1994 the central government began replacing the complex contract-based intergovernmental revenue system with a more transparent delineation of revenue sources for the central and local governments.[12] In addition, the National Tax Service was established to collect all central and shared taxes. The overall objective of these reforms is to raise the central government's share of total revenue and thereby enhance its macroeconomic capabilities; on the structural side, one of the objectives is to enable the central government to reduce regional fiscal disparities through grants. In order to avoid disrupting local government finances and facilitate the formation of a consensus on the reform programme, agreements were reached to phase in the new revenue-sharing system over several years.

Evaluation of Historical Experiences

The financial problems of the early confederations – the Confederate States of America, Switzerland, and Germany – were due to a variety of historically specific factors. In the Confederate States, much of the trouble derived from the disturbances of war, which were compounded by poor tax administration and the absence of a mechanism for collection of state contributions. But, as many economic historians have observed, it would be a mistake to conclude that the Confederate States were drifting toward ruin: at its heart, the country was economically sound, and relatively simple measures were sufficient to strengthen its finances. In Switzerland, the weaknesses of the financial system derived primarily from foreign interference and the need to raise revenue through customs duties and road and bridge taxes, generally the only tax bases available at the time. Thus, it would be wrong to argue that the trade barriers between cantons were erected because of confederate finances. Similarly, it would be wrong to attribute the problems of German public finances to the disproportionate financial power of the *Länder*. The states paid their contributions regularly and the central tax administration was sufficiently developed for the central government to collect a reasonable slack in revenues. The problem was clearly in the unrestrained military expenditure of the central government, which would have continued to plague German public finances even if the *Matrikularbeiträge* had been replaced by taxes. The problems that had led to the evolution of these confederations into federal states have become less important today due to better tax systems, more abundant revenue sources, and globalization of economic activity. Thus, one cannot conclude from these early experiences that confederations are inherently unstable.

The more recent episodes of confederate finances – the former Yugoslavia and China – are perhaps more instructive as an aid to thinking about the design of fiscal arrangements in future confederations. While not necessarily contributing to macroeconomic instability, the arrangements such as the reverse transfers, intergovernmental contracts, and the need for consensus on, or coordination of, fiscal policies and budgetary procedures unavoidably complicate macroeconomic policy-making. In the former

Yugoslavia and China, the basic macroeconomic policy infrastructure was not sufficiently developed to accommodate such complications. As a result, confederate arrangements led to negative spillovers of local policies, both vertically (by undermining macroeconomic management capabilities of the central government) and horizontally (by reducing allocative efficiency within a common economic space). Future confederations are likely to have a stronger infrastructure, necessary for indirect macroeconomic management, and fewer allocative distortions overall, and, hence, may be better equipped to cope with such spillover effects. However, as argued in Section V, the complications arising from policy coordination will continue to pose a major challenge for the design of confederate finances.

The Yugoslav experience is also instructive for two other reasons. First, it suggests that welfare surpluses from the integration of dissimilar regions into a common economic and political space cannot be taken for granted – however elaborate, the arguments on gains from economies of integration may be too simplistic when applied in practice. Second, this experience suggests that economic efficiency is not necessarily the most important dimension of public policy-making or of citizens' welfare – countries may sacrifice economic well-being to a certain extent, but not necessarily the political and legal sovereignty. This suggests an important role for constitutions and the right of secession as mutual insurance against negative-sum economic and social outcomes in confederations.

III   WHAT MAKES CONFEDERATIONS DIFFERENT?

In order to understand why there has been a resurgence of interest in unification and partition movements among countries and regions in recent years, it is important to clarify what it is that makes confederations different from federations. The above discussion has demonstrated that confederations cannot be neatly separated from federations. The political, constitutional and economic aspects of confederate and federal arrangements intersect and contain many joint elements. Nevertheless, some important differences can be discerned.

Political science literature has identified two underlying philosophies of federalism: federalism as 'the method of dividing powers so that the general and regional governments are each, within a sphere, co-ordinate and independent' (Wheare, 1963, p. 10); and federalism based on 'the principle of the general government being subordinate to the regional governments and dependent upon them' (ibid., p. 4). The first approach is embodied in the United States Constitution of 1787. The second approach is embodied in the Articles of Confederation of 1777, the Swiss

Constitution of 1848, the Constitution of the German Empire of 1867–1919, and, to a certain extent, the Yugoslav Constitution of 1974.[13] This approach typifies what is commonly referred to as a *confederation*, an alliance of sovereign states united to pursue some joint action such as defence or free trade (in German, *der Staatenbund*), the alliance of states, as opposed to *der Bundesstaat*, the federal state).

From the legal point of view, members of a confederation are completely separate subjects of international law, entering into association by international compact, and thus they cannot be subjected to a supra-state legal regime which would be expressed in a constitutional act characteristic of federal states (Pajić, 1991).[14] From the political point of view, the main difference is that member states of a confederation retain their own sovereignty and delegate only certain powers to the joint bodies, whereas in federations the central authority delegates powers to member states. In addition, members of a confederation retain the right to disengage themselves from the associative arrangement at their own will (King, 1982).[15] With regard to economic relations, member states of a confederation can set up, as well as enter or leave of their own will, any of a number of different forms of economic association: a free trade area, a customs union, a common market, or an economic union. In a federation, however, member states are basically forced to adopt the common associative arrangement, normally a currency union, the most integrated form of economic union.[16]

To conclude, what makes confederations different from federations – and, hence, attractive as a model around which countries may want to build their relations – is that member states of a confederation can exercise independent powers in all the key areas of sovereignty: political, legal, and economic. Members of a federation may exercise powers in some – but not all – of these areas concurrently. Historical experiences suggest that countries are often willing to relinquish certain economic powers to the joint authorities, but are reluctant to do so with respect to their political and constitutional rights. In what follows, it will be therefore assumed that members of a confederation have a lexicographic ordering of preferences over different aspects of sovereignty, placing the highest value on the political and constitutional sovereignty, while being prepared to give up certain economic powers to the joint bodies.

IV ECONOMIC RATIONALE FOR CONFEDERATIONS

In the traditional fiscal federalism literature, the question about the rationale for federal-type fiscal structures (or multilevel government more generally) has been typically posed as a question about why government intervention should take place at a decentralized level. In thinking about the rationale for confederate arrangements, the natural question to ask is why countries and regions should enter (or leave) such arrangements. At the theoretical level, there seem to be two main groups of motives to form confederations: the insurance motives and the standard integrationist motives.

In broad terms, countries will consider entering a confederation if the act of confederating is potentially Pareto-improving for their citizens.[17] How to evaluate a potential Pareto improvement is, of course, a complicated issue. Because such evaluations have to be made behind a Rawlsian 'veil of ignorance' about the future relative position of countries, one of the key issues that has to be addressed initially is mutual insurance against *ex post* bad outcomes. A major motive to enter a confederation may thus be credible promise (embedded, for example, in the joint constitution) that *ex post* 'lucky' states will help out those that experience a decline in their relative income position.[18] Another crucial constitutional provision is the right of secession, which may be seen as insurance against potentially catastrophic political and economic risks of the union.[19] These mutual insurance arguments have been largely neglected in the literature.[20]

The integrationist arguments have been elaborated mainly in the literature on the formation of optimum currency areas, and, to a lesser extent, in the public finance and transition economies literature. According to the standard argument on optimum currency areas, economic integration leads to more rational use of resources, an expanded set of consumer choice, greater likelihood of effective competition, and a larger area over which resources can move freely in response to changing economic conditions. Additional benefits can be derived in a currency union, because the adoption of a single currency eliminates the recourse to an inflation tax, thus making the costs of government activity more transparent and forcing governments to manage their debt prudently.[21] The literature on currency unions has also identified factors promoting the formation of such unions, including: (1) openness, industrial diversification among member countries or regions, and interdependence of regional economies; (2) labour and capital mobility; and (3) wage and price flexibility.[22] These factors are relevant when considering the costs of integration and, hence, the extent to which countries may be willing to integrate their policies. Thus, incentives to form a monetary union are small if countries or regions have relatively closed economies (as measured by the size of the non-traded goods sector); their economies are not diversified; and the volume of mutual trade is small. Under these conditions, there are potentially large gains from independent exchange rate changes, so fixing the exchange rate could result in welfare losses for some members of the union.[23]

From the perspective of the public finance literature, the costs of monetary union depend to a large extent on the need for countries to rely on an inflation tax. Different countries have different tax collection costs and different black market sectors; they also have different preferences with respect to the mix of taxes and the size of their government. In countries where the costs of collecting conventional taxes are relatively high and tax evasion is widespread, it is probably optimal to implement higher rates of inflation than would obtain in a monetary union (Rebelo, 1994). A recent strand of the public finance literature has focused on the role of country size in strategic tax design. While similarity in terms of size might point to greater ease of coordination (and, hence, the gains from integration), dissimilarity may imply greater gains from eliminating tax coordination (that is, pursuing non-cooperative behaviour).[24]

Additional considerations on the costs of integration apply in the case of transition economies, including: the need for strong and accepted administrative leadership; the significant differences in the degree of economic, human capital and institutional development; the need to experiment with different approaches to the transition problem; and mixed experience with past integration efforts (Gros, 1991; Palei and Petr, 1992). For many economies in transition, a careful evaluation of these considerations may lead to the conclusion that the net benefits of independence outweigh those of closer economic and political integration. As this literature points out, the standard integrationist argument rests on implicit assumptions on the substantial degree of cultural, economic and political agreement and stability within the integrated area, assumptions which may be unwarranted in many economies in transition. Preference for a larger degree of fragmentation in the short run does not preclude enhanced integration in the long run. Therefore, economies in transition cannot be ruled out as candidates for future confederations.

Finally, historical experiences and the political and economic dynamics behind the recent integrationist and separatist movements around the world suggest that a major attraction of confederations is that they are neither too 'tight' nor too 'loose' in terms of the degree of economic integration and policy disciplines that they impose on member countries. Moreover, the degree of integration is not irrevocably fixed and major rules on policy coordination can be adjusted relatively flexibly (at least in principle). Federal-type structures are generally too 'tight' in terms of the policy strictures that they impose and the relative fixity of institutional arrangements, while integrations such as customs unions or common markets may be too 'loose' to reap all the benefits of integration, especially in the case of small open economies. In view of the ongoing globalization of economic activity, the advantages of confederations are likely to assume increasing importance in the future.

V   ISSUES IN THE DESIGN OF CONFEDERATE FINANCES

This section examines how independent countries in a newly emerging confederation might want to arrange fiscal relations with each other and the confederate authority. The basic assumptions are: (1) members of a confederation would maintain a high degree of political and constitutional sovereignty; (2) the confederate authority would only perform the tasks and exercise the powers assigned to it by member states; (3) the horizontal and vertical fiscal arrangements at the confederate level would not interfere with the fiscal arrangements (federal or unitary) within member states; and (4) member states would establish a monetary union within the confederation. The main questions addressed in this section are, then, to what extent members of a confederation should centralize redistribution and stabilization functions, and what principles of expenditure and tax assignments they should follow.

Redistribution

Questions of fiscal equity and regional redistribution by means of intergovernmental transfers have occupied a great deal of attention in the early fiscal federalism literature. The usefulness of this discussion for confederations may be limited, however. As noted above, it is unlikely that countries entering a confederation would exhibit the relatively high degree of homogeneity in preferences for core public services, the mix of taxes, and the degree of regional redistribution that has evolved in mature federations and that has traditionally been assumed in the literature. The costs associated with uniformity in these areas are likely to be high and, therefore, the case for centralizing redistribution and social security functions at the confederate level is weak, at least in the early stages of integration. Issues such as the extent to which the population of different regions should (or could) be supplied with a similar level of public services and subjected to a similar burden of taxation are, therefore, not likely to be high on the integration agenda.

It must be recognized, however, that the issue of interregional equity is not simply a question of perceived social justice. Important as that issue may be in its own right, interregional equity is also necessary to help achieve a degree of convergence of economic performance required for a successful and stable economic integration. Moreover, failure to introduce fiscal systems which broadly aim for horizontal equity can induce flows of population which are socially disruptive and can lead to the inefficient use of mobile resources in an economy (Craig, 1995). Therefore, the interregional transfers of resources may actually be efficiency-improving rather than carrying an efficiency cost (Boadway and Flatters, 1982).

The design of interregional transfers will depend on the extent to which the regional distribution of net benefits from integration is perceived to be inequitable. In general, unconditional grants to the relevant jurisdictions may be appropriate. Such grants can be made either vertically by the confederation or horizontally by confederate members in line with an agreed formula. However, it is unlikely that a confederation would accommodate an elaborate system of specific-purpose, open-ended, matching grants to confederate members, as this would require too much central power and entail too high a cost of coordination. Where there is imperfect correspondence between the spatial distribution of benefits and interjurisdictional boundaries (for example, in the case of an interstate transportation system, training and education spending), conflicts over policies would have to be solved through *ad hoc* negotiation or in standing committees.

Stabilization

There are three reasons for suggesting that fiscal stabilization should remain a responsibility of member states of a confederation. First, because of the narrow scope of joint activities and revenue sources, the confederate budget would be small and lack effective capacity for deficit financing; in addition, the budget would lack social security functions and stabilizer-type revenue. Second, the incidence of asymmetric regional shocks, brought about by the growing internationalization of economic activity, is likely to be prevalent in confederations, because sectors that cause the instability or help to cushion it are unlikely to be distributed evenly throughout the confederation (Scott, 1964).[25] These two considerations suggest that stabilization initiatives at the level of confederate members' economies, based on broader instruments and better information about the nature of local shocks, can make a more effective contribution to stabilization than the centralized initiatives.

The third consideration is that the proposed mechanism for implementing centralized fiscal policy – that is, a system of stabilizing fiscal transfers that the centre would make to member states hit by asymmetric shocks – would be too complex to be timely and effective, and would require too much central power.[26] In particular, as the system of stabilizing fiscal transfers would essentially be an elaborate insurance scheme, a union-wide contingency fund would have to be established and financed by members. To be effective, such a fund would have to act fast, preferably automatically, hence requiring the control of stabilizer-type revenues by the confederate government. To overcome moral hazard problems, complex issues of measurement and trigger mechanism problems would have to be resolved. To minimize administrative costs and the misuse of funds by the politicians, transfers would have to be directed towards the affected individuals and channelled through existing transfer systems used to administer social security programmes. Such arrangements would run strongly counter to the idea that distributional policy should be a matter for the lower-level governments. Finally, there is strong evidence in the empirical literature that, even in the case of much more clear-cut transfers such as fiscal equalization grants, the structure of grant programmes and the distribution of grants are determined by political variables rather than stated programme objectives (Inman, 1988). This political risk is an additional reason for making fiscal stabilization in confederations a preserve of member states.

The proposals for subnational fiscal policy were originally formulated for regions within a federation. The instruments proposed included subnational 'rainy day' stabilization funds and subnational borrowing from designated trust funds (for example, the unemployment trust funds), under constraints on the stock of debt rather than on annual deficits (Gramlich, 1987). Of course, confederate members would also have at their disposal conventional revenue and expenditure measures to address macroeconomic disturbances. If necessary, a second tier of regional fiscal instruments could then be deployed to address local disturbances within members' economies.

The possibility of negative spillovers of members' stabilization actions on other countries raises the need for policy coordination. The question that arises in this context is whether coordination should be implemented on the basis of fixed rules or discretionary actions.

One view, expressed in the Delors Report on European Monetary Union, is that a monetary union can work only if some rules limiting the size of the national budget deficits or the government debt are imposed. More generally, while a procedure that enables fiscal policies to be coordinated flexibly has its advantages, it may be difficult to monitor, may be misinterpreted, and may not be put in place at the right time if it relies on discretion rather than on rules (Masson and Taylor, 1992). However, De Grauwe (1990) showed that the experience of a number of smaller EMS countries (Belgium and The Netherlands in particular) illustrated the need to maintain relatively flexible national fiscal policies, including the need to run large but temporary budget deficits when the country is hit by negative shocks. These actions did not undermine the credibility of these countries' fixed exchange rate commitments. More generally, it may be very difficult to define rules or institutionalized procedures appropriate to all situations.

Another view, which draws on the practice of existing federations, is that the most effective framework for policy coordination is to coordinate the development of agreements about broad fiscal rules (for example, on the debt to GDP ratios), establish mechanisms for regular discussion and coordination of budgetary strategies, and utilize automatic stabilizer properties of the tax system (Scott, 1964; Wiseman, 1965; Haller, 1968). This cooperative approach to coordination seems to be more relevant for confederations than the fixed-rule approach because of the important procedural characteristics of confederatism. Unlike in federations, reservation of separate powers to constituent members implies that the confederate authority cannot ignore conflicts over policy and overrule policy decisions by individual members (Dafflon, 1977). What one needs instead is a mechanism for securing coordination of members' policies and, possibly, sanctions for independent actions that impose excessive spillover costs on other constituent members (Walsh, 1992). Several models of policy coordination have been developed along these lines in the non-traditional fiscal federalism literature.

Drawing on the ideas first developed by Wiseman (1965) and Haller (1968), Dafflon (1977) elaborated a proposal for a two-tier organization of policy groups to ensure institutional efficiency in policy-making. The higher tier – the Budget Coordination Group – would contain representatives of both confederate and regional representatives and deal with the general structure and size of the confederate and members' budgets. The lower tier would consist of special policy groups in charge of significant but narrower issues such as stabilization policy, tax coordination, equalization policy, common standards and regional policy. Dafflon showed how coordination along these lines would increase the overall efficiency of macroeconomic policy while preserving the important procedural characteristics of confederatism.

A variant of the policy group model has been applied in Belgium. A committee for the financing needs of the nation was formed within the influential High Council for Finance to evaluate, each fiscal year, the size of the consolidated budget of the central and intermediate level of government against the prevailing macroeconomic environment (Moesen, 1993). To ensure its impartiality, the membership of this committee is limited to academics and top civil servants of the finance ministry and the central bank. The yearly report, published before the new budgets are elaborated, provides guidelines for the size of the consolidated budget deficit and its breakdown over the various units of government. Partly as a result of this coordination effort, the general government fiscal deficit has declined and stabilized since the late 1980s.

Another model of cooperative decision-making has been operative in Germany under the Economic Stability and Growth Law of 1967. This law was intended to strengthen, through the medium of fiscal policy, the ability of the national government to combat economic fluctuations and to ensure a high and sustainable growth rate. The law can thus be seen as a means of redressing the imbalance between the use of fiscal and monetary policies in currency unions. While preserving the right of the federal government and the states to be independent in their budgeting, this law mandated that: (1) both the federal government and states had to consider the requirements of macroeconomic stability ('total economic equilibrium') in their budgeting; (2) each level of government had to plan several years ahead; and (3) for purposes of business cycle control, the federal government could issue regulations with regard to government borrowing and the use of government funds held with the central bank.[27] As a result of the implementation of this law, a recession in 1967 was handled very effectively. Subsequent post-recession efforts at demand management proved less capable of reining back fiscal deficits. However, this problem could be relatively unimportant in confederations because large fiscal deficits at the confederate level are unlikely to occur. By setting clear rules defining the respective powers and responsibilities, this law could provide a useful model for devising institutionalized procedures for fiscal policy coordination in confederations.[28]

Expenditure Assignment

The 'layer cake' model of federalism, with expenditure functions and matching revenue sources neatly allocated to government agencies in distinct tiers (Oates, 1972), has become a pillar of the traditional approach to fiscal federalism. The subsequent work showed, however, that it is unlikely that the standard 'layer cake' model would emerge as an optimal solution to the assignment problem (Prud'homme, 1985; Hamlin, 1991). Many fiscal functions require joint commitment of several layers of government and coordination of tasks such as policy formulation, administration and financing, rather than constant reshuffling of these tasks between federal, state and local authorities.

The traditional model of expenditure and revenue assignment actually might be more relevant for the centre–state relations in confederations than for other multilevel government structures. By design, confederate members would delegate certain functions to the joint bodies, and provide financing for these functions. In addition to defence and trade, the most obvious confederate functions would be regulation of capital and labour movements, competition policy, enforcement of interstate private contracts, settlement of disputes between members and prudential supervision of financial institutions. The main challenge in this area would not be so much to create uniform rules as to avoid the disincentives to economic and other social activities that stem from over-regulation.

The major social security programmes would have to continue to be provided at the level of member countries, given the importance that members are likely to attach to distributional issues. However, for many public goods and services that are regional in character (transportation and communications, environment 'cultural affairs' and so on), more flexible forms of expenditure provision, such as regional cooperation agreements covering regions belonging to different states, are desirable. Such 'functional federalism' would lead to a regime where regions organize themselves in different jurisdictions for different purposes; moreover, jurisdictions may be overlapping, but without explicit ranking (Casella and Frey, 1992). A major advantage of this model would be that regions belonging to different states could form cooperative agreements without passing through the higher jurisdictional level, thus overcoming inefficiencies that are inherent in a more rigid, hierarchically structured organization of jurisdictions.

Tax Assignment

The main tax assignment issues in future confederations are likely to be the financing of joint activities – historically, the most contentious and destabilizing issue – and the extent of tax harmonization and tax competition. The first issue may be relatively unimportant in future confederations due to the more efficient and buoyant tax systems in existence today. The revenue needs of the confederate government will depend on the scope of joint activities, which – as noted above – is likely to be limited. The confederate budget should, therefore, be easily provisioned through agreed-upon lump-sum contributions by member states and, if necessary, sharing of the joint tariff or other revenue. To provide stability, the financing agreements would have to specify procedures for occasional revisions of the contribution and the tax-sharing formulae.

With assignment of stabilization and redistribution functions to member states and the confederate budget out of the picture due to its small size, the traditional normative case for tax centralization would be profoundly weakened.[29] However, the issues of tax harmonization and tax competition would arise, given that all major taxes – in particular, personal and corporate income taxes and major indirect taxes – would remain the preserve of member states. Recent empirical literature surveyed in Groenewegen (1988) suggests that the quantitative importance of the potentially distorting effects from unharmonized tax structures – that is, reduced tax neutrality, increased administrative and compliance costs, and tax exporting – is exaggerated. The differences in taxes are generally too small an element in business costs (or individuals' locational decisions); tax differentials reflecting differential quality and costs in local public services need not be inefficient; and subnational tax policy-makers often have a real fear of the potential effects of tax competition. It should also be recognized that in a world with increasing international mobility of labour and capital, central governments are beginning to lose control over rates and other features of their income taxes, as demonstrated by international reactions to the US income tax reform of 1986.

In summary, considerations of benefits and costs of tax competition suggest that, with properly functioning factor and commodity markets, tax competition is likely to bring about a gradual convergence of the tax burdens, so there would be no need for confederations to insist on tax harmonization.

VI CONCLUSIONS

The question of what motivates countries to enter and leave interjurisdictional fiscal arrangements has assumed increased importance in recent years. This chapter has argued that the guarantee of political sovereignty, as well as mutual insurance motives and potential efficiency gains from integration, may provide significant incentives for countries to enter confederate-type arrangements. How large these gains are, and what type of countries are likely to join such arrangements, will depend on both structural economic factors and socio-political and constitutional factors. While historical experience does not provide clear guidance with regard to the 'right' mix of these factors, it does suggest that there is no reason why arrangements based on confederate principles should not be economically viable.

The key complication in designing fiscal relations in confederations is the need to coordinate policies to prevent negative spillovers of members' stabilization actions. Because of the binding nature of constraints such as reservation of powers over fiscal policies to member states, a cooperative approach to coordination based on broad and relatively flexible fiscal rules, and implemented through regular discussions and coordination of budgetary strategies, is potentially more effective than the approach based on rigid fiscal rules. The need to coordinate distributive policies in confederations is less obvious, however. Apart from a role for interregional transfers to compensate for the effects of disruptive economic disparities, social policies should remain the preserve of confederate members. With a limited range of responsibilities, the confederate budget would be small, so issues of expenditure and revenue assignment would be straightforward. The small size of the budget, in turn, would be advantageous from the political economy perspective, in that the proportion of budgetary means available for discretionary use would be considerably lower than in federations. Confederations may thus secure a level and composition of public spending that is more in line with voter preferences – at least at the central level – than is the case in federations.

Notes

1. A noted nineteenth-century American historian, John Fiske, called the Confederation period the 'critical period' during which the 'nation was rapidly drifting toward anarchy' (quoted in Unger, 1978, p. 144). More recently, the confederate fiscal arrangements in the former Yugoslavia were seen as one of the factors contributing to the disintegration of the country (see, for example, Bogoev, 1991).
2. Madison noted in 1787 that the Delphian Amphictyony 'bore a very instructive analogy to the present confederation of the American states' (Wills, 1982, p. 84).
3. Other relevant cases include: Canada, which in terms of decentralization falls between the cases of the USA and Switzerland, on one side, and Germany, on the other; and the European Union, which is struggling with many of the same kinds of issues examined here. These cases were not considered in this chapter partly because it was not clear, at the time of writing, how the Quebec issue and European Monetary Union would evolve.
4. Charles A. Beard, a famous twentieth-century American historian, argued that the country was in many respects steadily recovering, and ultimately only one group suffered: those who held the wartime securities (quoted in Unger, 1978, p. 144). This small but powerful elite wanted the public debts repaid fully, and they therefore pushed for the creation of a strong central government that would have sufficient taxing power to collect the public debts.
5. The *Matrikularbeiträge* were originally of two kinds: payments by the states for some specific benefit conferred on them by the Reich; and the general contributions to be made irrespective of any such benefit and determined by the Reich at its own discretion.

6.   The middle part of this clause was interpreted differently by the Reich, which argued that the clause did not explicitly rule out the use of centralized direct taxes, and the states, which argued that the clause had established the tax separation principle. When the Reich introduced direct taxes in 1911, the overlapping of taxes by jurisdictions was scrupulously avoided.

7.   This section draws on Mihaljek (1993).

8.   Another sixth of total spending was financed by republics and autonomous provinces, and two-thirds by independent fiscal agencies that had their own tax powers and operated at a highly decentralized level.

9.   This section draws on Chapter IV in Tseng *et al.* (1994).

10. The remittance rates in these contracts were determined on the basis of actual performance in the current contract. A better performance in the current contract could lead to a higher remittance rate in the following contracts, which acted as a disincentive for local governments to outperform their current contract.

11. Since local governments maintained the power to restrict the inflow of goods from other provinces and to preempt the use of inputs produced in their own province, it was in their interest to shield locally owned enterprises from competition from other provinces.

12. For details, see Tseng *et al.* (1994).

13. Another well-known example is the 1867 *Ausgleich* of the Austro-Hungarian Empire.

14. For certain activities, however, lower levels of government in a federation or a unitary state can enter into international contracts (for example, contracts on the promotion of trade and investment).

15. Although federal constitutions in some countries grant member states the right to secede (for example, in Canada, Switzerland, the former Yugoslavia), such clauses are an exception rather than the rule.

16. A currency union is formed when countries agree to utilize a single currency and surrender control over monetary policy to a joint coordinating body. In a monetary union, countries retain their own currencies but they fix their exchange rates *vis-à-vis* each other and integrate their financial and banking markets.

17. For simplicity, it is assumed here that citizens in a given country have homogeneous preferences, so that the issue of compensating transfers for groups or individuals who stand to lose from integration does not arise.

18. This is one possible interpretation of the Belgian constitutional reform of 1988.

19. To insure against secessionist demands by countries or regions that experience *ex post* huge income windfalls (for example, resource-rich regions), constitutions may attach certain conditions to the right of secession.

20. For a discussion of constitutional rules for a united Europe, see Mueller (1994). Berkowitz (1996a, 1996b) discusses economic and non-economic factors that might drive a region to secede from an economically viable fiscal federation.

21. Other benefits of a single currency include eliminating exchange rate risk and speculative capital flows within the currency union; reducing costs of information, search and calculation; and enabling countries to pool their foreign exchange reserves and enlarge their foreign exchange market.

22. See Mundell (1961) and McKinnon (1963).
23. It is often argued that when labour and capital are not mobile and wages and prices are sticky, the exchange rate becomes a powerful policy tool. The work on rules versus discretion suggests, however, that even in the presence of nominal rigidities, the gains from discretionary exchange rate changes may be limited.
24. See, for example, Kanbur and Keen (1993), who show that the imposition of a minimum tax rate may benefit both large and small countries.
25. The asymmetric shocks can be defined as relative price changes which raise the rate of change of output and employment in some regions and lower it in others.
26. The proposal is based on the observation that exchange rate realignments – which are the most effective way to overcome temporary asymmetric shocks – are not available as a policy tool for individual countries in a monetary union. Given the rigidity of labour markets in many countries, the argument goes, the best way to deal with such shocks would be to put in place a system of stabilizing fiscal transfers (see, for example, Eichengreen (1990) and Wyplosz (1991)).
27. To help streamline decision-making and promote cooperation, the Business Cycle Council and the Financial Planning Council were set up under this law. The membership of each council was similar – two federal representatives, one from each of the states, and four municipal representatives.
28. Certain provisions of the Economic Stability and Growth Law that could result in considerable central government control over local fiscal policies would have to be amended in the case of confederations.
29. The tax assignment criteria developed in the traditional literature (Musgrave, 1983) favoured centralization of the income taxes, most indirect taxes and natural resource taxes largely on grounds of horizontal and vertical fiscal equity, factor mobility and stabilization policy.

References

Adarkar, Bhalchandra P. (1933) *The Principles and Problems of Federal Finance* (London: King & Son).

Aronson, J. Richard and John L. Hilley (1986) *Financing State and Local Governments*, 4th edn (Washington, DC: Brookings Institution).

Berkowitz, Daniel (1996a) 'Nationalism and Secession', forthcoming in D. Pines, E. Sadka and I. Zilcha (eds), *Topics in Economics* (Cambridge: Cambridge University Press).

—— (1996b) 'Regional Income and Secession', unpublished manuscript, Department of Economics, University of Pittsburgh.

Boadway, Robin and Frank Flatters (1982) 'Efficiency and Equalization Payments in a Federal System of Government: A Synthesis and Extension of Recent Results', *Canadian Journal of Economics*, vol. 15, pp. 613–33.

Boczek, Adam (1976) *Taxation in Switzerland* (Cambridge, Mass.: Harvard University Press).

Bogoev, Ksente (1991) 'The Dangers of Decentralization: The Experience of Yugoslavia', in Rémy Prud'homme (ed.), *Public Finance with Several Levels of*

Government, Proceedings of the 46th Congress of the International Institute of Public Finance (Brussels: Foundation Journal of Public Finance).

Breton, Albert and Anthony Scott (1978) *The Economic Constitution of Federal States* (Toronto: University of Toronto Press).

Bullock, Charles J. (1895) 'The Finances of the United States from 1775 to 1789, with Especial Reference to the Budget', *Bulletin of the University of Wisconsin*, vol. 1, pp. 117–273.

Casella, Alessandra and Bruno Frey (1992) 'Federalism and Clubs: Towards an Economic Theory of Overlapping Political Jurisdictions', *European Economic Review*, vol. 36, pp. 639–46.

Codding, George A. (1961) *The Federal Government of Switzerland* (Boston, Mass.: Houghton Mifflin).

Craig, Jon (1995) 'Horizontal Equalization Grants', in Ehtisham Ahmad, Gao Qiang and Vito Tanzi (eds), *Reforming China's Public Finances* (Washington, DC: International Monetary Fund).

Dafflon, Bernard (1977) *Federal Finance in Theory and Practice With Special Reference to Switzerland* (Bern: Verlag Paul Haupt).

Dewey, Davis Rich (1934) *Financial History of the United States* (New York: Longmans, Green & Co.).

Eichengreen, Barry (1990) 'Costs and Benefits of European Monetary Unification', Discussion Paper No. 453 (London: Centre for Economic Policy Research).

Gramlich, Edward M. (1987) 'Subnational Fiscal Policy', *Perspectives on Local Public Finance and Public Policy*, vol. 3, pp. 3–27.

De Grauwe, Paul (1990) 'Fiscal Discipline in Monetary Unions', Working Document No. 50 (Brussels: Centre for European Policy Studies).

Groenewegen, Peter (1988) 'Taxation and Decentralization: A Reconsideration of the Costs and Benefits of a Decentralized Tax System', in Geoffrey Brennan, Bhajan S. Grewal and Peter Groenewegen (eds), *Taxation and Fiscal Federalism: Essays in Honour of Russell Matthews* (Sydney: Australian National University).

Gros, Daniel (1991) 'Regional Disintegration in the Soviet Union: Economic Costs and Benefits', *Intereconomics*, vol. 26, pp. 207–13.

Haller, Heinz (1968) 'Wandlungen in den Problemen föderativer Staatswirtschaften', *Finanzarchiv*, vol. 27, pp. 249–70.

Hamlin, Alan P. (1991) 'Decentralization, Competition and the Efficiency of Federalism', *Economic Record*, vol. 67, pp. 193–204.

Inman, R.P. (1988) 'Federal Assistance and Local Services in the United States: The Evolution of a New Fiscal Order', in H. Rosen (ed.), *Fiscal Federalism: Quantitative Studies* (Chicago, Ill.: University of Chicago Press).

Kanbur, Ravi and Michael Keen (1993) 'Jeux Sans Frontières: Tax Competition and Tax Coordination When Countries Differ in Size', *American Economic Review*, vol. 83, pp. 877–92.

King, Preston (1982) *Federalism and Federation* (Baltimore, Md: Johns Hopkins University Press).

McKinnon, Ronald I. (1963) 'Optimum Currency Areas', *American Economic Review*, vol. 53, pp. 717–25.

Masson, Paul R. and Mark. P. Taylor (1992) 'Issues in the Operation of Monetary Unions and Common Currency Areas', in Morris Goldstein, Peter Isard, Paul R.

Masson and Mark P. Taylor (eds), *Policy Issues in the Evolving International Monetary System*, Occasional Paper No. 96 (Washington, DC: International Monetary Fund).

Mihaljek, Dubravko (1993) 'Intergovernmental Fiscal Relations in Yugoslavia, 1972–90', in Vito Tanzi (ed.), *Transition to Market: Studies in Fiscal Reform* (Washington, DC: International Monetary Fund).

Moesen, Wim A. (1993) 'Community Public Finance in the Perspective of EMU: Assignment Rules, the Status of the Budget Constraint, and Young Fiscal Federalism in Belgium', in Commission of the European Communities, *The Economics of Community Public Finance. European Economy*, vol. 5, pp. 167–90.

Mueller, Dennis C. (1994) 'The Constitution of the United States of Europe', unpublished manuscript, Department of Economics, University of Maryland.

Mundell, Robert A. (1961) 'A Theory of Optimum Currency Areas', *American Economic Review*, vol. 51, pp. 657–65.

Musgrave, Richard A. (1959) *The Theory of Public Finance* (New York: McGraw-Hill).

—— (1983) 'Who Should Tax, Where, and What?', in Charles E. McLure, Jr (ed.), *Tax Assignment in Federal Countries* (Canberra: The Australian National University).

Newcomer, Mabel (1937) *Central and Local Finance in Germany and England* (New York: Columbia University Press).

Oates, Wallace E. (1972) *Fiscal Federalism* (New York: Harcourt Brace Jovanovich).

Pajić, Zoran (1991) 'Yugoslavia and the Confederation Model: International Aspects', *Review of International Affairs*, vol. 42, pp. 5–7.

Palei, L.V. and Jerry L. Petr (1992) 'Integration versus Independence for the Successor States of the USSR: When Might Economics' Right Answers Be Wrong?', *Comparative Economic Studies*, vol. 34, pp. 1–12.

Prud'homme, Rémy (1985) 'Federalisme Fiscal et Politiques Sociales', in Guy Terny and A.J. Culyer (eds), *Public Finance and Social Policy* (Detroit, Mich.: Wayne State University Press).

Putkammer, Ellinor von (1955) *Föderative Elemente im deutschen Staatsrecht seit 1648* (Göttingen: Musterschmidt Verlag).

Rebelo, Sérgio (1994) 'Towards European Monetary Union without the EMS: Discussion', *Economic Policy*, vol. 9, pp. 174–8.

Schultz, William J. and M.R. Caine (1937) *Financial Development of the United States* (New York: Prentice-Hall).

Scott, Anthony (1964) 'The Economic Goals of Federal Finance', *Public Finance*, vol. 19, pp. 241–88.

Tseng, Wanda, Hoe Ee Khor, Kalpana Kochhar, Dubravko Mihaljek and David Burton (1994) *Economic Reforms in China: A New Phase*. Occasional Paper No. 114 (Washington, DC: International Monetary Fund).

Unger, Irwin (1978) *These United States: The Question of Our Past*, vol. I (Boston, Mass.: Little, Brown).

Walsh, Cliff (1992) 'Fiscal Federalism: An Overview of Issues and a Discussion of their Relevance to the European Community', Federalism Research Centre Discussion Paper No. 12 (Canberra: The Australian National University).

Wheare, Kenneth C. (1963) *Federal Government*, 4th edn (London: Royal Institute of International Affairs).

Wills, Gary (ed.) (1982) *The Federalist Papers by Alexander Hamilton, James Madison, and John Jay* (New York: Bantam Books).

Wiseman, Jack (1965) *The Political Economy of Federalism: A Critical Appraisal* (Ottawa: Canadian Royal Commission on Taxation). Reprinted in *Environment and Planning C: Government and Policy*, vol. 5, pp. 383–410.

Wyplosz, Charles (1991) 'Monetary Union and Fiscal Policy Discipline', Discussion Paper No. 488 (London: Centre for Economic Policy Research).

8 Reform and Coordination of Company Taxes in the European Union

Sijbren Cnossen[*]

I INTRODUCTION

In 1992, the Ruding Committee (1992), appointed by the European Commission to examine the need for company tax (CT) harmonization in the European Union (EU), presented its findings and recommendations.[1] Although the Committee concluded that differences in CTs distort the workings of the internal market – differences which most likely would not be eliminated by market forces or tax competition – it nonetheless proposed to leave the CTs in the EU essentially the same as it had found them, replete with their widely diverging domestic and cross-border treatment of different kinds of returns and different kinds of recipients of the various returns. As argued below, however, differential treatment will perpetuate the distortions inherent in the current CTs and erode the taxing authority of source states. A minimum statutory CT rate of 30 per cent, proposed by the Ruding Committee, and the adoption of the (draft) directives of the European Commission[2] are insufficient to repair the infringements of the neutrality and subsidiarity requirements, as applied to taxation, agreed to by the member states. More fundamental reform seems called for. Moreover, CT reform *in* the member states is a condition for CT coordination *between* the member states.

This chapter reviews the distortions and the tax-base erosion of the current CTs in the EU and examines various options for reform and coordination. The article falls into five sections. Following this introduction, Section II briefly reviews current CTs, distinguishing their treatment of the returns on equity (profits) from their treatment of the returns on debt

* The author is grateful to Michael Devereux and Charles McLure for valuable advice and encouragement, and to Richard Bird, Lans Bovenberg, Malcolm Gammie, Jeffrey Owens, Peggy Musgrave, Peter Sørensen and Emil Sunley for comments and suggestions.

(interest). The review shows that reform is called for if member states wish to continue taxing company earnings (and other capital income) in an even-handed manner. As explained in Section III, reforms should be guided by the neutrality criterion and the subsidiarity requirement (that is, member state tax autonomy), as laid down in the treaties establishing the single internal market. Subsequently, Section IV examines various alternatives to the current arrangements. These alternatives are full integration, dual imputation, dividend deduction, an allowance for corporate equity, a cash-flow tax, a comprehensive business income tax and the dual income tax. Section V explores the preferred alternative.

At the outset, it should be emphasized that the chapter focuses on desirable CT reform in a world of increasing capital mobility. Attempts to maintain global, residence-based, income taxes in a world of increasing capital mobility have resulted in complex, fragmentary and largely ineffective levies on company profits (and other capital income) that violate horizontal and vertical equity norms, as well as competitive conditions. It will be argued that across-the-board source taxation of all capital income at low proportional rates is most likely to ensure a greater degree of effective equity, as well as yield neutrality gains compared with the current situation by eliminating the tax discrimination of different types of investment and methods of financing. Specifically, company earnings on equity and on debt should be subjected to identical tax treatments. Coordination is essential for the survival of the CT. Agreement on the CT entitlement rules – who should tax, where and what – is a prerequisite for maintaining operational independence in implementing the tax.

II   REVIEW OF CURRENT COMPANY TAXES

The 15 member states of the EU tax different kinds of returns (retained profits, dividends, capital gains, interest, royalties) and different kinds of recipients of these returns (tax-liable residents, non-residents, exempt entities, companies, individuals) at widely diverging effective rates of tax. This is a source of distortion, discrimination and socially unproductive tax arbitrage.[3] These issues are dealt with below, following a brief survey of current CTs.

Survey of Company Taxes

Company taxes in the EU (and elsewhere) are commonly distinguished depending on whether and to what extent they reduce the double tax – CT and personal income tax (PT) – on distributed profits, that is, provide dividend relief.[4] As shown in Table 8.1, basically four approaches are being used.

- Six member states employ the imputation system, including the largest states: France, Germany, Italy and the United Kingdom (UK).[5] Under the imputation system, shareholders are permitted a full or partial tax credit against their PT for the CT that can be imputed to the dividends received by them. (Finland provides full relief; other member states offer less than full relief.) Two distinguishing features of imputation systems are (a) the gross-up of the net dividend by the tax credit (which is usually expressed as a fraction of the net dividend) and (b) the imposition of CT on exempt profits that are used to pay dividends (compensatory tax).
- Two member states use the tax credit method which, in contrast to the imputation system, either does not have the gross-up feature (Portugal) or permits the tax credit without ensuring that the underlying CT has been paid (Spain) – in other words, without levying a compensatory tax.
- Six member states provide dividend relief at shareholder level by taxing dividend income at a special, usually flat, PT rate. Since Greece exempts dividend income in the hands of shareholders, its special PT rate may be said to be zero. Luxembourg exempts half of dividends received; dividend income, in other words, is taxed at half of marginal PT rates.
- One member state, The Netherlands, regards companies as entities entirely separate from their shareholders and taxes them as such under what is called the classical system. Apart from a small exemption at shareholder level, dividend income is fully subject to the twin yoke of the CT and the PT.

Thus 14 out of 15 member states provide dividend relief at shareholder level. The imputation system is the most structured form of relief, because it reduces the double CT/PT burden on profit distributions in proportion to the marginal PT rates of all shareholders. In contrast, under the tax credit method without gross-up and the special PT rate schemes, the relief tends to be greater for high-income-bracket PT-payers than for low-income-bracket PT-payers. This regressive effect can be mitigated (as is done in Austria and Belgium) but not eliminated, by permitting low-income-bracket PT-payers, whose marginal ordinary PT rate is lower than the special PT rate, to opt for classical double taxation of their dividend

Table 8.1 European Union: taxes on company earnings in 1996 (in percentages)

CT system/ member state	CT (on retained profits)[a]	Dividend relief — Particulars	Dividend relief — As per cent of classical tax burden[b]	Ordinary top PT[n]	CT+PT on distributed profits[c]	Top PT on interest[d]	Top PT on capital gains[e,f] — Ordinary shares	Top PT on capital gains[e,f] — Substantial holdings
1. Imputation system	*Tax credit as fraction of net dividend*							
Finland	28	7/18	100	57.5	28	28**	28	28
France	36 2/3	1/2 (basic CT)	91	60.2	61.5	19.4*	19.4	19.4
Germany	56[g]	3/7 (CG/CT)	59	57	64.4	57*	–	rr[h]
Ireland[i]	38 (10)	23/77 (1/18)	49	48	58.1 (50.6)	42*	40	40[j]
Italy	53.2	37/63 (CG/CT)	66	51	58.7	12.5**	15	25
United Kingdom	33	1/4	51	40	49.8	40*	40	40
2. Tax credit method		*Tax credit*						
Portugal	39.6	60% of CT[k]	91	40	42.2	20**	–	rr[m]
Spain	36	40% of net div.[l]	71	56	60.6	56*	rr[m]	rr[m]
3. Special PT rate		*PT rate*						
Austria[n]	34	22	109	50	48.5	22**	–	Half of PT
Belgium[n]	40.2	25[o]	135	60.6	55.1	15**[o]	–	–
Denmark	34	40[p]	105	61	60.4	61	40	40
Greece	35	0	152	45	35	15**	–	–
Luxembourg[n]	40.3	Half of PT	62	51.3	55.6	51.3	–	25.6
Sweden	28	30	152	56	49.6	30	30	30
4. Classical system		*No relief*						
Netherlands	35	–[q]	0	60	74	60	–	20

Notes:

Abbreviations have the following meaning: CT = company income tax; PT = personal income tax; CG = central government; rr = reduced rate. Some information may be incomplete or out of date. Percentages have been rounded to one decimal place.

a   Rates include surcharges, surtaxes or profit (income) taxes levied by local governments (if different, an average or representative rate has been chosen). Net wealth or capital taxes – levied in Germany, Italy and Luxembourg – are not included.

b   Measured against the combined CT+PT under the classical system, according to the formula

$$\text{Dividend relief} = \frac{CT+PT \text{ without relief} - \text{Actual } CT+PT}{CT+PT \text{ without relief} - CT+PT \text{ with full relief}}$$

c   Calculated as: CT + [(1 – CT) PT] minus any tax credit, if available. Under the dual income tax in Finland, the top PT rate on capital income equals the CT rate of 28%. In countries with special PT rates on dividend income, obviously the special PT rate is taken as the top PT rate in calculating the CT + PT on distributions. Dividend payments to residents are subject to withholding tax in Austria (22%), Belgium (25%), Denmark (25%), Germany (25%), Italy (12.5%), Luxembourg (25%), The Netherlands (25%), Portugal (12.5%) and Spain (25%).

d   An asterisk (*) denotes that interest payments are subject to a withholding tax; a double asterisk (**) means that the withholding tax is final. Generally, royalty payments to residents are not subject to withholding tax, except in France (15%) and the UK (25%).

e   Usually, capital gains realized by companies are subject to CT at the normal rate; generally, the tax is deferred if the gain is reinvested.

f   Capital gains are adjusted for inflation in Ireland, Italy, Luxembourg and the UK. Alternatively, short-term and long-term gains are taxed at different (effective) rates in Denmark, France and Spain as well as in Ireland. PT rates shown are for long-term capital gains. Various countries exempt small amounts of capital gains.

g   A lower rate of 30% applies to distributed profits. This rate is 42% if the 7.5% surcharge and the 17% tax-exclusive, deductible, local tax are included. This form of partial dividend relief at company level is called the split-rate system. Overall, however, imputation is the dominant feature of Germany's CT/PT system.

h   Capital gains up to DM 30 million on substantial holdings (more than 25% of the share capital) are taxed at reduced rates.

i   The rates/fractions given in parentheses apply to profits/tax credits of qualifying manufacturing and processing companies.

j   In Ireland, the capital gains tax rate is 27% on the disposal of shares in unquoted companies held for at least five years.

k   In Portugal, 60% of the underlying CT is creditable against the PT without gross-up. Alternatively, a special (final) PT rate of 12.5% applies to net dividend income. This provides dividend relief at 70%, distributionns being taxed at a CT+PT rate of 47.2%.

l   In Spain, 40% of the net dividend is grossed up and credited against the PT. However, there is no compensatory tax on distributions out of profits not subject to CT.

m   Reduced rates are related to the length of the holding period and the amount of other income.

n   Austria, Belgium and Luxembourg permit a (limited) deduction from personal income of expenditures on the purchase of new shares.

o   In Belgium, the PT rate is 15% on dividends paid on shares issued after 1 January 1994 and 25% on interest paid on bonds issued before 1 March 1990.

p   Share income not exceeding DKr 33 800 (DKr 67 600 for married couples) is taxed at 25%.

q   Df 1000 dividend income is exempt from PT (Df 2000 for married couples).

Source: International Bureau of Fiscal Documentation, *European Taxation* (Amsterdam: loose-leaf).

income (with credit for the special PT withheld at source). Furthermore, more than full relief can be provided under the special PT rate schemes as well as the tax credit method, if dividends are paid out of exempt profits.[6]

Taxing Returns on Equity: Distortion and Discrimination

Finland and Greece are the only member states that tax profit distributions and retentions at the same marginal CT/PT rates. In all other member states the CT+PT on distributions is generally higher than the CT on retentions.[7] In comparing the effective tax rates, the PT on capital gains should be taken into account, of course. Generally, however, effective rates are (very) low or nil (see Table 8.1). Seven member states do not tax capital gains on ordinary shares. Other member states tax capital gains but only upon realization: a concession, equivalent in value to an interest-free loan. Gains on the sale of shares that represent a substantial holding, that is, a controlling interest, are taxed more widely but, again, deferral and preferential rates should result in relatively low tax burdens.

If, as appears to be the case, the CT+PT on profit distributions is higher than the CT (plus capital gains tax, if any) on retained profits, then dividend payout decisions will be distorted and new investment will be discouraged. At least, this should be the case under the 'traditional view' which holds that dividend payouts cannot be lowered without cost because they offer non-tax benefits, for instance by signalling shareholders that the company is financially healthy or by limiting financial discretion and hence potential misuse of funds by management.[8] Under the 'new view', on the other hand, the double tax does not affect dividend payout decisions or the effective rate of tax on investments financed by retentions, because the PT on dividend income 'trapped' in the company acts as a once-off wealth tax.[9] Most empirical studies support the traditional view over the new view (Poterba, 1987; Gerardi, Graetz and Rosen, 1990; Zodrow, 1991). Whatever view is adopted, taxing dividends twice always harms investments by new and emerging firms, which have to rely on new share issues to provide for their equity needs.

The distortions described above yield important EU-wide implications. First, the higher tax on dividends, which stimulates profit retention, reduces the amount of capital becoming available on European capital markets and thus hampers the development of EU share markets. Second, investments by old firms financed through retained earnings tend to yield a lower (before-tax) return than can be obtained elsewhere. In other words, resources are misallocated. Third, the tax bias in favour of old firms inhibits the entry of new firms, that is, the tax system infringes on competitive conditions, thereby jeopardizing the dynamics of the single internal market. In addition, current CT/PT systems have differential inter-member-state effects. The high tax on distributed profits, for instance, discriminates in favour of member states with many mature firms (which do not need new equity). Also, it confers an artificial advantage on member states with companies that conform to the 'conduit' model of the firm (with shareholders managing the company) and that, therefore, do not need to distribute a large portion of their profits to satisfy shareholders.

Last but not least, the discrimination between mature companies (able to rely on profit retention to finance investments) and new emerging companies (having to rely on new share issues) closely echoes the tax discrimination between the company form and the non-company form of doing business.[10] Under a CT with less than full imputation, the total tax on the equity income of new firms (having to distribute all profits), for which the company form is a *conditio sine qua non*, would generally be higher than the PT on the business income of the self-employed. Conversely, the CT (plus capital gains tax, if any) on the retained profits of mature companies would generally be lower than the PT on the business income of the self-employed, who cannot incorporate their businesses. Under financial neutrality, the CT+PT on the equity income of all companies, regardless of maturity, of course, should equal the PT on the business income of the self-employed.

Taxing Returns on Debt: the Hole in the CT Bucket

As Table 8.1 indicates, interest appears to be taxed positively, although generally at lower rates than the CT+PT on profit distributions. In reality, however, most interest is not taxed at all due to the symbiosis between interest deductibility at company (and personal) level and the existence of capital-rich tax-exempt investors, such as pension funds, life insurance companies and social security funds. Typically, interest income accruing to these institutional investors is not taxed, in contrast to returns on equity, which are taxed at source.[11]

The effective exemption of much interest has greatly stimulated debt finance (thin capitalization) and eroded the capital income tax base in most member states. In The Netherlands, for instance, in 1989 approximately Df 40 billion (8 per cent of GDP) of tax-deductible interest payments was 'washed out' by tax-exempt investors. On a net basis, the business sector accounted for 60 per cent of this amount (Cnossen, 1995). Furthermore, Sørensen (1988), reporting on the Danish situation, calculated that, in 1986, tax revenue collected on personal capital income was *minus* 1.6 per cent of GDP (11 per cent of total capital income computed on the basis of national accounts). Earlier, Hansson and Norman (quoted in Sørensen (1994a, p. 78) estimated that the yield of the Swedish tax on capital income was *minus* 0.3 per cent of household economic income. These findings are corroborated by Gordon and Slemrod (1988), who concluded that the complete exemption of capital income in the USA in 1983 would have raised revenue.[12]

The growing internationalization and liberalization of capital markets also suggest that interest is hardly taxed, because these developments increase opportunities for evading or avoiding the PT or CT on interest income. Whereas retained earnings are taxed at source through the CT, the tax authorities cannot be sure that cross-border interest payments are reported and taxed.[13] Moreover, withholding rates on cross-border interest payments (which vary by class of payer and payee, and by type of financial instrument – by itself a source of wasteful tax arbitrage) are very low.[14] As a result, as Huizinga (1994) concludes, 'international interest income to a large extent escapes taxation'. This favours international debt finance, violates neutrality, skews investors' portfolios and results in an arbitrary division of the interest income base between lending and borrowing countries.

The tax-favoured status of debt also discriminates against companies that face difficulties in attracting debt, because they do not yet enjoy a high credit rating, own mainly non-liquid assets (such as firm-specific machinery) against which it is difficult to borrow, or generate insufficient taxable profits to be able to deduct interest. Consequently, these companies, which tend to be fledgling enterprises, have to incur higher capital costs on account of taxation than do older, established companies with either easier access to debt financing or sufficient retained profits to finance new investments. Furthermore, at the EU level, the preferential treatment of debt favours member states with institutions (banks and large firms with liquid assets) that allow substantial debt finance.[15] In short, the equality of competitive conditions is violated.

Conclusion

This brief survey has raised three concerns. First, in nearly every member state, effective CT+PT rates on investment returns vary depending on the choice of financing (equity or debt), the company's dividend policy (distribution or retention), the form in which the investment is undertaken (the company form or the non-company form), the tax status of the recipient of the return (liable to the PT and/or the CT, or exempt) and the place of residence of the recipient of the return (at home or abroad). Broadly, as the OECD (1991) has pointed out, debt finance is favoured and individual investors are discriminated against.[16] Also, the taxing arrangements raise the entry costs of new companies which provide an important impetus to the development of entrepreneurial skills in the single internal market.

Second, even if the CT/PT systems would achieve neutrality with respect to different types of investment and methods of financing, they would still distort the level of investment. By taxing the opportunity cost of capital, the CT/PT reduces the incentive to invest, because investments that just yield a viable economic return before tax will not be worth undertaking after tax. This is the price that must be paid if it is considered desirable to tax investment returns.

Third, the symbiosis between interest deductibility and capital-rich tax-exempt domestic and foreign sectors and other opportunities for tax arbitrage erode the company (and capital) income tax base. This effect is reinforced by the substitution of hard-to-reach international debt (interest being taxed on the residence principle) for easier-to-tax equity (profits being taxed on the source principle). The toothless bite of capital income taxes, of course, greatly mitigates the distortions mentioned above, but at the expense of violating prevailing interpersonal and interjurisdictional equity norms.

III CRITERIA FOR REFORM AND COORDINATION

The previous section indicates that reform and coordination seem called for. As with other economic policy issues in the EU, the compass should be focused on the twin lodestars: neutrality and subsidiarity. This section examines these criteria more closely as they apply to company taxation.

Neutrality and Subsidiarity

The leitmotif of the Treaty of Rome (1957) is that competition should be the mechanism for allocating economic resources in the EU. Accordingly, tax neutrality should be its corollary in so far as it aims at ensuring that equal conditions for competitors are not distorted through the tax system. Neutrality *within* member states is an indispensable condition for neutrality *between* member states. As long as CTs distort the choice between debt and equity, distribution and retention, the company form and the non-company form of doing business within member states, they are bound to distort investment decisions across the EU.[17]

The Treaty of Maastricht (1992) enshrined subsidiarity as the guiding criterion in the discussion on the assignment of policy functions in the EU. Still evolving, subsidiarity proceeds from a presumption in favour of decentralization. Basically, policy functions, including taxation, should be exercised by the member states, but the states are obliged to consider the effects of their actions on other member states (Smith, 1993). While tax neutrality generally requires a substantial degree of tax coordination, subsidiarity, in contrast, implies that each member state should be permitted as much tax independence as is commensurate with the goals of free trade and free competition in the single internal market (Cnossen, 1990).

In taxation, subsidiarity seems to have two distinct but related dimensions. First and foremost, subsidiarity implies that member states should cooperate to establish the rules of the tax game. Basically, these rules should have regard to the allocation of the various tax bases in the EU to individual member states in such a way that overtaxation or undertaxation across member states is avoided. Also, unambiguous definitions and practices, that is, transparency, are essential. Second, and no less important, subsidiarity means that member states should be able to operate their own tax systems, designed in accordance with the agreed rules, without the need for day-to-day cooperation with other member states in the form of information exchange, cross-border audits, and so on. Operational independence has regard to legal concepts and practices, as well as assessment, collection and appeal procedures.[18] Viewed together, these two features of subsidiarity suggest that tax sovereignty has to be ceded in establishing the tax entitlement rules so that tax independence can be exercised more fully in administering these rules.[19]

Application to Company Taxation

Neutrality and subsidiarity are difficult to effect in the field of company taxation. For one thing, as amply illustrated in Section II, various kinds of return (retained profits, dividends, interest, royalties) and various kinds of recipients (tax-liable individuals, exempt entities, out-of-state residents) have traditionally been treated differently for tax purposes within and between member states. For another, while company profits are mainly taxed on the source basis, the claim to tax interest rests mainly on the residence principle. Thus company earnings are subject to different internal tax regimes and different interstate tax entitlement rules. Clearly, some fundamental rethinking must be done to straighten out these mixed sets of tax rules and practices in light of the new requirements.

Internal neutrality requires foremost that various kinds of company earnings, with respect to equity and debt, are subjected to identical tax treatments. The age-old distinction between debt and equity has become unrealistic and unworkable. Discriminatory and distortionary effects are exacerbated by the symbiosis of debt finance and capital-rich, tax-exempt sectors. Wasteful tax arbitrage and dead-weight losses may be sizeable. Half-baked solutions, such as prescribed debt–equity ratios, apart from bringing their own distortions along, will not solve the problem. The solution can be found only by viewing interest as another form of distributed company earnings.

External neutrality is even more difficult to achieve, because historically the CT has been levied on the source principle, instead of the residence principle. Company profits are taxed *where* they arise, that is, in the source state, instead of according to *who* they accrue to, that is, in the residence state. Unlike the residence state, however, the source state cannot ensure neutrality regarding EU-wide investment location decisions because, other things being equal, companies will tend to establish their profit-making activities in the state with the lowest CT instead of the state with the lowest production costs. While the source state can tax companies doing business on its territory alike (non-discrimination principle), it has no say over the out-of-state tax treatment of repatriated profits. In other words, the source state cannot equalize effective tax rates for all participants, taking account of any additional taxes they must pay in the residence state (capital import neutrality). Only the residence state can ensure efficiency in the EU-wide (and worldwide) allocation of resources (capital export neutrality).[20]

Capital export neutrality (embodied by the pure residence principle), on the other hand, is difficult to put into practice, particularly for the CT, in a single market with total freedom of trade and factor movements and a planned centralized monetary policy with a single currency. For one thing, source states would have to give up their historic right to tax company profits. For another, company profits would have to be taxed on an EU-wide basis as they accrue, and in accordance with the profit-determination rules of the residence state. Obviously, tax deferral, let alone tax exemption, cannot be allowed as it would imply the continuation of source taxation. Furthermore, residence states should be able to check the accuracy, in source states, of the reporting for out-of-state profits. All this suggests that residence-based CTs would violate the operational independence principle, because an inordinate degree of day-to-day interstate coordination (resembling the workings of a single, EU-wide CT administration) would be required. Clearly, at this juncture, the CTs in the EU should continue to be founded on the source entitlement principle.[21]

The primacy – perhaps the expediency – of the source entitlement principle establishes a case for exempting all inward dividend income from CT or PT and all outward dividend income from withholding tax. In other words, residence states should give up all claims to taxing out-of-state dividend income whether from direct investment or portfolio shareholding in the EU. Furthermore, the current residual right, for interpersonal equity purposes, of residence states to tax inward dividends violates financial neutrality and operational independency. Similarly, source states would have to renounce all claims to taxing out-of-state shareholders with respect to dividends paid to them. Likewise, imputation tax credits should not be extended to non-resident shareholders.

Neutrality and operational independence in taxing company equity income can largely be undone, however, by non-neutrality and operational dependence (that is, the need for day-to-day cooperation) in the tax treatment of interest (and royalties) payable to out-of-state residents. Full reliance on the residence principle means that interest (most likely) will not be taxed, because it accrues to tax-exempt out-of-state investors or is channelled through tax havens. Moreover, residence taxation of interest requires substantial day-to-day cooperation, because source states must inform residence states of outward interest payments. This weak spot in the CT bucket can only be repaired by taxing interest on the basis of the source principle. This is a clear breach with current practice, but an inevitable one if interest payments on inward debt are to be taxed at all.

Summing Up

In sum, most practical considerations imply that the choice is not between the source and the residence principle for taxing company profits, but between the source principle and no tax at all. Under the source principle, however, neutrality can be achieved only if the basic design of the various CTs is, by and large, harmonized and if statutory rates are approximately the same. If so, operational independence will largely be safeguarded because companies will have few incentives to relocate their profit-making activities to other member states, or to shift profits by manipulating their intercompany transfer prices (including overhead expenses) or their debt–equity structures. Moreover, the need for day-to-day cooperation would be minimized.

Specifically, neutrality and subsidiarity seem to imply the following criteria against which current CT systems and various alternatives, focusing on tax coordination through tax reform, should be evaluated:

- greater uniformity of the overall effective tax rates on the return to equity, whether retained or distributed, and the return to debt;
- greater uniformity of effective tax rates, regardless of whether the return of an investment accrues to domestic or foreign investors;
- minimization of the potential for tax avoidance and tax evasion, as well as the compliance and administrative costs of the CT regime; and, perhaps more controversially,
- allocation of the tax base for equity income as well as debt income primarily to the member state of investment (source state) instead of the state of the investor (residence state).

IV   OPTIONS FOR COORDINATING COMPANY TAXES

Which CT would best meet the criteria spelled out above? In trying to answer that question, this section reviews and evaluates various alternatives to the current CTs that have been proposed in the literature or put into practice. Some alternatives attempt to reduce or eliminate the discriminatory treatment of various forms of company earnings by adhering more closely to the requirements of a global, progressive income tax. Full integration, dual imputation and dividend deduction are examples of this approach. Other options, such as an allowance for corporate equity and a cash-flow tax, emphasize the desirability of neutrality. Specifically, only pure profits or rent income should be taxed, not the opportunity cost of capital. A third set of alternatives occupies the middle ground by taxing all company earnings (retentions, distributions, interest) in full, but at the same low, proportional CT/PT rate. The comprehensive business income tax and the dual income tax are examples of this approach.

Full Integration

Proponents of the global concept of income, as formulated by Schanz, Haig and Simons, argue that the CT should be fully integrated with the PT of shareholders.[22] Under full integration, all company earnings (distributed as well as retained profits, and interest) would be allocated to shareholders and debtholders and taxed at their marginal PT rate. Because all company earnings would be taxed alike, for new investment, the distinction between equity and debt, profit retention and distribution or the company form and the non-company form of doing business would become irrelevant.

Full integration has been proposed by the Royal (Carter) Commission in Canada (1966), the US Department of the Treasury (1979 – *Blueprints*) and the Campbell Committee (1981) in Australia. Under both the voluntary CT- and PT-rate alignment plan (Carter) and the mandatory partnership methods (*Blueprints*, Campbell), all corporate equity income would be allocated to shareholders and taxed in their hands with a full credit for the CT paid on their behalf. To prevent double taxation of retentions, the basis for corporate shares would be written up by the amount of the allocation net of the tax credit. Profit distributions would be considered repayment of capital up to the amount of the written-up basis; further repayments would be considered taxable capital gains.

These plans, however ingenious, have never left the drawing board, primarily because they are considered impracticable (McLure, 1979; US Department of the Treasury, 1992). The administrative objections relate to the precise and timely allocation of company profits to shareholders and, perhaps even more important, to the ascertainment of true economic income under which capital allowances would reflect actual economic depreciation and capital gains would be taxed as they accrued. In practice, this would require that all assets be revalued each year to measure the real loss or gain. In the presence of inflation, moreover, adjustments would have to be made to the real value of the outstanding debt.[23] Further complications arise when cross-border investments are taken into consideration. Under global, fully integrated CTs, the returns on these investments should be taxed on the basis of the residence principle – an extremely demanding administrative requirement, as argued above.

The administrative objection to full integration also has an economic counterpart. The economics literature has argued that, from a national point of view, the greater mobility of capital compared with labour means that it is not optimal to tax capital income at the same (high) rate as labour income, since this does not take account of the greater elasticity of supply of capital compared with labour (in terms of sensitivity to changes in the net real interest rate and the net real wage rate, both after tax, respectively).[24] High tax rates would induce capital flight and saddle labour with the burden in the form of lower productivity and lower real wages. Although capital is not fully mobile, especially in its physical form, moderation (or worldwide coordination) nonetheless seems to be required.

Dual Imputation

The dual imputation system focuses especially on the effective, one-level taxation of interest and dividend income.[25] Under this system, interest is treated in the same fashion as dividends are under current (full) imputation systems. In other words, interest would not be deductible at company level, but debtholders would be permitted a tax credit for the underlying CT against their PT (or CT) on their taxable interest income (grossed up by the tax credit). Alternatively, but equivalently, interest could continue to be deductible in computing taxable company profits, but it would be subjected to a withholding tax at a rate equal to the CT rate. Eleven member states already tax interest at source, but without regard to the comparable implications of dividend imputation systems. Exempt entities, for instance, are entitled to a refund of interest withheld. In contrast, under most imputation systems (Ireland and the UK are exceptions), exempt entities do not have the right to claim refunds of unused tax credits. The same rule should apply to interest, if equal treatment is to be ensured. To block an obvious avoidance route, the withholding tax on non-residents would have to be raised.

A dual imputation system would put dividend and interest on the same tax footing, but would maintain the favourable tax treatment of retained profits. The effective tax rate on debt-financed investment would increase, but the tax rate on equity-financed investment (assuming statutory rates to remain unchanged) would decrease in member states that do not yet have an imputation system. There would be few technical transition problems, but tax treaties might have to be renegotiated to extend the tax credit to debtholders in other member states. This would complicate the workings of the system and infringe on the operational independence principle. The greatest drawback of a dual imputation system – indeed, of any scheme that reduces the tax benefits to debt finance – is that the effective taxation of interest at the lender's CT rate or his (higher) PT rate would reduce the post-tax return to saving or instead raise the cost of capital to a level that could have detrimental effects on capital formation in the EU.

Dividend Deduction

Greater equality in the current treatment of dividend and interest can also be achieved by allowing a deduction for dividends paid in calculating taxable profits. The dividend deduction system is not found in the EU, but was in use in most Nordic countries before they switched to the imputation system.[26] Unless the goal is to stimulate equity investment by non-residents, a drawback of the dividend deduction system is that the relief is automatically extended to foreign shareholders, who do not pay the (additional) national PT incurred by domestic shareholders.[27] To prevent this, a dividend withholding tax could be introduced (or increased). This would make the dividend deduction system equivalent to an imputation system. Without a withholding complement, the dividend deduction system would jeopardize the effective, one-level taxation of distributed profits.

Furthermore, a deduction for dividends paid on new share issues has received strong support from proponents of the new view, particularly in the USA.[28] Until 1991, Sweden also permitted a deduction for dividends paid on newly issued shares. The total cumulative amount could not exceed the paid-in capital, and the concession expired 20 years after the year of issue. Furthermore, it should be noted that Austria, Belgium and Luxembourg permit a (limited) deduction from personal income for expenditures on the purchase of new shares, a concession which can be viewed as an alternative to a dividend deduction scheme for new share issues. In practice, it appears difficult to draw an effective distinction between new equity and old equity.

Allowance for Corporate Equity

Full integration, dual imputation and dividend deduction all tax the opportunity cost of capital – often referred to as 'normal profits'. This implies, however, that the level of saving and investment would continue to be distorted. If the CT is not to interfere with the level of economic activity, only 'pure profits' or 'economic rents' should be taxed. The ACE system, conceived by Boadway and Bruce (1984) but made operational by the IFS Capital Taxes Group (1991), purports to achieve this by providing an Allowance for Corporate Equity in computing taxable profits, equal to the product of 'shareholders' funds' (generally, the company's total equity capital, including taxable profits net of CT) and an 'appropriate nominal interest rate', set by the government but reflecting a normal market rate of return on, say, medium-term government bonds.[29] Since the allowance would approximate normal profits, its deduction from total taxable profits means that the CT would be confined to pure profits from intramarginal investments.

Proponents of the ACE allowance (Devereux and Freeman, 1991; Gammie, 1992b) point out that in present-value terms its tax base is identical to the base of an annual pure profits tax, for two reasons. First, the equity allowance permits any schedule of depreciation allowances without altering the present value of the tax payments associated with the cash flow of an investment. High depreciation allowances result in a lower amount of shareholders' funds and hence a lower allowance, and vice versa. Second, both companies and shareholders can borrow at the appropriate nominal interest rate to offset different profiles of tax payments or distributions, respectively. Furthermore, the ACE allowance preserves neutrality under inflation, because the interest rate is set at its full nominal level.

A form of ACE allowance has been adopted in Croatia where it is called the interest-adjusted income tax (IAIT) (Rose and Wiswesser, this volume). Under the IAIT, companies that keep proper accounts are permitted to deduct an imputed normal return, called 'protective interest' (equal to the rate of growth of manufacturing prices plus 3 percentage points), on their equity from taxable profits as conventionally computed. The self-employed, who may not have proper accounts, are permitted to deduct a similar return, which, however, is calculated by reference to the book value of depreciable assets. Savings of individual taxpayers are included in the tax base, but the normal return on them is exempt (prepayment method). Pension contributions, on the other hand, are deductible from taxable income, while payouts are taxed (standard method). The IAIT was implemented on 1 January 1994. Reports on the Croatian experience are not in yet.

Undoubtedly, the ACE allowance has attractive neutrality properties. The neutrality conditions, however, are met only if capital markets are perfect. If dividends continued to be taxed under present PTs, the ACE system would favour retentions even more strongly over distributions than do the current systems. To be fully neutral, the ACE allowance requires the reform of the PT, along the lines of an extended personal equity plan (IFS Capital Taxes Group, 1989) or the IAIT in Croatia. But the move to a full expenditure tax would fundamentally change the debate and greatly complicate the reform.[30] Under current PT taxing arrangements, the ACE allowance would erode the source entitlement principle – resembling the erosion of the residence principle due to interest deductibility. The ACE allowance might be given consideration if express or tacit coordination on taxing capital income cannot be achieved, yet the existing bias against equity is a serious problem.

Cash-Flow Tax

Usually, a tax on the pure profits of an investment is associated with cash-flow taxation. As has been shown in the literature (Meade Committee, 1978), a tax on the flow of funds into and out of any investment is equivalent in present-value terms to an annual pure profits tax levied over the lifetime of the investment. Under the cash-flow tax, companies would be denied a deduction for interest as well as dividends paid (if not already denied), but they would be allowed an immediate write-off of the cost of business assets. As a result, only pure profits or rent income would be taxed, not normal profits. In particular, the return on marginal investments, just making a viable economic return, would be exempted. Again, full neutrality, generally, cannot be achieved if, at the same time, current PTs are not replaced by personal consumption taxes, under which all savings or, alternatively, the yield of all savings are exempted from PT.[31]

Full neutrality is also achieved under the cash-flow equivalent, subtraction-VAT type of origin-based direct tax, which has been proposed in the USA (Hall and Rabushka, 1995) in replacement of the current personal and company income taxes. Under the 'flat tax', value added, consisting of wages and capital income, is determined by deducting purchases (including investment goods) from sales. Subsequently, wages are deducted and taxed separately at the individual level, permitting a basic exemption (and effective progressivity). Remaining capital income is taxed at the flat rate without basic exemption. Again, pure profits would be taxed, but the return on inframarginal investments would be exempted. For the time being, it seems unlikely that the USA will introduce a flat tax. Apart from the fear of the unknown, transitional difficulties and international problems (for example, obtaining a foreign tax credit for it) seem to preclude its adoption.[32]

Comprehensive Business Income Tax[33]

The dividend deduction system and the ACE allowance (without a personal expenditure tax complement) continue to favour retained profits over dividends and interest, and exempt entities and foreign shareholders and debtholders over domestic holders. A cash-flow tax, on the other hand, would be costly up front to revenue (the immediate write-offs generally would call for rebates and positive tax payments would be delayed) and out of step with conventional concepts of determining profits. In view of these drawbacks, perhaps the focus should be on a more even-handed taxation of profits, conventionally computed, and interest at company level. Taxation at company level would keep the tax intact on normal profits as well as corporate earnings paid to tax-exempt and foreign shareholders, that is, shore up the source entitlement principle.

On the basis of this philosophy, the comprehensive business income tax (CBIT), proposed by the US Department of the Treasury (1992), taxes all company earnings at company level. The CBIT proceeds from the fundamental equivalence between a CT levied at source and an equal-rate PT on company earnings with full credit for the underlying CT. Accordingly, under the CBIT, CT and PT are integrated by not allowing deductions, at company level, for dividends and interest paid to shareholders and debtholders, and not taxing these income items at the level of the recipients, be they individuals or companies. This makes the debt–equity distinction irrelevant, and greatly reduces the distinction between retained and distributed earnings (depending on the treatment of capital gains). Extending the CBIT to proprietorships and partnerships – more difficult to achieve – would also make the distinction between companies and non-companies irrelevant for tax purposes.

The CBIT can be introduced while largely maintaining the present rules for determining taxable profits, including those applicable to depreciation and inventory accounting. Exempt entities and non-residents would be treated like resident individuals or companies. They would not be eligible for a refund of the CBIT, nor would they have to pay any additional CBIT in the form of a withholding tax or otherwise. Companies receiving CBIT income also would not be taxable on such income. To ensure that dividends and interest are not paid out of exempt earnings, a compensatory tax (already in place under various imputation systems in the EU) should be levied on exempt income (made available for distribution as dividends or interest).[34] Capital gains on shares would only be taxed to the extent that they exceed the acquisition cost stepped up by the company's retained profits net of the CT.

The CBIT, as proposed, would reduce the relative tax burden on new equity-financed investment and increase the burden on debt-financed investment. Established firms and institutional investors would face a relatively higher tax burden, as would tax haven countries, but new, growing firms would be taxed less heavily. The CBIT would eliminate the incentives for thin capitalization and the bias against profit distributions. The exemption of dividend income at shareholder level and the taxation of interest at source should reduce the need for concerted tax coordination at the central EU level. In other words, operational independence would be promoted, although substantial non-subsidiarity (cooperation) is required to get there, especially as regards interest on inward debt investment (Gammie, 1992c). To alleviate the effects on current debt–equity structures, the CBIT could be introduced gradually. The US Department of the Treasury (1992), for instance, proposes a 10-year phase-in period. Initially, say, 10 per cent of interest payments would be disallowed, while dividend income would be taxed on a schedular basis at a rate that would be reduced over time.

Dual Income Tax

The CBIT could function properly in the USA, where the CT rate does not differ much from (or is equal to) the top PT rate. The situation in the EU, however, is markedly different. While most CT rates do not exceed the US CT rate, PT rates in the EU are considerably higher than EU CT rates, as well as the US PT rate. If it is not possible to reduce PT rates on all income, other approaches to CT reform must be explored.

An imaginative solution to the problems posed by the CT/top-PT differential has been found by the Nordic countries.[35] Denmark and Sweden, but especially Finland and Norway, have transformed their CTs and PTs into dual income taxes, under which capital income is treated separately for tax purposes from labour income (see Table 8.2).[36] To limit possibilities for tax arbitrage and to deal with growing capital mobility, all capital income, conventionally ascertained, is taxed once, no more and no less, at a uniform flat rate, that is, the CT rate, while labour income continues to be taxed at progressive rates. Full imputation, as in Finland and Norway, ensures that distributed profits are always subject to CT or PT. Capital gains are taxed in a similar fashion to that under the CBIT. Capital income accruing in proprietorships and closed companies is determined as the product of equity for tax purposes and a presumptive rate of return; remaining 'profits' are taxed as labour income.[37] To limit opportunities for tax arbitrage, the CT rate equals the lowest PT rate on labour income. In the course of the reforms, labour and capital income tax rates were substantially reduced (see Table 8.2), although revenue increased.[38]

The Nordic countries noted that the lower flat tax on capital income would mitigate the lock-in effect of a capital gains tax that induces capital owners to postpone realization, thereby frustrating the workings of the capital market. Furthermore, a lower rate eases the effects of applying the tax to inflationary gains, which should not be taxed but for which it is difficult to correct on practical grounds.[39] It has also been pointed out (Sørensen, 1994a) that horizontal equity implies that capital income should be taxed lower than labour income. After all, on the assumption of equal income-earning capacities, a global income tax that taxes savings twice weighs more heavily on people who save or who enter the labour market early than on people who consume their income early or start working later in life. In this situation, a lower tax rate on capital income lessens the horizontal discrimination between taxpayers with different patterns of consumption or different earnings profiles.

The treatment of capital income under the dual income tax strongly resembles its treatment under the CBIT, and effects should be similar. Labour income, however, is subject to higher (progressive) tax rates and capital income is taxed at a flat rate. Furthermore, interest is taxed at the level of the recipient instead of at company level. A non-refundable withholding tax on interest, set at the level of the CT rate as in Finland, would make the treatment of capital income paid to resident PT- or CT-liable

Table 8.2   Tax rates on labour and capital income in the Nordic countries[a] (%)

	Labor income	Capital income	
		Personal income	*Company income*
Sweden			
Before 1991	36–72	36–72	52
In 1991[b]	31–51	30	30
Norway			
Before 1992	26.5–50	26.5–40.5	50.8
In 1992	28–41.7	28	28
Finland			
Before 1993	25–57	25–57	37
In 1993	25–57	25	25[c]
Denmark			
Before 1994	50–68	50–56	50
In 1994	38–58	38–44/58[d]	34

[a] Inclusive of local taxes.
[b] Effective 1 January 1995, tax rates on labour income were increased to 32–56 per cent, whilst the company profits rate was reduced to 28 per cent. Furthermore, the double tax on dividends was reinstated and the reduced rate on capital gains was abolished.
[c] In 1995, the CT rate was increased to 28 per cent.
[d] The highest marginal tax rate on capital income less than Dkr 20 000 (Dkr 40 000 for married couples) cannot exceed 44 per cent.
Source: P.B. Sørensen (1994a) 'From the Global Income Tax to the Dual Income Tax: Recent Tax Reforms in the Nordic Countries', *International Tax and Public Finance,* vol. 1, p. 59.

individuals or investors identical to its treatment under the CBIT. A very important difference with the CBIT is that the Nordic countries do not tax interest on the source basis. (Withholding tax rates on interest paid on inward debt investment are nil.) To do so would require extensive discussion with other EU member states and other countries, as well as with participants in international debt markets.[40]

V   PREFERRED SOLUTION

In terms of the neutrality and subsidiarity criteria developed in Section III – equality of effective CT+PT rates on various forms of company earnings, regardless of the tax status of the recipients – full integration, dual imputation and dividend deduction do not seem to be serious prototypes for coordinating the CTs in the EU. All of these prototypes place undue reliance on the residence principle for taxing the full return on capital. It does not seem that this principle could be adequately implemented in a world of greatly increased capital mobility and financial innovation, offering a multitude of opportunities for domestic and cross-border tax arbitrage.

Without a personal expenditure tax complement, the ACE allowance and the cash-flow tax similarly rely on the residence principle in taxing the normal return on equity at the individual level. In view of the opportunities for cross-border arbitrage, this implies giving up on the effective taxation of normal profits, as has *de facto* been done with the taxation of interest. A personal expenditure tax complement would sanction the exemption of normal (and pure) profits and interest at company and individual level. But again, opportunities for tax arbitrage and evasion raise doubt as to whether the consumption of these returns would ever be taxed.

More importantly, the body politic in the EU (and the USA), thus far, seems to favour the taxation of the normal return to capital. The CT is looked upon as a progressive element in most tax systems and an essential complement to the PT. There appears to be no compelling reason, moreover, to eliminate the CT (and other taxes on capital income) on efficiency grounds.[41] If so, the remaining contenders for the present CTs are the CBIT and the dual income tax. To meet the neutrality and subsidiarity criteria, however, the dual income tax, like the CBIT, would have to be levied in full on the source basis.[42] This can be achieved through the imposition of a withholding tax on interest at company level, which would not be rebatable to exempt entities and non-residents.

Unlike the CBIT, the dual income tax continues to tax labour income at progressive rates over and above the proportional rate applicable to capital (and labour) income. Most EU member states may wish to do so, for two reasons. First, they have a preference for a fairly large public sector; in other words, the demand for revenue is large. Relatively immobile tax bases, such as labour, will then have to be exploited more intensively than in, for example, the USA. Second, separate taxation of labour and capital income leaves open the option of lowering the tax rate on capital income further (without, at the same time, having to lower the rate on labour income), should capital become even more mobile than it is at present. A vertical equity argument for higher taxes on labour income, moreover, is that most income differences in modern economies seem to be due more to differences in human capital than to differences in financial capital. Furthermore, efficiency considerations support progressive taxes on labour income, because they may moderate wage demands in unionized countries (Lockwood and Manning, 1993).

The dual income tax seems more or less in line with conventional methods of ascertaining profits or income, and existing forms of CT/PT systems. Six member states already have an imputation system. This system, or an equivalent compensatory tax, would also have to be introduced by the other member states upon the adoption of an EU-wide dual income tax. All states would have to deny the imputation credit to out-of-state shareholders and exempt entities. Another six member states already tax company profits, whether retained or distributed, at flat rates; they would have to eliminate the special PT rate on dividend income. All but four member states already apply a withholding tax to interest payments. This withholding tax would have to be introduced by all member states, but exemptions or tax refunds for non-residents and exempt entities would have to be abolished. Moreover, nearly all member states (Finland is the exception) should align the taxation of all forms of capital income with their CT rates. Finally, residence countries should exempt out-of-state dividend, interest and royalty income.

Under the dual income tax, all equity and debt income earned by companies is taxed only once: at shareholder and debtholder level through imputation (dividends) and withholding (interest, royalties) techniques. Also, such income would be taxed only by the source state. As a point of immediate policy relevance, this suggests that the parent–subsidiary directive (no source dividend tax on intercompany profit distributions) should be welcomed, but that the draft interest–royalty directive (no source tax on interest and royalties) should not be adopted. After all, the parent–subsidiary directive eliminates an undesirable extra layer of tax, but the draft interest–royalty directive prohibits a desired single layer of tax.

The proportional *in rem* taxation of all company earnings would obviate the need for thin capitalization rules. Also, the lack of external neutrality of current imputation systems would be a thing of the past. Tax credits would not be extended to out-of-state shareholders, because the proportional rate in source states and the exemption of capital income in domicile states would approximately ensure non-discriminatory treatment. Manipulation of transfer prices (prices charged to foreign affiliated companies) would still be possible to influence the allocation of profits (and thus CT revenues) between the member states, but a minimum CT rate, as proposed by the Ruding Committee, should reduce the incentive for this form of tax arbitrage (Daly and Weiner, 1993). In this connection, it should be emphasized that approximation of statutory tax rates seems more important than approximation of effective tax rates. Differences in statutory rates are important for exploiting opportunities for tax avoidance (transfer pricing, thin capitalization). Effective tax rates, on the other hand, have regard to the ascertainment of taxable profits (depreciation, inventory valuation) with respect to less mobile physical capital. Tolerable differences in effective tax rates would increase the operational independence of the member states.

The dual income tax would reduce the cost of equity-financed investment and increase the cost of debt-financed investment. This should benefit new, starting enterprises. The lower cost (and therefore the higher relative return) of equity should promote shareholding, make mergers (to avoid the double tax on dividends) less attractive, induce pension funds to change the composition of their portfolios in favour of shares, and form a natural barrier against easy foreign acquisition of domestic firms. In short, the dynamics of the market would be strengthened and ownership patterns would more closely reflect underlying market forces. Finally, the dual income tax should reduce the need for taxing capital gains on substantial shareholdings, because the profit of closely-held companies is split into a capital and a labour component with annual taxation of the proceeds from employment performed by management. This should improve the workings of the capital market, because profits of closely-held companies can be distributed without incurring tax.

Phase-in issues should be given due attention. Although the more effective taxation of interest income is clearly a goal worth pursuing, gradual and concerted action-is called for. Caution is advisable because the current tax-induced changes in corporate financing patterns may to a large extent serve to reduce the distortions of real investment and saving decisions. Higher before-tax interest rates, moreover, would dampen (debt-financed) investment demand. Coordination with the USA and Japan would be essential in order to prevent tax-induced capital outflows from reducing the post-tax return to saving or instead raising the cost of capital in the EU, and to jointly constrain tax haven practices.[43] A start could be made with a common minimum EU withholding rate. Interest paid to out-of-state residents should be included in the base. The low level of the rate would minimize changes in the interstate distribution of tax revenues. Additional revenues, moreover, would be likely to be positive for all member states in view of the present arrangements, which closely resemble the proverbial sieve.

This chapter has argued that domestic and cross-border investment decisions in the EU are distorted by a crazy quilt of widely diverging tax rates on company earnings (and other capital income). Tax neutrality, an important leitmotif in the Treaty of Rome, requires a more even-handed approach to the taxation of retained profits, distributions and interest, as well as capital gains, royalties and other forms of capital income. Current dividend relief systems repair only a minor defect (of doubtful pain for mature companies) of classical CT/PT systems and greatly complicate the treatment of outward and inward dividend income. More importantly, the deductibility of interest at company level, in conjunction with the existence of capital-rich exempt domestic and foreign sectors, creates an enormous loophole in the CT and greatly distorts the debt–equity choice.

Tax subsidiarity, an important leading thought in the Treaty of Maastricht, requires agreement on the allocation of tax bases throughout the EU and on the basic structure of the instruments for tapping those bases. The allocation of the CT base should probably be based on the primacy of the source entitlement principle, extended to all company earnings – profits as well as interest and royalties. A CT structure, agreed upon along these lines, would permit substantial operational independence; in other words, the need for day-to-day coordination would be minimized. The EU VAT is a good example of the way in which these distinct but related dimensions of subsidiarity have been effected. The Sixth Directive provides for a common VAT structure, yet member states enjoy nearly full independence in operating their VATs. Perhaps the CTs in the EU should be coordinated in similar fashion.

Notes

1. For early reviews of the report of the Ruding Committee (1992), see Devereux (1992), Gammie (1992a) and McLure (1992a). For a prior analysis, see Tanzi and Bovenberg (1990). For a general analysis of tax coordination in the European Community, see Kopits (1992). For some further thoughts, see also Cnossen and Bovenberg (1997).
2. For a review of the directives and other EU measures affecting the coordination of the income taxes, see Easson (1992).
3. For reviews of various theoretical and empirical studies, see OECD (1991, ch. 2); and US Department of the Treasury (1992, ch. 13).
4. See Mintz (1995) for an exposition of the various reasons for levying the CT.
5. For an analysis of the imputation system and other methods of dividend relief, see the classical analysis by McLure (1979) as well as US Department of the Treasury (1992).
6. Whether or not tax preferences at company level should be passed through to shareholders is a difficult policy issue that is not discussed here. For a good treatment, see McLure (1979, ch. 4).
7. Note that the following simplifying assumptions have been made in calculating the effective CT+PT rates on distributed profits: (a) CTs are borne by profits; (b) after-CT profits are fully distributed; (c) dividends are received

by resident PT-liable individuals; (d) individuals and companies face the maximum CT and PT rates, inclusive of taxes levied by subordinate levels of government; (e) CT and PT rates remain unchanged; and (f) the amount of pre-tax company income available for distribution remains the same, regardless of the level of tax rates or the degree of mitigation. See OECD (1991, p. 254).

8.   For fairly recent treatments of the signalling effect and the 'principal–agent' problem, see Williams (1988) and Easterbrook (1984), respectively.

9.   For reviews and analyses of these views, see Poterba and Summers (1985), Sinn (1985 and 1991), Zodrow (1991) and Sørensen (1994b and 1995). As Head (1997) points out, the policy implications of these two views are quite different. Under the new view, in contrast to the traditional view, any CT reform aimed at greater integration with the PT is of doubtful relevance from an efficiency point of view, but must clearly be rejected on equity grounds because it results in windfall gains to existing shareholders. The strong conclusions of the new view, however, rest entirely on the assumption that equity earnings must eventually be distributed as PT-liable dividends. Furthermore, it should be noted that the double tax also should not affect the cost of capital in a small open economy in which the required return on equity before PT is exogenously determined from abroad. The main effect of the PT on equity income is then to make shareholding less attractive relative to debtholding.

10. Gravelle and Kotlikoff (1989) have noted that the distortions of the business form are greater than shown by earlier estimates, because the CT/PT also distorts the relative importance of company producers (able to exploit economies of scale) and non-company producers (able to apply greater entrepreneurial skills) within an industry.

11. The tax-exempt status of institutional investors should affect their portfolio choice and thereby the ownership structure of firms. In the USA, for instance, 95 per cent of all company debt is thought to be owned by tax-exempt investors, compared with half of all equity (Graetz, 1989, p. 722).

12. It should be noted that Gordon and Slemrod (1988, p. 105) compare the tax revenue collected under the actual tax system with the tax revenue that would have been collected under a cash-flow tax. The cash-flow tax effects are simulated by 'allowing new investments to be expended and then taxing at ordinary rates any resulting cash flow from the investments, including the sales price if the assets are sold'. In terms of revenue raised, therefore, existing US income taxes do not tax the normal return to saving and investment, but they may tax any return over and above this – as a cash-flow tax would.

13. Earlier Bird and McLure (1990) drew attention to the erosion of the capital income base through the combination of interest deductibility, financial innovation, international tax arbitrage and evasion. For a general treatment, see also Owens (1993). Recently, the European Commission (1996) has expressed its concern with the situation. The problem is compounded by the use of increasingly sophisticated financial instruments.

14. Generally, withholding rates range from 0 to 10 per cent. In spite of various efforts (OECD, 1974; European Commission, 1989) to stem the tide, the general level of interest withholding taxes has declined since the 1980s.

15. German banks, for example, often resemble holding companies that are closely involved in the activities of German businesses. In this situation, the high CT rate (or the lower rate on distributed profits plus the withholding rate) does not discourage domestic investment, but mainly acts as a protective device against foreign take-overs and foreign ownership of domestic firms, because foreigners do not have the same easy access to bank finance.

16. It should be pointed out that the King–Fullerton type of model used by the OECD takes no account of behavioural responses (Fullerton, 1986). In other words, it is not known to what extent the potential distortions are actual effects on investment (and saving) decisions. The significant differential effects are confirmed, however, by the results of a survey, commissioned by the Ruding Committee (1992, pp. 100–9), among 6100 companies (of which 16 per cent responded) in the EU and the countries of the European Free Trade Association (EFTA).

17. It should be emphasized that tax neutrality, as interpreted here, abstracts from various next-best issues, such as differences in mobility, asymmetric information, and so on. For a broad treatment of the welfare economics of tax coordination, see Keen (1994).

18. McLure (1992b) is the *auctor intellectualis* of the operational (or, as he calls it, administrative) independence principle. The way in which I try to give body to the subsidiarity principle in this chapter owes much to his pioneering contribution.

19. The value-added tax (VAT) seems a good application of the neutrality and subsidiarity requirements. The tax credit and invoice mechanism generally ensures that producer or consumer choices are not distorted within member states and that products entering intra-EU trade are not affected by the tax. Moreover, agreement on the entitlement to tax consumption on a destination basis in accordance with uniform rules (as laid down in the EU's Sixth Directive on Value Added Tax) ensures operational independence in administering the VAT.

20. Most economists tend to favour capital export neutrality, which promotes efficiency in the allocation of investment, over capital import neutrality, which promotes efficiency in the allocation of savings. The reason is that users of capital, that is, business firms, tend to be more sensitive to differences in returns than are suppliers of capital, that is, savers. Hence, distortions in deviating from capital export neutrality tend to be greater. Businessmen and governments, on the other hand, tend to favour capital import neutrality which they associate with the source principle. Capital export neutrality, however, would not be achieved with a source-based CT unless there were harmonization. In considering these positions, note that as capital and capital owners become increasingly more mobile in the EU, the distinction between capital export and capital import neutrality is blurred. For a useful treatment, see Devereux and Pearson (1990).

21. See especially Musgrave (1987), who is the most vocal academic proponent of the source entitlement principle in allocating the CT base as a matter of inter-nation equity. For strong arguments in favour of the source principle, see also Vogel (1990). Brean (1992) rightly points out that the precise source of income may sometimes be difficult to pinpoint.

22. For the classical exposition of the S–H–S income concept, see Goode (1975). For the normative inference of full integration, see Musgrave and Musgrave (1984).
23. For a useful treatment, see Boadway, Bruce and Mintz (1982).
24. Here, the emphasis is on physical capital. See Atkinson and Sandmo (1980) and King (1980). As an extension, it has been suggested that a small, open economy in a world of full capital mobility acts optimally by placing the marginal tax burden exclusively on the immobile factor, labour (Razin and Sadka, 1989). It should be pointed out, however, that these studies assume that there is no coordination of capital income taxes.
25. The system's name was coined by Graetz (1989). Warren (1991) came out in favour of the system in his report to the American Law Institute.
26. Iceland still permits a dividend deduction up to an amount equal to 10 per cent of paid-in capital plus any later issue of stock dividends. Also, the US Treasury Department Report to the President (1984) included a proposal for a 50 per cent deduction (later reduced to 10 per cent) for dividends paid. It should be noted that a partial dividend deduction system is equivalent to the split-rate method – part of the German imputation system.
27. An interesting aspect of the US Treasury Department dividend deduction proposal (see note 26) was that the automatic extension of the benefit to non-residents was seen to be positive, because it would help finance the US deficit on current account. (Mentioned by Charles McLure in his comments on a draft of this article.)
28. Andrews (1979 and 1989), reporting for the American Law Institute, has proposed a limited deduction (determined by applying a risk-free rate of interest) for dividends on new equity, as well as a corporate excise tax on redemptions. Warren (1981 and 1993), however, has argued that the proposal would not be feasible.
29. Bond and Devereux (1995) have shown that the rate of relief for the ACE allowance should be the risk-free rate, provided that taxable profits and losses are treated symmetrically and that the tax rate is a known constant.
30. For a thorough comparison of a personal consumption tax and a PT, see Bradford (1986).
31. The combination of a cash-flow CT and a traditional PT would yield neutrality towards company financing decisions only if the marginal PT rates on interest, dividends and accrued capital gains on shares were identical. See OECD (1991, p. 32).
32. See McLure and Zodrow (1996) for arguments why taxation based on cash flow has administrative and economic advantages over a conventional income tax. For a discussion of implementation problems, see Mintz and Seade (1991) and Shome and Schutte (1993).
33. See the detailed treatment in US Department of the Treasury (1992, ch. 3). For reviews of the US Treasury study, see Goode (1992) and Sunley (1992).
34. The US Department of the Treasury (1992) advocates also imposing the compensatory tax on foreign source income, while retaining current foreign tax credit rules. To avoid double taxation, this should not, of course, be done in the EU, where the exemption method would apply to foreign source income.
35. See the surveys and evaluations by Lodin (1993) and Sørensen (1994a).

36. For individual country reviews, see Pedersen (1993) for Denmark, Tikka (1993) for Finland, Skaar (1991) for Norway, and Grosskopf (1990), Mutén (1992) and Andersson and Mutén (1994) for Sweden. For an outline of a Dutch dual income tax aimed at reducing the wedge on labour income and eliminating the highly differentiated taxation of capital income, see Cnossen (1995).
37. For a good treatment of the issues, see Hagen and Sørensen (forthcoming).
38. CT and PT receipts from capital income increased, for example in Sweden by 2.7 percentage points of GDP: at the same time, the highly distortionary tax burden on labour income was reduced – by 5.6 percentage points of GDP over a period of three years. See OECD (1994, Table 3), in conjunction with the Swedish Ministry of Finance (1991).
39. To illustrate, if the nominal return on an asset is 10 per cent and the rate of inflation is 4 per cent, then a PT rate of 50 per cent must be reduced to 30 per cent [0.5(0.1 – 0.04)/0.1] if only the real return is to be taxed.
40. As Malcolm Gammie pointed out to me, international debt markets generally operate on a gross interest payment basis and most existing loan instruments have gross-up clauses and clauses permitting early repayment if the taxation basis for interest changes. These clauses would be likely to be triggered, however low withholding tax on interest were introduced (or increased).
41. On the efficiency costs of the CT and its effect on the tax burden distribution, see Gravelle (1994, especially ch. 2).
42. Source taxation increases the importance of properly defining the source of income. Formula-based taxation to determine the source of income of companies operating throughout the EU would be a much more far-reaching alternative. See McLure (1989) and Weiner (1992). Formula-based taxation, however, would require an overarching EU CT.
43. The prospects of international coordination are not as bleak as they seem to be at first sight. The USA, for instance, has already debated the merits of the CBIT, which closely resembles the dual income tax.

References

Andersson, K. and L. Mutén (1994) 'The Tax System of Sweden', *Tax Notes International*, 10 October, pp. 1147–63.

Andrews, W.D. (1979) ALI Federal Income Tax Project, *Tentative Draft No. 2, Subchapter C – Corporate Distributions* (Philadelphia, Penn.: American Law Institute).

—— (1989) ALI Federal Income Tax Project, *Reporter's Study Draft – Subchapter C (Supplemental Study)* (Philadelphia, Penn.: American Law Institute).

Atkinson, A. B. and A. Sandmo (1980) 'Welfare Implications of the Taxation of Savings', *Economic Journal*, vol. 90, pp. 529–49.

Bird, R.M. and C.E. McLure Jr. (1990) 'The Personal Income Tax in an Interdependent World', in S. Cnossen (ed.), *The Personal Income Tax: Phoenix from the Ashes?* (Amsterdam: North-Holland).

Boadway, R. and N. Bruce (1984) 'A General Proposition on the Design of a Neutral Business Tax', *Journal of Public Economics*, vol. 24, pp. 231–9.

—, — and J. Mintz (1982) 'Corporate Taxation in Canada: Toward an Efficient System', in W.R. Thirsk and J. Whalley (eds). *Tax Policy Options in the 1980s* (Toronto: Canadian Tax Foundation).

Bond, S.R. and M. Devereux (1995) 'On the Design of a Neutral Business Tax under Uncertainty', *Journal of Public Economics*, vol. 58, pp. 57–91.

Bradford, D.F. (1986) *Untangling the Income Tax* (Cambridge: Harvard University Press).

Brean, D.J.S. (1992) 'Here or There? The Source and Residence Principles of International Taxation', in R.M. Bird and J.M. Mintz (eds), *Taxation to 2000 and Beyond* (Toronto: Canadian Tax Foundation).

Campbell Committee (1981) *Final Report of the Committee of Inquiry into the Australian Financial System* (Canberra: Australian Government Publishing Service).

Cnossen, S. (1990) 'The Case for Tax Diversity in the European Community', *European Economic Review*, vol. 4, pp. 471–9.

— (1995) 'Towards a New Tax Covenant', *De Economist*, vol. 143, pp. 285–315.

— and L. Bovenberg (1997) 'Company Tax Harmonization in the European Union: Some Further Thoughts on the Ruding Committee Report', in M.I. Blejer and T. Ter-Minassian (eds), *Macroeconomic Dimensions of Public Finance: Essays in Honour of Vito Tanzi* (London: Routledge).

Daly, M. and J. Weiner (1993) 'Corporate Tax Harmonization and Competition in Federal Countries: Some Lessons for the European Community', *National Tax Journal*, vol. 46, pp. 441–61.

Devereux, M. (1992) 'The Ruding Committee Report: An Economic Assessment', *Fiscal Studies*, vol. 13, no. 2, pp. 96–107.

— and H. Freeman (1991) 'A General Neutral Profits Tax', *Fiscal Studies*, vol. 12, no. 3, pp. 1–15.

— and M. Pearson (1990) 'Harmonising Corporate Taxes in Europe', *Fiscal Studies*, vol. 11, no. 1, pp. 21–35.

Easson, A. (1992) 'Harmonization of Direct Taxation in the European Community: From Neumark to Ruding', *Canadian Tax Journal*, vol. 40, pp. 600–38.

Easterbrook, F.H. (1984) 'Two Agency-Cost Explanations of Dividends', *American Economic Review*, vol. 74, pp. 650–9.

European Commission (1989) *Proposal for a Council Directive on a Common System of Withholding Tax on Interest Income*, COM (89) 60/3/Revision final (Brussels).

—— (1996), *Taxation in the European Union*, Discussion Paper for the Informal Meeting of ECOFIN Ministers, SEC (96) 487 final (Brussels).

Fullerton, D. (1986) 'The Use of Effective Tax Rates in Tax Policy', *National Tax Journal*, vol. 39, pp. 285–92.

Gammie, M. (1992a) 'The Harmonisation of Corporate Income Taxes in Europe: The Ruding Committee Report', *Fiscal Studies*, vol. 13, no. 2, pp. 108–21.

—— (1992b) 'Corporate Tax Harmonisation: An "ACE" proposal', *European Taxation*, vol. 31, pp. 238–42.

—— (1992c) 'Reforming Corporate Taxation: An Evaluation of the United States Treasury Integration Proposals and other Corporate Tax Systems in an International Context', Parts 1 and 2, *British Tax Review*, nos 3 and 4, pp. 148–73 and 243–76.

Gerardi, G., M.J. Graetz and H.S. Rosen (1990) 'Corporate Integration Puzzles', *National Tax Journal*, vol. 43, pp. 307–14.

Goode, R. (1975) *The Individual Income Tax*, 2nd edn (Washington, DC: Brookings Institution).

—— (1992) 'Integration of Corporate and Individual Taxes: A Treasury Report', *Tax Notes* (Special Report), 30 March, pp. 1667–71.

Gordon, R.H. and J. Slemrod (1988), 'Do We Collect Any Revenue from Taxing Capital Income?', in L.H. Summers (ed.), *Tax Policy and the Economy*, vol. 2 (Cambridge, Mass.: MIT Press).

Graetz, M.J. (1989) 'The Tax Aspects of Leveraged Buyouts and Other Corporate Financial Restructuring Transactions', *Tax Notes*, 6 February, pp. 721–6.

Gravelle, J.G. (1994) *The Economic Effects of Taxing Capital Income* (Cambridge, Mass.: MIT Press).

Gravelle, J.G. and L.J. Kotlikoff (1989) 'The Incidence and Efficiency Costs of Corporate Taxation When Corporate and Noncorporate Firms Produce the Same Good', *Journal of Political Economy*, vol. 97, pp. 749–90.

Grosskopf, G. (1990) 'The Swedish Tax Reform: Rules and Effects', *Bulletin for International Fiscal Documentation*, August/September, pp. 366–85.

Hagen, K.P. and P.B. Sørensen (forthcoming) 'Taxation of the Self-Employed: Taxation Principles and Tax Reforms in Scandinavia', in P.B. Sørensen (ed.), *Tax Policy in the Nordic Countries*.

Hall, R.E. and A. Rabushka (1995) *The Flat Rate*, 2nd edn (Stanford, Calif.: Hoover Institution Press).

Head, J.G. (1997) 'Company Tax Structure and Company Tax Incidence', *International Tax and Public Finance*, vol. 4, pp. 61–99.

Huizinga, H. (1994) 'International Interest Withholding Taxation: Prospects for a Common European Policy', *International Tax and Public Finance*, vol. 1, pp. 277–91.

IFS Capital Taxes Group (1989) *Neutrality in the Taxation of Savings: An Extended Role for PEPs*, Commentary No. 17 (London: Institute for Fiscal Studies).

—— (1991) *Equity for Companies: A Corporation Tax for the 1990s*, Commentary No. 26 (London: Institute for Fiscal Studies).

Keen, M. (1994) 'The Welfare Economics of Tax Co-ordination in the European Community: A Survey', *Fiscal Studies*, vol. 14, no. 2, pp. 15–36.

King, M.A. (1980) 'Saving and Taxation', in G.A. Hughes and G.M. Heal (eds), *Public Policy and the Tax System* (London: Allen & Unwin).

Kopits, G. (ed.) (1992) *Tax Harmonization in the European Community: Policy Issues and Analysis*, IMF Occasional Papers No. 94 (Washington, DC: International Monetary Fund).

Lockwood, B. and A. Manning (1993) 'Wage Setting and the Tax System: Theory and Evidence from the United Kingdom', *Journal of Public Economics*, vol. 52, pp. 1–29.

Lodin, S.-O. (1993) *The Nordic Reforms of Company and Shareholder Taxation* (Federation of Swedish Industries).

McLure, C.E., Jr (1979) *Must Corporate Income Be Taxed Twice?* (Washington, DC: Brookings Institution).

—— (1989) 'Economic Integration and European Taxation of Corporate Income at Source: Some Lessons from the U.S. Experience', *European Taxation*, vol. 29, August, pp. 243–50.

—— (1992a) 'Coordinating Business Taxation in the Single European Market: The Ruding Committee Report', *EC Tax Review*, vol. 1, pp. 13–20.

—— (1992b) 'Substituting Consumption-based Direct Taxation for Income Taxes as the International Norm', *National Tax Journal*, vol. 45, pp. 145–54.

McLure, C.E. and G.R. Zodrow (1996) 'A Hybrid Consumption-based Direct Tax for Bolivia', *International Tax and Public Finance*, vol. 3, pp. 97–112.

Meade Committee (1978) *The Structure and Reform of Direct Taxation* (London: Institute for Fiscal Studies).

Mintz, J. (1995) 'The Corporation Tax: A Survey', *Fiscal Studies*, vol. 16, no. 4, pp. 23–68.

Mintz, J. and J. Seade (1991) 'Cash Flow or Income? The Choice of Base for Company Taxation', *The World Bank Research Observer*, vol. 6, pp. 177–90.

Musgrave, P.B. (1987) 'Interjurisdictional Coordination of Taxes on Capital Income', in S. Cnossen (ed.), *Tax Coordination in the European Community* (Deventer: Kluwer).

Musgrave, R.A. and P.B. Musgrave (1984) *Public Finance in Theory and Practice*, 4th edn (New York: McGraw-Hill).

Mutén, L. (1992) 'The Fiscal Revolution in Sweden – Tax Reform in Preparation for European Integration', *Tax Notes International*, 16 November, pp. 1045–52.

OECD (1974) 'Report on Taxation of Loan Capital', unpublished (Paris).

—— (1991) *Taxing Profits in a Global Economy: Domestic and International Issues* (Paris: Organisation for Economic Cooperation and Development).

—— (1994) *Revenue Statistics in OECD Member Countries 1965–1993* (Paris: Organisation for Economic Cooperation and Development).

Owens, J. (1993) 'Globalisation: The Implications for Tax Policies', *Fiscal Studies*, vol. 14, no. 3, pp. 21–44.

Pedersen, B.M. (1993) 'Denmark: Tax Reform', *Bulletin for International Fiscal Documentation*, December, pp. 711–15.

Poterba, J.M. (1987) 'Tax Policy and Corporate Saving', *Brookings Papers on Economic Activity*, vol. 2, pp. 455–515.

Poterba, J.M., and L.H. Summers (1985) 'The Economic Effects of Dividend Taxation', in E. Altman and M. Subrahmanyam (eds), *Recent Advances in Corporate Finance* (Homewood, Ill.: Irwin).

Razin, A. and E. Sadka (1989) 'International Tax Competition and Gains from Tax Harmonization', National Bureau of Economic Research, Working Paper No. 3152.

Rose, M. and R. Wiswesser (this volume) 'Tax Reform in Transition Economies: Experiences from the Croatian Tax Reform Process of the 1990s'.

Royal (Carter) Commission on Taxation (1966) *Report* (Ottawa: Queen's Printer).

Ruding Committee (1992) *Conclusions and Recommendations of the Committee of Independent Experts on Company Taxation* (Luxembourg: Commission of the European Communities).

Shome, P. and C. Schutte (1993) 'Cash-Flow Tax', *IMF Staff Papers*, vol. 40, pp. 638–62.

Sinn, H.-W. (1985) *Capital Income Taxation and Resource Allocation* (Amsterdam: North-Holland).

—— (1991) 'Taxation and the Cost of Capital: The "Old" View, the "New" View and Another View', in D.F. Bradford (ed.), *Tax Policy and the Economy*, Vol. 5 (Cambridge, Mass.: MIT Press for the National Bureau of Economic Research).

Skaar, A.A. (1991) 'Norway Enacts Tax Reform of the Century', *Tax Notes International*, November, pp. 1169–72.

Smith, S. (1993) '"Subsidiarity" and the Co-ordination of Indirect Taxes in the European Community', *Oxford Review of Economic Policy*, vol. 9, no. 1, pp. 67–94.

Sørensen, P.B. (1988) 'Wealth Taxation, Income Taxation, and Saving', University of Copenhagen, Institute of Economics, *Blue Mimeo*, no. 163.

—— (1994a) 'From the Global Income Tax to the Dual Income Tax: Recent Tax Reforms in the Nordic Countries', *International Tax and Public Finance*, vol. 1, pp. 57–79.

—— (1994b) 'Some Old and New Issues in the Theory of Corporate Income Taxation', *Finanzarchiv*, vol. 51, pp. 425–56.

—— (1995) 'Changing Views of the Corporate Income Tax', *National Tax Journal*, vol. 48, pp. 279–94.

Sunley, E.M. (1992) 'Corporate Integration: An Economic Perspective', *Tax Law Review*, vol. 47, pp. 621–43.

Swedish Ministry of Finance (1991) *The Swedish Tax Reform of 1991* (Stockholm: Norstedts Tryckeri).

Tanzi, V. and L. Bovenberg (1990) 'Is There a Need for Harmonizing Capital Income Taxes within EC Countries?', in H. Sieber (ed.), *Reforming Capital Income Taxation* (Tübingen: Mohr for the World Economic Institute, Kiel).

Tikka, K.S. (1993) 'Finland: Fundamental Tax Reform (25 percent Rate on Capital Income and Corporate Income)', *Bulletin for International Fiscal Documentation*, June, pp. 348–53.

US Department of the Treasury (1979) *Blueprints for Basic Tax Reform* (Washington, DC: US Government Printing Office).

—— (1984) *Tax Reform for Fairness, Simplicity, and Economic Growth* (Washington, DC: US Government Printing Office).

—— (1992) *Integration of the Individual and Corporate Tax Systems: Taxing Business Income Once* (Washington, DC: US Government Printing Office).

Vogel, K. (1990) 'World-wide vs. Source Taxation of Income: A Review and Reevaluation of Arguments', in McLure, Musgrave *et al.*, *Influence of Tax Differentials on International Competitiveness* (Deventer: Kluwer).

Warren, A.C. (1981) 'The Relation and Integration of Individual and Corporate Income Taxes', *Harvard Law Review*, vol. 94, pp. 719–800.

—— (1991) Reporter's Memorandum No. 3, ALI Federal Income Tax Project, *Integration of the Individual and Corporate Income Taxes* (Philadelphia, Penn.: American Law Institute).

—— (1993) Reporter's Study of Corporate Tax Integration, ALI Federal Income Tax Project, *Integration of the Individual and Corporate Income Taxes* (Philadelphia, Penn.: American Law Institute).

Weiner, J. (1992) 'Tax Coordination and Competition in the United States of America', Annex 9C in Ruding Committee, *Conclusions and Recommendations* of the Committee of Independent Experts on Company Taxation (Luxembourg: Commission of the European Communities).

Williams, J. (1988) 'Efficient Signalling with Dividends, Investment, and Stock Repurchases', *Journal of Finance*, vol. 43, pp. 737–47.

Zodrow, G.R. (1991) 'On the "Traditional" and "New" Views of Dividend Taxation', *National Tax Journal*, vol. 44, pp. 497–510.

Part IV
Economies in Transition: Raising Revenue and Allocating Property Rights

9 Tax Reform in Transition Economies: Experiences from the Croatian Tax Reform Process of the 1990s

Manfred Rose and Rolf Wiswesser*

I NTRODUCTION

Economies in the process of transition from centrally planned to market-oriented all suffer heavily from a lack of real capital – concerning both fixed assets in business and human capital in the labour force. The success of the transformation process crucially depends on overcoming this deficiency. In order to maximize the prospects for increasing real capital, one has to focus on the main sources of capital from domestic investment and to attract capital from the developed Western countries. To this end, the tax system has to exhibit the following important properties: it has to guarantee that the cost of capital is protected from being taxed and it has to be attractive from a foreign investor's point of view.

During 1990, immediately after becoming independent, Croatia started to reform the fiscal system it inherited from the former Yugoslavia. In July 1990, an antiquated schedular system of direct taxes on income and a hybrid tax on the sale of goods and services was enacted. In addition, a tax on overall personal income was introduced, which burdened net income from all sources exceeding a threshold of three times the annual average salary level. Finally, in September 1990, a war tax on net wages and other personal income was imposed. Taking into account special community

---

* The research on which this chapter is based has been supported by the Deutsche für Schungsgemeinschaft. We are grateful to Clive Bell, Mike Browne, Armin Schmutzler and George Zodrow for comments on an earlier draft of this chapter. Two referees provided useful suggestions.

wage taxes, all taxes on income added up to marginal tax rates of more than 90 per cent for top incomes. As a consequence, tax evasion, especially among high-income earners and businessmen, emerged on a large scale. Furthermore, a multitude of tax concessions was given to different groups of taxpayers. This exacerbated distortions.

Since 1992, the Croatian Ministry of Finance, in close cooperation with the German KNS tax reform group,[1] has taken up the tremendous task of overcoming these inefficiencies and of introducing a new system of taxation which is better adjusted to the development of a young market economy. As a result of the combined efforts of Croatian and German tax experts, a new personal income tax and a new business profit tax were enacted and have been in use since the beginning of 1994.

II   CRITERIA FOR THE NEW TAX SYSTEM

In order to evaluate an existing tax system and to develop alternatives for reform, criteria for a 'good' tax system are needed. These criteria can be inferred from the basic goals of fiscal policy and the associated functions of taxation, as well as a knowledge of the tax incidence (tax burdens). The demand for a criteria-oriented tax reform is of particular importance for the former socialist countries of Central and Eastern Europe, which usually have no experience with taxes as the main source of financing the government budget in the new framework of democracy and social market economy.

The committee for tax reform at the Croatian Ministry of Finance, following a KNS group blueprint, has designed its basic tax system and tax laws – which are described below – to meet the following criteria:

Criteria to guarantee goal-oriented taxation

C_1: Taxes should supply the public authorities with sufficient revenue to cover their expenses so that state debt financing is restricted to a minimum and so that the government does not rely on inflation-inducing money creation.

C_2: Tax bases should be consumption-oriented, as far as possible, in order to directly absorb part of consumer purchasing power from the market. Moreover, adjusting tax bases to the real burden of taxes, which ultimately are sacrifices in private consumption, helps consumers to identify the total burden of taxation they bear (transparency of tax burden).

C_3: The taxation of income from capital should contribute to an attractive environment for foreign investment in Croatia without discriminating against domestic entrepreneurs.

Criteria to guarantee efficiency in taxation

C_4: Taxes should be as simple as possible in order to keep collection costs low, taking into account the skills of the tax administration; a simple tax system should also keep compliance costs at a minimum, that is, it should help the taxpayer to easily calculate his tax burden and understand his rights under the tax laws.

C_5: Taxes should not distort or hamper the efficient functioning of the economy in transition towards market conditions, that is, taxes should be decision-neutral with respect to the ranking of economic alternatives in order to minimize dead-weight losses from tax-distorted behaviour.

C_6: Taxes should naturally adjust as automatically as possible to changes in economic conditions, in order to avoid or at least minimize the need for new legislation. Automatic adjustments of tax bases, tax brackets and tax rates for the effects of inflation are necessary in order to guarantee that the tax burden is automatically linked to real income.

Criteria to guarantee fairness in taxation

C_7: Only individuals (or income units) whose income exceeds the level needed to purchase the subsistence basket of commodities should be taxed. Therefore, there must be no tax on the subsistence level of family consumption.

C_8: Any purchasing power derived from activities in markets should be taxed only once during the time in which it was earned and used to finance lifetime consumption. Thus, in accordance with the principle of horizontal equity, discriminatory double taxation of any type of income should be avoided.

C_9: The total burden of taxation should be fairly distributed among citizens. We interpret this to imply a modest amount of progressivity in the marginal rate structure.

A detailed discussion of these criteria is beyond the scope of this chapter. We will, however, look at the criterion of decision neutrality in greater detail because politicians and tax reformers often disregard this topic.

The goal underlying the criterion of neutrality in decision-making (C_5) is the formation of efficiently functioning markets. It is of central importance for the functioning of a free market economy in the early stages of development that the tax system be relatively neutral in order to avoid as far as possible the undesired effects of distortionary taxes. In order to ensure the neutrality of a tax system with respect to the economic decisions of consumers, workers, producers and investors, the taxpayer must be able to neglect the tax burden in his individual decision-making because it has no effect on the choice of alternatives. Roughly speaking, this means that ideally the tax system should not prompt anyone to act differently from how he would have under no-tax conditions where he only obeys market signals. The theory of optimal taxation tells us that complete neutrality cannot be achieved because first-best taxation via lump-sum taxes is not possible. Instead, the relevant question is what kind of tax system is closest to second-best. In other words, what are the implications of optimal tax theory for tax policy which, according to Slemrod,[2] should be oriented to an optimal tax system? When dealing with this problem, one has to consider many other aspects of taxation such as collection costs, evasion and avoidance opportunities, and equity properties. We will present the Croatian solution to this issue below.

III   THE NEW CROATIAN SYSTEM OF TAXING PERSONAL INCOME AND BUSINESS PROFIT

General Framework: Efficiency and Decision-Neutrality Properties of Alternative Tax Systems

In designing a rational system of bases for taxing personal income and business profits, the criterion of neutrality with respect to decision-making (C_5) was the starting point.

If personal income taxation is to be neutral, one primary concern relates to the timing of consumption and the incentive to work: the tax system should ideally not interfere with an individual's decision regarding the time pattern of consumption and the labour/leisure choice. For taxing income from business in a decision-neutral way, the profit tax, coordinated with the personal income tax, should not alter the investor's choice between alternative investments. From a theoretical point of view, this implies the requirement of intertemporal neutrality, which is satisfied if, as in the pre-tax situation, the ratio of exchange between present and future consumption (the rate of time preference) is equivalent to one plus the gross rate of return on investment in competitive markets.

The relative virtues of the consumption-based and accretion-based approaches of taxation have long been debated in the literature.[3] We will not repeat the discussion here except to mention two frequently advocated reasons for rejecting the traditional accrual approach to taxing income comprehensively and for favouring consumption-oriented tax bases.

The first argument is related to saving and investment. According to the comprehensive income taxation approach, interest from previously taxed and saved income has to be taxed in full – which effectively imposes a double tax on savings. Thus it is no longer sufficient for the return from an investment to compensate for the consumption forgone – only investments which can also cover tax on interest will appeal to companies, and investments which cannot carry this additional burden will be shelved. A conventional income tax thus raises the capital costs facing companies, which in turn leads to the abandonment of socially desirable investments.

The intertemporal neutrality of consumption-based tax systems, in contrast, is likely to produce a higher level of private savings, a lower deadweight loss,[4] and a greater amount of private investment in the economy.

The second relative virtue of a consumption-based income tax concerns the criterion of fairness (C_8). Taxpayers who are alike in all respects except the timing of their consumption should bear the same tax burden. By taxing income from interest a comprehensive income tax discriminates against savers (late consumers or early earners) in comparison to those who prefer present consumption. Thus, the traditional concept of income taxation, with its uniform taxation of income from labour and interest, is not only inefficient, but also unfair. In comparison, a consumption tax in its ideal form and in its actually implementable forms is more consistent with the principle of horizontal equity.[5]

Many recommendations for designing a consumption-based system of taxing personal and business income have already been put forth in the literature. In the following pages, however, we focus only on the two approaches which Croatian tax reformers and the KNS group discussed when planning the Croatian tax reform.

The first is the cash-flow consumption tax (also known as the consumed income tax). When assessing the cash-flow consumption tax at the individual level, one has to apply the tax rate schedule to the difference between the taxpayer's cash receipts from various sources and the total amount of transfers into all kinds of reserve funds, that is, to saving accounts, life insurance reserves, pension funds, security deposits, and so on. All reductions of reserve funds are dealt with as taxable cash inflows. At the business level, the cash-flow consumption tax should be designed as a tax on net distributions (DT) paid by any taxable business entity, while providing full credit to domestic shareholders. Since taxable income is calculated by subtracting the total net savings from the gross income a taxpayer receives during the year, one can speak of a savings-adjusted personal income tax (SAIT).

In recent discussions concerning a tax system which is equitable and appropriate to a free market economy, another approach has gained increasing attention; this approach is also consistent with the principle of taxing consumption and – in contrast to the SAIT – offers simplicity in collection. This is the interest-adjusted personal income tax (IAIT) and the interest-adjusted business profit tax (IAPT). Such a system exempts from taxation those components of earnings which coincide with the 'normal' (standard) return on capital. Although this does not constitute direct taxation of personal annual consumption, it achieves taxation of personal lifetime consumption comparable to that achieved by a savings-adjusted income tax. The most important points are that the interest-adjusted tax system (a) leads to a prepayment of taxes on future consumption, which eliminates the discrimination against savings of the traditional income tax; and (b) guarantees that the deductible costs of capital in present-value terms correspond to the amount of investment expenditure, and therefore makes a firm's investment decision independent of depreciation allowances and the tax rate.

Using the well-known concept of effective tax rates, it will be shown below that the interest-adjusted (IA) approach meets the criterion of intertemporal neutrality (C_5).

The effective marginal tax rate can be used to assess the impact of taxation on savings and investment. The effective marginal tax rate measures the tax-induced difference between the pre-tax real rate of return on investment (RI) and the post-tax real rate of return to the saver (RS); if intertemporal neutrality holds, the effective marginal tax rate is zero. The effective marginal tax rate is defined as

$$\tau_{eff} = \frac{RI - RS}{RI} \tag{9.1}$$

To calculate the effective marginal tax rate one has to determine RI and RS. In a tax system where interest earned by savers is tax-free, RS equals the real interest rate r, which is equal to the nominal market rate of interest i minus the inflation rate π:

$$RS = r = i - \pi \tag{9.2}$$

The calculation of *RI* is slightly more difficult, as one has to consider the decision to invest one unit of capital (here capital is used as numéraire) into an enterprise. The initial gross marginal rate of output arising from this increment to the capital stock is *c*. With economic depreciation at the rate of δ, the output at time *t* equals $c\,e^{-\delta t}$, with the capital stock employed being $e^{-\delta t}$. For simplicity, we assume a constant rate of inflation at π. Thus the nominal output rate amounts to $c\,e^{-\delta t}\,e^{\pi t}$. This nominal output is subject to a profit tax at constant rate τ, allowing deductions for depreciation as well as interest expense on all capital employed. Taking γ as the constant rate of depreciation for tax purposes, the book value of the capital remaining in this enterprise is $e^{-\gamma t}$ at time *t*. Therefore the tax liability at time *t* amounts to

$$T(t) = \tau(ce^{-\delta t}e^{\pi t} - \gamma e^{-\gamma t} - ie^{-\gamma t}) \tag{9.3}$$

with $\gamma e^{-\gamma t}$ being depreciation for tax purposes and $ie^{-\gamma t}$ being the interest deduction on capital employed.[6] It should be noted that an interest deduction is allowed for, no matter whether the capital is financed by equity or by debt. Consequently, there is no tax discrimination between debt financing and equity financing. At the same time, the tax system does not differentiate between different uses of profits. All profits are taxed at rate τ whether retained or distributed. As a result the tax system is neutral towards different ways of financing investment.

To calculate *RI* one has to compare the cost of investment (which in our case is one) with the post-tax return on investment, taking into account that the capital employed in the enterprise would otherwise yield a return at the constant rate of interest *i*. Therefore, all returns are discounted at rate *i*. The arbitrage condition, then, is

$$1 = \int_0^\infty \left[ce^{-\delta t}e^{\pi t} - \tau\left(ce^{-\delta t}e^{\pi t} - \gamma ce^{-\gamma t} - ie^{-\gamma t}\right)\right]e^{-it}dt \tag{9.4}$$

Explicit integration leads to

$$1 = \frac{c(1-\tau)}{i - \pi + \delta} + \frac{\tau(\gamma + i)}{\gamma + i} \tag{9.5}$$

Solving for $c - \delta$, we get the expression for *RI* guaranteeing that no arbitrage profit remains:

$$RI = c - \delta = i - \pi = r \tag{9.6}$$

The result is that *RI* equals *RS*, leading to an effective tax rate of zero. This proves that the combination of IAIT at the personal level and IAPT at the business level fulfils the criterion of intertemporal neutrality.

From equation (9.6) it can also be deduced that the IA approach of taxing income is neutral towards investment decisions, a result that holds regardless of the inflation rate and the rate of depreciation. The choice of the depreciation method which, under the traditional regime of profit taxation, is always a matter of discussion between tax authorities and taxpayers, would no longer exercise any particular influence on the size of the effective tax burden. Tax savings resulting from an accelerated depreciation automatically lead to a smaller book value of equity capital, which has the effect of diminishing the additional valuation item of the imputed capital interest accordingly. Thus, under the IA approach, accelerated depreciation would not provide a significant advantage for real investment and would therefore be degraded to a nearly ineffective fiscal policy instrument for stimulating and hence distorting private investment.[7]

On the other hand, the fiscal authorities can use depreciation rules as an instrument to influence the time pattern of tax revenue (see criterion C_1) without considerably influencing the profitability of investment. This is the decisive advantage of the IAPT compared to the dividend tax which matches the SAIT. With the dividend tax, the time pattern of tax revenue is entirely dependent on the dividend policy of corporations. Thus, revenue from the business tax crucially depends on private behaviour, which can undergo dramatic fluctuations. The same is true for the real cash-flow business tax which, in conjunction with the IAIT, is proposed by McLure and Zodrow (1990). In their view this system is particularly suitable for developing countries in which administrative capabilities are extremely scarce. However, treating the total amount of investment as an expense in the year it is made which is essential to the cash-flow tax, reduces the tax base substantially at the beginning of the investment period and postpones tax liabilities into the future. The resulting time pattern of tax payments will certainly increase government budget deficits in the years following the enactment of the tax. This could cause crucial fiscal problems, especially in fast-growing countries, where investment is expected to be relatively high at the beginning of the transformation process toward a market economy.[8]

From an efficiency and an equity point of view, the two consumption based tax system – SAIT/DT and IAIT/IAPT – are virtually equivalent to each other. The main reason is that under both tax regimes, capital income is effectively only burdened once. Within the SAIT/DT framework interest is taxed as income when withdrawn from qualified accounts; within the

IAIT/IAPT system, however, tax on interest is prepaid in the year of investment. In both cases, individual lifetime consumption is taxed and, assuming uniform tax rates, the same tax burden in present-value terms will arise.[9]

However, the two systems differ as far as criterion C_4 is concerned. With the SAIT, several monitoring problems have to be solved to ensure taxation of individual annual consumption. A system must, for example, be established to record and control the uses of assets enjoying cash-flow tax treatment. It must be ensured that assets placed with banks and similar financial institutions are taxed when they are sold and the proceeds used for consumption. Administrative measures of this kind are also important because of the need to ensure that all assets on qualified accounts are taxed if the taxpayer clears them entirely for the purposes of transferring his domicile abroad. Problems will also arise in the framework of double taxation agreements, because the definition of taxable kinds of income differs substantially from the definition used in the OECD Model Tax Convention for double taxation agreements. In contrast, the IAIT is easy to administer, even more so because it reduces the number of traditionally taxable kinds of income.

Furthermore, for a long time after its implementation, the SAIT/DT system of taxing income would probably require higher marginal rates or higher additional public debt financing than an IAIT/IAPT system to yield the same total revenue. This is because of the SAIT/DT's narrower tax base. These higher tax rates within the cash-flow tax harm work incentives more than an interest-adjusted income tax.

Taking into account both the urgent need for revenue (in part arising from the war) and the limited capacity in tax administration, the tax reform committee of the Croatian Ministry of Finance followed the recommendation of the KNS group to implement an IAIT/IAPT system as the best choice out of all alternative consumption-based approaches of taxing income from market activities.

Finally, another important issue regarding decision neutrality in taxation has to be mentioned. Croatian tax reformers were determined to avoid as far as possible tax preferences in the income and profit tax codes which are aimed at influencing the decisions of domestic consumers/savers and investors. The widespread use of tax expenditures, familiar to Western countries, was seen as undesirable for the new system. Though they are entirely justifiable where they help to correct market failures, it is very difficult to administer tax preferences in a way which improves the results that the market would have achieved if left to itself.

Details of the Personal Income Tax

The income tax is imposed on the sum of all taxable incomes derived worldwide within the tax year by any individual – which is the tax unit – with domestic residence. The taxable types of income of non-residents are restricted to those from domestic sources. Taxable items include income from employment (paid in cash or as a fringe benefit), income from self-employment (derived from small business, professional work, and from farming and forestry), income from property (movable and immovable real assets) and property rights (patents, copyrights, and so on).

Any payment in cash or kind that the employee receives from his employer is subject to withholding. Personal allowance factors which are entered into the wage tax card of the employee are used by the employer to calculate the monthly personal allowance of his employees (see below, Section IV). All contributions to social security are treated as expenses for acquiring income from employment. In order to simplify tax collection, other kinds of income-related expenses are deductible only in cases of reimbursement by the employer. However, the deductibility of reimbursements, for example, concerning expenses for commuting between home and work, is limited to certain amounts according to a decree by the Minister of Finance. This provision makes it possible to accomplish the taxation of most income from employment through withholding and the payment of the wage tax by employers. Only when additional income is received from other sources (for example, rents from real estate) must the employee visit the relevant tax office.

A consumption-based tax system – being administratively feasible at the personal level – should provide for both the tax-free formation of human capital and the taxation of all returns on these investments. The taxpayer, therefore, should be entitled to deduct all expenditures for investment in education. But such an entitlement would create serious problems for the tax administration because of the need to audit each personal item claimed for deduction. It would have to be verified, for example, whether an expenditure is directed to the formation of human capital or used for private consumption. Moreover, this would bring about thousands of tax declarations which are usually avoided due to withholding tax on wages. With this in mind, Croatian tax reformers decided not to allow for expending of investment in human capital. It was also taken into account that the Croatian public education system is free of charge.

For pensions paid by statutory social security agencies, the savings-adjusted concept of taxing was applied. This means that all contributions to the social security funds are completely deductible from current wages, and all pensions subsequently paid out are taxed in full as income from previous employment. The taxation of pensions is handled by the social security agencies on the basis of tax cards. Thus, the collection of income tax on pensions follows the same lines as that on income from employment. Because not only employees but also self-employed people are obliged to contribute to social security, nearly all pensioners can take the advantage of a personal allowance. Hence, both in working life and in retirement a certain subsistence minimum of consumption is protected from being taxed, as demanded by the criterion of fairness (C_7).

For taxation of retirement income from voluntary contributions to private pension schemes, the tax prepayment approach of taxing consumption was chosen. Voluntary saving for retirement is made from taxed income, so that the tax on consumption in retirement has already been paid in the period in which the pension rights are acquired; in effect, the tax on retirement consumption has actually been paid during the pensioner's working life.

Note that the favourable properties of the IA system are achieved by exempting income from capital only up to the standard rate of interest. It is advisable here to adjust the tax-exempt standard interest income annually by a fixed procedure based on the rate of interest on government bonds or other government securities which are traded in fully functioning capital markets. Because such market rates of interest do not yet exist in the Croatian economy, the standard rate was approximated as follows: assume an arbitrary value for the real rate of interest at 5 per cent per year, that is, $r = 0.05$, take the rate of inflation π from statistics on the monthly reported prices for industrial products, and use these two figures in the Fisher Equation to calculate

$$z = 0.05 \, (1 + \pi) + \pi \qquad (9.7)$$

Applying such a basis of taxation in practice requires only a simple administrative change in the conventional assessment of income and profit. The new system of taxing income, therefore, guarantees that income from capital up to the amount of imputed interest is protected from being taxed wherever capital is invested. In Croatia, z is called 'the protective rate of interest'.

Taxation of income derived from privately owned interest-bearing capital was abolished for reasons of simplicity. This is linked to the fact that, on average, there is virtually no difference between actual interest on capital and imputed interest which systematically has to be kept tax-free.[10] But it is important to note that interest from savings is indirectly burdened as a result of the taxation of income from employment and so on. This is because the income tax on savings from taxed income will cause the return to be smaller than it would have been without taxation.

Income from self-employment is composed of entrepreneurial wages and income from real capital invested in business. For the purpose of determining income from self-employment according to the interest-adjusted approach, it must be ensured that all capital costs are left untaxed. Therefore, the imputed interest on equity must be included in addition to conventional deductions. As it is not reasonable, however, to demand that small-scale businessmen, professionals and farmers should be obliged to undertake accrual-based financial accounting, a simplified cash-based accounting was introduced. But there is immediate write-off of purchased capital goods only if the assets are intended for use in business within one year. For long-term capital goods, depreciation allowances are granted in order to spread the cost of wear and tear of these assets over their estimated useful life according to the straight-line method. Furthermore, the book value of real assets which are not subject to cash-flow treatment is multiplied by the protective rate of interest – z – so as to allow for the deductibility of financing costs of the real assets used in business. Hence, interest paid on bank loans and so on is not deductible. A register of all real assets has to be kept in order to document the total basis for all deductible costs of capital (that is, depreciation allowances and interest costs). If the book values of assets are adjusted according to the rate of inflation, the deduction for interest is calculated by applying a fixed real rate of 5 per cent to the adjusted book values at the end of the year.

To sum up, income from small-scale business and professional work is taxed within the income tax according to a modified real cash-flow concept which implies a presumptive determination of tax-free 'normal' income from capital; the remaining taxable income is then attributed to labour and 'excessive profits'. In the case of debt financing, the actual interest may be higher than interest based on the imputed return, z. Thus, investment decisions may be distorted when the actual rate of interest paid on debt differs from the standardized one.[11] But if entrepreneurs are not satisfied with the deductions according to the protective interest rate, they can opt for assessment under the profit tax. Then they can take advantage of the full scheme of interest adjustment, that is, being entitled to deduct all kinds of interest paid on debt capital and the imputed interest on equity capital as well.

The income from property only includes income derived from real capital (rented movables and immovables) which is not normally taxable business income. The taxpayer is entitled to deduct 30 per cent of the rental as costs, or to apply the general rules of taxing business income. Capital gains from the sale of immovables are only taxed if these are sold within a three-year period.

The income from rights to private property, that is, income that is gained mainly from inherited proprietory rights (copyrights, patent rights, and so on), is calculated according to the net cash flow without regard to expenses for capital.

The Base of the Personal Income Tax
Income from employment
+ Income from self-employment
+ Income from (real) property and rights to property
= Total income
− Loss carry-forward, adjusted with the protective rate of interest
− Personal allowances, composed of the basic allowance and additional credits per dependent (non-working spouse, children, etc.) of the tax-payer's immediate family
= Income tax base

If taxpayer's business losses cannot be set off against any other income of the current year, the excess may be carried forward to each of the five succeeding taxable years. A loss is adjusted with the protective rate of interest in each year of its carry-forward. If the carry-forward does not exceed five years, this provision guarantees that the cost of equity-financed real capital in present-value terms is independent of the year in which it is deducted. Thus, the interest adjustment of loss carry-forward is essential to establish the appropriate tax conditions for the neutrality of the firm's investment decision (C_5).

The deduction of personal allowances from taxable income is advantageous from a fairness point of view. Generally speaking, when personal allowances correspond to the subsistence level of consumption of the taxpayer and his dependents, the tax base can be seen as income available for 'excessive' consumption, the progressive taxation of which may be justified. But the personal allowance itself gives rise to a progression in terms of the average tax burden on total taxable income.

The income tax schedule comprises constant marginal rates within two income brackets. In the first bracket, a rate of 20 per cent is applied. The second bracket, where a rate of 35 per cent is applied, starts at an income of Kuna 28 800 ($\approx$ US\$4600). Cities with more than 40 000 inhabitants are entitled to impose a surtax on their share in revenue from income tax. Hence, the top marginal tax rate might be marked up to 37.6 per cent in these cities, and in Zagreb, if the city council exhausts its special surtax entitlements, even up to 44.5 per cent. On the other hand, all communities and cities are entitled to reduce the tax burden of their inhabitants – at the cost of a lower share in their revenue – resulting in a reduction of the top rate of 35 per cent to 32.4 per cent. The tax burden, therefore, will differ according to the taxpayer's residence. This means that individuals with equal income pay different amounts of tax and the criterion of fairness (C_9) is not met. Of course, this could be compensated by differences in the provision of public goods.

Details of the Business Profit Tax

All enterprises (sustainable profit-oriented activities in markets), whether personally held or as legal entities, which are statutorily obliged to keep commercial financial accounts, are subject to the profit tax. Individual entrepreneurs and closely held companies (partnerships and so on) that are taxed under the income tax are entitled to opt for the profit tax if they fulfil all requirements for full accounting (double-entry book-keeping, preparing balance sheets, and so on). Thus, the new Croatian business profit tax satisfies the demand for decision neutrality with respect to different legal forms of entrepreneurial activities (C_5).

Generally speaking, the basic procedure for determining taxable profits is based on the German model, that is, the method of net worth (equity according to balance sheet) comparison applies. It is important to note that the equity at the end of the year also contains the gains from the inflation adjustments of real assets to which the companies are entitled under the Croatian law on accounting. The addition of gains from indexation to the tax base is indispensable in order to avoid a double adjustment for inflation, for both the paid interest expenses on debt and the imputed interest expenses on equity at the beginning of the year already contain an inflation element. Hence, the deduction of the cost of real capital arising from inflation is taken into account via the depreciation from inflation-adjusted values.

If a company holds shares in another company, the parent has no tax liability whatsoever with respect to either dividends received or capital gains/losses on the shares in the subsidiary. Thus, because the profit derived from balance sheets includes gains/losses on shares, the tax base has to be corrected for these items in order to avoid double taxation of profits of affiliated companies. But this correction does not apply to profits which a parent derives from shares in companies subject to income tax.

Personally held companies subject to profit tax are permitted to deduct an entrepreneurial wage for the owner and for each joint owner respectively in order to make it possible for these individuals to use the personal allowances of the income tax. Therefore, with respect to protecting the subsistence level of consumption, all entrepreneurs, whether subject to income tax or to profit tax, are treated equally. There are currently no restrictions concerning the deductibility of entrepreneurial wages.

The Base of the Business Profit Tax

Profit according to the accrual-method of commercial financial accounting (equity at the end of the year – equity at the beginning of the year – new equity issues + with-drawals of any kind)

+/– Convential corrections concerning depreciation allowances, hidden dividends, owner-related and representation-related expenses etc.

– Gains (+ losses) on shares in another company subject to profit tax

– Imputed entrepreneurial wage in cases of personally held companies

+ Amount of excessive interest on debt to creditors not subject to profit tax

– Protective interest on equity

– Interest-adjusted loss carry-forward

= Profit tax base

Excessive interest on debts to creditors which are not subject to profit tax are not deductible. This provision is made to prevent the transformation of a company's profit into tax-free private income from interest through appropriate debt arrangements between the company and individuals who are related to the entrepreneurs or to shareholders. Excessive interest is the amount by which the interest according to the terms of a loan exceeds the interest which a company's bank pays on deposits of equal term.

The decisive correction (starting from the conventional determination of taxable profit) is of course the deduction of interest on equity.[12] The allowance for interest on equity is calculated by applying z (see p. 267) on the equity at the beginning of the year. The value of shares in other companies subject to profit tax is deducted from the equity in order to avoid a double allowance for protective interest. Furthermore, the amount of this imputed interest is corrected for interest on equity issues, dividends received from other companies, net acquisitions of shares in other companies, and withdrawals of any kind of equity during the year on a monthly basis. Payments of profit tax are also part of withdrawals for interest adjustment. For the assessment of profit tax at the end of the year, however, the monthly tax prepayments may be offset against the final amount of tax liability at interest-adjusted values. Note that the correction for interest on equity inflows and outflows also works against tax planning with the aim of artificially increasing equity value at the beginning of the year.

With regard to the consistency of the tax system, the personal income and profit taxes should be integrated both with respect to the base and to the rate. As we have shown, the tax bases are almost perfectly integrated. In order to get an integrative solution concerning tax rates, the rate of the profit tax should be set at the top rate of the personal income tax. Hence, the Ministry of Finance proposed a profit tax rate of 35 per cent. But the Croatian government did not follow this recommendation and submitted to the Croatian parliament an amendment with a rate of 25 per cent, which was passed. The main reason was that – from an international point of view – a low profit tax rate would be an appropriate signal to attract foreign investors (C_3). Because of this difference in tax rates the Croatian Tax Administration observed various activities of firms and their employees aimed at transforming highly taxed labour income into dividends which are subject to a lower burden. In order to stop such tax avoidance strategies the Croatian Parliament changed the profit tax law in 1996. Since 1 January, 1997, the rate of the profit tax is 35 per cent.

IV   ADJUSTMENTS FOR THE EFFECTS OF INFLATION

A major deficiency in traditional concepts of direct taxation is their lack of inflation neutrality. When tax brackets and allowances, expressed in nominal values, are not constantly adapted to inflation, bracket creep occurs, that is, average effective tax rates increase though real income remains unchanged because taxpayers move into higher tax brackets as nominal income increases.

Of greater severity are the effects of capital income taxation under conditions of inflation when capital income is defined in nominal rather than real terms. Even at low rates of inflation, real rates of return soon become negative. This leads to a dramatic flight of capital. A perfect system of indexation at all levels of income would be needed to correct for inflation, but can hardly be administered in countries in transition. Here, the system of interest-adjusted taxation proves to be very advantageous. When nominal interest up to the market rate i remains tax-free at all levels of business and private income, illusory paper profits are not part of the tax base. In the first part of Section III it was shown that IABT is intertemporally neutral regardless of the inflation rate and the method of financing. An interest-adjusted definition of the tax base makes it unnecessary to index the balance sheet and thereby to give up with the nominal-value principle. When the indexation of depreciable assets is applied according to the Croatian law of accounting, however, the interest-adjusted profit tax remains inflation-neutral, as indexation profits are taxable (see the last part of Section III) and depreciation allowances are calculated at indexed values. To sum up, the IABT automatically adjusts itself to inflation through nominal interest deduction for equity as well as debt-financed investment, thereby fulfilling criterion C_6.

The Croatian income tax allows for relief with regard to the taxpayer himself, the taxpayer's non-working spouse and the children. Additional allowances are provided for dependent disabled members of the immediate family. These allowances must be adjusted to changing consumer prices in order to prevent inflation-induced erosion of their real value. Frequent indexation of personal allowances, however, calls for significant administrative effort, as the wage tax cards on which they are recorded may require alterations – even on a monthly basis – in times of high inflation. Since alterations to the wage tax card may only be carried out by authorized civil servants (local or community revenue authority officials), such an indexing process causes substantial additional administrative burdens to all parties. For this reason, a simpler alternative is used in Croatia, whereby the individual's circumstances are accounted for by way of allowance factors instead of nominal rebate amounts. The wage tax card records a personal allowance factor which corresponds to the sum of various allowance factors. This personal allowance factor then (either from the employer or the tax office) has to be multiplied by the prevailing basic allowance in order to calculate the personal allowance.

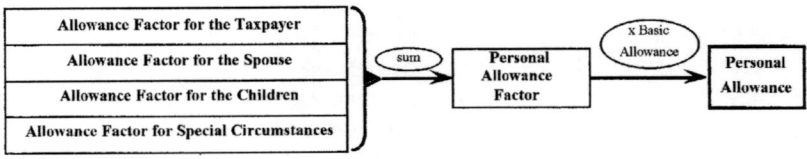

Figure 9.1 Determination of the personal allowance in the Croatian tax system

This process does not require alterations in the wage tax card records in order to adjust for rates of inflation. If inflation occurs, indexation of the personal allowance is easily achieved by indexing the basic allowance. Thus alterations are required only in the case of changes in personal/family circumstances.

The same procedure is used to define the tax brackets. The 35 per cent tax bracket is reached when taxable income exceeds three times the amount of the basic allowance. By indexing the basic personal allowance, all credits and the tax brackets are corrected for inflation without any alteration in the wage tax card. If the Croatian tax law provided for a regulation to adjust automatically the personal allowance for inflation, then criterion C_6 would be met. But the Croatian government did not take that measure, for fear that inflationary expectations could be provoked when indexation was explicitly mentioned in the tax law. One can accept this when inflation rates are fairly low. On the other hand, the explicit provision of indexation rules in the tax law is found even in countries with low inflation.[13]

V   CONCLUDING REMARKS

The IAIT/IAPT came into force on 1 January 1994, which means that the evaluation time for the Croatian tax system is rather short. The immediate feedback is that the new system of taxing income and profits in Croatia is widely accepted among the population and enterprises. The main reasons for the acceptance are: the increase in transparency relative to the previous system, lower marginal tax rates, and tax bases that are more reasonable from an economic point of view. Despite the cut in tax rates, income tax revenue rose by approximately 25 per cent compared to the expected revenue from the old system. The increase in tax revenue is mainly due to the broadening of the tax base by way of abolishing a huge number of tax preferences. Greater tax revenue was a crucial step towards controlling the government budget deficit and achieving price stability. In conjunction with a stabilization programme, it was possible to reduce the inflation rate from 1250 per cent in 1993 to –3 per cent in 1994.

Focusing on simplicity and ease of tax administration when designing the new income and profit tax was the precondition for successful implementation of the new tax laws. Despite the dramatic changes in tax regulations, the introduction of a wage tax card and the ongoing restructuring process within the tax administration, no major difficulties occurred with the implementation of the new tax regulations. This was another reason for the increase in tax revenue.

By implementing the new tax system, the Croatian Ministry of Finance aimed at establishing an environment attractive to domestic and foreign investors by tax-exempting those parts of profit which correspond to the protective rate of interest.

Even though the tax system has only been implemented in 1994, due to its high level of acceptance by foreign and domestic investors the desired effect of stimulating capital formation, employment and economic development has actually been realized.

Notes

1. KNS is the acronym for *Konsumorientierte Neuordnung des Steuersystems* (consumption-oriented reorganization of the tax system). The Heidelberg KNS tax reform group of German tax experts (from various branches of tax science and tax administration) came together at the beginning of 1990, right after the Heidelberg Congress on Taxing Consumption of 1989 (Rose, 1990). The goal of the group is to design practical working tax systems of the consumption-based type, and also to help Central and Eastern European countries reform their tax systems in order to produce sufficient revenue in an administratively feasible way – without hampering the development of new market economies.

2. We share the opinion of Slemrod (1990, p. 158), who argues that 'a theory of optimal tax systems has the promise of addressing some of the fundamental issues of tax policy in a more satisfactory way than the theory of optimal taxation'.

3. See Bradford (1986) and Rose (1990).

4. This view is shared by many other economists; see for example Sinn (1987, pp. 281ff.) and McLure and Zodrow (1990, pp. 336–7). For a critical discussion of this assumption see, for example, Slemrod (1990, pp. 161 and 174). Results from applied general equilibrium analysis also support the assumption that a consumption-based income tax system is less wasteful than the traditional system of comprehensive income taxation. See Ballard *et al.* (1985) and Duschek and Rose (1994).

5. For discussions of the issue of horizontal equity see Kay (1990) and Zodrow (1990).

6. It is important to distinguish between the real capital employed in the company $e^{-\delta t}$ and the value the tax ascribes to that capital $e^{-\gamma t}$ at time t. For the determination of the tax base, one always has to refer to the value calculated for tax purposes. Both can differ due to accelerated depreciation as well as to indexation.

7. The 'irrelevance result' for depreciation allowances is not restricted to the case of exponential depreciation. In order to illustrate this point, let us assume an arbitrary set of yearly depreciation allowances $\{A_0, A_1, ..., A_N\}$ for the asset A which is invested in year 0, where

$$A = A_0 + A_1 + ... + A_N$$

Furthermore, there is an interest allowance I_n in each year n of the investment period calculated according to

$$I_n = iB_n$$

Where B_n denotes the book value of the asset at the beginning of year n. The present value of the stream of deductions then is

$$A_0 + \frac{A_i + iB_1}{1+i} + \frac{A_2 + iB_2}{(1+i)^2} + \dots + \frac{A_N + iB_N}{(1+i)^N} =$$

$$A_0 + \frac{A_1 + i(A - A_0)}{1+i} + \frac{A_2 + i(A - A_0 - A_1)}{(1+i)^2} + \dots +$$

$$\frac{A_N + i(A_0 - A_1 - \dots - A_{N-1})}{(1+i)^N} =$$

$$A_0 + \frac{A_1 + i(A - A_0)}{1+i} + \frac{A_2 + i(A - A_0 - A_1)}{(1+i)^2} + \dots + \frac{A_N + iA_N}{(1+i)^N} =$$

$$A_0 + \frac{A_1 + i(A_1 + A_2 + \dots + A_N)}{1+i} + \frac{A_2 + i(A_2 + A_3 + \dots + A_N)}{(1+i)^2} + \dots +$$

$$\frac{A_N}{(1+i)^{N-1}} =$$

$$A_0 + A_1 + \frac{i(A_2 + A_3 + \dots + A_N)}{1+i} + \frac{A_2 + i(A_2 + A_3 + \dots + A_N)}{(1+i)^2} + \dots +$$

$$\frac{A_N}{(1+i)^{N-1}} = \sum_{n=0}^{N} A_n = A$$

For all methods of depreciation applied it holds that the present value of the allowed deductions is equal to the amount of investment. The result is that real cash-flow tax – which provides for immediate write-off of real assets – is one possible version of the an interest-adjusted business profit tax. One should note, however, that we assume an allowance for interest on capital at rate z which equals the market rate i and which the investor applies in discounting future earnings and costs. If z is not equal to the discount rate i, the irrelevance of alternative methods of depreciation does not hold any longer. In the case of $z < i$, for example, accelerated depreciation will be more advantageous than linear depreciation. If z is – according to the tax law – determined to be not much below i, however, an extra depreciation allowance would not prompt entrepreneurs to increase their investment activities substantially.

8. In order to reduce revenue shortfalls during the first years following the enactment of a cash-flow tax and the likelihood of a negative cash flow as well, McLure and Zodrow (1996) propose including loan proceeds and interest income in the business tax base and, consequently, to deduct repayments of debt principal and interest expense.

9. For a discussion of this point see McLure and Zodrow (1990, pp. 372–6). The equivalence, however, is strictly given only under certainty with respect to future returns on savings, a rate of return equal to the discount rate and a constant tax rate over the individual's lifetime. For testing the equivalence

theorem under conditions of uncertainty see Zodrow (1995).

10. Note that this assumption only holds true if the imputed rate of interest, which has to be protected from being taxed, is based on capital market conditions.

11. For alternative approaches to calculating the cost of capital used by the self-employed to derive income, see Sørensen (1994, p. 23).

12. The concept of the interest-adjusted business profit tax goes back to Boadway and Bruce (1984) and Wenger (1983). See also the proposal for a corporation tax with an 'Allowance for Corporate Equity' (ACE), suggested by the Institute for Fiscal Studies (1991). The KNS group initially put forward its proposal for a general interest-adjusted business profit tax for the reform of the Hungarian tax system (Deutsche Gesellschaft für Technische Zusammenarbeit/KNS Tax Reform Group, 1992). The two independently developed proposals aim at the same goal – to achieve neutrality both between different investments and between different sources of their financing.

13. Legal provisions for the indexation of rate schedules and/or reliefs can be found in the USA, Canada, the United Kingdom, Switzerland, Sweden, The Netherlands, Luxembourg, Belgium, Greece, Italy and France (OECD, 1993, p. 43).

References

Ballard, C.L., D. Fullerton, J.B. Shoven and J. Whalley (1985) *A General Equilibrium Model for Tax Policy Evaluation* (Chicago University of Chicago Press).

Boadway, Robin and Neil Bruce (1984) 'A General Proposition on the Design of a Neutral Business Tax', *Journal of Public Economics*, vol. 24, pp. 231–9.

Bradford, David F. (1986) *Untangling the Income Tax* (Cambridge, Mass.: Harvard University Press).

Deutsche Gesellschaft für Technische Zusammenarbeit (GTZ) GmbH and KNS Tax Reform Group (1992) '*Recommendations on the Reform of Hungary's Tax System*', unpublished report, Heidelberg, Eschborn.

Duschek, Klaus, Thomas Farken and Manfred Rose (1994) 'Welfare Effects of Abolishing the German Business Taxes – An Applied General Equilibrium Analysis', in W. Eichhorn (ed.), *Models and Measurement of Welfare and Inequality* (Berlin, Heidelberg, New York: Springer-Verlag) pp. 252–85.

Institute for Fiscal Studies (1991) *Equity for Companies: A Corporation Tax for the 1990s* (London: Chameleon Press).

Kay, John (1990) 'Consumption and Income Taxation: Horizontal Equity and Life Cycle Issues', in Rose (1990) pp. 85–115.

McLure, Charles E., Jr and George R. Zodrow (1990) 'Administrative Advantages of the Individual Tax Prepayment Approach to the Direct Taxation of Consumption', in Rose (1990) pp. 337–89.

(1996) 'A Hybrid Consumption-based Direct Tax Proposed for Bolivia', *International Tax and Public Finance*, vol. 3, pp. 97–112.

Organization for Economic Co-operation and Development (1993) *Taxation in OECD Countries* (Paris: OECD).

Rose, Manfred (ed.) (1990) *Heidelberg Congress on Taxing Consumption* (Heidelberg, New York, London: Springer-Verlag).

Sinn, Hans-Werner (1987) *Capital Income Taxation and Resource Allocation* (Amsterdam, New York, Oxford, Tokyo: North-Holland).

Slemrod, Joel (1990) 'Optimal Taxation and Optimal Tax Systems', *The Journal of Economic Perspectives*, vol. 4, no. 1, pp. 157–78.

Sørensen, Peter (1994) 'From the Global Income Tax to the Dual Income Tax: Recent Tax Reforms in the Nordic Countries', *International Tax and Public Finance*, vol. 1, pp. 57–79.

Wenger, Ekkehard (1983) 'Gleichmäßigkeit der Besteuerung von Arbeits- und Vermögenseinkünften', *Finanzarchiv*, vol. 41, pp. 207–52.

Zodrow, George R. (1990) 'The Individual Tax Base: Efficiency and Horizontal Equity Aspects of the Choice Between Income and Consumption', in S. Cnossen and R.M. Bird (eds), *The Personal Income Tax: Phoenix from the Ashes?* (Amsterdam: North-Holland).

—— (1995) 'Taxation, Uncertainty, and the Choice of a Consumption Tax Base', *Journal of Public Economics*, vol. 58, pp. 257–65.

10 The Sales Policy of the *Treuhandanstalt* as a Privatization Strategy

Gerlinde Sinn*

I INTRODUCTION

At the end of 1994 the *Treuhandanstalt* closed its doors. In less than four years it had officially completed its task of helping transform the East German economy from a centrally planned system into a decentralized market economy. The incredible speed with which the privatization of the East German economy was carried out has no historical precedent. Neither the previously most comprehensive Chilean privatization, which reversed the nationalizations of the Allende government, nor the major privatization programmes undertaken by the Thatcher government in Britain had succeeded in pushing through their privatization programmes as quickly as the *Treuhand*,[1] which had been established only in 1990.

The impressive speed of privatization is advantageous as it makes it less likely that the transformation process will be reversed. Speed is only one aspect of the *Treuhand's* policy. The underlying goals of privatization given in the *Treuhand* Law were the promotion of competition and the creation of jobs that increased competition would encourage. With respect to these goals the *Treuhand's* policy appears less impressive.

Post-unification East Germany has become a deindustrialized region. Prior to unification, Saxony had the highest industrial employment in the whole of Europe.[2] Since then, however, the proportion of those employed in industry has fallen below the levels of Ireland and Portugal. As yet, no significant East German industry has developed along with privatization.

Rapid change of ownership was supposed to be associated with strong investment. As in former socialist countries, capital was scarce in East

---

* I gratefully acknowledge the comments of the editor and an anonymous referee and also of Juli Leβmann who not only translated the chapter but helped with her advice.

Germany and the level of capital stocks was actually falling in the last socialist decade; there had in fact been disinvestment.[3]

Because of the shortfall in capital in East Germany, high returns on capital could be expected and an investment boom was anticipated which was supposed to bring East Germany's economic performance up to the West German levels. Privatization policy was aimed at supporting these goals. This chapter will look at whether the privatization policy chosen was the one best suited to achieving this aim.

II   SUCCESSFUL PRIVATIZATION

The success of any privatization policy must be judged in terms of its objectives and there can be many of these. However, what counts in the end are gains in welfare. These gains can accrue from efficiency increases in the country privatizing its 'communally owned' assets. They can occur in other countries too if assets are transferred at rock-bottom prices to new owners from outside the region. In East Germany it was mainly West Germans who benefited from privatization so most of the welfare gains went to them.

To evaluate the increase in efficiency, some might argue that it is enough to simply look at the public share of total output. Any decline in the public sector increases efficiency and leads to welfare gains. In this context the most successful privatization policy would then be the one with the biggest fall in government activity. Accordingly any fall in public sector employment, or at least in the ratio of public to overall employment, must be seen as an improvement regardless of where it comes from.

In terms of economic policy it does matter whether, with changes in public employment, the overall employment rate stays constant or whether the change in public employment leads to a decline in total employment. In the first case those formerly employed in the public sector become absorbed by the private sector. In the second case the private sector only partially absorbs those laid off, if at all. In East Germany there was a drop in public employment accompanied by an even sharper decline in overall employment from 8.8 million people in 1990 to 6.4 million in 1995[4] thus *increasing* the ratio of public employment from 22.8 per cent to 24.6 per cent. The social costs of a structural change largely depend on these employment effects. A specific privatization policy is superior to another one if it achieves its goals, a certain decreased level of government activity and public employment with lower social costs.

Social welfare is optimized when no increase in economic efficiency is possible by transferring available resources from the public to the private sector.[5] If net economic gains result from such a transfer, then further privatization is worthwhile. However, any assessment of the welfare gains must consider not only the discounted future returns from increased efficiency brought about by resource shifts but also the short-term costs associated with these shifts. As Keynes said, 'in the long run we are all dead', and even when the long-run benefits clearly outweigh the short-run costs, these costs nevertheless have to be taken into account. When they *are* considered, privatization, as it was carried out in East Germany, appears less beneficial.

Privatizations in the Western market economies, not only in Great Britain and France but also in West Germany, came about in a comparatively settled environment with low unemployment. The waves of privatization there[6] coincided with the increasing influence of new economic liberalism, which emphasized that productive efficiency could be improved by means of deregulation and privatization.

In a way the transformation of the centrally planned economies into competitive market economies can be interpreted as a major success for economic liberalism. The collapse of the centrally planned economies occurred primarily because their goods production was inefficient, and their citizens were increasingly dissatisfied with the low levels of consumption resulting from a faulty form of economic organization and a deficient system of incentives.

When the Iron Curtain came down, attempts were made in the countries of the former Eastern Bloc to promote, quickly and in various ways, entrepreneurial activities and competitiveness, and to develop[7] new incentive structures. Decision-making power was decentralized and transferred to local government authorities and to large firms. The allocative function of prices which reflect scarcities was recognized, and prices were freed in order to improve the supply of goods to the consumers.

However, the most important incentive in a market economy – the opportunity to make profit – was largely ruled out. Profits are major rewards of entrepreneurial activity and the willingness to bear risk. The idea of transferring socialist property rapidly from common to personal ownership and allowing individuals to gain profits was regarded with suspicion by many of those formerly in power. The remarkably rapid privatization of 70 per cent of industry available for privatization in Russia can be put down to the fact that such privatization often benefited the former combine managers, that is, the former *Nomenklatura*.[8]

III   THE HISTORY OF THE TREUHAND

The former GDR had decided as early as February 1990 on a programme for restructuring the East German economy[9] by means of a new system of incentives. The aim there again was to increase economic efficiency. The main emphasis was on introducing market elements into the production and distribution of goods, though a new distribution of assets was not altogether excluded.[10]

To improve the economic structure and to smooth the path to a decentralized, competitive type of economy, large parts of the communally-owned property in the GDR were transferred to what was called a *Treuhandanstalt* (trust agency). The former government combines and firms transferred to the *Treuhand* were split up into about 8300 legally independent decision-making units in the form of corporations. Quasi-market structures were to be created by the decentralization of decision-making power. The planners estimated that about two years would be needed for the transition to the new, but still socialist, type of economy.[11] The first changes had hardly been made when political developments in East Germany forced these plans to be revised.

In March 1990 the first democratic government of the disintegrating GDR was elected. Three months after it had been elected the original *Treuhand* concept was changed.[12] Restructuring *and* privatization of the communal assets were now declared to be the primary aims of transformation and the socialist property system was abandoned. The work of the *Treuhand* was now being carried out in terms of these two-pronged goals. After the unification of Germany in October 1990 the *Treuhand*, now with a new manager – Detlev Rohwedder – who was responsible to the Federal Ministry of Finance, continued to work towards achieving these goals. A political decision was made to give priority to privatization rather than to restructuring.

The *Treuhand*'s decision about priority was a reversal of the sequence of restructuring and privatization usually chosen for privatization programmes in Western market economies. It was contrary to the view of Sir Alan Walters, who had been closely associated with the large Thatcher government privatizations and who had clearly come down in favour of first restructuring and then privatizing the former communally-owned firms in Central and Eastern Europe.[13]

In East Germany, as in the former socialist countries generally, the enormous size of the privatizations argued against the sequence recommended by Walters.[14] Under the British method the process would have taken several decades to complete. During this time, major sectors of the

East German economy would not be subject to the free play of market forces, but to government or semi-government decisions. Any attempt to restructure the whole East German economy by means of a super planning and restructuring authority would be little different from a continuation of the planned economy combined with high efficiency losses.

To prevent what was, in practical terms, a continuation of the planned economy, the *Treuhand* tried to put its new concept of restructuring by means of privatization into practice quickly.[15] It decentralized the restructuring of the East German economy by transferring the responsibility for this to the future owners. In line with market economy incentives, the returns from restructuring would accrue to those who had borne the burden.

The *Treuhandanstalt* did not only try to shift the cost and returns of restructuring to the new owners, it also decided to sell the assets rather than give them away to the East German people. Its aim in doing this was to produce revenues from sales. At the start of the privatization process, it was expected that the revenues from the sales of *Treuhand* property could cover its expenses. The then manager of the *Treuhand*, Rohwedder, estimated that the sales revenues it could expect would be in the order of 600 billion Deutschmarks because East Germany was in a far better situation than the other countries undergoing transformation. The way unification was effected had made privatization much easier.

IV   THE TREUHAND'S ADVANTAGE FROM ITS INITIAL SITUATION

The initial situation of the *Treuhand* when it started work under West German management in 1990 seemed very favourable compared to that of the other transitional countries and, as mentioned above, the revenues from selling its properties were expected to be high. Under paragraph 23 of the German Constitution, the five East German *Länder* became equal partners in the West German economic and social system. This meant that West German institutions, in particular the economic and legal systems, were transferred to East Germany immediately the two states became one. Institutions are said to determine a country's long-term economic development.[16] The West German institutional system had proved itself over the 40 years that had elapsed since the establishment of the Federal Republic in 1949 and was thus able to offer all the security of an established, well-known economic and legal entity.

The security offered to future participants in the market gave East Germany a clear advantage for potential investors over other countries in the disintegrating Eastern Bloc. Access to world capital markets through West Germany's integration in international markets appeared to confirm this.

The development of investment in East Germany since unification seems to support these expectations. Investors were attracted and capital stocks were built up as a result of strong investment.

Given the secure institutional framework, it is not surprising that the bulk of direct investment by Western investors in the former Eastern Bloc countries was in East Germany. Since 1989 foreign direct investment by Western countries in Eastern and Central European countries has been only US$133.6 in per capita terms, while in East Germany it has been US$1082.[17] How much of the investment in East Germany can be attributed to the *Treuhand* privatization policy is an open question. In any case the massive investment subsidies given by the German government for new investment in East Germany must have had a considerable effect. They made investment profitable even if the gross returns on the investment were negative[18] and may well explain the bulk of it.

V   THE PRIVATIZATION METHODS OF THE *TREUHANDANSTALT*

New capital to East Germany was needed to restructure both reprivatized property and newly privatized property. *Reprivatization*, restitution in kind, is the return of expropriated property to its former owners; *privatization* is the transfer of property to new owners by means of sales. Restitution in kind was a seemingly natural way of returning property to its former owners or their heirs, but it failed to take account of the fact that 45 years under a socialist regime had completely altered the production units. This meant that many questions relating to dividing up the units and allocating the parts to the eligible owners remained unsolved. This discouraged many potential new investors who were, understandably, unwilling to make financial commitments when the property rights were unclear.[19] These limitations on the willingness to invest slowed down both the transformation and the upswing in the East German economy and could only be offset by large government investment subsidies. Financing these subsidies has put heavy burdens on present and future taxpayers. The restitution in kind thus reduced the advantages that East Germany initially had.

East Germany's attractiveness as a location for industry was also reduced by the *Treuhand*'s sales privatizations. The sales policy put the capital market under enormous strain. It was combined with an unafford-able wage policy which consequently reduced employment in the former *Treuhand* firms to about one-third of what it was originally.[20] Although the negative consequences of privatizing by means of sales were very quickly recognized, and although the expected revenues from sales soon dropped to a fraction of their initial value, the *Treuhand* persisted in using this method right up to the official completion of its work in 1994. This can partly be explained by assuming that the *Treuhand* was trying to change the management in the old East German firms as quickly as poss-ible, that it was convinced that it could offer potential investors optimal locational conditions, and that it acted with complete confidence in the omnipotence of the international capital markets.

VI THE SALES POLICY OF THE TREUHANDANSTALT

Of all the countries undergoing transformation, only in East Germany did the privatization policy involve attempting to sell off the whole economy at once.[21] The *Treuhand's* experience with privatization through sales pro-vided very few grounds for optimism though. Believing that it is possible to achieve both speed and large sales revenues from privatizing a whole economy is rather like believing that it is possible to square the circle.

The difference between the returns expected from the privatization and those actually received confirm this dilemma. As previously mentioned, at the start of the *Treuhand* operations in the autumn of 1990 the returns from sales were estimated at 600 billion Deutschmarks.[22] In the event, at the completion of the sales the total returns turned out to be 66.6 billion Deutschmarks,[23] or only about one-tenth of the original estimate.

Asset Values and the *Treuhand's* Revenue from Sales

The large gap between the returns expected and those realized was to a large extent caused by the *Treuhand's* sales policy itself, although various other explanations have been given for this divergence. One popular explanation is the 'junk' hypothesis which argues that few of the former socialist firms were able to command a positive price under market condi-tions because their market value, that is, the present value of their expected future returns, was close to zero, or even negative.

Even if the situation of the East German economy did turn out to be much worse than originally expected,[24] this argument fails to consider several important points. First, it is hardly surprising that firms whose supply and demand conditions were determined by central planning needed to make some adjustments before they could operate effectively in the decentralized market economy at completely new prices.[25] Many of the East German firms did indeed try to adjust to the new price system. The success of these restructuring measures is evident from the increase in productivity in the East German economy following unification.[26] However, the positive effects of these efforts on the firms' market values were counteracted by changes in other determining factors.

Furthermore, after the economic and monetary union the existing debt of East German firms was subject to western interest rates which were more than twice their previous eastern levels. Even though the old debt was devalued to half its original level the increase in interest rates meant that the market values of many East German firms declined. Further increases in the interest rates due to debt financing of the unification costs reinforced this effect.

In addition, after unification, East German demand shifted to the West German products that had previously been unavailable. Although it was not clear whether this demand shift represented a long-term change in preferences or only a temporary change in demand resulting from consumers' curiosity about the newly available goods, firms' actual and expected future revenues, that is, firms' market values, dropped.

One aspect of the *Treuhand* privatization policy that drove down the market values of the East German firms has received little attention. In Britain, the government firms were initially transformed into public companies, and shares were then issued through a consortium of banks.[27] The *Treuhand*, however, tried to sell the firms it controlled as single units. According to its final statistics the *Treuhand* privatized 6546 firms and 8054 production units, and liquidated 3700 units.[28] In addition more than 25 000 units were privatized under 'small privatization'.[29] The *Treuhand* apparently hoped to replicate the West German owner-managed firm structure and believed that this would bring in the fresh investment capital needed. Unfortunately there was no well-functioning market for big firms. At best, there was a demand for small firms as a whole. Only a few firms, and even fewer individuals, have sufficient uncommitted resources to buy a whole firm. Mostly only large, well-established joint stock companies can loosen their credit constraints significantly and undertake such large investments. They can try to expand their capital base by issuing new shares through the stock exchange. The sale of whole units reduced overall demand for East German assets because many potential purchasers were excluded.

Finally, the currency conversion of the East German mark caused a fourfold increase in wages in the export sector and the market values of export sector firms, which in 1989 had been responsible for 40 per cent of East German GDP,[30] crashed. The fall in market values caused by the appreciation of wages which resulted from the currency revaluation was only the start of the wage-determined slide in the market values of the East German firms. Shortly after unification, the first East German union wage negotiations were completed. East German union wages were to be brought up to the level of West German wages in just four or five years.[31] Only the *Treuhand* could have prevented the devaluation of the old East German capital stock caused by high wage increases, but it did not participate in the wage negotiations. The explosion of East German wages to more than ten times their original level within four years led to the implosion of the East German firms' market values.[32]

The Sale of a Whole Economy

Using the sum of the microeconomic-based expected market values as an estimate for the potential *Treuhand* revenues led to further miscalculation. It neglected to take into account the fact that the *Treuhand* was attempting to sell the whole East German economy at once. The expected 600 billion Deutschmarks from sales revenues could only have been financed under very restrictive assumptions: either if investors were planning an asset exchange in their portfolios, or if the sales revenues were used to repay government debt – both these alternatives were unlikely – or if there had been sufficient savings from forgoing present consumption.

The actual capital stock of an economy represents the accumulated savings over many prior periods. Current period savings not only provide for net investment, but also for the government budget deficit and possibly an export of capital. There would only have been scope for financing the sale of the *Treuhand* properties through current savings if one of these variables had been cut back or if current savings had been increased – current savings in West Germany at the time of unification amounted to only 30 per cent of the value of the additional East German capital stock needed for the East–West adjustment.[33]

There is even little evidence that the variables which absorb the current savings changed in the direction needed for financing the *Treuhand* assets.

Savings did not increase nor did the West German net investment decline in the first few years after unification. On the contrary, the aggregate savings rate fell from 14.7 per cent in 1990 to 12.3 per cent in 1994.[34] Net investment in West Germany was still increasing after unification; in per capita terms it grew even faster than net investment in East Germany, thus widening the gap in capital intensity. Only since 1993 has there been any change. The massive investment subsidies for East German projects transferred resources from West to East Germany. Even the government budget deficit, the only use of savings that can be directly influenced by the government, did not change in the direction required. The high unification costs caused it to increase suddenly and, far from taking a smaller share of West German savings, it claimed an even larger one.

The only variable that changed in the right direction following unification was the international flow of capital. In 1989, Germany exported 135 billion Deutschmarks[35] capital. In 1991 the flow of capital changed direction as a result of rising interest rates and by 1992, Germany had capital imports of 90 billion Deutschmarks.[36] Even if all capital imports had been used for buying *Treuhand* assets they could only have covered a minor share of the *Treuhand* revenues expected.

The effect of rising interest rates, on the one hand changed the direction of international capital flows and, on the other hand, significantly affected the capital values. An existing capital stock normally generates a current revenue stream with a present value which falls with rising interest rates, but usually remains positive. New investment, however, is characterized by high initial expenditures and, with increasing interest rates, its capital value can easily become negative. Purchases of firms that had formerly been communal assets were just this kind of interest rate-sensitive new investment with high initial expenditure. With rising interest rates many of the sales were cancelled. In the end the *Treuhand* had to give away its properties and the 'buyers' frequently only made token payments.

Privatization and New Property Ownership

Even though much of the *Treuhand* assets had been given away at very low prices, East Germans were almost entirely excluded from participating in the *Treuhand's* sales. The hardly unexpected result was that only about 6 per cent of the privatizations, measured in terms of East German jobs retained, went to East Germans over the whole period of the sales.[37] East Germans did not have the resources needed to buy the *Treuhand* firms. They had neither the financial assets nor the securities required for external borrowing. This was partly an effect of the lack of incentive and opportunity to accumulate private financial assets in the socialist system and partly the result of East German savings losing value when the currency was converted.[38] A new system of property ownership for the former socialist property which excluded its own citizens, or gave them only a very limited share in it, was – unlike in the other former socialist countries – politically only feasible in East Germany. This is due to the fact that it was the West Germans, that is, German citizens and voters, who benefited most.[39]

The huge transfer payments that were made to East Germany may be seen as compensation for the small share of East Germans as a group in the *Treuhand* privatizations. The transfers partly finance the high union wages and the resulting costs of unemployment. Whether they can be seen as *adequate* compensation for the negative effects of the privatization policy is questionable. Privatization defines property rights in productive assets, which produce a steady stream of future returns. If temporary resource flows, that is, short-term income subsidies, were equivalent to stocks then the recipients of the transfers would have been in a position to use the short-term payments to purchase the stocks in the market-place. In concrete terms, this means that the payments to the East Germans should have enabled them to buy up the existing stocks of communal assets, which they clearly could not.[40]

For the East Germans after unification, a capitalism without capitalists emerged. The dream of many of the intellectual Left – a decentralized economy with no significant private ownership of productive resources – became reality as far as the East Germans were concerned, although not exactly in the form the proposers had meant.

Competitive Effects of the Sales Privatization

Initially, it was thought that integrating the separate East and West German markets would increase competition.[41] However, this did not happen, as the results of privatization show. Of the 85 per cent of the *Treuhand* properties that were sold to West Germans, 90 per cent took the form of mergers with West German firms in the same industry branches.[42] The West German purchasers, who were buying the firms primarily as supplements to their owns firms, tried to lower the production costs of the plants they bought by introducing new labour-saving processes.[43]

Research that would result in both process and product innovations was needed for East German firms to become competitive and be able to enter new markets. This chance was reduced with the splitting up of the *Treuhand* firms into 'saleable' parts. In this process research departments were often disbanded. The overall employment in research and development departments in East Germany fell to 10 per cent of its previous level.[44]

Furthermore, the sale of whole firms as single units erected quite unnecessary barriers to entry and excluded many new potential purchasers. With this specific privatization method German industry became more concentrated.[45]

The Fiscal Consequences of Sales Policy

The sales method used by the *Treuhand* would have been justified if it had been successful in achieving other goals such as minimizing the fiscal burden of transformation.[46] The sales method of privatizing did not. As the sales policy reduced the possible revenues it created an extra fiscal burden.

If state-owned assets are sold at a price below their value, wealth is transferred from the state to the new owners and a fiscal loss occurs. With given public expenditures, this fiscal loss must be offset by increased taxes or by government borrowing. The danger of 'underpricing' when selling government firms, and the burden this could impose on future taxpayers, was fully discussed when the privatizations in the Western countries were being carried out[47] but was not taken seriously in the East German privatization process.

Future German taxpayers will have to pay twice for East German privatization – once for the likely loss in public revenues caused by sales at rock-bottom prices and once for avoidable unification costs. Unification costs could have been lower with a lower unemployment rate. The high unemployment rate in East Germany is due to a mistaken wage-based distribution policy that can be seen as a consequence of the specific privatization policy chosen. The extremely low participation of East Germans in the whole privatization process possibly encouraged the destructive wage policy – a wage policy that turned East Germany into a *Mezzogiorno* and resulted in permanent flows of net transfers from West Germany. There was no justification in fiscal terms for using the sales method for East German privatization.

Privatization and Distribution

Transition periods always change distribution a significant way. German unification, too, brought about an enormous redistribution. East German assets were transferred to West Germany and West German tax revenues were transferred to East Germany. The political aim of rapidly adjusting East German living standards to West German levels led to a distribution policy that prevented East German resources being allocated rationally and thus created economic losses.

A wage-based distribution policy was chosen, which adapted East German wages to those in West Germany without taking factor scarcities into account. However, the competition between economic systems had shown that payment according to need, or to the subjective contributions made by workers, leads to a suboptimal resource allocation. The decision, on political grounds, to introduce the 'just' western wages completely ignored this conclusion and brushed aside the allocative effects of the policy.

If a society wants to have a well-balanced system of consumption possibilities applicable to all its members, the distribution of personal income based on factor endowment must provide the standard. The communist state had allowed only very few East Germans to own private property in the form of real capital and real estate and the value of the human capital accumulated within the socialist system fell after unification occurred. The necessary distribution of property rights in the former socialist assets provided an opportunity for using market principles for the East–West redistribution policy and such a policy could have narrowed the gap between factor endowments in East and West Germany. The distribution that, in the event, was chosen made the gap larger.

VII WERE THERE ALTERNATIVE WAYS OUT OF THE DILEMMA?

Was there a privatization strategy which would have been more appropriate to the aims set out for the transformation of the East German economy?

The politically motivated goal of raising living standards to Western levels made building a strong, productive economy a necessity and involved attracting investment to restructure and renovate the East German capital stock. The old East German capital stock was estimated at 578 billion Deutschmarks in 1990. A net investment of 962 billion Deutschmarks would have been needed in the year of unification to make East German capital intensity equal to that in West Germany.[48] If this had happened wages could have been adjusted. The impossibly large amount of net investment needed to equalize the capital intensities ensured that the wage adjustment was not feasible economically.

An alternative would have been to let East Germans take part in the future upswing through property rights in the existing capital stock and to raise wages in East Germany gradually in line with increases in labour productivity. This alternative had already been suggested shortly following unification.[49]

The basic idea combined a better privatization policy with a better distribution policy. In accordance with this the *Treuhand* assets could have been distributed freely either in the form of shares in funds or even shares in firms. The recipients of the shares would have been the residents of East

Germany. The German government too could have participated in the East German economic recovery by retaining some of the shares. The value of these shares would have increased with the upswing and the government would not have depended for its revenue on taxes only.

In this way efficiency too could have been improved. A give-away scheme for German privatization would have expanded investment in East Germany. Such a method could help to overcome some credit constraints which could not be loosened simply by lowering the sales prices which is what the *Treuhand* tried to do.[50]

Such a give-away scheme could have been combined with an attempt by the *Treuhand* to find investors with the know-how necessary to restructure the firms and to exercise effective control over them. It was evident that the amount of capital needed for East Germany, both real and human, in the form of real investment and technical and managerial know-how, was expected to far exceed the value of the old East German capital stock. Joint ventures could have been undertaken in which investors could have been given majority shares in these ventures equal to their total investment. The East German residents could have received non-voting minority shares equal to the overall value of the old capital stock.

As most former combines were split up into joint stock or limited liability companies as late as 1991 such a procedure could have been easily carried out. In the case of joint stock companies shares in the companies could have been distributed freely. In the case of limited liability companies the residents would be given credit claims on the companies. These credits could have been free of interest in the initial transformation stages in order to provide risk-sharing advantages similar to those of equity.

The shares the East Germans received could have been traded off against smaller increases in wages. Smaller wage increases would have made more firms viable and total employment could have been higher. Giving East Germans an endowment of capital assets would have been a better use of scarce capital and would have allowed a more adequate distribution policy to be introduced. The overall costs of transformation could thus have been substantially reduced.

Notes

1. *Treuhandanstalt* and *Treuhand* are used synonymously.
2. Some of the jobs in industry were certainly obsolete, and when market relations were established the loss of these jobs increased overt unemployment. However it should not be forgotten that before the Second World War Saxony was Germany's most industrialized region.
3. For this see Kusch and Montag (1991, p. 22).

4. The actual number employed in 1990 before unification is uncertain though. Some estimate it at about 10 million, including employment in the secret activities of the state for which no employment figures are available.

5. There is no one appropriate level of government activity *per se*. A look at the present Western market economies is sufficient to see that the weight of the government sector differs considerably among these countries. For East Germany, the choice of the correct government share which depends on the preferences of the people was not an issue, because the nature and amount of government activity in West Germany was the reference point.

6. Both during and after the Second World War, substantial parts of the economies of these three countries were nationalized. Since the end of the 1970s many of these nationalizations have been reversed.

7. See Winicki (1992, p. 275).

8. According to Henryk Kierzkowski in an address given at the University of Munich in April 1995.

9. See Roesler (1993, p. 20).

10. For this, new forms of common property owned by local government authorities or by firms were to be developed, (ibid., p. 21).

11. This estimate was only slightly different from the initial optimistic estimates made by the West German politicians for the time needed for the transformation of a planned economy.

12. See the Second *Treuhand* Law, 17 June 1990.

13. Walters (1990).

14. Tador, the leader of the Hungarian Free Democratic Party, estimated that his country would take 100 years to carry out privatization on the British pattern. See Walters (1992, p. 104), though Walters questioned the validity of Tador's estimates.

15. This recommendation was made by the Sachverständigenrat zur Begutachtung der gesamtwirtschaftlichen Entwicklung (1990) and by the Wissenschaftlichen Beirat beim Bundesministerium für Wirtschaft (1991).

16. See North (1992, p. 127).

17. A major factor in this comparison is of course the enormous population of the former Soviet Union. See Jermankowicz (1995, p. 43) and BMWI (1994, p. 18).

18. For this see H.-W. Sinn (1995, p. 39).

19. This problem often arose, especially in the decisive early period immediately following unification.

20. Employment in *Treuhand*, and former *Treuhand*, firms fell from 4.5 million in 1990 to 1.6 million at the end of 1994.

21. Hungary, of course, has been using the sales method to privatize its economy, but these sales have been spread out over a long period. Since the beginning of 1995 even Hungary has discontinued sales privatization, although this is because it fears that further sales could result in the domination of its economy by foreigners. The other countries of the former Eastern Bloc have preferred different redistribution methods for privatizing their communal property. Most of these involved distributing shares to the population as a whole.

22. Made by the President of the *Treuhand*, Rohwedder, to the Bundeskammer in Vienna, according to an ADN report of October 1990. By the end of 1991

the estimate was already down to DM 115 billion, but even then this estimated sum was still twice the amount which was finally received.

23.   *Abschlußstatistik der Treuhandanstalt* (1995, p. 5). The numbers found in the actual literature vary however as the *Treuhand* statistics are inconsistent. Sometimes the 'sales revenues' include compensation claims guaranteed to the purchasers when the firms were sold, sales of agricultural land or clearing prices for assets handed over to other public organizations.

24.   See Sinn and Sinn (1993, p. 54).

25.   Harberger (1992) argued in favour of introducing new prices gradually into Eastern Europe because he believed that failure to do so would mean that at least half the Eastern European firms would be unable to survive, an evaluation that might have held for East Germany too.

26.   For the increase in productivity in the East German economy, see Burda and Funke (1993).

27.   Vickers and Yarrow (1988, p. 171).

28.   *Abschlußstatistik der Treuhandanstalt* (1995, p. 5).

29.   Wegner (1995, p. 124). Small privatization included very small businesses, for example, shops and so on.

30.   See Sinn and Sinn (1993, p. 46).

31.   The outcome of the wage negotiations was strongly influenced by West German unions and employers' organizations which took charge of the bargaining process. They supported a rapid wage increase to adjust eastern to western wages in their own interest. The unions wanted to avoid the immigration of an East German industrial reserve army and the employers' organizations wanted to hinder low price competition from their backyard.

32.   Even a well-functioning West German firm would have experienced a drastic fall in its market values under these conditions and in all likelihood would have been summarily ejected from the market.

33.   *Monthly Report of the Deutsche Bundesbank*, no. 3/March 1995, p. 6*.

34.   Ibid., p. 66.

35.   Germany was then the country with the most exports, a fact which permitted many politicians and others to believe, wrongly, that unification could be accomplished almost painlessly.

36.   This came about in response to the large increase in interest rates caused by the sudden rise in the budget deficit. *Monthly Report of the Deutsche Bundesbank*, March 1995, p. 68*.

37.   See G. Sinn, (1994, p. 25).

38.   Sinn and Sinn (1993, p. 87).

39.   H.-W. Sinn (1995, p. 36).

40.   These transfers from West to East Germany are being financed through the budget deficit and the current beneficiaries in East Germany as future taxpayers will later have to help pay for their own benefits.

41.   Kantzenbach (1992, p. 128).

42.   Müller (1993, p. 396).

43.   Meith (1994, p. 15).

44.   Wölfing (1994, p. 113).

45.   Of course this development might be advantageous from the point of view of global competition.

46. That borrowing was given preference over taxes for financing the unification costs certainly had very little to do with the public finance principle of intergenerational justice. Rather, the decision was made with an eye to the next election, for government borrowing places hardly any burden on current taxpayers and voters.
47. Vickers and Yarrow (1988, pp. 177 and 180).
48. See Sinn and Sinn (1994, p. 43).
49. Ibid., p. 194.
50. For this see Schöb (1996). Lowering the sales prices only attracts riskier investments and results in higher equity rates demanded by the financing banks.

References

BMWI (1994) *Informationen* from 18 August 1994, Bonn.

Burda, M. and M. Funke (1995) 'Eastern Germany – Can't We Be More Optimistic?', *ifo Studien – Zeitschrift für empirische Wirtschaftsforschung*, no. 3, Munich.

Cornelsen, D. (1991) 'Privatization – The Example of East Germany', unpublished paper given at WEFA Group International Economic Outlook Conference on Eastern Europe and the Soviet Union in Berlin from 22 to 26 April 1991.

Deutsche Bundesbank (1995) Monatsberichte, no. 3, March 1995, Frankfurt.

European Bank for Reconstruction and Development (1994) *Transition Report* (London).

Guzek, M. (1995) 'Privatization in Poland', in J. Hölscher *et al.* (eds), *Bedingungen ökonomischer Entwicklung in Zentralosteuropa* (Marburg: Metropolis).

Harberger, A. (1992) 'Strategies for the Transition', in C. Clague and G.C. Rausser (eds), *The Emergence of Market Economies in Eastern Europe* (Cambridge, Mass. and Oxford: Blackwell).

Kantzenbach, E. (1992) 'Von der Plan- zur Marktwirtschaft – Eine Zwischenbilanz, Initiierung des Wettbewerbs', in B. Gahlen and H. Hesse (eds), *Von der Plan- zur Marktwirtschaft – Eine Zwischenbilanz* (Tübingen: J.C.B. Mohr (Paul Siebeck).

Mieth, W. (1994): 'Die Wachstumsschwäche des verarbeitenden Gewerbes in Ostdeutschland und ihre Folgen', Regensburger Discussion Paper Series in Economics, No. 262.

Müller, J. (1993): 'Strukturelle Auswirkungen der Privatisierung durch die Treuhandanstalt', in W. Fischer *et al.* (eds), *Treuhandanstalt – Das Unmögliche wagen*, (Berlin: Akademie).

Newbery, D. (1991) 'Sequencing the Transition', in H. Siebert (ed.), *The Transformation of Socialist Economies* (Tübingen J.C.B. Mohr (Paul Siebeck)).

Quaisser, W. (1992) 'Die polnische Wirtschaftsentwicklung im Jahre 1991/92', Working Paper No. 153, East European Institute (Osteuropa-Institut), Munich.

Roesler, J. (1993) 'Die Treuhandanstalt: Wirtschaftsimperium oder Politikinstrument?', in R. Liedtke (ed.), *Die Treuhand und die zweite Enteignung der Ostdeutschen* (Munich: Spangenberg).

Schmörgernova, B. (1995) 'Privatization in the Czech Republic and in the Slovak Republic', in J. Hölscher *et al.*, (eds), *Bedingungen ökonomischer Entwicklung in Zentralosteuropa* (Marburg: Metropolis).

Schöb, R. (1996) 'Kreditrationierung und Treuhandpolitik', *Jahrbücher für Nationalökonomie und Statistik 215* (Tübingen:).

Sinn, G. (1994) 'Politikversagen bei der wirtschaftlichen Vereinigung', in Institut für Wirtschaftsforschung Halle (ed.), *Wirtschaft im Systemschock* (Berlin: Analytica).

Sinn, G. and H.-W. Sinn (1993) *Kaltstart – Volkswirtschaftliche Aspekte der deutschen Vereinigung*, 3rd rev. edn (München Beck) (English edition: *Jumpstart* Cambridge, Mass. and London: MIT Press).

Sinn, H.-W. (1995) 'Schlingerkurs – Lohnpolitik und Investitionsförderung in den neuen Bundesländern' in G. Gutmann (ed.), *Conference Papers on the Annual Meeting 1994 of the German Economic Society* (*Verein für Socialpolitik*) (Berlin: Jena, Duncker & Humblot).

Treuhandanstalt (1995) *Abschlußstatistik zum 31.12.1994* (Berlin: Bundesanstalt für vereinigungsbedingte Sonderaufgaben).

Vickers, J. and G. Yarrow (1988) *Privatization – An Economic Analysis* MIT Press).

Walters, A. (1990) 'How Fast Can Market Economies be Introduced?', *European Business Forum*, Financial Times Conference, 26–27 Novembers, Rome.

Walters, A. (1992) 'The Transition to a Market Economy', in C. Clague and G.C. Rausser (eds), *The Emergence of Market Economies in Eastern Europe* (Cambridge, Mass. MA and Oxford: Blackwell).

Wegner, M. (1995) *Bankrott und Aufbau – Ostdeutsche Erfahrungen* (Baden-Baden Nomos).

Winiecki, J. (1992) 'Privatization in East–Central Europe: Avoiding Major Mistakes', in C. Clague and G.C. Rausser (eds), *The Emergence of Market Economies in Eastern Europe* Cambridge, Mass. and Oxford: Blackwell).

Wölfling, M. (1994) 'Nachholende Modernisierung in der ostdeutschen Industrie – das Beispiel Sachsen-Anhalt', in Institut für Wirtschaftsforschung Halle (ed.), *Wirtschaft im Systemschock* (Berlin, Analytica).

Index

ability-to-pay taxation   39
ad valorem tax rate   134
Adarkar, B.P.   198–9
age (employment)   160–1, 180
Alesina, A.   93
Algeria   61–2
Alisan, S.M.   75
Allende government   279
Allingham, M.G.   75
allocation problems   94
allowance for corporate equity
   236–7, 238, 242
Andre, C.   55
Argentina   62–3
Aronson, J.R.   197
Arrow, K.J.   47
Asia   1
assets   31, 32, 285–7
assimilation   179
Atkinson, A.B.   40, 73, 75, 92, 165
Australia
   Campbell Committee   234
   employment   102, 103
   government expenditure   54
   labour market programmes   114
   unemployment   129, 130, 139, 140,
     141, 145
Austria
   company tax   223, 224, 236
   government expenditure   54
   labour market programmes   114
   unemployment   128, 139, 141, 146

Baltic republics   168
Bamberg, G.   75
Barone, E.   47
Barr, N.   78
Becker, G.S.   88
Beckerath, E. von   43
Belgium   21
   company tax   223, 224, 236
   government expenditure   55

High Council of Finance   211–12
   labour market programmes   114
   stabilization   211
   unemployment   130, 139, 141, 145
benefit taxation   37, 39
Bentham, J.   40
Bergson, A.   40
Bernstein, E.M.   65
Beveridge curve   134, 136, 138
Bismarck, O. von   45
Blanchard, O.J.   128
Boadway, R.W.   91, 167, 209, 236
Boczek, A.   197
Böhm-Bawerk, E. von   83
Booth, A.   137
Borjas, G.J.   179
Bovenberg, A.L.   135, 138, 142
Bowen, H.   38
Bradford, D.F.   162–3
Brazil   61–2
Brennan, G.   47, 164
Breton, A.   194
Bruce, N.   236
Bruni, F.   56
Buchanan, J.M.   5, 37, 38, 47, 76,
   164, 167
Bucholz, W.   75
Budget Coordination Group   211
budgetary subsidies   65
Bulgaria   168
Bullock, C.J.   196
Bulow, J.I.   76
business profit taxation   270–2
Butlin, N.G.   55

Caine, M.R.   195
Campbell Committee   234
Canada
   employment   102, 103
   factor mobility   166
   government expenditure   54
   labour market programmes   114

Canada – *continued*
  Royal (Carter) Commission   234
  unemployment   113, 139, 140, 141
  capital   22–6, 152, 173
  capital and labour   153, 154, 156, 157
  confederations   213
  factor mobility   160, 165
  see also migration
Carter Commission   234
Casella, A.   213
cash tax-transfer   153
cash-flow consumption tax   28, 261
cash-flow tax   25, 237–8, 242
CBIT   *see* comprehensive business
    income tax
Central Europe   131, 258, 282, 284
central government   19, 21, 167–8,
    171, 201, 202
Chamley, C.   63
Chile   62, 279
China   20, 130, 155, 201–4
Cnossen, S.   16, 22–6, 28, 221–49
Coase, R.   168, 171
Codding, G.A.   197
Colm, G.   45
Colombia   61
communal state   4, 35, 36, 41–6
company taxes in European Union
    24, 221–49
  allowance for corporate equity
    236–7
  application   230–2
  cash-flow tax   237–8
  comprehensive business income tax
    238–9
  dividend deduction   235–6
  dual imputation   234–5
  dual income tax   239–41
  full integration   233–4
  neutrality and subsidiarity   229–30
  preferred solution   241–5
  survey   222–6
  taxing returns on debt   227–8
  taxing returns on equity   226–7
compensatory finance   41
compensatory tax   223
comprehensive business income tax
    25, 238–9, 240, 241, 242
confederations   193–217

China   20, 201–4
  differentiation   204–5
  economic rational   205–8
  expenditure assignment   212–13
  as fiscal constitution   19–22
  former Yugoslavia   20
  Germany   20, 21, 198–9, 203
  redistribution   208–9
  stabilization   209–12
  Switzerland   20, 197–8, 203
  tax assignment   213–14
  United States   20, 195–7, 203
  Yugoslavia   199–201, 203–4
consumption-based taxation   27, 28,
    261, 266
corporate income   25
corporate tax, minimum   24
corruption   53
Costa Rica   61
Cote d'Ivoire   62
Craig, J.   209
Croatia   27, 29, 237
  Ministry of Finance   258, 265, 266,
    272, 274
  Tax Administration   272
  see also tax reform in Croatia
crowding-out effect   77–8
Cruciger, G.   80
currency unions   206

Dafflon, B.   194, 211
Daly, M.   243
De Grauwe, P.   210
De Melo, M.   59, 60–1
De Viti de Marco, A.   37
debt finance   22
Delorme, R.   55
Delors Report   210
Denmark
  company tax   224, 227–8, 240, 241
  labour market programmes   114
  unemployment   139, 140, 141
depreciation   28, 263, 264
Devereux, M.   236
Dewey, D.   196
Diamond, P.H.   41, 75
disability schemes   131
distribution policy   290–1
dividend deduction   235–6, 238

dividends 22
Dixit, A.K. 65, 177
Domar, E. 75, 80, 87
dual income tax 25, 26, 239–41, 242–4
Dupuit, J. 40

earned income tax credit 14, 127, 141–2, 144–5, 146
earnings *see* wages and earnings
Easterly, W. 63
Eastern Europe 1, 52
   factor mobility 169, 170, 176, 181
   privatization 29, 282, 284
   revenue raising and property rights
      allocation 26
   tax reform 258
   unemployment 131
Eaton, J. 75
economic unions 168–71
economies in transition 64, 207
   revenue-raising and property rights
      allocation 26–32;
      privatization 29–32; tax
      system, design of 26–9
   see also tax reform in Croatia
Edgeworth, F.Y. 39–40
education and training 7, 179
   Eastern Europe 144–6, 147
   Europe 127, 128, 129, 131
   United States 103, 113
effective marginal tax rate 262
efficiency *see* factor mobility and
   redistributive policy
Egypt 62–3
Ehrlich, I. 88
Einaudi, L. 37
EITC *see* Earned Income Tax Credit
employers' associations 30
employment
   Germany 30
   United States 102–3
   see also welfare state,
      entrepreneurship and
      employment
employment-based marginal subsidy
   11–12, 116–18, 120
EMS 210
energy taxes 143–4

entitlement principle 231–2
entrepreneurship 146
   see also welfare state,
      entrepreneurship and
      employment
environmental taxation 14, 142–4, 147
equity *see* factor mobility and
   redistributive policy
Europe 2
   continental 4
   factor mobility 166
   political and constitutional
      constraints 193
   welfare state 11–15
   see also Central; Eastern; European;
      unemployment; Western
European Free Trade Area 114, 129, 130, 131
European Union 66
   capital income taxation 22
   factor mobility 168, 169, 170, 181
   labour market programmes 114
   unemployment 103
   see also company taxes
expenditure assignment 21, 212–13
expenditure instruments 56
explicit labour tax 143, 144
explicit taxes 64, 66

factor market integration and factor
   allocations 155–6
factor market integration income
   distribution 156–9
factor mobility 16–19
   labour 19, 166, 167, 182, 183
factor mobility and redistributive
   policy 151–88
   fiscal aspects 161–71; central
      government transfers 167–8;
      curtailment of redistributive
      policy 164–5; economic
      unions and jurisdiction
      formation 168–71; income
      redistribution cost increase
      162; redistributive policy,
      reduction of benefits of 165–7
   labour mobility, fiscal impacts of
      171–82; migration 172–7;

factor mobility and redistributive
    policy – *continued*
    migration, dynamic fiscal impact of
        179–82; migration dynamics:
        market integration and factor
        aggregation 177–9
    mobility effects on efficiency and
        equity 154–61; factor market
        integration and factor
        allocations 155–6; factor
        market integration and income
        distribution 156–9; factor
        mobility and income risk
        insurance 159–61
family 180, 181
federalism 196, 200, 204, 207, 208,
    212
    cooperative 194
    functional 213
federations 19, 20, 193, 195, 205
Feldstein, M. 75, 87
Fichte, J.G. 42
financial repression 6
Finanzwissenschaft tradition 4
Finland
    company tax 223, 224, 226, 240,
        241, 243
    factor mobility 168
    labour market programmes 114
    unemployment 130, 139, 140, 141
fiscal consolidation 142–4
fiscal incentives for entrepreneurs
    146
fiscal instruments 7, 65
fiscal policies 18, 21, 151–2
fiscal theory 47–8
fiscal tools 6
Fisher, I. 83
flat tax 238
Flatters, F.R. 167, 209
flawed state 35, 36, 46–8
Flora, P. 55
Ford, H. 80
former Soviet Union 131, 168, 181,
    281
former Yugoslavia 62–3, 257
    confederation 20, 199–201, 203–4,
        205
France

company tax 223, 224
employment 102, 103
government expenditure 54
labour market programmes 114
privatization 281
unemployment 130, 139, 140, 141,
    146
Freeman, H. 236
Frey, B. 213
Friedman, M. 76, 91
Fry, M.J. 61–3
full-time employment 128

Gammie, M. 236, 239
gender (and employment) 180
general equilibrium model 8, 65
Gerardi, G. 226
Germany
    communal state 36, 44
    company tax 223, 224
    confederation 20, 21, 198–9, 203,
        205
    Constitution 283
    Economic Stability and Growth Law
        (1967) 212
    employment 102, 103
    factor mobility 158, 168, 178, 181
    Federal Ministry of Finance 282
    Finanzwissenschaft 42, 43, 44, 45,
        46
    government expenditure 54
    KNS tax reform group 258, 261,
        265
    labour market programmes 114
    pensions 74
    privatization 29, 30, 31, 32
    tax reform 270
    unemployment 128, 130, 139, 140,
        141, 146
    see also Treuhandanstalt
Ghana 62–3
Giovannini, A. 59, 60–1
Gordon, R.H. 76, 228
government
    budget 2
    communal state 45
    factor mobility and redistributive
        policy 17
    failure 5, 47

revenue 2
see also central government; *and*
    government *below*
government, alternative perceptions of
    2–6
  historical perspective 3–5
  impact, definining and measurement
    of 5–6
government role 51–2
government, role of in fiscal theory
    35–48
  communal state 41–6
  market failure correction: service
    state 36–9
  policy failure: flawed state 46–8
  welfare state: adjusting distribution
    39–41
government role and policy
    instruments efficiency 60–3
  see also quasi-fiscal
Graetz, M.J. 226
Gramlich, E.M. 210
Greece 60, 61–2
  company tax 223, 224, 226
  labour market programmes 114
  unemployment 128, 139, 140, 141
Groenewegen, P. 214
Gros, D. 207
gross domestic product 6, 52, 59, 60,
    63, 64
  China 201
  company tax 227–8
  Germany 30
  policy instruments 56
  social insurance, incentives and risk-
    taking 77
  stabilization 211
  unemployment 113
gross national product 120

Haig, A. 41, 233
Hall, R.E. 238
Haller, H. 211
Hamburg 80
Hamilton, B.W. 164
Hamlin, A.P. 212
Hansen, A. 41
Hansson, I. 228
Harberger, A.C. 41, 156

Harsanyi, J.C. 40, 76
Hatton, T.J. 156
Haveman, R.H. 7, 9–11, 12, 14,
    101–24, 129, 147
Head, J. 38
Hecksher–Ohlin tradition 153–4, 182
Hegel, G.W.F. 42, 43
Helms, L.J. 75
Hermann, F. 43, 44
Hernandez, A. 55
Hicks, Sir J.R. 178
Hilley, J.L. 197
hiring schedule 134
Huizinga, H. 228
Hume, D. 3, 36–7, 38, 42, 44
Hungary 168

Iceland 130
IFS Capital Taxes Group 236
immigration 152, 169–70, 182
implicit labour tax 143, 144
implicit subsidies 59, 167
implicit taxes 59, 60, 63, 66
import restrictions, quantitative 59
in-kind benefits 153
income
  aggregate 158
  communal state 44
  distribution 3, 4, 6, 16, 91, 156–9;
    and migration 159; policy
    instruments 56
  distribution, pre-tax 91
  per capita 160
  post-tax 91
  redistribution role 51, 52
  risk 159–61, 166
  see also income tax
income tax 94
  credit, earned 14, 127, 141–2,
    144–5, 146
  dual 25, 26, 239–41, 242–4
  personal 223–4, 226–9, 232–5,
    237–8, 240–3, 245, 266–70
  savings-adjusted personal 28, 262,
    264
India 61–2
indifference curve 83, 86, 88, 89,
    91–2, 93, 95
Indonesia 61–2

inequality 91–4
inflation 61, 272–4
   rate 264
   tax 207
Inman, R.P. 210
institutional failure 5
insurance 79–87
   line 90
   market 75–9, 81, 84
   private 8, 77, 78, 79, 81, 97
   social 2, 7–9, 75–9
integration 206–7
interest-adjusted business profit tax
   262, 264, 272–3, 274
interest-adjusted personal income tax
   28, 237, 262, 264, 274
interest-adjusted tax system 267
intergovernmental grants 152, 168
interregional transfers 209
investment 30, 143, 284, 287–8, 291
Ireland
   company tax 224, 235
   government expenditure 54
   labour market programmes 114
   privatization 279
   unemployment 128, 130, 139, 140,
      141
Italy
   company tax 223, 224
   employment 102, 103
   flawed state 36
   government expenditure 55
   labour market programmes 114
   unemployment 128, 130, 139

Jackman, R. 133, 137
Jacob, L.H. von 43
Jamaica 61
Japan
   capital income taxation 25
   company tax 244
   employment 102
   government expenditure 54
   labour market programmes 114
   policy instruments 56
   unemployment 128, 129, 130, 131,
      139, 140, 141
job vouchers 145
Johansen, L. 53

joint stock companies 292
Jordan 61
jurisdiction formation 168–71
jurisdictional boundaries 151–2

Kaldor, N. 79
Kanbur, R. 75, 91
Kant, I. 42, 76
Kaplow, L. 76
Keynes, J.M. 41, 281
King, P. 205
KNS tax reform group 258, 261, 265
Konrad, K. 76
Korea 61–2, 168
Krugman, P. 161

labour
   income 25
   –leisure choice 94
   market activity 7
   markets 2
   see also capital and labour;
      employment; factor mobility
      and redistributive policy;
      migration
Latin America 169, 170
Layard, R. 133, 137
Lerner, A. 41
Lindahl, E. 38
List, F. 42
local property tax 162–3
Locke, J. 39, 40, 42
Lockwood, B. 137, 243
Luxembourg 114, 223, 224, 236

Maastricht Treaty 22, 230, 245
MacLeod, W.B. 147
McLure, C.E. Jr 234, 264
Malaysia 61–2
Malcolmson, J.M. 147
male work patterns (United States)
   104–5
Manning, A. 137, 243
marginal utility theory of value 37
market failure 3, 4, 5
   correction 36–9
   policy instruments 56
market insurance 75–9, 81, 84
Marshall, A. 40

Marx, K. 47
Masson, P.R. 219
Mazzola, U. 37
Meade Committee 237
means-tested subsidies 142
Meisel, F. 42
Mexico 60, 61–3, 176, 178
Meyer, S. 75
Mieszowski, P. 162
migration 18–19, 172–7
  confederations 21
  dynamic fiscal impact 179–82
  dynamics: market integration and
    factor aggregation 177–9
  factor mobility 157–8, 160, 161,
    162, 166, 171
  and income distribution 159
  unemployment 131
Mihaljek, D. 16, 19–21, 193–217
Mill, J.S. 3, 37, 39
Mirrlees, J.A. 41, 75
Mitchell, B. 55
Moesen, W.A. 211
moral hazard 8, 9, 74, 87–90, 92, 93
  confederations 210
  optimal tax 94
  social insurance, incentives and risk-
    taking 80, 86
Morocco 61–2
motivation 44
Mueller, D.C. 53
Müller, A. 43
Musgrave, R.A. 2–3, 5, 6, 7, 17,
  35–48, 51, 75, 80, 87, 194

National Tax Service 202
net distributions tax 261–2, 264, 265
Netherlands
  company tax 223, 224, 227
  employment 102, 103
  government expenditure 55
  labour market programmes 114
  stabilization 211
  unemployment 129, 130, 139, 140,
    141, 146
neutrality 22–3, 24, 27
New Jobs Tax Credit programme
  116, 117
new property ownership 288–9

New Zealand 54, 114, 141
Newcomer, M. 198
Nickell, S. 133, 137
Nigeria 62
NJTC *see* New Jobs Tax Credit
  programme
non-fiscal instruments 57
Nordic countries 25, 169, 235
  see also under individual countries
Norman, E. 228
North Africa 176
North America 1, 2
  factor mobility 166, 169, 181
  labour market programmes 114
  unemployment 129, 130, 131
  see also Canada; United States
Norway
  company tax 240, 241
  factor mobility 168
  government expenditure 54
  labour market programmes 114
  unemployment 130, 139, 140, 141

Oates, W.E. 194, 212
Ohlin, B.G. 153–4, 182
oil price shocks 128
opportunity line 85, 86, 88, 89, 93
optimal taxation 41, 94–6
Organisation for Economic
  Cooperation and Development 7
  company tax 229
  factor mobility 182
  Model Tax Convention 265
  unemployment 113, 126–31, 139,
    140, 143, 145, 147

Pajilc, Z. 205
Pakistan 61–2
Palei, L.V. 207
Panama 61
Panteleoni, M. 37
Papua New Guinea 61
Pareto, A. 47
Pareto harmful 170
Pareto improvement 7, 79, 86, 206
Pareto optimality 8, 39, 45, 48, 65,
  86, 89
part-time employment 128, 129, 130
Penati, A. 56

pensions 74, 131, 181, 237, 266–7
Perotti, R. 93
personal income tax 223–4, 226–9,
 232–5, 237–8, 240–3, 245,
 266–70
 savings-adjusted 28, 262, 264
Persson, T. 93
Peru 62–3
Petr, J.L. 207
Phelps, E. 65, 134
Philippines 61–2
Pigou, A.C. 38, 40–1, 44, 57, 83
Pindyck, R.S. 177
Pinto, B. 63
Pissarides, C.A. 134
Ploeg, F. van der 7, 11–15, 126–48
Poisson matching probability 134
Poland 168
policy failure: flawed state 46–8
policy instruments 52–7, 60–3
 government expenditure 54–5
Porta, A. 56
Portugal 60, 61–2
 company tax 223
 labour market programmes 114
 privatization 279
 unemployment 130, 139, 140, 141
post-tax incomes 91
post-tax inequality 92, 93, 96
post-tax risk 95
Poterba, J.M. 226
poverty 9, 119
 traps 117, 142
pre-insurance mean 82
pre-tax distribution 95
pre-tax income distribution 91
pre-tax inequality 92, 93, 94, 96
principal–agent problems 53
private insurance 8, 77, 78, 79, 81,
 97
privatization 29–32
 see also Treuhandanstalt
probability distributions 91
progressive taxes 147
property rights 291
 allocation 2, 26–32
protective rate of interest 267
Prud'homme, R. 212
PT *see* personal income tax

public goods theory 46
public sector failure 46
public spending 64
Putkammer, E. von 198
Puviani, A. 47

quasi-fiscal activities and regulations
 6, 7, 57–60, 64, 65, 66
 policy instruments 56–7
 through financial system 59–60
 through foreign exchange system 58–9
quotas 170

Rabushka, A. 238
Rau, K.-H. 43
Rawls, J.A. 40, 76, 206
Rebeol, S. 207
reciprocity 43
redistribution line 84–5, 88, 89,
 92–3, 95, 96
redistributive taxation 8, 9, 13, 73,
 74, 75–9, 79–87, 93, 94, 97
 confederations 208–9
 and inequality 91–4
 policies 15, 16–19; *see also* factor
  mobility and redistributive
  policy
 social insurance, incentives and risk-
  taking 90
 welfare state policies 7
rent 13
 controls 6, 58
 –seeking 5, 53, 164
reprivatization 31, 284
residence principle 22
resource allocation 6, 16, 65
 government role 51, 52
 Pareto-optimal 8
 social insurance, incentives and risk-
  taking 76
revenue-raising 26–32
Revolutionary Debt Obligations 196
Richter, W.F. 75
risk-taking 7, 7–9, 76, 79–87, 166–7
Ritschl, H. 45
Rochet, J.Ch. 75
Rodríguez, C.A. 63
Rodrik, D. 93
Rohwedder, D. 282, 283

Romania 168
Rose, M. 26–9, 237, 257–77
Rosen, H.S. 75, 226
Royal (Carter) Commission 234
Ruding Committee 221, 243

SAIT *see* savings-adjusted income tax
sales revenue 285–7
Samuelson, P.A. 3, 38
Sandmo, A. 75
savings 143, 287–8
savings-adjusted personal income tax 28, 262, 264
Sax, E. 37, 45
Scandinavia 36
    see also under individual countries
Schäffle, A. 4, 43–4
Schanz, G. 44, 233
Schelling, F.W.J. von 42
Schiantarelli, F. 137
Schmidt-Hebbel, K. 63
Schultz, W. 195
Schumpeter, J.A. 43, 45
Scott, A. 194, 209, 211
seigniorage 6, 61
self-employment 28, 130, 268
self-insurance line 83, 85, 86, 89, 92–3, 94, 95, 96
service state 3, 35, 36–9, 45
Shavell, S. 88
Simons, H.C. 44, 233
Sinn, G. 26, 29, 30–2, 279–95
Sinn, H.-W. 7, 8–9, 73–98, 165
Sixth Directive 245
Slemrod, J. 228, 260
Smith, A. 3, 4, 36, 37, 38–9, 43, 44, 45
Smith, S. 230
Snower, D.J. 145
social indifference curve 91
social insurance 2, 7–9, 75–9
social policy 45
social services programmes 165
Somalia 63
Sørensen, P.B. 1–32, 227, 228, 240, 241
source principle 22–3
South Africa 155
sovereignty 205, 214

Spain
    company tax 223
    government expenditure 55
    labour market programmes 114
    unemployment 128, 129, 130, 139, 140, 141
Spann, O. 43
Sri Lanka 61–2
stabilization 21, 51, 52, 209–12
state governments 21
Stein, L. von 4, 43
Stigler, G.J. 162
Stiglitz, J.E. 53, 87
subsidiarity 22–3
subsidies 58
    budgetary 65
    employment-based marginal 11–12, 116–18, 120
    implicit 59, 167
    means-tested 142
Summers, L.H. 76, 128
Sweden
    company tax 224, 228, 236, 240, 241
    employment 102, 103
    government expenditure 54
    labour market programmes 114
    policy instruments 56
    unemployment 139, 140, 141
Switzerland
    confederation 20, 197–8, 203, 204–5
    factor mobility 168
    government expenditure 54
    unemployment 139, 140, 141, 146

Tabellini, G. 93
Tanzania 62
Tanzi, V. 2–3, 5, 6, 7, 51–67
Targeted Jobs Tax Credit 117
Tariff Law (1879) 198
tax 2, 12, 56, 59, 61, 65
    ability-to-pay 39
    ad valorem 134
    assignment 194, 213–14
    benefit 37, 39
    business profit 270–2
    capital income 22–6
    cash-flow 25, 237–8, 242

tax – *continued*
  cash-flow consumption 28, 261
  China 201, 202
  communal state 42, 43, 44, 45
  compensatory 223
  comprehensive business income
    25, 238–9, 240, 241, 242
  confederations 203
  consumption-based 27, 28, 261,
    266
  credit, earned income 14, 127,
    141–2, 144–5, 146
  distortions in competitive labour
    markets 132–3
  double of dividends 22
  dual income 25, 26, 239–41,
    242–4
  energy 143–4
  environmental 14, 142–4, 147
  explicit 64, 66
  explicit labour 143, 144
  flat 238
  implicit 59, 60, 63, 66
  implicit labour 143, 144
  inflation 207
  interest-adjusted business profit
    262, 264, 272–3, 274
  interest-adjusted personal income
    28, 237, 262, 264, 274
  level effect 144
  local property 162–3
  market failure in service state 38
  minimum corporate 24
  net distributions 261–2, 264, 265
  optimal 4, 41, 94–6
  personal income 223–4, 226–9,
    232–5, 237–8, 240–3, 245,
    266–70
  policy 21
  progressive 147
  quasi-fiscal activities 58
  rate, effective marginal 262
  rates, average and marginal 13, 14
  revenue 63
  savings-adjusted personal income
    28, 262, 264
  shifting effect 144
  Switzerland 197
  system 3, 23, 26–9, 126

  system, interest-adjusted 267
  theory 40–1
  –transfer rates 7, 8
  –transfer system 2, 7, 9
  see also company tax; redistributive;
    tax reform; unemployment in
    Europe
tax reform in Croatia 257–77
  business profit tax 270–2
  criteria for new tax system 58–60
  efficiency and decision-neutrality
    properties of alternative tax
    systems 260–5
  inflation 272–4
  personal income and business profit
    taxation 260–77
  personal income tax 266–70
  taxpayer equity 27
  Taylor, M.P. 219
  temporary employment 129, 130
  Teulings, C.A. 147
  Thailand 61–2
  Thatcher government 279
  Timm, H. 79
  Tinbergen, J. 53, 65
  trade policy 1
  trade unions 30, 147
  Treaty of Rome 22, 229, 244
  Treuhandanstalt 29–32
    advantage from initial situation
      283–4
    history of *Treuhand* 282–3
    privatization methods 284–5
    sales policy 279–95; asset values
      and sales revenue 285–7;
      competitive effects of sales
      privatization 289; fiscal
      consequences 290;
      privatization and distribution
      290–1; privatization and new
      property ownership 288–9;
      whole economy, sale of 287–8
    successful privatization 280–1
  Tullock, G. 38, 76
  Tunisia 61
  Turkey 60, 61–2, 141, 168, 169

  unemployment 178
    compensation 12

education 147
ethnic minorities 147
Europe 11–15
schemes 131
structural 2
see also unemployment in Europe;
    unemployment in United States
unemployment in Europe 11–15,
    101, 102, 110, 112, 126–48
active labour market policies 144–6
age 128
anatomy 127–31
apprenticeships 127, 128–9, 146,
    147
benefits 139–42
earned income tax credit 138–42
education and training 127, 128,
    129, 131, 144–6
fiscal consolidation and
    environmental tax reform
    142–4
fiscal incentives for entrepreneurs
    146
policy conclusions 146–8
tax distortions in competitive labour
    markets 132–3
taxation 133–8; hiring 134–5;
    matching jobs and vacancies
    133–4; policy implications
    136–8; surplus, sharing of
    135
unemployment in United States
    9–11, 101–24, 128, 131, 139, 140,
    146, 147
age 103, 109
earning inequality: policy response
    110–14
education and training 103, 113
employer-based marginal
    employment subsidy 116–18
employment growth 102–3
ethnic/racial groups 103
male work patterns and
    unemployment 104–5
poverty 119
trends 103–4
wage and earnings inequality
    105–9
wage rate subsidy 118–19

United Kingdom
communal state 42
company tax 223, 224, 235
employment 102, 103
government expenditure 54
government role in fiscal theory 35
labour market programmes 114
privatization 279, 281, 282, 286
unemployment 128, 130, 137, 139,
    140, 141, 145
United States 12
capital income taxation 25
communal state 44
company tax 228, 236, 238, 240,
    242, 244
confederation 20, 195–7, 203, 204
Department of the Treasury 234,
    238, 239
employment 102
factor mobility 160–1, 163–4,
    166–8, 170, 176, 178–9, 181–2
government expenditure 54
government role in fiscal theory 36
labour market programmes 114
policy instruments 56–7
see also unemployment in United
    States
utility function 81, 87, 94, 95

value creation 43
Varian, H.R. 75, 165
VAT structure 245
Venezuela 62
Venice 80, 81
Voltaire, F.M.A. de 152
von Neumann–Morgenstern utility
    function 81, 87
voting imperfections 47

wages and earnings 101, 178
differentials 12
Germany 291
growth 12
inequalities 2, 10, 104–5, 110–14
moderation 129
policy 30
subsidies 11, 14, 15, 118–19, 145,
    147
Wagner, A. 4, 43, 44, 45, 79

Walsh, C.　211
Walters, A.　282
Warsaw Pact countries　182
Weiner, J.　243
welfare economics　5, 38, 75
welfare state　2, 3–4, 35, 36, 45, 73,
　　74, 76, 97
　adjusting distribution　39–41
　Europe　11–15
　social insurance, incentives and risk-
　　taking　78, 80, 89, 90, 94
　tax-transfer systems　7
welfare state, entrepreneurship and
　　employment　6–15
　Europe　11–15
　social insurance and risk-taking
　　7–9
　United States　9–11

Wellisch, D.　169
Western Europe　1, 2, 10
　factor mobility　169, 176, 182
　revenue raising and property rights
　　allocation　26
Wheare, K.C.　204
Wicksell, K.　3, 37, 38, 40, 41, 47
Wieser, F. von　37
Wildasin, D.E.　16–19, 21, 91,
　　151–88
Williamson, J.G.　156
Wiseman, J.　194
Wiswesser, R.　26–9, 237, 257–77

Zaire　61–3
Zambia　63
Zimbabwe　60, 61
Zodrow, G.R.　226, 26